Cisco CCNA Routing and Switching 200-120

Flash Cards and Exam Practice Pack

Eric Rivard

Cisco Press
800 East 96th Street
Indianapolis, IN 46240 USA

Cisco CCNA Routing and Switching 200-120 Flash Cards and Exam Practice Pack

Eric Rivard

Copyright© 2014 Pearson Education, Inc.

Published by:
Cisco Press
800 East 96th Street
Indianapolis, IN 46240 USA

Printed in the United States of America 1 2 3 4 5 6 7 8 9 0

First Printing July 2013

Library of Congress Control Number: 2013941281

ISBN-13: 978-1-58720-400-5

ISBN-10: 1-58720-400-2

Warning and Disclaimer

This book is designed to provide information about late-stage preparation for the Cisco CCNA 200-120 exam. Every effort has been made to make this book as complete and as accurate as possible, but no warranty or fitness is implied.

The information is provided on an "as is" basis. The authors, Cisco Press, and Cisco Systems, Inc., shall have neither liability nor responsibility to any person or entity with respect to any loss or damages arising from the information contained in this book or from the use of the discs or programs that may accompany it.

The opinions expressed in this book belong to the author and are not necessarily those of Cisco Systems, Inc.

Trademark Acknowledgments

All terms mentioned in this book that are known to be trademarks or service marks have been appropriately capitalized. Cisco Press or Cisco Systems, Inc. cannot attest to the accuracy of this information. Use of a term in this book should not be regarded as affecting the validity of any trademark or service mark.

Corporate and Government Sales

The publisher offers excellent discounts on this book when ordered in quantity for bulk purchases or special sales, which may include electronic versions and/or custom covers and content particular to your business, training goals, marketing focus, and branding interests. For more information, please contact: **U.S. Corporate and Government Sales** 1-800-382-3419 corpsales@pearsontechgroup.com

For sales outside the U.S., please contact: **International Sales** international@pearsoned.com

Feedback Information

At Cisco Press, our goal is to create in-depth technical books of the highest quality and value. Each book is crafted with care and precision, undergoing rigorous development that involves the unique expertise of members from the professional technical community.

Readers' feedback is a natural continuation of this process. If you have any comments regarding how we could improve the quality of this book, or otherwise alter it to better suit your needs, you can contact us through e-mail at feedback@ciscopress.com. Please make sure to include the book title and ISBN in your message.

We greatly appreciate your assistance.

Publisher: Paul Boger

Business Operation Manager, Cisco Press: Jan Cornelssen

Associate Publisher: Dave Dusthimer

Executive Editor: Brett Bartow

Senior Development Editor: Christopher A. Cleveland

Managing Editor: Sandra Schroeder

Copy Editor: John Edwards

Senior Project Editor: Tonya Simpson

Technical Editors: Brian D'Andrea, Desiree Lindfield

Editorial Assistant: Vanessa Evans

Proofreader: Sarah Kearns

Book Designer: Mark Shirar

Composition: Mary Sudul

CISCO.

Americas Headquarters
Cisco Systems, Inc.
San Jose, CA

Asia Pacific Headquarters
Cisco Systems (USA) Pte. Ltd.
Singapore

Europe Headquarters
Cisco Systems International BV
Amsterdam, The Netherlands

Cisco has more than 200 offices worldwide. Addresses, phone numbers, and fax numbers are listed on the Cisco Website at **www.cisco.com/go/offices**.

CCDE, CCENT, Cisco Eos, Cisco HealthPresence, the Cisco logo, Cisco Lumin, Cisco Nexus, Cisco StadiumVision, Cisco TelePresence, Cisco WebEx, DCE, and Welcome to the Human Network are trademarks; Changing the Way We Work, Live, Play, and Learn and Cisco Store are service marks; and Access Registrar, Aironet, AsyncOS, Bringing the Meeting To You, Catalyst, CCDA, CCDP, CCIE, CCIP, CCNA, CCNP, CCSP, CCVP, Cisco, the Cisco Certified Internetwork Expert logo, Cisco IOS, Cisco Press, Cisco Systems, Cisco Systems Capital, the Cisco Systems logo, Cisco Unity, Collaboration Without Limitation, EtherFast, EtherSwitch, Event Center, Fast Step, Follow Me Browsing, FormShare, GigaDrive, HomeLink, Internet Quotient, IOS, iPhone, iQuick Study, IronPort, the IronPort logo, LightStream, Linksys, MediaTone, MeetingPlace, MeetingPlace Chime Sound, MGX, Networkers, Networking Academy, Network Registrar, PCNow, PIX, PowerPanels, ProConnect, ScriptShare, SenderBase, SMARTnet, Spectrum Expert, StackWise, The Fastest Way to Increase Your Internet Quotient, TransPath, WebEx, and the WebEx logo are registered trademarks of Cisco Systems, Inc. and/or its affiliates in the United States and certain other countries.

All other trademarks mentioned in this document or website are the property of their respective owners. The use of the word partner does not imply a partnership relationship between Cisco and any other company. (0812R)

About the Author

Eric Rivard is a professional services manager for CDW overseeing an industry expert team of consultants who implement advanced Cisco, Microsoft, data center, virtualization, and storage solutions to enterprise customers. Over the years, he has taught professionals in both academic and industry settings on topics of SCADA, Windows, networking, and IT security. Eric has 15 years of experience in the IT industry, ranging from a network administrator to senior Cisco engineer to IT director. Eric is also a professor at National University, teaching networking and IT classes. He is the author of the first, second, and third editions of the *CCNA Flash Card Practice Pack*.

He holds a B.S. in information technology from the University of Phoenix and a master's in business management from Redlands University. Eric also volunteers serving the young men ages 12 through 18 in his church. Eric is an Eagle Scout and currently works with the Boy Scouts in his area. He lives with his wife and five children in Oceanside, California.

About the Technical Reviewers

Brian D'Andrea started his career working as a bench technician for a large computer manufacturer. He then progressed to a consultant position for various financial and medical institutions across Pennsylvania, New Jersey, and Delaware. He is now a long-time instructor and courseware developer of Cisco courses that include CCNA Routing & Switching, CCDA, CCNA Security, CCNP Routing & Switching, and CCDP. He has been privileged to be part of several Cisco Press–published materials. He enjoys sharing his knowledge and 17 years of experience in the information technology field.

Desiree Lindfield is a Cisco Certified Systems Instructor (CCSI) and provides official Cisco training for Boson and Global Knowledge. She has delivered technical training for numerous vendors and technologies for teams located around the globe. In addition to training, Desiree serves on a team of consultants providing design, installation, and troubleshooting services. Recent implementations include Nexus 7000 switches and the Cisco Unified Computing System. Desiree is a regular attendee of Cisco Live, B-Sides, and Defcon conferences.

Dedications

I dedicate this edition to my beloved family: my beautiful wife, Tammy, and my children, Ellie, Collin, Reegin, Averie, and Sadie. I am the man I am today because of you. You are my everything! Tammy, I could not have found a more perfect partner to spend my life and all eternity with. I am deeply in love with you. Thank you for your support, understanding, love, and patience. To my children, you are such a blessing to your mother and me and we love you more than you will ever know. Always remember how special you are. Always choose the right path and help others. I love you so much!

Finally, I would like to dedicate this edition to my father-in-law, Paul M. Hatch. Thank you for your love, support, and righteous example through the years. I feel so blessed to be called your son. We love you. God be with you until we meet again.

Acknowledgments

First and foremost, I would like to thank my Father in Heaven for Your love and tender mercies. You have always been there for me. To my beautiful wife, thank you for being understanding during the long nights and hours I had to put in while working on this edition. It is not easy raising five kids, let alone trying to do it on your own while I was working late. You are an amazing mother and woman. To my children, everything I do, I do for you. Thank you for being such great kids. I am lucky to be your father.

To my parents, brothers, and in-laws. You guys are so amazing and I love you dearly. I am truly blessed to have you in my life.

To Brett Bartow, Executive Editor, thank you for your efforts in ensuring that this project was a success. It is always a pleasure to work with you.

To Christopher Cleveland, thank you for your efforts and working with me on this edition.

To the team at Cisco Press that helped with all the behind-the-scenes work to make this edition happen, thank you. To the technical reviewers, Brian and Desiree, thank you for your hard work and time. Your efforts were paramount.

Contents

Icons

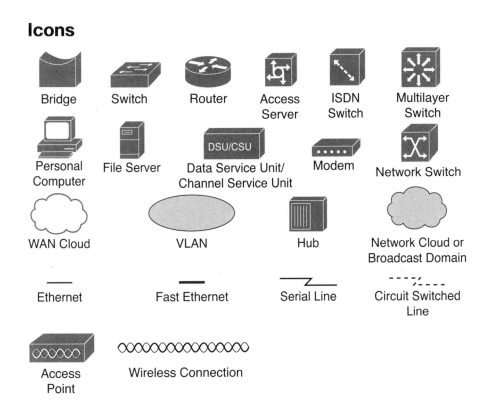

Bridge   Switch   Router   Access Server   ISDN Switch   Multilayer Switch

Personal Computer   File Server   Data Service Unit/ Channel Service Unit   Modem   Network Switch

WAN Cloud   VLAN   Hub   Network Cloud or Broadcast Domain

Ethernet   Fast Ethernet   Serial Line   Circuit Switched Line

Access Point   Wireless Connection

Command Syntax Conventions

The conventions used to present command syntax in this book are the same conventions used in the IOS Command Reference. The Command Reference describes these conventions as follows:

- **Boldface** indicates commands and keywords that are entered literally, as shown. In actual configuration examples and output (not general command syntax), boldface indicates commands that are manually input by the user (such as a **show** command).
- *Italics* indicate arguments for which you supply actual values.
- Vertical bars (|) separate alternative, mutually exclusive elements.
- Square brackets [ ] indicate optional elements.
- Braces { } indicate a required choice.
- Braces within brackets [{ }] indicate a required choice within an optional element.

Introduction

Since the Cisco career certification programs were announced in 1998, they have been the most sought-after and prestigious certifications in the networking industry. For many, passing the ICND exams is crucial in building a rewarding career in networking or obtaining career advancement.

Notorious as being some of the most difficult certifications in the networking industry, Cisco exams can cause much stress to the ill-prepared. Unlike other certification exams, the Cisco exams require that students truly understand the material instead of just memorizing answers. This pack is best used after you have used another, primary method of study for the CCNA certification, and need a mode of self-assessment and review to bring you confidently to test day.

The Purpose of Flash Cards

For years, flash cards have been recognized as a quick and effective study aid. They have been used to complement classroom training and significantly boost memory retention.

The flash cards in this pack serve as a final preparation tool for the CCNA exam. They work best when used in conjunction with official study aids for the CCNA exam. They might also be useful to you as a quick desk- or field-reference guide.

Who These Flash Cards Are For

These flash cards are designed for network administrators, network engineers, Cisco Networking Academy Program students, and any professional or student looking to advance his or her career through achieving Cisco CCNA certification.

How to Use These Flash Cards

Review one section at a time, reading each flash card until you can answer it correctly on your own. When you can correctly answer every card in a given section, move on to the next.

These flash cards are a condensed form of study and review. Don't rush to move through each section. The amount of time you spend reviewing the cards directly affects how long you'll be able to retain the information needed to pass the test. A couple of days before your exam, review each section as a final refresher. Although these flash cards are designed to be used as a final-stage study aid (30 days before the exam), they can also be used in the following situations:

- **Pre-study evaluation:** Before charting out your course of study, read one or two questions at the beginning and end of every section to gauge your competence in the specific areas.
- **Reinforcement of key topics:** After you complete your study in each area, read through the answer cards (on the left side of the pages) to identify key topics and to reinforce concepts.

- **Identify areas for last-minute review:** In the days before an exam, review the study cards and carefully note your areas of weakness. Concentrate your remaining study time on these areas.

- **Post-study quiz:** By flipping through this book at random and viewing the questions on the right side of the pages, you can randomize your self-quiz to be sure that you're prepared in all areas.

- **Desk reference or field guide to core concepts (Quick Reference Guide sections only):** Networking professionals, sales representatives, and help-desk technicians alike can benefit from a handy, simple-to-navigate book that outlines the major topics aligned with the CCNA certification.

Quick Reference Guide

At the end of each part of the book, after the flash cards, you will find the Quick Reference Guide, which can serve as both a study guide for the CCNA exam and as a companion reference to the text. For readers who seek CCNA certification, this Quick Reference Guide is well suited to reinforce the concepts learned in the text rather than as a sole source of information. For readers who have either already obtained CCNA certification or simply need a basic overview, the study sheets in this guide can serve as a standalone reference.

What Is Included on the CD-ROM

The CD-ROM included with this book provides you with access to the Pearson IT Certification Practice Test (PCPT) software as well as the Pearson IT Certification Cert Flash Cards Online application.

The PCPT software comes complete with more than 200 exam-realistic practice test questions that help you assess your knowledge and exam-readiness. The software is fully customizable, enabling you to focus on individual topic areas or take completed, timed exams. You can work in study mode, which allows you to review answers and full explanations, or in practice exam mode, which simulates the actual exam experience. You can take notes on questions or bookmark questions to create your own custom question databases. This powerful assessment engine also tracks your performance and provides feedback on a chapter-by-chapter basis, laying out a complete assessment of your knowledge to help you focus your student where it is needed most.

The Cert Flash Cards Online allows you to access all the flash cards from the book in a customizable online application. This flexible application lets you enter your answer to each question and compare what you entered to the correct answer. You can choose to view cards in order or at random, and you can create custom sets from the entire bank of cards. The engine provides you with the ability to mark each question correct or incorrect and provides a detailed score report by category for each session. You can even write notes on each question and then get a printable PDF of all your notes aligned to the relevant questions. Best of all, the application is accessible by any device that has an Internet connection, allowing you to study at home on your desktop or on the go on your smartphone or tablet.

PART I   ICND1

Section 1
Exploring the Functions of Networking

Section 2
Introducing LANs

Section 3
Understanding Ethernet and Switch Operations

Section 4
Understanding TCP/IP

Section 5
Routing

Section 6
Managing Traffic Using Access Lists

Section 7
Enabling Internet Connectivity

Section 8
Managing Network Device Security

Section 9
Implementing VLANs and Trunks

Section 10
WAN Technologies

Section 11
Implementing OSPF

Section 12
Introducing IPv6

ICND1 Quick Reference Guide

Section 1
Exploring the Functions of Networking

Today's compute environment is exciting and changing quickly. Within a five-year period, we have seen technology innovation move from the business sector to the consumer sector. During this time, we have also seen virtualization increase the consolidation and mobility of systems, cloud computing, and consumer devices being used in the business.

All of this evolution of computing have one thing in common—the network. The network is the foundation that enables virtualization, cloud computing, and end users to bring their own devices to work. As such, the network plays a critical role to ensure the possibility of today's compute environment.

This section reviews the foundational functions of networking, including the OSI model and the TCP/IP model.

Question 1

What is a network?

Question 2

What four major categories make up the physical components of a network?

Question 3

What are the four major resources that are shared on a computer network?

Answer 1

A network is a collection of devices and end systems.

Networks consist of computers, servers, and network devices, such as switches, routers, wireless access points, and firewalls that are interconnected, communicating with each other and sharing resources with each other. They are found in homes, small business, and large enterprises.

Answer 2

The four major categories found in networks are

- **Endpoints:** These devices receive data and are endpoints of the network. Examples include PCs, servers, laptops, tablets, and so on.

- **Interconnections:** The components that provide a means for data to travel across the network. This includes network interface cards (NIC), network media, and connectors.

- **Switches:** Provide network access for compute devices and other network devices.

- **Routers:** Interconnect networks.

Answer 3

The four major resources that are shared on a computer network are as follows:

- **Data and applications:** Consist of computer data and network-aware applications such as e-mail

- **Resources:** Include input and output devices such as cameras and printers

- **Network storage:** Consists of directly attached storage devices (physical storage that is directly attached to a computer and a shared server), network attached storage, and storage-area networks

- **Backup devices:** Can back up files and data from multiple computers

Question 4

What are common network user applications on today's networks?

Question 5

List three categories of network applications.

Question 6

What are three types of network-monitoring software?

Answer 4

Common network user applications on today's networks are

- Email
- Web (this includes web applications or any application the uses HTTP/HTTPS)
- Instant messaging
- Video/collaboration
- Databases
- File sharing

Answer 5

Three categories of network applications are as follows:

- **Batch applications:** Examples are FTP and TFTP. They are started by a person and complete with no other interaction. Bandwidth is important but not critical.
- **Interactive applications:** Include database updates and queries. A person requests data from a server and waits for a reply. Response time depends more on the server and storage than the network.
- **Real-time applications:** Include VoIP and video. Network bandwidth is critical because these applications are time sensitive. Quality of service (QoS) and sufficient network bandwidth are mandatory for these applications.

Answer 6

Three types of network-monitoring software are

- **Protocol analyzers:** Capture network packets between network devices and decode the packets so that one can view what applications are being transmitted on a network.
- **Sniffers:** Work like a wiretap and allow one to observe network communication and view the data that is being transmitted.
- **Availability and performance programs:** Use protocols use as ICMP and SNMP to view the availability of network devices and performance in real time.

Question 7

Your company wants to provide streaming video services to all branches and sales representatives. What two network characteristics are the most critical to achieving this goal?

Question 8

When describing the characteristics of a network, what does speed refer to?

Question 9

When describing the characteristics of a network, what does cost refer to?

Answer 7

The most critical characteristics are bandwidth and latency.

Time-sensitive applications such as video and VoIP are dependent on bandwidth and latency to function properly. When implementing time-sensitive applications, one needs to ensure that the network has enough bandwidth and low delay to ensure a proper end-user experience.

Answer 8

Speed refers to how fast data is transmitted over the network.

Today's networks consist of speeds of 100 Mbps, 1Gbps, 10 Gbps, 40 Gbps, and 100 Gbps.

Answer 9

Cost refers to the general financial value of network components, installation, and maintenance.

NOTE   Do not confuse this with cost that is associated with dynamic routing protocols such as OSPF.

Question 10

When describing the characteristics of a network, what does security refer to?

Question 11

When describing the characteristics of a network, what does availability refer to?

Question 12

Your CIO wants to know the network availability of your company's network for the past year. During the past year, the network was down for 30 minutes. What was the total availability of the network?

Answer 10

Security refers to protecting the network devices and data from both internal and external sources.

Answer 11

Availability is the measurement of the network uptime compared to its downtime.

Network availability percentage can be calculated using the following formula, which calculates the number of minutes of downtime compared to the number of minutes in a year:

([525,600 – Minutes downtime] / [525,600]) * 100

Answer 12

The total availability was 99.994%.

([525,600 – 30] / [525,600]) * 100 = 99.994%

NOTE Network availability percentage is calculated using the following formula, which calculates the number of minutes of downtime compared to the number of minutes in a year:

([525,600 – Minutes downtime] / [525,600]) * 100

Question 13

When describing the characteristics of a network, what does scalability refer to?

Question 14

When describing the characteristics of a network, what does reliability refer to?

Question 15

What is the difference between the physical and logical network topology?

Answer 13

Scalability refers to how well the network can accommodate more users and more data—in other words, how easily the network can grow and expand.

Answer 14

Reliability refers to the dependability of the devices that make up the network (switches, routers, computers, servers, access points, software, and so on).

Answer 15

Physical topology defines the physical layout of devices and network media—cables, network devices, computers, and so on—and how these components are physically connected and configured.

Logical topology refers to the data path or logical paths of the network in which data accesses the media and transmits packets across it. This includes IP addresses as well as routing paths.

Question 16

What are the six types of physical topologies implemented in today's networks?

Question 17

What physical network topology connects all devices to one cable?

Question 18

Describe a ring physical network topology.

Answer 16

The six types of physical topologies implemented in today's networks are

- Star
- Extended star
- Mesh
- Partial mesh
- Bus
- Ring

NOTE   See the study sheets located at the back of the flash cards for a diagram of each of these physical topologies.

Answer 17

The bus topology connects all devices to one cable.

This cable connects one computer to another. In a logical bus topology, only one packet can be transmitted at a time.

Answer 18

In a ring topology, all hosts and devices are connected in the form of a ring or circle. The following two types of ring networks exist:

- **Single-ring:** In a single-ring network, all devices share a single cable and data travels in one direction. Each device waits its turn to send data over the network.
- **Dual-ring:** A dual-ring network has a second ring to add redundancy and allows data to be sent in both directions.

Question 19

Describe a star and extended star physical topology.

Question 20

What physical network topology connects all devices to each other?

Question 21

What is the difference between a full-mesh and a partial-mesh topology?

Answer 19

Star and extended star physical topologies are made up of a central connection point, such as a hub or switch, where all cable segments connect. A star topology resembles spokes in a bicycle wheel and is the network topology of choice in Ethernet networks.

When multiple star topologies are connected to a common independent centralized device, it is called an extended star topology.

Answer 20

A mesh network topology connects all devices to each other for fault tolerance and redundancy.

Answer 21

A full-mesh topology connects all nodes to one another for full redundancy. In a partial-mesh topology, at least one node maintains multiple connections to all other devices and one node cannot connect to all other nodes as well.

Question 22

What are the seven layers of the OSI reference model? Include the layer number and name of each layer in your answer.

Question 23

What are six reasons that the OSI reference model was created?

Question 24

What is the function of the physical layer (Layer 1) in the OSI model? Give some examples of physical layer implementation.

Answer 22

The seven layers of the OSI reference model are as follows:

- Layer 7: Application layer
- Layer 6: Presentation layer
- Layer 5: Session layer
- Layer 4: Transport layer
- Layer 3: Network layer
- Layer 2: Data link layer
- Layer 1: Physical layer

Answer 23

Six reasons that the OSI reference model was created are as follows:

1. To ensure that different vendors' products can work together
2. To create standards to enable ease of interoperability by defining standards for the operations at each level
3. To clarify general functions of internetworking
4. To divide the complexity of networking into smaller, more manageable sublayers
5. To simplify troubleshooting
6. To enable developers to modify or improve components at one layer without having to rewrite an entire protocol stack

Answer 24

The physical layer defines the physical medium. It defines the media type, the connector type, and the signaling type (baseband versus broadband). This includes voltage levels, physical data rates, and maximum cable lengths. The physical layer is responsible for converting frames into electronic bits of data, which are then sent or received across the physical medium. Twisted-pair, coaxial, and fiber-optic cable operate at this level. Other implementations at this layer are repeaters/hubs.

Question 25

What is the responsibility of the data link layer (Layer 2)?

Question 26

The Institute of Electrical and Electronics Engineers (IEEE) defines what sublayer of the data link layer?

Answer 25

The data link layer defines how data is formatted from transmission and how access to the physical media is controlled. This layer also typically includes error correction to ensure reliable delivery of data.

The data link layer translates messages from the network layer into bits for the physical layer, and it enables the network layer to control the interconnection of data circuits within the physical layer. Its specifications define different network and protocol characteristics, including physical addressing, error notification, network topology, and sequencing of frames.

Data-link protocols provide the delivery across individual links and are concerned with the different media types, such 802.3. The data link layer is responsible for putting 1s and 0s into a logical group. These 1s and 0s are then put on the physical wire. Some examples of data link layer implementations are IEEE 802.3, packet trailer (for Ethernet, frame check sequence [FCS] or cyclic redundancy check [CRC]), Fiber Distributed Data Interface (FDDI), High-Level Data Link Control (HDLC), and Frame Relay.

Answer 26

The IEEE defines the Media Access Control (MAC) sublayer of the data link layer.

Question 27

What functions does the Media Access Control (MAC) sublayer provide?

Question 28

What are examples of network devices that operate at the data link layer (Layer 2)?

Question 29

Describe the function of the network layer (Layer 3) of the OSI model. Give some examples of network layer implementations.

Answer 27

The MAC sublayer specifies how data is placed and transported over the physical wire. It controls access to the physical medium.

The MAC sublayer communicates downward directly to the physical layer. Physical addressing (MAC addresses), network topologies, error notification, and delivery of frames are defined at the MAC sublayer.

Answer 28

Bridges and switches operate at the data link layer.

Both devices make decisions about what traffic to forward or drop (filter) by MAC addresses; logical network address are not used at this layer. Data link layer devices assume a flat address space.

Answer 29

The network layer provides internetwork routing and logical network addresses. It defines how to transport traffic between devices that are not locally attached.

The network layer also supports connection-oriented and connectionless service from higher-layer protocols.

Routers and multilayer switches operate at the network layer. IP and IPv6 are examples of network layer implementations.

Question 30

Are network layer addresses physical or logical?

Question 31

What is the transport layer (Layer 4) of the OSI model responsible for? Give some examples of transport layer implementations.

Question 32

What layer of the OSI model handles the reliability of network communications between hosts using flow control, sequencing, and acknowledgments?

Answer 30

Network layer addresses are logical.

These addresses are logical addresses that are specific to the network layer protocol being run on the network. Each network layer protocol has a different addressing scheme. They are usually hierarchical and define networks first and then hosts or devices on that network. An administrator typically assigns network layer addresses either by static configuration or dynamic configuration.

An example of a network address is an IP address. For example, IPv4 has 32-bit addresses often expressed in decimal format. An example of an IPv4 address in decimal format is 192.168.0.1.

Answer 31

The transport layer segments and reassembles data from upper-layer applications into data streams. It provides reliable data transmission to upper layers.

End-to-end communications, flow control, multiplexing, error detection and correction, and virtual circuit management are typical transport layer functions. Some examples include Transmission Control Protocol (TCP) and User Datagram Protocol (UDP).

NOTE   Not all transport protocols perform error detection and correction. For example, UDP does not perform error detection or correction.

Answer 32

The transport layer handles this reliability.

The transport layer uses acknowledgments and sequence numbers for reliable delivery of data. Flow control is used to avoid network or host congestion.

Question 33

What is flow control, and what are the three methods of implementing it?

Question 34

How do network devices use buffering for flow control?

Question 35

What are the functions of the session layer (Layer 5) of the OSI model? Provide some examples.

Answer 33

Flow control is the method of controlling the rate at which a computer sends data, thus preventing network congestion.

The three methods of implementing flow control are as follows:

- Buffering
- Congestion avoidance
- Windowing

Answer 34

Buffering is used by network devices to temporarily store bursts of extra data in memory until they can be processed and sent. Buffering can handle occasional data bursts; however, buffer overflows can occur if data bursts are continuous.

Answer 35

The session layer is responsible for creating, managing, and ending communication sessions between presentation layer entities.

These sessions consist of service requests and responses that develop between applications located on different network devices. Some examples include Structured Query Language (SQL), remote-procedure call (RPC), and SSL.

Question 36

What is the responsibility of the presentation layer (Layer 6)?
Give some examples of Layer 6 implementations.

Question 37

What does the application layer (Layer 7) of the OSI model do,
and what are some examples of this layer?

Question 38

How do the different layers of the OSI model communicate with
each other?

Answer 36

Also known as the translator, the presentation layer provides coding and conversion functions to application layer data. This guarantees that the application layer on one system can read data transferred from the application layer of a different system. Some examples of the presentation layer are

- Compression, decompression, and encryption
- JPEG, TIFF, GIF, PICT, QuickTime, MPEG, EBCDIC, and ASCII file types

Answer 37

The application layer is the layer that is closest to the user. This means that this layer interacts directly with the software application. The application layer's main functions are to identify and establish communication partners, determine resource availability, and synchronize communication. Some examples include TCP/IP applications protocols such as Telnet, FTP, Simple Mail Transfer Protocol (SMTP), and HTTP.

NOTE   An application must have a communicating component, such as FTP, to be relevant to internetworking.

Answer 38

Each layer of the OSI model can communicate only with the layer above it, below it, and parallel to it (a peer layer on a remote host).

For example, the presentation layer can communicate with only the application layer and session layer on the local host, and the presentation layer on the remote host. These layers communicate with each other using service access points (SAP) and protocol data units (PDU). The SAP is a conceptual location at which one OSI layer can request the services of another OSI layer. PDUs control information that is added to the user data at each layer of the model. This information resides in fields called headers (the front of the data field) and trailers (the end of the data field).

NOTE   SAPs apply to OSI layer application protocols and do not apply to TCP/IP.

Question 39

Which layer of the OSI model uses the hardware address of a device to ensure proper message delivery to a host on a LAN?

Question 40

Which network layer protocols are responsible for path determination and traffic switching?

Question 41

At which layer on the OSI model is a logical path created between two host systems?

Answer 39

The data link layer uses physical addresses or hardware addresses for message delivery on a LAN.

Answer 40

Routing protocols are responsible for path determination and traffic switching.

Answer 41

The network layer creates a logical path between two host systems.

The logical path consists of logical addresses. Logical addresses are also known as network layer addresses.

Question 42

At which layers of the OSI model do WANs operate?

Question 43

What are the four layers of the TCP/IP stack?

Question 44

On what layer are physical data rates, connectors, and MAC addresses located in the TCP/IP stack?

Answer 42

WANs operate at the data link and physical layers.

The physical and data link layers work together to deliver data across a variety of types of physical networks like LANs, MANs, and WANs.

Answer 43

The four layers of the TCP/IP stack are as follows:

- Application
- Transport
- Internet
- Network Access

Answer 44

Physical data rates, connectors, and MAC addresses are located on the network access layer.

Question 45

What are some protocols that operate at the TCP/IP Internet layer?

Question 46

What is data encapsulation as it relates to the OSI model?

Answer 45

Some protocols that operate at the TCP/IP Internet layer are as follows:

- IP
- ICMP (Internet Control Message Protocol)
- ARP (Address Resolution Protocol)
- RARP (Reverse Address Resolution Protocol)

IP is the main connectionless routed protocol at the Internet layer (or OSI network layer). IP has various associated protocols, such as ICMP, ARP, and RARP.

Answer 46

Encapsulation wraps data with the necessary protocol information before network transmission.

A protocol data unit (PDU) can include different information as it goes up or down the OSI model. It is given a different name according to the information it is carrying (the layer where it is located). When the transport layer receives upper-layer data, it adds a TCP header to the data; this is called a segment. The segment is then passed to the network layer, and an IP header is added; thus, the data becomes a packet. The packet is passed to the data link layer, thus becoming a frame. This frame is then converted into bits and is passed across the network medium. This is data encapsulation. For the ICND test, you should know the following:

- Session layer and higher: Data
- Transport layer: Segment
- Network layer: Packet
- Data link layer: Frame
- Physical layer: Bits

Question 47

What is the process that data goes through when a host transmits data across a network to another host?

Answer 47

This process is known as encapsulation.

Encapsulation wraps data with the necessary protocol information before network transmission. For data to be transferred to other hosts on a network, it is encapsulated into a PDU.

Section 2
Introducing Local-Area Networks

Today's ultra-connected society requires that Internet access be provided almost anywhere. Because of this, networks play a central role in today's business and compute environment. In short, the network touches everything. Without the network, we would not have the Internet, cloud computing, video streaming to our homes, or social media. In general, there are three types of networks:

- Local-area networks
- Wide-area networks
- Storage-area network

Local-area networks (LAN) are an inexpensive way to connect and share resources. In today's environment, LANs are found almost everywhere: homes, small business, enterprises, schools, hospitals, and universities.

Wide-area networks (WAN) connect LANs together over many distances and media types.

Storage-area networks (SAN) are networks that connect storage arrays to servers providing high-speed access to data using protocols such as Fibre Channel, iSCSI, and Fibre Channel over Ethernet. SANs are not covered in ICND1 or ICND 2.

LANs provide high-speed connections to end users and are relatively easy to maintain. This section provides an overview of LAN technologies as well as Cisco IOS features, enhanced IOS editing commands, and basic Cisco router and switch configuration.

Question 1

What are local-area networks?

Question 2

What are LAN standards?

Question 3

What are the typical components found in LANs?

Answer 1

Local-area networks (LAN) are high-speed, low-error data networks that cover a small geographic area.

LANs are usually located in a building or campus and do not cover a large distance. They are relatively inexpensive to develop and maintain. LANs connect computers, printers, and other devices in a single building or a limited area.

Answer 2

LAN standards define the physical media and connectors used to connect to the media at the physical layer and the way devices communicate at the data link layer.

LAN standards encompass Layers 1 and 2 of the OSI model. An example of a LAN standard is Ethernet, which is also known as 802.3.

Answer 3

Typical components found in LANs are

- **Computers:** PCs, servers, tablets
- **Interconnections:** NICs, media
- **Network devices:** Switches, routers, access points
- **Protocols:** Ethernet, IP, ARP, DHCP

Question 4

What is the logical topology of Ethernet?

Question 5

What are two types of Layer 1 network devices?

Question 6

What are some network devices that operate at the data link layer (Layer 2)?

Answer 4

Bus. Ethernet uses a logical bus topology and either a physical bus or star topology.

Answer 5

Two types of Layer 1 network devices are as follows:

- **Repeaters:** Regenerate and retime network signals, allowing the signal to travel a longer distance on a network media.
- **Hubs:** Known as a multiple-port repeaters, hubs also regenerate and retime network signals. The main difference between a hub and a repeater is the number of ports a hub has. A repeater typically has two ports, whereas a hub has from 4 to 48 ports.

NOTE In Ethernet networks, both hubs and repeaters share the LAN bandwidth. All devices compete to use network bandwidth, and only one device can access the network at a time. For example, if you have ten devices connected to a 100-Mbps hub, all ten devices share the 100 Mbps of bandwidth.

Answer 6

Bridges and switches are network devices that operate at the data link layer. Both devices make decisions about what traffic to forward, flood, or drop (filter) by MAC addresses, and logical network addresses are not used at this layer. Data link layer devices assume a flat address space.

Typically, a bridge is designed to create two or more LAN segments and is software implemented.

A switch is a hardware version of a bridge, has many more ports than a bridge, and is designed to replace a hub while providing the filtering benefits of a bridge.

Question 7

What is a LAN segment?

Question 8

What devices can you use to extend a LAN segment?

Question 9

How do collisions occur on an Ethernet LAN?

Answer 7

A LAN segment is a network connection made by a single unbroken network cable.

Segments are limited by physical distance because, after a certain distance, the data transmission becomes degraded because of line noise and the reduction of signal strength.

Answer 8

To extend a LAN segment, you can use the following devices:

- Hubs
- Repeaters
- Bridges
- Switches

Answer 9

Collisions occur on a shared LAN segment when two devices try to communicate at the same time. In a shared Ethernet segment, only one device can transmit on the cable at a time. When two devices try to transmit at the same time, a collision occurs.

When a collision occurs, a jam signal is sent from a workstation. A collision affects all the machines on the segment, not just the two that collided; when the jam signal is on the wire, no workstations can transmit data. The more collisions that occur in a network, the slower it will be, because the devices must resend the packets that collided.

Question 10

What are collision domains?

Question 11

What happens when you segment the network with hubs/repeaters?

Question 12

What is the advantage of segmenting a LAN with switches?

Answer 10

A collision domain is set of LAN interfaces whose frames could collide with each other. For example, all devices connected to a hub are in the same collision domain.

Answer 11

Hubs and repeaters operate at the physical layer of the OSI model; segmenting a network with these devices appears as an extension to the physical cable.

Hubs and repeaters are transparent to devices; they are unintelligent devices. All devices that connect to a hub/repeater share the same bandwidth. Hubs/repeaters create a single broadcast and collision domain.

Answer 12

Switches operate at Layer 2 of the OSI model and filter and forward by MAC address. Each port on a switch provides fully dedicated bandwidth and creates a single collision domain. Because switches operate at Layer 2 of the OSI model, they cannot filter broadcasts, and they create a single broadcast domain.

Question 13

What devices are used to break up collision domains?

Question 14

In an attempt to extend your Ethernet LAN segment, you add a 24-port hub. How many collision domains will you have in the segment with the addition of the hub?

Question 15

In an attempt to extend your Ethernet LAN segment, you add a 24-port switch. How many collision and broadcast domains will you have in the segment with the addition of a switch?

Answer 13

Switches, bridges, and routers are used to break up collision domains. They create more collision domains and result in fewer network collisions. Each port on a bridge, switch, and router creates one collision domain. For example, if you have a switch with 24 ports, you have 24 separate collision domains.

Answer 14

You will have one collision domain.

A hub only extends the Ethernet segment, and all devices share the same segment bandwidth. As a result, a hub does not create more collision domains.

Answer 15

You will have 24 collision domains and one broadcast domain.

Switches operate at Layer 2 of the OSI model, and they divide the network into different segments, thus creating more collision domains. Each port on a switch creates one collision domain. Also, because a switch operates at Layer 2 of the OSI model, it cannot filter broadcasts. As such, a switched network will have one broadcast domain.

Question 16

What are broadcast domains?

Question 17

You install a six-port router on your network. How many collision domains and broadcast domains will be created on the network with the addition of the six-port router?

Question 18

What is a broadcast storm?

Answer 16

A broadcast domain defines a group of devices that receive each other's broadcast messages. As with collisions, the more broadcasts that occur on the network, the slower the network will be. This is because every device that receives a broadcast must process it to see whether the broadcast is intended for that device.

NOTE Although too many broadcasts can slow your network, they are used by many protocols for communications. To avoid excessive broadcasts, segment your network with routers or Layer 3 switches.

Answer 17

Six collision domains and six broadcast domains will be created.

Each interface on a router creates a collision domain and a broadcast domain.

Answer 18

Broadcast storms occur when many broadcasts are sent simultaneously across all network segments. They are usually caused by Layer 2 loops because of spanning tree misconfigurations, a bad network interface card (NIC), a faulty network device, or a virus.

Question 19

What three primary functions do Layer 2 switches provide?

Question 20

How does a switch differ from a hub?

Question 21

A fundamental concept behind LAN switching is that it provides microsegmentation. What is microsegmentation?

Answer 19

The three primary functions that Layer 2 switches provide are as follows:

- MAC address learning
- Frame forwarding/filtering
- Loop avoidance with the Spanning Tree Protocol

Answer 20

Switches are Layer 2 devices and make forwarding decisions based on Layer 2 information. Hubs operate on Layer 1. Switches make forwarding decisions based on Layer 2 information by learning MAC addresses on incoming frames and storing these frames in a MAC address table.

Answer 21

Microsegmentation is a network design (functionality) where each workstation or device on a network gets its own dedicated segment (collision domain) to the switch. Each network device gets the full bandwidth of the segment and does not have to contend or share the segment with other devices. Microsegmentation reduces collisions because each segment is its own collision domain.

Question 22

What advantages are offered by LAN segmentation using LAN switches?

Question 23

What are the three switching methods (frame transmission modes) in Cisco Catalyst switches?

Question 24

What is the Cisco Catalyst store-and-forward switching method?

Answer 22

A switch considers each LAN port to be an individual segment. The advantages offered by LAN segmentation using LAN switches are as follows:

- Collision-free domains from one larger collision domain
- Efficient use of bandwidth with full duplex
- Low latency and high frame-forwarding rates at each interface port

Answer 23

The three frame operating modes to handle frame switching are as follows:

- Store-and-forward
- Cut-through
- Fragment-free

Answer 24

In the store-and-forward switching method, the switch's incoming interface receives the entire frame before it forwards it. The switch compares the last field in the datagram, the cyclic redundancy check (CRC), against its own frame check sequence (FCS) calculations to make sure that the frame is free from physical and data-link errors. If the switch observes any errors in the FCS calculations, the frame is dropped. If the frame is a runt (less than 64 bytes, including the CRC) or a giant (more than 1518 bytes, including the CRC), the switch discards it. Because the switch stores the frame before forwarding it, latency is introduced in the switch. Latency through the switch varies with the size of the frame.

Question 25

What is the Cisco Catalyst cut-through switching method?

Question 26

What is the Cisco Catalyst fragment-free switching method?

Question 27

What are six ways to configure a Cisco device?

Answer 25

In cut-through switching mode, the switch only checks the frame's destination address and immediately begins forwarding the frame out the appropriate port. Because the switch checks the destination address in only the header and not the entire frame, the switch forwards a frame that has a bad CRC calculation.

Answer 26

Also known as modified cut-through, fragment-free switching checks the first 64 bytes of the frame before forwarding the frame. If the frame is less than 64 bytes, the switch discards the frame. Ethernet specifications state that collisions should be detected during the first 64 bytes of the frame. By reading the first 64 bytes of the frame, the switch can filter most collisions, although late collisions are still possible.

Answer 27

Six ways to configure a Cisco device are as follows:

- Console connection
- Auxiliary connection (through a modem)
- Telnet connection
- HTTP/HTTPS connection
- Secure Shell (SSH) Connection
- Cisco Prime

Question 28

What type of cable do you need to connect to a Cisco device's console port?

Question 29

What are the console configuration settings needed to connect to a Cisco device's console port?

Question 30

What two EXEC modes are supported in Cisco IOS?

Answer 28

You need an RJ-45–to–RJ-45 rollover cable. A rollover cable is a cable that has each pin wired to its opposite number at the other end.

Answer 29

The COM port configuration settings needed to connect to a Cisco device's console port are as follows:

- **Speed:** 9600 bits per second
- **Data bits:** 8
- **Parity:** None
- **Stop bit:** 1
- **Flow control:** None

Answer 30

The two Cisco IOS EXEC modes are

- User EXEC mode (user mode)
- Privileged EXEC mode (enable or privileged mode)

Question 31

What is user EXEC mode in Cisco IOS?

Question 32

In Cisco IOS, what is privileged EXEC mode?

Question 33

When you are in privilege EXEC mode, how do you return to user EXEC mode?

Answer 31

User EXEC mode allows a person to access only a limited number of basic monitoring commands. This mode is limited and is mostly used to view statistics. You cannot change a router's configuration in this mode. By default, the greater-than sign (>) indicates that you are in user mode. This is how the router prompt looks in user mode:

```
RouterA>
```

NOTE   You can change the default user-mode prompt and enable-mode prompt by using the **prompt** global mode command.

Answer 32

In privileged EXEC mode, you can view and change the configuration in a router; you have access to all the router's commands and the powerful **debug** commands.

To enter privileged mode, enter the **enable** command while in user mode. By default, the pound symbol (#) indicates that you are in privileged mode. This mode is usually protected with a password. Here is an example of how to enter privileged mode. You also see the output of the prompt:

```
Router> enable
Password:
Router#
```

Answer 33

You can return to user EXEC mode by using the **disable** IOS command. Here is an example of using the disable command:

```
Router# disable
Router>
```

Question 34

What two types of context-sensitive help are available in the Cisco IOS?

Question 35

You enter a command in EXEC mode and receive the following error:

```
% Ambiguous command:
```

What does this error mean?

Question 36

From EXEC mode, you issue the show ip command. After pressing Enter, you receive the following error:

```
% Incomplete command
```

Why did you get this error?

Answer 34

Two types are word help and command syntax help.

Word help uses a question mark (?) and identifies commands that start with a character or sequence of characters. For example, the following router output shows the use of word help for any IOS command that starts with the letters "cl":

```
Router# cl?
clear   clock
```

Command syntax help is when you use a question mark (?) after a command so that you can see how to complete the command. For example:

```
Router# clock ?
  set   Set the time and date
```

Answer 35

"% Ambiguous command" means that not enough characters were entered for the IOS to recognize the command.

Answer 36

You received the error because you did not enter all the values or keywords that IOS requires for this command.

In this case, IOS does not know which **show ip** command you want to view.

Question 37

Upon entering a command in EXEC mode, you receive the following error:

```
% Invalid input detected at '^' marker
```

Why did you get this error?

Question 38

What are Cisco IOS global commands?

Question 39

How do you enter global configuration mode?

Answer 37

You received the "% Invalid input detected at '^' marker" error because you entered the command incorrectly. For example, if you entered **sjow ip** instead of **show ip**, you would receive this error.

Answer 38

Global configuration commands are commands that affect the entire device. They can be executed only in global configuration mode.

Answer 39

To enter global configuration mode, you enter the **configure terminal** command from privileged EXEC mode, as follows:

```
Router# configure terminal
Enter configuration commands, one per line.  End with CTRL-Z.
Router(config)#
```

NOTE   Notice how the command prompt changes to (config)# in global configuration mode.

Question 40

On a Cisco IOS device, name the enhanced editing commands that do the following:

- Move the cursor to the beginning of the line
- Move the cursor to the end of the line
- Move the cursor forward one word
- Move the cursor forward one character to the right
- Move the cursor back one character
- Delete all characters from the cursor back to the beginning of the command line

Question 41

What Cisco IOS command would you use to view a list of the most recently used commands?

Answer 40

The enhanced editing commands are as follows:

- Move the cursor to the beginning of the line: Ctrl-A
- Move the cursor to the end of the line: Ctrl-E
- Move the cursor forward one word: Esc-F
- Move the cursor forward one character to the right: Ctrl-F
- Move the cursor back one character: Ctrl-B
- Delete all characters from the cursor back to the beginning of the command line: Ctrl-U

Answer 41

The **show history** command, by default, displays the last ten commands used. You can also use the up-arrow key (or press Ctrl-P) to display the very last command you entered and the down-arrow key (or press Ctrl-N) to display the previous commands you entered. As you use the up- or down-arrow keys, you are scrolling through the history buffer. The following is an example of the **show history** command:

```
Router# show history
      en
      show running-config
      show history
      enable
      show version
      show clock
      show history
Router#
```

Question 42

Command history is enabled by default and records ten commands in its history buffer for the current session. How do you edit the number of commands that are stored in the Cisco IOS device's history buffer?

Question 43

How can an administrator determine whether a switch has been configured when it is first powered up?

Question 44

Where on a Cisco device are the names of the two configuration files?

Answer 42

To edit the number of command lines stored for the current session, use the **terminal history** [**size** *number-of-lines*] command in privileged EXEC mode.

For example, the following changes the history size to 20 lines:

```
Router# terminal history size 20
```

NOTE   The maximum number of lines you can set for the current session is 256, but doing so wastes device memory.

Answer 43

When first powered up, an unconfigured switch enters the setup mode.

Answer 44

The names of the two configuration files are

- **Running configuration:** The current configuration of the device
- **Startup configuration:** The configuration file in NVRAM that is loaded when a Cisco device is powered up or rebooted

Question 45

What can cause a switch to enter setup mode?

Question 46

Which router component stores the routing tables, packet buffer, and ARP cache?

Question 47

What is the function of ROM on a Cisco device?

Answer 45

A switch enters setup mode if any of the following occur:

- The switch is a new switch, with no previous configuration.
- No configuration is stored in NVRAM.
- The **setup** command was issued from the privileged mode prompt.

Answer 46

RAM holds the router's routing table, packet buffers, and ARP cache. The running config is also stored in RAM. On most Cisco routers, the IOS is loaded into RAM as well.

Answer 47

On a Cisco device, ROM starts and maintains the router or switch.

Question 48

What is flash memory used for on a Cisco device?

Question 49

What is the function of NVRAM on a Cisco switch or router?

Answer 48

Flash memory stores the Cisco IOS Software image and, if room exists, multiple configuration files or multiple IOS files for backup purposes. Flash memory is not erased when the router or switch is reloaded.

Answer 49

Nonvolatile random-access memory (NVRAM) holds the saved router or switch configuration. This configuration is maintained when the device is turned off or reloaded. NVRAM also stores boot system commands and the configuration register.

Question 50

What Cisco IOS command displays the contents of flash memory?

Question 51

How do you display the amount of flash and RAM available on a Cisco router or switch?

Answer 50

The **show flash** command displays the contents of flash memory. This includes the images stored in flash memory, the images' names, bytes used in flash memory, bytes available, and the total amount of flash memory on your router, as follows:

```
cnat2-2901-1# show flash
-#- --length-- -----date/time------ path
1      74856492 Apr 5 2012 18:43:10 +00:00 c2900-universalk9-
                                             mz.SPA.151-4.M3.bin
2          2903 Apr 5 2012 18:51:04 +00:00 cpconfig-29xx.cfg
3       3000320 Apr 5 2012 18:51:20 +00:00 cpexpress.tar
4          1038 Apr 5 2012 18:51:34 +00:00 home.shtml
5        122880 Apr 5 2012 18:51:44 +00:00 home.tar
6       1697952 Apr 5 2012 18:52:04 +00:00 securedesktop-ios-
                                             3.1.1.45-k9.pkg
7        415956 Apr 5 2012 18:52:20 +00:00 sslclient-
                                             win-1.1.4.176.pkg
8          3982 May 3 2012 21:46:52 +00:00 BW
9      87224236 May 4 2012 18:53:26 +00:00 c2900-universalk9-
                                             mz.SPA.152-3.T.bin
10           27 May 9 2012 16:11:40 +00:00 LISP-MapCache-
                                             IPv4-00000000
11         4687 May 9 2012 20:59:32 +00:00 lisp

89137152 bytes available (167350272 bytes used)
```

Answer 51

The **show version** command displays the amount of flash and RAM available on a router and switch.

Question 52

What IOS command would you use to back up the running configuration on a Cisco IOS device to a TFTP server?

Question 53

How do you restore your Cisco IOS router to its factory defaults?

Answer 52

To back up the running configuration to a TFTP server, use the **copy running-config tftp** privileged EXEC command, which can also be shortened to **copy run tftp**. The example that follows shows this command in action:

```
RouterB# copy run tftp
Address or name of remote host []? 192.168.0.2
Destination filename [routerb-confg]?
!!
780 bytes copied in 6.900 secs (130 bytes/sec)
```

Answer 53

The **erase startup-config** privileged EXEC command, as follows, erases your router's configuration, thus bringing it back to its factory defaults:

```
RouterB# erase startup-config
Erasing the nvram filesystem will remove all files! Continue?
  [confirm]
[OK]
Erase of nvram: complete
```

NOTE   To complete the process, you need to reload the router. To restore a Cisco router to its factory defaults, you need to erase the startup config file and the VLAN.dat file, too.

Question 54

How do you restore the configuration file from a TFTP server to your Cisco IOS device's RAM?

Question 55

What IOS command is used to enter interface configuration mode?

Answer 54

The **copy tftp running-config** privileged EXEC command merges the previously backed up and running configuration into your Cisco device's RAM, so any commands not explicitly changed or removed will remain in the running configuration. Sample command output is as follows:

```
RouterB# copy tftp running-config
Address or name of remote host []? 192.168.0.2
Source filename []? routerb-confg
Destination filename [running-config]?
Accessing tftp://192.168.0.2/routerb-confg...
Loading routerb-confg from 192.168.0.2 (via Ethernet0): !
[OK - 780/1024 bytes]
780 bytes copied in 4.12 secs (195 bytes/sec)
RouterB#
01:40:46: %SYS-5-CONFIG: Configured from tftp:
  //192.168.0.2/routerb-confg
```

Answer 55

To enter interface configuration mode, use the **interface** *interface-id* command.

To enter interface mode, you first need to be in global configuration mode. The *interface-id* parameter is the type and number of the interface you want to configure.

For example, to configure gigabit interface 0/1, enter the following:

```
switch(config)# interface g0/1
switch(config-if)#
```

Question 56

What IOS command would you use to issue a switch the host name of "BuildingB-Switch"?

Question 57

As a network administrator, you have a new Catalyst switch. You want to assign it the IP address of 192.168.0.10/24. What IOS commands do you need to enter the IP address to the switch?

Question 58

How do you configure a Catalyst switch with a default gateway?

Answer 56

The **hostname BuildingB-Switch** global configuration mode IOS command allows you to configure this switch with a host name.

Answer 57

To assign the IP address to the switch, enter the following commands:

```
interface vlan1
         ip address 192.168.0.10 255.255.255.0
         no shutdown
```

Follow these steps to assign the IP address to the switch:

1. Enter the VLAN 1 interface. This is a logical interface used for management.

2. Assign the IP address and subnet masks.

3. Enable the interface by issuing the **no shutdown** command.

Answer 58

To configure the default gateway, use the **ip default-gateway** *ip-address* global configuration command. The following example configures the switch to use IP address 192.168.0.1 as its default gateway:

```
Switch(config)# ip default-gateway 192.168.0.1
```

NOTE   To remove the default gateway, use the **no ip default-gateway** command.

Question 59

Because a switch operates at Layer 2 of the OSI model, why do you need to configure a default gateway on the switch?

Question 60

What is the purpose of assigning an IP address to a switch?

Question 61

The system LED is amber on a Cisco Catalyst switch. What does this indicate?

Answer 59

You need to configure a default gateway on the switch to allow remote networks to manage the switch.

Although a switch does not see Layer 3 and above information, a default gateway is configured on a switch to allow administrators to remotely administer and configure the switch.

Answer 60

Assigning an IP address to a switch allows remote management of the switch.

Answer 61

The switch is malfunctioning.

The System (SYST) LED provides a quick overall status of the switch with three states:

- **Off:** The switch is not powered on.
- **On (green):** The switch is powered on and operational.
- **On (amber):** System malfunction. One ore more power-on self-tests errors occurred and the Cisco IOS did not load.

Question 62

How do you display the current active configuration on a switch?

Question 63

What command allows you to view the statistics for all interfaces on a switch?

Answer 62

You display the current active configuration on a switch by issuing the **show running-configuration** or **sh run** privileged command.

Answer 63

The **show interfaces** privileged command allows you to view the statistics for all interfaces configured on the switch.

Question 64

What command displays the switch's configured IP address, subnet mask, and default gateway?

Question 65

By default, Telnet access to a switch is disabled. How do you enable Telnet access and configure a password to secure access to a switch?

Answer 64

The **show ip interface** user and privilege EXEC command displays all IP information configured for all interfaces on the switch. Following is the output of the **show ip interface** command:

```
Switch# show ip interface
Vlan1 is up, line protocol is down
  Internet address is 192.168.0.10/24
  Broadcast address is 255.255.255.255
  Address determined by setup command
  MTU is 1500 bytes
  Helper address is not set
  Directed broadcast forwarding is disabled
  Outgoing access list is not set
  Inbound  access list is not set
  Proxy ARP is enabled
```

Answer 65

To enable a password for Telnet access, enter the **line vty 0 15** global configuration command, the **login** command, and finally the **password** line subcommand. The password is case sensitive.

In this example, the Telnet password is set to CCNA:

```
Switch(config)# line vty 0 15
Switch(config-line)# login
Switch(config-line)# password CCNA
```

NOTE   Without the **login** command, the switch will not let you log on through Telnet, even if a password is set.

Question 66

How many vty lines exist on a Catalyst switch?

Question 67

Privileged EXEC mode allows you to make global configuration changes to a switch. Because of this, best practice is to restrict access to privileged EXEC mode to authorized users. How do you restrict access to privileged EXEC mode?

Question 68

A network administrator issues the following commands on a Catalyst switch:

```
Cat2960(config)# enable password Cisco
Cat2960(config)# enable secret cisco1
```

What password will the switch use to enter privileged EXEC mode?

Answer 66

A Cisco Catalyst switch has 16 vty lines.

Answer 67

To restrict access to privileged EXEC mode, assign a password to privileged mode.

This is done in one of two ways: by either using the **enable password** global command or the **enable secret** global command.

Cisco recommends that you use the **enable secret** global command versus the **enable password** command because the **enable secret** command encrypts the password.

Answer 68

The switch will use cisco1 to enter privileged EXEC mode.

When a switch has the enable password and enable secret password configured, the switch will use the enable secret password as the password to enter privileged EXEC mode.

Question 69

When you view the configuration on Cisco IOS devices, only the enable secret password is encrypted. How do you encrypt the console, Telnet, and enable passwords?

Answer 69

To encrypt the passwords, use the **service password-encryption** global command, as follows:

```
Switch(config)# service password-encryption
```

Question 70

What Cisco switch IOS command displays the system hardware, software version, names of configuration files, and boot files?

Answer 70

The **show version** switch IOS command displays the system hardware, software version, boot images, and configuration register. The following is the output of the **show version** command:

```
cnat-2921-1# sh version
Cisco IOS Software, C2900 Software (C2900-UNIVERSALK9-M),
   Version 15.1(4)M2, RELEASE SOFTWARE (fc1)
Technical Support: http://www.cisco.com/techsupport
Copyright (c) 1986-2011 by Cisco Systems, Inc.
Compiled Mon 26-Sep-11 17:37 by prod_rel_team

ROM: System Bootstrap, Version 15.0(1r)M9, RELEASE SOFTWARE (fc1)

cnat-2921-1 uptime is 1 week, 5 days, 17 hours, 38 minutes
System returned to ROM by power-on
System restarted at 15:23:13 CST Sun Feb 10 2013
System image file is
   "flash0:c2900-universalk9-mz.SPA.151-4.M2.bin"
Last reload type: Normal Reload


<text omitted>

Cisco CISCO2921/K9 (revision 1.0) with 2285536K/73728K bytes of
memory.
Processor board ID FTX1549ALHF
4 Gigabit Ethernet interfaces
2 terminal lines
1 cisco Embedded service engine(s)
1 Services Module (SM) with Services Ready Engine (SRE)
   Cisco SRE-V Software 2.0.1.0 in slot/sub-slot 1/0
DRAM configuration is 64 bits wide with parity enabled.
255K bytes of non-volatile configuration memory.
255744K bytes of ATA System CompactFlash 0 (Read/Write)
<text omitted>
-----------------------------------------------------------------
Technology    Technology-package          Technology-package
              Current      Type           Next reboot
-----------------------------------------------------------------
--
ipbase        ipbasek9     Permanent      ipbasek9
security      None         None           None
uc            None         None           None
data          None         None           None

Configuration register is 0x2102
```

Question 71

As a system administrator, you want to view how long the switch has been running since its last reboot. What command do you issue to view the uptime of the switch?

Question 72

How do you display the MAC address table on a Catalyst 2960 switch?

Answer 71

Issue the **show version** EXEC command to view the uptime of the switch.

In addition to displaying the switch hardware configuration and software version information, the **show version** command displays switch uptime, switch platform information including RAM, switch serial number, and MAC address.

```
cisco2960-1# sh version
Cisco IOS Software, C2960 Software (C2960-LANBASEK9-M), Version
   15.1SE3, RELEASE SOFTWARE (fc1)
Technical Support: http://www.cisco.com/techsupport
Copyright (c) 1986-2010 by Cisco Systems, Inc.
Compiled Thu 02-Dec-10 08:16 by prod_rel_team
Image text-base: 0x00003000, data-base: 0x01800000

ROM: Bootstrap program is C2960 boot loader
BOOTLDR: C2960 Boot Loader (C2960-HBOOT-M) Version 15.1SE3,
   RELEASE SOFTWARE (fc1)

cisco2960-1 uptime is 27 weeks, 4 days, 20 hours, 4 minutes
System returned to ROM by power-on
```

Answer 72

You display the MAC address table on a Catalyst 2960 by issuing the **show mac-address-table** privileged command, as follows:

```
Switch-1# show mac-address-table
            Mac Address Table
-------------------------------------------------

Vlan    Mac Address       Type        Ports
----    -----------       --------    -----
 All    0000.0000.0000    STATIC      CPU
 All    000b.469d.c900    STATIC      CPU

  10    0002.b3ef.c687    DYNAMIC     Po1
  10    0007.e980.d7a6    DYNAMIC     Fa0/7
  10    000d.65ac.507f    DYNAMIC     Po1
  10    000f.207a.008c    DYNAMIC     Po1
  10    0010.db72.b08f    DYNAMIC     Fa0/24
<text omitted>
```

NOTE   Static addresses are MAC addresses assigned to specific ports and not aged out. The Po1 port is a logical port used by EtherChannel. EtherChannel is discussed in ICND2.

Question 73

How do you add a password to the console terminal line?

Question 74

How do you add a message of the day (MOTD) banner on a Cisco IOS device?

Answer 73

To add a password to the console terminal line, use the **line console 0** global configuration command, followed by the **login** and **password** *password* line configuration mode commands, as follows:

```
Cat2960(config)# line console 0
Cat2960(config-line)# login
Cat2960(config-line)# password CCNA
```

The **login** subcommand forces the router to prompt for authentication. Without this command, the router will not authenticate a password. The **password CCNA** subcommand sets the console password to CCNA. The password set is case sensitive.

NOTE Sometimes, when people type **login,** they tend to want to type **login local,** which looks for a username/password statement in the local router configuration. If you do not have a username and password configured locally and you type in **login local,** the only way to access the system would be through password recovery.

Answer 74

You add an MOTD banner by entering the **banner motd #** *text* **#** global configuration command.

The pound signs (#) are delimiting characters. They can be any character of your choice, but they must be the same and cannot be included in your text. They signify the beginning and end of your text. The following example shows the **banner motd** command:

```
Cat2960(config)# banner motd #
Enter TEXT message.  End with the character '#'.
Warning only authorized users many access this switch.
#
Cat2960(config)#
```

NOTE The MOTD banner is displayed to anyone who connects to the router through VTY, the console port, or the auxiliary port.

Section 3

Understanding Ethernet and Switch Operations

Ethernet is the technology of choice for today's LANs. It is fast, has low costs, and is easy to maintain. Today's Ethernet standards support speeds of 10 Mbps, 100 Mbps, 1 Gbps, 10 Gbps, and 40 Gbps.

Ethernet functions at Layers 1 and 2 of the Open Systems Interconnection (OSI) model. As such, Ethernet standards specify cabling, signaling, and data link layer addressing.

Because most LANs use Ethernet as the primary Layer 2 technology, most switches today are Ethernet switches. This section covers the fundamentals of Ethernet technologies and describes how switches operate.

Question 1

What does BASE mean in 100BASE-T and 1000BASE-T?

Question 2

What is carrier sense multiple access collision detect (CSMA/CD)?

Question 3

What is UTP cabling?

Answer 1

BASE in 100BASE-T and 1000BASE-T refers to the baseband signaling method. Baseband is a network technology in which only one carrier frequency is used. This means that when a device transmits, it uses the entire bandwidth on the wire and does not share it during the single time interval.

Answer 2

CSMA/CD describes the Ethernet access method.

In CSMA/CD, many stations can transmit on the same cable, and no station has priority over any other. Before a station transmits, it listens on the wire (carrier sense) to make sure that no other station is transmitting. If no other station is transmitting, the station transmits across the wire. If a collision occurs, the transmitting stations detect the collision and run a random backoff algorithm. The random backoff algorithm is a random time that each station waits before retransmitting.

Answer 3

Unshielded twisted-pair (UTP) cabling is a type of twisted-pair cable that relies solely on the cancellation effects produced by the twisted wire pairs to limit electromagnetic interference (EMI) and radio frequency interference (RFI).

UTP cable is often installed using an RJ-45 connector, and UTP cabling must follow precise specifications dictating how many twists are required per meter of cable. The advantages of UTP are ease of installation and low cost. A disadvantage of UTP is that it is more prone to EMI than other types of media.

Question 4

What is the maximum cable length for UTP?

Question 5

What is a straight-through Ethernet cable, and when would you use it?

Question 6

What is a crossover Ethernet cable, and when would you use it?

Answer 4

The maximum length is 100 meters or 328 feet.

Answer 5

A straight-through Ethernet cable is wired the same way at both ends. This cable uses pins 1, 2, 3, and 6. The send and receive wires are not crossed.

You should use a straight-through Ethernet cable when connecting dissimilar devices (for example, data terminal equipment [DTE] to data communications equipment [DCE]). Examples include connecting PCs (DTE) to switches or hubs (DCE) or a router (DTE) to a switch or a hub (DCE).

Answer 6

A crossover Ethernet cable is a cable that has the send and receive wires crossed at one of the ends. In a Category 5 cable, the 1 and 3 wires are switched and the 2 and 6 wires are switched at one end of the cable.

You should use a crossover cable when connecting similar devices (DCE to DCE or DTE to DTE), such as connecting a router to a router, a switch to a switch or hub, a hub to a hub, or a PC to a PC.

NOTE In today's networks, most Catalyst switches have auto-mdix, which can automatically detect the type of cable connected to the interface and automatically configure the connection appropriately.

Question 7

What are the different UTP categories?

Question 8

What is the difference between single-mode fiber (SMF) and multimode fiber (MMF)?

Question 9

What are three ways that LAN traffic is transmitted?

Answer 7

The categories of UTP cable are as follows:

- **Category 1:** Used for telephone communications.
- **Category 2:** Capable of data transmission speeds of up to 4 Mbps.
- **Category 3:** Used in 10BASE-T networks. Speeds up to 10 Mbps.
- **Category 4:** Used in Token Ring networks. Speeds up to 16 Mbps.
- **Category 5:** Capable of data transmission speeds of up to 100 Mbps.
- **Category 5e:** Supports speeds of up to 1 Gbps.
- **Category 6:** Consists of four pairs of 24-gauge copper wires. Speeds up to 1 Gbps.
- **Category 6a:** Supports speeds up to 10 Gbps.

Answer 8

The primary difference between SMF and MMF is the ability of the fiber to send light for a long distance at high bit rates. In general, MMF supports shorter distances than SMF.

Answer 9

LAN traffic is transmitted one of the following three ways:

- **Unicast:** Unicasts are the most common type of LAN traffic. A unicast frame is a frame intended for only one host.
- **Broadcast:** Broadcast frames are intended for all hosts within a broadcast domain. Stations view broadcast frames as public service announcements. All stations receive and process broadcast frames.
- **Multicast:** Multicasts are traffic in which one transmitter tries to reach only a subset, or group, of the entire segment.

Question 10

How many bits are in an Ethernet address?

Question 11

What portion of the MAC address is vendor specific?

Question 12

What portion of the MAC address is vendor assigned?

Answer 10

Also called a MAC address, an Ethernet address is the Layer 2 address associated with the Ethernet network adapter. Typically burned into the adapter, the MAC address is usually displayed in a hexadecimal format, such as 00-0d-65-ac-50-7f.

Answer 11

The first half or first 24 bits of the MAC address are vendor specific.

A MAC address is 48 bits and is displayed in hexadecimal. The first half of the address identifies the vendor or manufacturer of the card. This is called the Organizational Unique Identifier (OUI). The last half of the address identifies the card address.

Answer 12

The last 24 bits are vendor assigned.

Question 13

What are the first 24 bits in a MAC address called?

Question 14

What is an example of a Layer 2 address?

Question 15

What is an example of a Layer 3 address?

Answer 13

These bits are the Organizational Unique Identifier (OUI).

Answer 14

An example is a MAC address.

Answer 15

An example is an IP address.

Question 16

If a sending device does not know the MAC address of the destination device, what protocol is used to find the MAC address of the receiving device?

Question 17

Host A wants to send data to host B. Host B is on a different segment from host A. The two segments are connected to each other through a router. What will host B see as the source MAC address for all frames sent from host A?

Question 18

Switching uses a process outlined by the IEEE as transparent bridging. What are the five processes transparent bridges use for determining what to do with a frame?

Answer 16

Address Resolution Protocol (ARP) is used to find the MAC address of the receiving device.

ARP is a local broadcast sent to all devices on the local segment to find the MAC address of a host.

Answer 17

Because host B is on a different segment that is separated by a router, the MAC address of all frames sent from host A will be the MAC address of the router. Anytime a frame passed through a router, a router rewrites the MAC address to the MAC address of the router's exit interface for the segment and then sends the frame to the local host.

In this case, the router will change the source MAC address of the frame sent from host A with the MAC address of its interface connecting to the segment host B is on. Host B will see that the frame came from the MAC address of the router with the IP address of host A.

Answer 18

The five processes of transparent bridging as defined in IEEE 802.1d are

1. Learning
2. Flooding
3. Filtering
4. Forwarding
5. Aging

Question 19

What is the transparent bridging learning process?

Question 20

What is the transparent bridging flooding process?

Question 21

What is the transparent bridging filtering process?

Answer 19

When a frame enters a switch, the switch adds the source Ethernet MAC address and source port into its MAC address table. The process of recording the source MAC address and the source port in the table whenever a switch sees a frame is called the learning process.

Answer 20

When a switch receives a unicast frame and it does not have the destination MAC address and port in its bridging table, or a broadcast or multicast frame, the switch will forward this frame out all ports, except the port it received the unicast frame on. This is called the flooding process.

Answer 21

The filtering process occurs when a switch receives a frame and the source and destination hosts reside on the same interface. When this occurs, the switch filters or discards the frame.

Question 22

What is the transparent bridging forwarding process?

Question 23

What is the transparent bridging aging process?

Question 24

For what two purposes does the Ethernet protocol use physical addresses?

Answer 22

A switch forwards a frame when the destination address is in the switch's MAC address table and the source and destination are on different interfaces. This is the forwarding process.

Answer 23

When a switch learns a source address, it time-stamps the entry in the MAC address table. Every time the switch sees a frame from the same source, the timestamp is updated. The aging process occurs when the switch does not see a frame from the source before the aging timer expires. When this happens, the switch removes the entry from the MAC address table.

Answer 24

Ethernet uses physical addresses to

■ Uniquely identify devices at Layer 2

■ Allow communication between different devices on the same Layer 2 network

Question 25

What will an Ethernet switch do if it receives a unicast frame with a destination MAC that is listed in the switch table?

Question 26

Under what conditions would a switch flood a frame?

Answer 25

The switch will forward the frame to a specific port.

Switches use the transparent bridging process to determine how to handle frames. The process is as follows:

1. A frame is received.

2. If the destination is a broadcast or multicast, the switch will forward the frame to all ports except to the port the frame was received.

3. If the destination is a unicast and the address is not in the MAC address table, the switch forwards the frame to all ports except the receiving port.

4. If the destination is a unicast, the address is in the MAC address table, and the associated interface in the MAC address table is not the receiving interface, the switch forwards the frame to the correct interface.

5. If the above rules do not occur, filter the frame.

Answer 26

A switch will flood a frame if the MAC address table is full, if the destination MAC address has not been learned by the switch, or if the frame is a broadcast or multicast frame.

Question 27

What is the switch MAC address table used for?

Question 28

Describe full-duplex transmission.

Answer 27

The switch MAC address table forwards traffic out the appropriate interface.

Because switches operate at Layer 2 of the OSI model, they switch traffic by MAC address. Instead of flooding traffic out all interfaces, a switch learns the MAC address of devices on each interface and only forwards traffic destined to the host on the interface. The learned MAC addresses are stored in the switch's MAC address table.

Answer 28

Full-duplex transmission is achieved by setting switch interfaces, router ports, and host NICs to full duplex. Microsegmentation, where each network device has its own dedicated segment to the switch, ensures that full duplex will work properly. Because the network device has its own dedicated segment, it does not have to worry about sharing the segment with other devices. With full-duplex transmission, the device can send and receive at the same time, effectively doubling the amount of bandwidth between nodes.

Three points to remember about the operation of full-duplex communication are

■ There are no collisions in full-duplex mode.

■ A dedicated switch port is required for each full-duplex node.

■ The host network card and the switch port must be capable of operating in full-duplex mode.

Question 29

What are the advantages of using full-duplex Ethernet instead of half-duplex?

Question 30

How does replacing a hub with a switch affect CSMA/CD behavior in an Ethernet network?

Answer 29

Full-duplex provides faster data transfer by being able to send and receive simultaneously and operates without collisions.

NOTE   By enabling full-duplex on a port, you are disabling CSMA/CD on the segment.

Answer 30

It effectively eliminates collisions.

Replacing a hub with a switch effectively eliminates collisions because each switch port is a separate collision domain. One device per switch port and configured for full-duplex operation eliminates the need for CSMA/CD.

Question 31

What command allows you to view the duplex and speed settings configured for a switch port?

Question 32

Can a network hub be connected to a switch port in full-duplex mode?

Answer 31

To view the duplex and speed setting configured for a switch port, enter the **show interface** *interface-id* command, as follows:

```
Cat2960# show interface f0/1
FastEthernet0/1 is up, line protocol is up
  Hardware is Fast Ethernet, address is 0019.e81a.4801
    (bia 0019.e81a.4801)
  MTU 1500 bytes, BW 10000 Kbit, DLY 1000 usec,
    reliability 255/255, txload 1/255, rxload 1/255
  Encapsulation ARPA, loopback not set
  Keepalive set (10 sec)
  Auto-duplex, Auto-speed, media type is 10/100BaseTX
  input flow-control is off, output flow-control is unsupported
  ARP type: ARPA, ARP Timeout 04:00:00
```

Answer 32

No. Because a hub shares access to the segment, it must connect to a switch port in half-duplex mode to be able to detect collisions.

NOTE CSMA/CD is not enforced when full-duplex is configured.

Question 33

When troubleshooting a switch interface operating in full-duplex mode, which error condition can be immediately ruled out?

Question 34

An end user complains of slow access to the network. You issue the show interface command on the port the end user is connected to and you see a lot of collisions and runts on the interface. What is most likely the cause of the problem?

Question 35

An end user complains of slow access to the network. You issue the show interface command on the port the user is connected to and you see a lot of collisions and cyclic redundancy check (CRC) errors on the interface. What can be several causes for the problem?

Answer 33

Collisions can be ruled out.

Remember, collisions occur only on half-duplex links. There are no collisions on full-duplex links.

Answer 34

A duplex mismatch is most likely the cause.

Although there are many things that can cause network slowness, the key here is when you issue the **show interface** command, you see many collisions and runts. A duplex mismatch will not only cause the end user to experience network slowness but also cause many collisions and runts on the switch interface.

Answer 35

The most likely causes of the problem are a bad network cable, damaged media, or EMI.

Excessive collisions and CRC errors usually indicate a problem with the network cable attached to the port, or outside interference.

Question 36

You connect two switches using a straight-through UTP Cat 6 cable. The port link lights between the switches are not coming on. What is the problem?

Question 37

You have a port on your switch that is not working properly. You enter the show interface command on the faulty port and the port status says "errDisable." What are some possible causes for this error?

Question 38

Traffic between two switches is slow. You issue the show interface command on the uplink between the two switches and you see the following:

```
!output omitted!
0 input packets with dribble condition detected
     180749 packets output, 8004302 bytes, 0 underruns
     0 output errors, 45345 collisions, 0 interface resets
     0 babbles, 45345 late collision, 0 deferred
     0 lost carrier, 0 no carrier
     0 output buffer failures, 0 output buffers swapped out
```

What are several possibilities for this problem?

Answer 36

The problem is with the cable. A straight-through cable is used to connect data terminal equipment (DTE) devices to data communications equipment (DCE) devices. A switch is considered a DCE device, and so are hubs. DTE devices include computers, printers, servers, and routers. For two like devices to connect to each other, a crossover cable is needed. In this case, replacing the cable with a crossover cable will fix the problem.

Answer 37

If you are having connectivity issues and the port state shows "errDisable," the following issues can be causing this error:

- EtherChannel misconfiguration.
- Duplex mismatch.
- Bridge protocol data unit (BPDU) port guard has been enabled on the port.
- Unidirectional Link Detection (UDLD).
- A native VLAN mismatch.

Answer 38

The switch port is receiving a lot of late collisions. The problem can be a duplex mismatch or a faulty port, or the distance between the two switches might exceed the cable specifications.

NOTE   Duplex mismatches occur when the connecting ends are set to different duplex modes, or when one end's duplex is configured and the other end is set to autonegotiation.

Question 39

What is the cause of multiple collisions on a port?

Question 40

While troubleshooting a switched network, you see the following on a switch interface that is having connectivity problems:

```
!output omitted!
  5 minute input rate 10000 bits/sec, 8 packets/sec
  5 minute output rate 10000 bits/sec, 7 packets/sec
      1476671 packets input, 363178961 bytes, 0 no buffer
      Received 20320 broadcasts (12683 multicast)
      2345 runts, 0 giants, 0 throttles
      0 input errors, 0 CRC, 0 frame, 0 overrun, 0 ignored
```

What could be the cause of the problem?

Answer 39

Multiple collisions are the number of times the transmitting port had more than one collision before successfully transmitting a frame. If you experience multiple collisions on a port, the problem usually lies with an oversaturated medium.

Answer 40

The switch is receiving a lot of runts. Runts are frames smaller than 64 bytes with a bad frame check sequence (FCS). Bad cabling or inconsistent duplex settings usually cause runts.

Section 4
Understanding TCP/IP

TCP/IP was created by the Defense Advanced Research Projects Agency (DARPA) to run as the protocol for the ARPANET in 1974. TCP/IP is the most widely used protocol suite in the world today. It is the protocol suite used on the Internet, and most network operating systems (NOS) require TCP/IP to run to communicate with other nodes. TCP/IP is the protocol suite you will encounter the most as a network engineer. You must thoroughly understand TCP/IP and know how it works.

As you can tell by its name, TCP/IP is a suite of protocols, with its major protocols being TCP and IP. TCP provides reliable delivery, and IP provides network addressing and routing.

Currently, two versions of IP exist: IP version 4 (IPv4) and IP version 6 (IPv6). IPv4 is the most widely used implementation of IP. IPv4 has a 32-bit network address, and IPv6 has a 128-bit network address. Currently, IPv4 addresses are exhausted. As a result, IPv6 is being implementing in the Internet. This section focuses on IPv4 addresses unless otherwise noted.

Variable-length subnet masking (VLSM) is a way to divide larger subnets into smaller subnets. VLSM was introduced as a way to save IP addresses from being wasted and can combine networks to summarize routes. Route summarization reduces the size of routing tables and improves convergence time by advertising the entire summary route instead of each individual route. For example, a large company is using the IP range 192.168.1.0 to 192.168.255.255, instead of advertising all 255 networks, the company could summarize one route to all its networks: 192.168.0.0 255.255.0.0 to other routers.

Question 1

What is the Internet Protocol (IP)?

Question 2

What is an IP address used for?

Question 3

How many bits are in an IPv4 address? In an IPv6 address?

Answer 1

IP is a connectionless protocol that provides best-effort delivery and routing of packets. IP has the following characteristics:

- Operates at Layer 3 (network) of the Open Systems Interconnection (OSI) reference model and the Internet layer of the TCP/IP (Internet) model.
- Is connectionless, providing best-effort delivery of packets.
- Uses hierarchical addressing.
- Has no built-in data recovery.
- Each packet is treated independently; thus each packet can travel a different way to its destination.
- Operates independently of the medium that is carrying the data.

Answer 2

An IP address uniquely identifies a device on an IP network.

Answer 3

IPv4: 32 bits

IPv6: 128 bits

Question 4

An IP address is a hierarchical address that consists of what two parts?

Question 5

What are the different classes of IP addressing and the address ranges of each class?

Answer 4

An IP address is a hierarchical address that consists of the following two parts:

- **Network ID:** Describes the network to which the IP address or device belongs
- **Host ID:** The ID that identifies a specific host

NOTE   IP addresses include the use of a subnet mask that is responsible for deciphering which part of the IP address is the network and which part is the host.

Answer 5

The different classes of IP addressing and their ranges are as follows:

- **Class A:** 1.0.0.0 to 126.255.255.255
- **Class B:** 128.0.0.0 to 191.255.255.255
- **Class C:** 192.0.0.0 to 223.255.255.255
- **Class D:** 224.0.0.0 to 239.255.255.255 (Multicasting)
- **Class E:** 240.0.0.0 to 255.255.255.254 (Reserved)

NOTE   127.0.0.0 is also a Class A network, but it is reserved for the loopback, or "localhost," IP—the IP address of the TCP/IP software itself.

Question 6

What are the five types of reserved IPv4 addresses?

Question 7

What does RFC 1918 define?

Answer 6

The five reserved IPv4 addresses are

- **Network address:** The address of the network is an IP address that has binary 0s in all the host bit positions.

- **Direct broadcast address:** An address for each network that allows communication to all hosts on a network. The direct broadcast address has all 1s in the host bit positions.

- **Local broadcast address:** Used to allow hosts to communicate with all hosts on a local network. The address used is 255.255.255.255.

- **Local loopback address:** Used to let the system send a message to itself for testing. This address is 127.0.0.1.

- **All zeros address:** Used to indicate hosts in "this" network and used only as a source address.

Answer 7

RFC 1918 defines reserved (private) networks and addresses that are not routed on the Internet.

These addresses are as follows:

- 10.0.0.0 to 10.255.255.255
- 172.16.0.0 to 172.31.255.255
- 192.168.0.0 to 192.168.255.255

They are used as internal private addresses within a corporation or home network. Private addresses are widely used today, and they employ mechanisms such as Network Address Translation (NAT) and Port Address Translation (PAT) to assist with "stretching" the current IPv4 address space. This stretching is done by translating private IP addresses to public routable IP addresses on the Internet, thus ensuring that private hosts can communicate externally without having a public IP address directly configured.

Question 8

If an IP addressed device wants to communicate with all devices on the local network, what is the destination IP address of its broadcast?

Question 9

What is special about IP address 127.0.0.1?

Question 10

In a default Class A network, how many octets are used for host addresses?

Answer 8

The destination IP address is 255.255.255.255.

This address is also called the local broadcast address.

Answer 9

127.0.0.1 is the loopback address.

The loopback address is used to test the proper installation of the IP stack.

Answer 10

Three octets are used for host addresses. One octet consists of 8 bits; thus a default Class A network uses 24 bits for host addresses. The maximum number of hosts a Class A network can have is 16,777,214 (2^{24} − 2).

Question 11

How many hosts are available for use in a default Class B network?

Question 12

How many hosts are available for use in a default Class C network?

Question 13

What is DNS?

Answer 11

65,534 addresses are available.

A default Class B network uses 16 bits for host addresses; thus $2^{16} - 2 = 65,534$.

Answer 12

254 hosts are available.

A default Class C network uses 8 bits for host addresses. Thus $2^8 - 2 = 254$.

Answer 13

The Domain Name System (DNS) converts domain names or host names into IP addresses.

Instead of having to remember a host's IP address, DNS allows you to use a friendly name to access the host. For example, it is easier to remember http://www.cisco.com than 198.133.219.25.

Question 14

On a Windows computer, what command can you use at the command prompt to view the IP information assigned to the PC?

Question 15

On a Windows computer, what commands do you use to release an IP address obtained from DHCP and request a new address?

Question 16

Convert the binary number 01100100 to decimal.

Answer 14

You can use the **ipconfig** command.

Answer 15

- To release the IP address: **ipconfig /release**
- To request a new address: **ipconfig /renew**

Answer 16

Converting a binary number to decimal is just the reverse of converting a decimal number to binary. When converting from binary, look at the numbers that are considered ON and then find their place value. In the binary number 01100100, the place values 64, 32, and 4 are ON. If you add these place values together, you get the decimal number of 100.

Question 17

Convert the binary number 0101011011000010 to hexadecimal.

Question 18

What is the range of binary values for the first octet in Class B addresses?

Question 19

What is the role of the subnet mask in an IP network?

Answer 17

Converting binary to hex is easier than it looks. No matter how large the binary number, always apply the following conversion: Break the binary number into groups of four, starting from the right and moving left. If the binary number is not divisible by four, add 0s to the left end or until you have four digits in every group.

Using this equation, 0101011011000010 is broken into the following groups: 0101 0110 1100 0010. After you have created the groups, you can convert the digits to hex. 0101 is 5 in hex, 0110 is 6, 1100 is C, and 0010 is 2, so this binary number looks like the following in hex: 0x56C2.

Answer 18

The first octet for a Class B IP address is 128–191 in decimal, which is 10000000– 10111111 in binary.

If you see similar questions on the ICND 1 exam, remember the following:

■ Class A addresses always have the high-order bit as 0. For example, 0xxxxxxx.

■ Class B addresses always have the high-order bit as 1 and the second bit as 0. For example, 10xxxxxx.

■ Class C addresses always have the high-order bit and second bit as 1. The third bit is 0. For example,110xxxxx.

Answer 19

The subnet mask identifies the network and host portion of an IP address. It is used by hosts to identify the destination IP address as either local or remote and is also used by routers to determine the path to route packets.

Question 20

How many usable IP addresses are provided in a default Class C network address?

Question 21

Convert the decimal number 167 to binary.

Answer 20

254 usable IP addresses are provided. The default subnet mask for a Class C address is 255.255.255.0, or /24. This means that 24 bits are used for the network number and 8 bits are reserved for hosts. $2^8 = 256$. However, because two addresses are reserved for the network address and broadcast address, the amount of usable IP addresses is 254. The formula to calculate usable IP addresses is 2^n-2, where n is the number of host bits.

Answer 21

Binary uses only two symbols (1 or 0) instead of ten symbols like decimal. In binary, 1 signifies ON and 0 signifies OFF. To convert a decimal number to binary, each digit represents the number 2 raised to a power exponent based on its position. The following table converts decimal to binary:

Base Exponent	2^7	2^6	2^5	2^4	2^3	2^2	2^1	2^0
Place Value	128	64	32	16	8	4	2	1

To convert a decimal number to binary, first find the largest power of 2 that can fit into the decimal number. If you have the decimal number 167, 128 is the largest power of 2 that fits into this binary number, so 128 is considered ON. Subtracting 128 from 167 leaves you with 39. The next largest power that can fit into 39 is 32, so 32 is considered ON. Subtracting 32 from 39 leaves you with 7, so 4, 2, and 1 are considered ON. This leaves you with the following binary number: 10100111.

Question 22

What is the correct network address for host
192.168.10.72/26?

Question 23

What is the purpose of the default gateway?

Question 24

A host computer has been correctly configured with a static IP
address, but the default gateway is incorrect. Which layer of
the OSI model is first affected by this misconfiguration?

Answer 22

The correct network address is 192.168.10.64.

A 26-bit subnet mask is 255.255.255.192. A quick way to find the network of a given subnet mask is to subtract the last portion of the subnet mask from 256. In this case, 256 – 192 = 64. Assuming that the **ip subnet zero** command is enabled on the router, the usable networks for a 26-bit subnet mask are as follows:

- 192.168.10.0
- 192.168.10.64
- 192.168.10.128
- 192.168.10.192

Host 192.168.10.72 falls in the 192.168.10.64 network.

Answer 23

The default gateway allows hosts to communicate with hosts that are on a different network segment.

All data that is not destined for the same network of the sending device is sent to the default gateway for delivery.

Answer 24

Layer 3 is affected first.

The default gateway sends IP packets to a remote network and functions at Layer 3 of the OSI model.

Question 25

As a network administrator, you have a Class B address. Assuming that the ip subnet zero **command is enabled on the router, what subnet mask allows you to have 100 subnetworks with at least 500 usable hosts?**

Question 26

How many usable subnets and usable hosts do you have if you subnet the network address 192.168.1.0 with the subnet mask 255.255.255.240?

Answer 25

The subnet mask is 255.255.254.0.

255.255.254.0 in binary is as follows:

11111111.11111111.11111110.00000000

All you care about are the last two octets. So you have 7 bits for the network and 9 bits for host addresses. Seven bits of subnetting provide 128 subnets, and 9 bits of host subnetting provide 510 hosts per subnet.

Answer 26

You have 16 subnets with 14 hosts in each network.

If you subnet 192.168.1.0 with a 28-bit mask (255.255.255.240), you have 16 networks with 14 hosts in each network. If you look at the network address and subnet mask in binary, you can see that in the last octet, you have 4 bits for networks and 4 bits for hosts, as follows:

11000000.10101000.00000000.00000000

11111111.11111111.11111111.11110000

You can apply these bits to the following formula, where x is the amount of borrowed bits:

Amount of subnets $= 2^x$

Amount of hosts $= 2^x - 2$

Therefore, $2^4 - 2 = 14$ subnets.

You can then apply the same equation to determine that the number of hosts is also 14.

Question 27

Your Internet provider has given you the IP network address of 172.16.0.0/16. You have 18 networks, each with 1200 hosts. You want to assign one IP range per subnet, leaving room for future growth. Assuming that the ip subnet zero command is enabled on all routers, what subnet mask would best achieve your goals?

Question 28

What are the benefits of variable-length subnet masking (VLSM)?

Question 29

What is CIDR?

Answer 27

The subnet mask of 255.255.248.0 would best achieve your goals.

If you look at this subnet mask in binary, you can see that you have 5 subnet bits for the network address:

11111111.11111111.11111000.00000000

If you use the subnet equation $2^5 = 32$, 32 available networks will be provided with the subnet mask, which fulfills the requirement for 18 networks and allows adequate growth. This leaves you with 11 bits to be assigned to hosts. This gives you 2046 ($2^{11} - 2$) addresses, giving you more than enough IP addresses to be assigned to hosts. If you use a subnet mask of 255.255.240.0, you will meet the requirement of 1200 hosts ($2^{12} - 2 = 4094$ available hosts) but not have enough networks ($2^4 = 16$ available networks).

Answer 28

VLSM gives a network administrator the option of including more than one subnet mask within a network and of subnetting an already subnetted network address. VLSM benefits include

- **More efficient use of IP addresses:** Without VLSM, companies must implement a single subnet mask within an entire Class A, B, or C network number.

- **Better-defined network hierarchical levels:** VLSM allows more hierarchical levels within an addressing plan and allows aggregation of network addresses.

Answer 29

Classless interdomain routing (CIDR) is an addressing scheme for the Internet that allows more efficient use of IP addresses than the old Class A, B, and C scheme. It is more flexible and offers route aggregation (supernetting). A CIDR address is a network address that does not use original Class A, B, and C rules. For example, a CIDR address can look like this: 192.168.2.0/29.

Question 30

What does route aggregation mean when referring to VLSM?

Question 31

What functions does the transport layer perform?

Question 32

What two common protocols function at the transport layer of the TCP/IP model?

Answer 30

Route aggregation means combining routes to multiple networks into one larger IP network or aggregated IP subnets within the class rules.

Answer 31

The transport layer performs the following functions:

- Session multiplexing
- Identification of different applications
- Segmentation
- Flow control
- Connection-oriented
- Reliability

Answer 32

Two protocols that function at the transport layer of the TCP/IP model are as follows:

- **TCP (Transmission Control Protocol):** A connection-oriented, reliable protocol
- **UDP (User Datagram Protocol):** A connectionless and unacknowledged protocol

NOTE   TCP deals with the three-way handshake. Reliability deals with acknowledgments (ACK) and NAKs. TCP uses ACKs and NAKs that are used by other protocols if there is a problem. UDP is characterized as connectionless and does not include a mechanism to guarantee data delivery. UDP uses a best-effort delivery and, on most networks today, can send a packet with minimal to no packet loss without the overhead of TCP.

Question 33

What is session multiplexing?

Question 34

What is the purpose of flow control?

Question 35

How do TCP/IP protocols identify applications?

Answer 33

Session multiplexing is a process that allows a host with a single IP address to support multiple sessions simultaneously. A session is created when a source host needs to send data to a destination host.

Answer 34

Flow control provides a mechanism for the receiver to control the transmission speed.

TCP implements flow control by using the SYN and ACK fields in the TCP header, along with the Window field. The Window field is a number that implies the maximum number of unacknowledged bytes allowed to be outstanding at any time.

Answer 35

TCP/IP protocols identify applications through port numbers.

Question 36

How do TCP and UDP perform segmentation?

Question 37

Which has more overhead: UDP or TCP?

Question 38

What is the IP protocol number for TCP and UDP?

Answer 36

TCP performs segmentation by taking data chunks from applications and breaking them into smaller segments that will fit in the maximum transmission unit (MTU) of the underlying network layers.

UDP does not perform segmentation; instead it expects the application process to send data in correct sizes.

Answer 37

TCP has more overhead. Because UDP segments are not acknowledged, they do not carry the overhead that TCP does, thus allowing faster transmissions.

Answer 38

TCP: 6

UDP: 17

NOTE IP protocol numbers are the link in the IP header that points to upper-layer protocols such as TCP and UDP.

Question 39

What is reliable versus best-effort delivery?

Question 40

What is the purpose of TCP and UDP port numbers?

Question 41

What are well-known port numbers?

Answer 39

Reliable delivery is connection oriented, and best-effort is connectionless.

Answer 40

To pass information (such as email) to upper layers, TCP and UDP use port numbers. These port numbers are predefined and keep track of different conversations among different hosts at the same time. Originating source port numbers are dynamically assigned by the source host using a number in the range of 49,152 to 65,535.

Answer 41

Well-known port numbers are used for fundamental applications such as email and DNS. They have a range from 0 to 1023.

Question 42

What is the port number for SMTP?

Question 43

What is the port number for DNS?

Question 44

What are the port numbers for FTP?

Answer 42

25

Answer 43

53

Answer 44

20 and 21

FTP uses port 20 for data transfer and port 21 is the command port.

Question 45

What is the port number for TFTP?

Question 46

What is the port number for Telnet?

Question 47

What is the port number for SSH?

Answer 45

69

Answer 46

23

Answer 47

22

Question 48

What protocol(s) and port numbers does DNS use?

Question 49

What is a TCP/IP socket?

Question 50

What are the three mechanisms TCP uses to accomplish a connection-oriented connection?

Answer 48

DNS uses both TCP and UDP using port number 53.

DNS uses UDP to carry simple queries and responses and TCP to guarantee the correct and orderly delivery of large amounts of bulk data between DNS servers for synchronization of databases.

Answer 49

A TCP/IP socket is an IP address combined with a TCP or UDP port number.

When a host wants to talk to another host, it sends its IP address along with the application (port number) it wants to communicate with. For example, if host 192.168.0.3 wants to talk to host 192.168.0.2 by email, host 192.168.0.3 sends its IP address and destination port number (192.168.0.3:1023) to host 192.168.0.2 with the port number it wants to communicate with (192.168.0.2:25).

Answer 50

The three mechanisms TCP uses to accomplish a connection-oriented connection are as follows:

- Packet sequencing
- Acknowledgments, checksums, and timers
- Windowing

Question 51

What are the steps for the TCP three-way handshake?

Question 52

What is the purpose of the TCP three-way handshake?

Question 53

What is a TCP window?

Answer 51

The steps of the TCP three-way handshake are as follows:

1. The source host sends a SYN to the destination host.

2. The destination host replies to the source with an ACK. At the same time, it sends a SYN to the source host.

3. The source host replies with an ACK.

NOTE   For the exam, remember: Step 1: SYN, Step 2: SYN/ACK, Step 3: ACK.

Answer 52

The three-way handshake creates a connection-oriented virtual circuit between two devices, and establishes an initial sequence number and window size.

Answer 53

A TCP window determines the number of segments that can be sent before an acknowledgment is required.

NOTE   TCP uses a "sliding window" technique to specify the number of segments that the recipient can accept. Sliding means that the window size is negotiated dynamically during the TCP session.

Question 54

What is the purpose of TCP sequencing?

Question 55

What are the most common fields that are included in the TCP header?

Question 56

What transport layer protocols are best suited for the transport of VoIP data?

Answer 54

The purpose of sequencing is to provide reliability by requiring the recipient to acknowledge receipt of a group of segments before a timer expires. Sequencing is also used to provide proper ordering or segments.

Answer 55

The most common used fields included in the TCP header are as follows:

- Acknowledgment Number
- Sequence Number
- Source/Destination Port
- Window Size
- TCP Checksum

Answer 56

UDP and RTP are best suited.

VoIP uses a combination of UDP and RTP for transport of data. VoIP is time sensitive and uses UDP because UDP uses less overhead than TCP.

Section 5
Routing

Routing is the process of finding a path to a destination and moving data across this path from source to destination. Routers are used to connect different IP networks and are essential devices that help make communication on the Internet. Routers are a major component of the routing process. Without routing, we would not be able to send emails, view our favorite websites, listen to music streams, or watch videos on the Internet.

In general, routing is considered a hop-by-hop paradigm. Some exceptions to this exist, such as multicast routing, but the ICND exams do not cover multicasting. Data is moved from router to router until it reaches the destination. A router's main function is path determination and packet forwarding.

This section covers the most basic terminology of routing and introduces you to the basics of static routing and configuring a Cisco router with basic IP information. Additionally, CDP is discussed. CDP is a Cisco-proprietary protocol that provides discovery of directly connected Cisco devices.

Question 1

Provide a brief description of routing.

Question 2

What are the two key functions that a router performs?

Question 3

How does a router determine the path a packet should take to reach its destination?

Answer 1

Routing is the process of finding a path to a destination and moving information across an internetwork from the source to the destination.

Answer 2

The two key functions that a router performs are path determination (routing) and packet forwarding (switching). Routing protocols used by the routing process are responsible for learning and maintaining awareness of the network topology. The switching function is the process of moving packets from an inbound interface to an outbound interface.

Answer 3

A router determines a path a packet should take to reach a destination by picking the best path to the destination. The best path a packet should take is determined by one of the following methods:

- Static routing
- Dynamic routing
- Default routing

Question 4

What are the three packet-forwarding mechanisms supported by Cisco routers?

Question 5

Define processing switching.

Question 6

What is fast switching?

Answer 4

The three packet-forwarding mechanisms supported by Cisco routers are

- Process switching
- Fast switching
- Cisco Express Forwarding

Answer 5

Processing switching is the oldest forwarding mechanism supported on Cisco routers. Every packet processed by the router requires a full lookup in the routing table.

Answer 6

Fast switching is a process that uses the cache to speed routing. When a packet is received for a destination, the first packet is process switched and an entry is created in the router's cache. Subsequent packets are switched in the interrupt code using the cache to improve performance.

Question 7

Define Cisco Express Forwarding.

Question 8

What is the difference between a routed and a routing protocol?

Question 9

What are six types of information stored in routing tables?

Answer 7

Cisco Express Forwarding (CEF) is the preferred Cisco IOS packet-forwarding mechanism. CEF consists of two key components: the Forwarding Information Base (FIB) and adjacencies. The FIB is similar to the routing table created by the router but maintains only the next-hop address for a particular route. The adjacency table maintains Layer 2 information linked to a particular FIB entry, avoiding the need to do an ARP request for each table lookup.

Answer 8

A routed protocol is a protocol that provides the information in its network layer to allow a packet to direct traffic and defines the use of fields within a packet. Examples of routed protocols are IPv4 and IPv6.

A routing protocol finds routes in an internetwork and maintains route awareness. Routing protocols aid in building and maintaining routing tables that routers will use to determine how routed protocols are routed. Routing Information Protocol v2 (RIPv2), Enhanced IGRP (EIGRP), Intermediate System–to–Intermediate System (IS-IS), Open Shortest Path First (OSPF), and Border Gateway Protocol (BGP) are examples of routing protocols.

Answer 9

The following are six types of information stored in routing tables:

- Destination network address
- Next-hop address
- Exiting interface
- Metric
- Administrative distance
- Routing source

Question 10

How do routing protocols maintain their routing tables with each other?

Question 11

What are the four types of routes found in a routing table?

Question 12

When a router is powered on, what three tasks does the router perform?

Answer 10

Routing protocols maintain their routing tables through the transmission of messages. These messages are exchanged between routers at periodic intervals or when a change in the network topology occurs. The information contained in the messages varies from routing protocol to routing protocol.

Answer 11

The four types of routes found in a routing table are as follows:

- **Directly connected networks:** Route entries that a router is directly connected to.
- **Static routes:** Routes entered manually by an administrator.
- **Dynamic routes:** Routes learned and populated by a routing protocol.
- **Default route:** Used to route packets when the router does not have a specific destination for packets in its routing table. The default route is entered manually or dynamically.

Answer 12

The router performs the following tasks when powered on:

1. Runs a power-on self-test (POST) to test the hardware
2. Finds and loads the IOS
3. Finds and applies the router configuration file, if one exists

Question 13

Upon first boot, a new router does not have a configuration file to load. In the event that a router has no configuration file, what happens?

Question 14

On a Cisco router, how do you display the configuration running in RAM?

Question 15

On a Cisco router, how do you view the configuration stored in nonvolatile RAM (NVRAM)?

Answer 13

If a router does not find a configuration file, the router runs setup mode, a question-driven configuration process that allows you to configure basic router parameters.

NOTE   The system configuration dialog is run if the router does not find a configuration file in NVRAM or if the **setup** privileged mode command is entered at the router's command prompt.

Answer 14

You display the configuration running in RAM using the **show running-config** privileged mode command.

Answer 15

You view the configuration stored in NVRAM using the **show startup-config** privileged mode command.

Question 16

How do you store the active configuration of a Cisco router to NVRAM?

Question 17

How do you give a Cisco router a name?

Question 18

What is the correct command to add the description "Link to West LA" to an interface on a Cisco router?

A. name Link to West LA

B. interface description Link to West LA

C. description Link to West LA

D. interface name Link to West LA

Answer 16

To save the running config to the startup config, use the **copy running-config startup-config** privileged mode command.

Answer 17

The **hostname** *name* global configuration command configures a name on a Cisco router.

For example, the following command changes the router's host name to RouterA:

```
Router(config)# hostname RouterA
RouterA(config)#
```

Answer 18

C. The command to add a description to an interface is the **description** *interface-description interface* configuration command.

NOTE   Adding a description to an interface on a Cisco router does not have any performance effects. It just adds a description to help identify the interface.

Question 19

How do you administratively disable an interface on a Cisco router?

Question 20

When configuring a router interface for the first time, is the interface administratively disabled?

Question 21

What are some of the things that the show interface *interface-type number* command displays?

Answer 19

You administratively disable an interface on a Cisco router by issuing the **shutdown** interface configuration command.

In this example, the serial interface is issued the **shutdown** command:

```
RouterA(config)# interface g0
RouterA(config-if)# shutdown
00:27:14: %LINK-5-CHANGED: Interface GigabitEthernet0, changed
state to administratively down
```

NOTE   To administratively enable an interface, use the **no shutdown** interface configuration command.

Answer 20

Yes. By default, router interfaces on Cisco routers are administratively disabled. They must be enabled using the **no shutdown** interface command.

Answer 21

The **show interface** command displays the following:

- Whether the interface is administratively down
- Whether the line protocol is up or down
- An Internet address (if one is configured)
- Maximum transmission unit (MTU) and bandwidth
- Traffic statistics on the interface
- Interface encapsulation type

Question 22

How do you display the status of interface F0 only?

Question 23

Packets are not being forwarding from one segment to another on your Cisco router. You enter the show interface g0 command and notice that the interface is administratively down. What does this mean, and how do you fix it?

Question 24

You are configuring an interface on a router and the interface says "Interface is up, line protocol is down." What does this tell you regarding the interface?

Answer 22

The IOS commands to display the status of interface F0 only are as follows:

- **show interface f0**
- **show ip interface f0**
- **show protocols f0**

Answer 23

When an interface is administratively down, it has been shut down manually or was never enabled. To remedy this, enter the interface command **no shutdown**.

Answer 24

If an interface says "Interface is up, line protocol is down," the interface is experiencing Layer 2 problems. This could be caused by not receiving keepalives, no clocking received, or encapsulation mismatch.

NOTE   If the interface says, "Interface is down, line protocol is down" and it is not administratively disabled, the interface is having Layer 1 problems.

Question 25

How would you configure a Fast Ethernet interface 0 with an IP address of 192.168.0.1/24 on a Cisco router?

Question 26

What is the Cisco Discovery Protocol (CDP)?

Question 27

List at least five types of information obtained from CDP.

Answer 25

To configure a Fast Ethernet interface 0 with an IP address of 192.168.0.1/24 on a Cisco router, issue the following commands from global configuration mode:

```
Router(config)# interface f0
Router(config-if)# ip address 192.168.0.1 255.255.255.0
Router(config-if)# no shutdown
```

NOTE   By default, every interface on a router is administratively disabled and needs to be enabled using the **no shutdown** command. If you receive any simulators on the exam, you will get the question wrong if you do not manually enable the interface.

Answer 26

CDP is a Cisco-proprietary protocol that runs on all Cisco IOS–enabled devices by default. It gathers information about directly connected Cisco devices. CDP operates at Layer 2 of the OSI model and is media independent.

With CDP, you can tell the hardware platform and device capability, device identifier, Layer 3 addresses of the connected interface, software version, and interface of the remote device that your Cisco device is attached to. CDP is enabled by default on all Cisco equipment. CDP is a Layer 2 frame that is not routable.

NOTE   Frame Relay interface by default will disable CDP.

Answer 27

The types of information obtained from CDP are as follows:

- Neighbor device ID (host name of remote device)
- Layer 3 address list of remote devices
- Device platform
- Device capabilities (router, switch, and so on)
- Local interface type and outgoing remote port ID
- Hold time value
- IOS version of remote device

Question 28

List two reasons to disable CDP.

Question 29

How do you disable CDP on Cisco routers?

Question 30

What does the show cdp command display?

Answer 28

Two reasons to disable CDP are as follows:

- To save network resources by not exchanging CDP frames.
- Security. CDP multicasts information about the device every 60 seconds. Sniffers and other devices can view these multicasts to discover information about your network.

Answer 29

Two commands disable CDP on a Cisco router. To disable CDP on the entire device, use the **no cdp run** global command, as follows:

```
RouterB(config)# no cdp run
```

To disable CDP on an interface only, use the **no cdp enable** interface command, as follows:

```
RouterB(config)# int f0
RouterB(config-if)# no cdp enable
```

This disables CDP on Fast Ethernet interface 0.

Answer 30

The **show cdp** command displays global CDP information about the device. It tells you how often the device will send CDP packets and the CDP holdtime:

```
RouterB# show cdp
Global CDP information:
        Sending CDP packets every 60 seconds
                Sending a holdtime value of 180 seconds
                Sending CDPv2 advertisements is enabled
```

NOTE   For the exam, remember that the default time interval a device sends out CDP information is 60 seconds, and the default holdtime is 180 seconds.

Question 31

What does the show cdp neighbors detail **command display?**

Question 32

What does the show cdp traffic **command display?**

Answer 31

The **show cdp neighbors detail** and **show cdp entry** * commands show the same output. They both display the following:

- Device ID (host name) of the remote neighbor
- Layer 3 addresses of the remote device interface that is connected to the local device
- Device platform and capabilities
- Local interface and outgoing port ID
- Local holdtime that is associated to the remote device
- IOS type and version

Answer 32

The **show cdp traffic** command, as follows, displays information about interface traffic. This includes the number of CDP packets sent and received and CDP errors:

```
RouterB# show cdp traffic
CDP counters :
        Total packets output: 550, Input: 682
        Hdr syntax: 0, Chksum error: 0, Encaps failed: 0
        No memory: 0, Invalid packet: 0, Fragmented: 0
        CDP version 1 advertisements output: 0, Input: 0
                CDP version 2 advertisements output: 550, Input: 682
```

Question 33

What does the show cdp interface **command display?**

Question 34

What Cisco IOS router command can you use to see a neighbor router's IP address?

Answer 33

The **show cdp interface** command, as follows, displays the status of CDP on all CDP-enabled interfaces on your device:

```
RouterB# show cdp interface
Ethernet0 is up, line protocol is down
  Encapsulation ARPA
  Sending CDP packets every 60 seconds
  Holdtime is 180 seconds
Serial0 is up, line protocol is up
  Encapsulation HDLC
  Sending CDP packets every 60 seconds
  Holdtime is 180 seconds
Serial1 is up, line protocol is up
  Encapsulation HDLC
  Sending CDP packets every 60 seconds
  Holdtime is 180 seconds
```

Answer 34

To see a neighbor router's IP address, you must use the **show cdp neighbor detail** or **show cdp entry** * user EXEC mode or privileged EXEC command.

Question 35

What is an example of a Layer 2 address?

Question 36

What is the Address Resolution Protocol (ARP)?

Answer 35

An example is a MAC address.

Ethernet interface manufacturers assign MAC addresses to end devices and are used for communication over the local network. MAC addresses are hard-coded into the network card and Ethernet interfaces.

Answer 36

ARP is used to resolve a known destination IP address to its associated MAC address on the local network.

For a host to communicate with another host, it must know the MAC address of the destination host. If the hosts are on the same subnet, the sending host will send an ARP request to the destination asking for its MAC address. The destination host will reply with its MAC address. If the sending host and the destination host are on a different subnets, the ARP request is sent to default gateway. The default gateway will reply to the ARP request with its MAC address on the local subnet of the sending host and the logical address of the destination host.

NOTE   ARP takes the destination IP address and resolves it to the MAC address on the local network through a local broadcast. For the exam, remember that ARP is used when a device knows the destination IP of another device and needs to learn the destination MAC address of that device on the local network.

Question 37

What is the ARP table?

Question 38

What three configuration settings does a host on a TCP/IP network require to communicate with hosts on a remote TCP/IP network?

Question 39

You want to test TCP/IP connectivity between two hosts. What TCP/IP tools can you use to do this?

Answer 37

The ARP table stores the reference of each known IP address to its MAC address on the local Layer 3 network.

The ARP table is created and maintained dynamically but can also include static ARP entries.

Answer 38

The three configuration settings needed to communicate with hosts on a remote TCP/IP network are

- IP address
- Subnet mask
- Default gateway address

Answer 39

You can use ping and traceroute.

Ping is a tool that that sends Internet Control Message Protocol (ICMP) packets to test network layer connectivity between two hosts. Ping sends an ICMP echo request packet to the target host and listens for an ICMP echo response.

Traceroute also uses ICMP, and it maps the path packets use to reach a destination.

Question 40

What two utilities test IP connectivity?

Question 41

What are static routes?

Question 42

What are dynamic routes?

Answer 40

Two utilities are ping and traceroute (tracert).

Ping and traceroute are ICMP utilities. ICMP specifically tests Layer 3 connectivity. Traceroute uses UDP when sending packets and ICMP when responding to the request of connectivity.

Answer 41

Static routes are routes to a remote destination that are manually configured on a router. They are administrator-defined routes and allow precise control over routing behavior.

Answer 42

Dynamic routes use a routing protocol to dynamically learn routes to remote networks and add them to the routing table. The routing protocol automatically updates route knowledge whenever new topology information is received.

Question 43

List three advantages and disadvantages of static routes when compared with dynamic routing.

Question 44

How do you configure a static route on a Cisco router?

Question 45

What is a default route?

Answer 43

Three advantages of static routing are

- They conserve routing resources that are consumed when using a routing protocol.
- Simple to configure in a small network.
- Quick to implement.

Three disadvantages are

- Scalability is limited. Static routes should be used for small networks or stub networks.
- A lot of manual configuration is required for larger networks.
- Do not automatically adapt to network changes.

Answer 44

To configure a static route on a Cisco router, enter the **ip route** *destination-network mask* {*next-hop-address* | *outbound-interface*} [*distance*] [**permanent**] global command. Here's an example:

```
RouterB(config)# ip route 172.17.0.0 255.255.0.0 172.16.0.1
```

This example instructs the router to route to 172.16.0.1 any packets that have a destination of 172.17.0.0 to 172.17.255.255.

Answer 45

Also known as the gateway of last resort, a default route is a special type of route with an all-0s network and network mask. The default route directs any packets for which a destination network is not specifically listed in the routing table. By default, if a router receives a packet to a destination network that is not in its routing table, it drops the packet. When a default route is specified, the router does not drop the packet. Instead, it forwards the packet to the IP address specified in the default route.

Question 46

How do you configure a default route to point out interface Fast Ethernet 0/0?

Question 47

What IOS command displays the entries in the routing table?

Answer 46

Use the following command to configure the default route:

```
RouterB(config)# ip route 0.0.0.0 0.0.0.0 fastethernet0/0
```

Answer 47

The following command displays the entries in the routing table:

```
show ip route
```

Section 6
Managing Traffic Using Access Lists

Access lists can be used to protect specific networks from certain users or other networks. You can even use them to block web traffic or any other type of TCP/IP traffic.

Access lists are used for many reasons. Cisco security devices, such as firewalls and Virtual Private Network (VPN) concentrators, use access lists to define access to the network. For example, Cisco firewalls use access lists to define rules to specify traffic and ports that are allowed through the firewall. Access lists define the traffic that a firewall or VPN concentrator will encrypt. Cisco routers also use access lists for quality of service (QoS), route filters, and Network Address Translation. In short, as a network administrator, you will see access lists used in many Cisco devices.

When implementing access lists in your network, remember that access lists use excess router processing time. The longer the access list, the greater the burden it puts on the router processor. Before you implement an access list, make sure that it will not significantly degrade the router's performance. Also, try to keep access lists short.

This section breaks down access lists and covers the required access control list (ACL) topics you will see on the ICND exam. Additionally, the section provides you with the information you need to successfully implement access lists in your network.

Question 1

What are six common types of IP access lists that can be configured on a Cisco router?

Question 2

How are access lists processed?

Question 3

What is at the end of each access list?

Answer 1

The following are common types of IP access lists: numbered (including standard and extended), named, dynamic, reflexive, and time-based access lists.

Answer 2

Access lists are processed in sequential, logical order, evaluating packets from the top down, one statement at a time. As soon as a match is made, the permit or deny option is applied, and the packet is not applied to any more access list statements. Because of this, the order of the statements within an access list is significant.

Answer 3

An implicit deny any statement is at the end of each access list. An implicit deny statement denies any packet that is not matched in the access list.

NOTE   You can override the implicit deny with an extended ACL with a **permit ip any any** command at the end of the access list.

Question 4

What criteria do standard IP access lists use to filter packets?

Question 5

What criteria do extended IP access lists use to filter packets?

Question 6

What are the number ranges that define standard and extended IP access lists?

Answer 4

Standard IP access lists filter packets by the source IP address. This results in the packets being permitted or denied for the entire protocol suite based on the source network, subnet, or host IP address.

NOTE   Because standard IP access lists filter by source address, you should place the access list as close to the destination network as possible. Doing this helps avoid denying unnecessary traffic and ensures that the source still has access to other, nonfiltered destinations.

Answer 5

Extended IP access lists use any combination the source address, destination address, and protocols to filter packets.

If the protocols specified in the extended access lists are TCP or UDP, port numbers can be included in the criteria. If ICMP is the protocol specified, specific ICMP message types can be filtered.

NOTE   Extended access lists should be placed as close to the source as possible. This prevents unwanted traffic from passing through the network.

Answer 6

The number ranges that define standard and extended IP access lists are as follows:

- **Standard IP access lists:** 1 to 99 and 1300 to 1999 (expanded range)
- **Extended IP access lists:** 100 to 199 and 2000 to 2699 (expanded range)

Question 7

What are reflexive access lists?

Question 8

What are dynamic access lists?

Question 9

What are time-based access lists?

Answer 7

Reflexive access lists allow IP packets to be filtered based on upper-layer session information. They allow outbound traffic and limit inbound traffic in response to sessions that originate from a network inside the router.

Reflexive ACLs contain only temporary entries that are created when a new IP session begins and are removed when the session ends. Reflective ACLs are *not* applied directly to an interface, but are "nested" within an extended named IP ACL that is applied to an interface.

Answer 8

Dynamic access lists (lock-and-key) dynamically create access list entries on the router to allow a user who has authenticated to the router through Telnet to access resources that are blocked behind the router.

Dynamic access lists depend on the user authenticating to the router and on extended access lists. Considered lock-and-key, the configuration starts with an extended ACL that blocks traffic through the router. A user who wants to traverse through the router is blocked by the extended ACL until he authenticates to the router through Telnet with a username and password. After the user is authenticated, the Telnet connection is dropped, and a single-entry dynamic ACL entry is added to the extended ACL to permit the user to traverse through the router.

Answer 9

Time-based ACLs are an enhancement to extended access lists that additionally consider the time of day when making a filtering decision.

Question 10

In what two ways can IP access lists be applied to an interface?

Question 11

How any access lists can be applied to an interface on a Cisco router?

Answer 10

IP access lists can be applied inbound or outbound.

Inbound access lists process packets as they enter a router's interface and before they are routed.

Outbound access lists process packets as they exit a router's interface and after they are routed.

NOTE   Inbound access lists, when compared to an outbound access list, conserve CPU processing by filtering packets before being processed against the routing table. Outbound and inbound access lists process packets going into or out of a router, but not traffic originating from the router when the access list is applied to an interface. For the ICND exam, if a question asks which type of access list is more effective—inbound or outbound—the more correct answer would be inbound.

Answer 11

Only one access list per protocol, per direction, per interface can be applied on a Cisco router. Multiple access lists are permitted per interface, but they must be for different protocols or applied in different directions.

NOTE   You should first create an access list and then apply it to an interface; an empty access list when applied to an interface permits all traffic. The reason for all traffic being permitted is that the implicit deny does not exist within an ACL until at least one statement is defined.

Question 12

What two things must one do to activate an access list?

Question 13

What things should one should consider when configuring access lists?

Answer 12

To activate an access list, you must perform the following steps:

1. Create the access list.

2. Apply or reference the access list.

Answer 13

Things one should consider when configuring access lists are

- The ACL type (standard or extended) determines the criteria used for filtering.

- Only one ACL per interface, per protocol, per direction is allowed.

- Access-list ordering is important during configuration. Poor ordering can create undesired results; therefore, always ensure that specific references to a subnet or network appear before those that are generalized. Also, when possible, place more often matched statements toward the top of an ACL and less frequent ones to the bottom of the list, to help with router CPU processing.

- Every ACL needs at least one permit statement because of the implicit "deny any any" at the end of each ACL.

- When placing an ACL, place extended ACLs close to the source. Standard ACLs should be placed close to the destination.

- An ACL can filter traffic going through a router when the ACL is applied to an interface or traffic to and from the router when the ACL is applied to a VTY line.

- By default, all new statements added to an access list are appended to the bottom, before the implicit deny, of the ACL.

- When applying an ACL to an interface, consider applying the ACL in the inbound direction to save processing through the routing table.

Question 14

What is the IOS command syntax that creates a standard IP access list?

Question 15

When implementing access lists, what are wildcard masks?

Question 16

What is the Cisco IOS command syntax that creates an extended access list?

Answer 14

The command syntax that creates a standard IP access list is as follows:

```
access-list access-list-number {permit | deny} source-address
  [wildcard-mask]
```

In this syntax, *access-list-number* is a number from 1 to 99 or 1300 to 1999.

For example:

```
RouterA(config)# access-list 10 deny 192.168.0.0 0.0.0.255
```

This command creates access list number 10, which denies any IP address between 192.168.0.0 and 192.168.0.255.

Answer 15

Wildcard masks define which of the 32 bits in the IP address must be matched.

Wildcards are used with access lists to specify a host, network, or part of a network. In wildcard masks, when binary 0s are present, the corresponding bits in the IP address must match. Wildcard mask bits with a binary value of 1 do not require matching bits within the IP address. For example, if you have an IP address of 172.16.0.0 with a wildcard mask of 0.0.255.255, the first two octets of the IP address must match 172.16, but the last two octets can be in the range of 0 to 255.

NOTE   Remember that a wildcard mask bit of 0 means to check the corresponding bit value of the IP address or network address it is paired with. The opposite is true of a wildcard mask bit of 1: to ignore the corresponding bit value of the IP or network address.

Answer 16

To create an extended access list in IOS, use the following command:

```
access-list access-list-number {permit | deny} protocol
  source-address
    source-wildcard-bits [operator port] destination-address
      destination-wildcard-bits
    [operator port]
```

In this syntax, *protocol* examples include IP, TCP, User Datagram Protocol (UDP), Internet Control Message Protocol (ICMP), and generic routing encapsulation (GRE).

The *operator port* value can be **lt** (less than), **gt** (greater than), **eq** (equal to), or **neq** (not equal to) and a TCP or UDP port number.

Question 17

What does the following access list do?

```
access-list 110 deny ip host 172.16.0.2 any
access-list 110 permit ip any any
```

Question 18

After you create a standard or extended IP access list, how do you apply it to an interface on a Cisco routers?

Answer 17

The access list denies any traffic from the host 172.16.0.2 and permits all other traffic.

Answer 18

Use the **ip access-group** interface command, as follows:

```
ip access-group access-list-number {in | out}
```

For example:

```
RouterA(config)# int g0/0/0
RouterA(config-if)# ip access-group 10 in
```

This applies access list 10 to gigabit interface 0/0/0 as an inbound access list.

NOTE To remove an access list from a router, first remove it from the interface by entering the **no ip access-group** *access-list-number direction* command. Then remove the access list by entering the **no access-list** *access-list-number* global configuration command. To remove one line from an access list, you need to specify the ACL entry sequence number you want to edit.

Question 19

What IOS commands will create an extended access list that denies web traffic to network 192.168.10.0/24?

Question 20

You have a router that has its Gigabit Ethernet interface G0/0 connected to the network 192.168.1.0/24. As the network administrator, you want to block all Telnet traffic originating from the network 192.168.1.0/24 while permitting all other IP traffic. You create the following access list and apply it to Gigabit interface 0/0:

```
access-list 101 deny tcp 192.168.1.0 0.0.0.255 any eq 23
```

After you apply the access list, hosts connected to the router's Gigabit interface cannot communicate to remote networks. Why might this be?

Answer 19

To create an extended access list that denies web traffic to network 192.168.10.0, enter the following:

```
access-list 101 deny tcp any 192.168.10.0 0.0.0.255 eq www
access-list 101 permit ip any any
```

NOTE This denies any web traffic to network 192.168.10.0 and permits any other IP traffic. Because access lists are processed in sequential order, the first statement denies web traffic and the last statement permits all other IP traffic. If the last statement were not included, all IP traffic would be denied because of the implicit deny any at the end of each access list. Access lists should always have one permit statement.

Answer 20

Hosts attached to network 192.168.1.0/24 cannot communicate with remote networks because the access list is denying all IP traffic. At the end of each access list is a deny all statement. Thus access list 101 is not only denying Telnet traffic but is also denying all IP traffic as well. To resolve the problem, the access list needs to be configured as follows:

```
access-list 101 deny tcp 192.168.1.0 0.0.0.255 any eq 23
access-list 101 permit ip any any
```

Question 21

Create a named access lists that only blocks pings from networks 172.16.0.0/22 to host 192.168.0.101.

Question 22

Which IOS command will display all the configured access lists on a Cisco router?

Answer 21

To create a named access list that only blocks pings from networks 172.16.0.0/22 to host 192.168.0.101, enter the following:

```
ip access-list extended block-ping
deny icmp 172.16.0.0 0.0.3.255 host 192.168.0.101 echo
ip permit any any
```

When you create a named access list, you use the **ip access-list extended** *name* global configuration command. Issuing this command places you in named extended IP access list subcommand mode, which then allows you to enter the access list statements.

NOTE A shortcut to find the wildcard mask is to subtract the subnet mask from 255.255.255.255.

Answer 22

To display all access lists, enter the **show running-config** or the **show access-list** command, as follows:

```
RouterA# show access-list
Standard IP access list 10
    deny   192.168.0.0, wildcard bits 0.0.0.255
Extended IP access list 101
    permit tcp any any eq www
    permit udp any any eq domain
    permit udp any eq domain any
    permit icmp any any
    deny tcp 192.168.10.0 0.0.0.255 any eq www
RouterA#
```

NOTE The **show ip access-list** command shows all configured IP access lists on a router but does not show any access lists configured for different protocols.

Question 23

What IOS command can you use to see whether an IP access list is applied to an interface?

Answer 23

To determine whether an IP access list is applied to an interface, enter the following command:

show ip interface *interface-type interface-number*

For example:

```
RouterA# show ip interface s0
Serial0 is up, line protocol is up
  Internet address is 192.168.1.2/24
  Broadcast address is 255.255.255.255
  Address determined by non-volatile memory
  MTU is 1500 bytes
  Helper address is not set
  Directed broadcast forwarding is enabled
  Multicast reserved groups joined: 224.0.0.9
  Outgoing access list is not set
  Inbound  access list is 10
  Proxy ARP is enabled
  Security level is default
  Split horizon is enabled
  --Text Omitted--
```

Section 7
Enabling Internet Connectivity

The Internet has transformed how businesses operate today. From communications such as email, voice, and video, to consumer-to-business and business-to-business transactions and mobile computing, the Internet is a critical component for many businesses today.

Businesses and home users connect to the Internet in many different ways. These include DSL, cable, and fiber technologies such as FIOS, dedicated leased lines, satellite, and wireless technologies.

This section provides an overview on how to connect to the Internet for a small business. Most Internet services come from connecting to an Internet service provider (ISP) and use technologies such as Network Address Translation (NAT) and Port Address Translation (PAT) to allow several computers to connect to the Internet through one or more public IP addresses at a time. Basic WAN topics, DHCP, and NAT terminology are covered.

Question 1

What is Dynamic Host Configuration Protocol (DHCP)?

Question 2

What are the three mechanisms that DHCP uses for IP address allocation?

Question 3

When connecting a router to the Internet, what are the two options for configuring a public IP address from the ISP?

Answer 1

DHCP is a protocol that is based on a client-server model that dynamically allocates the assignment of IP addresses.

The DHCP server is a device that is configured to allocate IP addresses and network configuration.

A DHCP client is a host that requests IP address, subnet mask, default gateway, and other information from a server.

Answer 2

The three mechanisms that Dynamic Host Configuration Protocol (DHCP) uses for IP address allocation are as follows:

- **Automatic allocation:** Assigns a permanent IP address to a client
- **Dynamic allocation:** Assigns an IP address to a client for a set period of time, for example, 7 days
- **Manual allocation:** Assigns a specific IP address to a client as defined by the administrator using the client's MAC address

Answer 3

The two options are statically or dynamically using DHCP.

Configuring an IP address statically is done by manually configuring the router interface connecting to the ISP with the public IP address provided to you by the ISP.

Dynamic configuration is done by configuring the router interface connecting to the ISP to be a DHCP client.

Question 4

How do you configure your Cisco router with a statically assigned IP address?

Question 5

How would you configure Gigabit Ethernet interface 0/0 on your Cisco router to be a DHCP client?

Question 6

What are private IP addresses?

Answer 4

To configure a Cisco router with a statically assigned address, from global configuration, you would use the **ip address** *ip-address subnetmask* interface command.

For example, to configure Gigabit Ethernet interface 0/0 with an IP address of 192.168.0.1/24, you would issue the following commands:

```
Router(config)# interface g0/0
Router(config-if)# ip address 192.168.0.1 255.255.255.0
Router(config-if)# no shutdown
```

Answer 5

The **ip address dhcp** interface command configures an interface to be a DHCP client. To configure Gigabit Ethernet interface 0/0 as a DHCP client, the following commands would be issued on the router:

```
Router(config)# interface g0/0
Router(config-if)# ip address dhcp
Router(config-if)# no shutdown
```

Answer 6

Private IP addresses are defined in RFC 1918 and define blocks of IP addresses that can be used for private use within an organization. These IP addresses are not routable on the Internet, and any organization using private IP addresses that wants to connect to the Internet must use NAT for IP address translation.

Question 7

What are the three private IP address ranges?

Question 8

What is Network Address Translation (NAT)?

Question 9

What are three benefits of NAT?

Answer 7

The three private address ranges are as follows:

- **Class A:** 10.0.0.0 to 10.255.255.255
- **Class B:** 172.16.0.0 to 172.31.255.255
- **Class C:** 192.168.0.0 to 192.168.255.255

Answer 8

NAT is a mechanism where private, nonroutable IP addresses are translated to public routable IP addresses and vice versa.

Answer 9

Three benefits of NAT are as follows:

- Eliminates readdressing overhead of hosts that require external access
- Conserves IP addresses through application port-level multiplexing
- Hides the internal network, providing a small level of network security

Question 10

What are five drawbacks to using NAT?

Question 11

Define the following Cisco NAT terminology:

- Inside local address
- Inside global address
- Outside local address
- Outside global address

Question 12

What is static NAT?

Answer 10

Five drawbacks to using NAT are

- Some applications depend on end-to-end functionality without modified packets.
- End-to-end IP traceability is lost.
- Complicates tunneling protocols like IPsec.
- Some services that require the initiation of TCP connections from the outside or stateless protocols might be disrupted.
- Increases switching delay.

Answer 11

These terms are defined as follows:

- **Inside local address:** The IP address assigned to a host on the inside, private network. This is usually a private (RFC 1918) IP address.
- **Inside global address:** A registered, Internet-routable IP address that represents one or more inside local IP addresses to the outside world.
- **Outside local address:** The IP address of an outside host as it appears to the inside, private network.
- **Outside global address:** The IP address assigned to a host on the outside network by the host's owner. This is usually a routable IP address.

Answer 12

Static NAT provides a one-to-one mapping, translating one private IP address to one public IP address.

Question 13

What is dynamic NAT?

Question 14

What is overload NAT?

Question 15

How many internal hosts can be translated to one routable IP address through PAT?

Answer 13

Dynamic NAT provides a many-to-many mapping, translating private IP addresses to public IP addresses from a group of public IP addresses.

Answer 14

Overload NAT is another term for Port Address Translation (PAT). It has a many-to-one or many-to-many mapping using different port numbers to add uniqueness.

NOTE   Other types of NAT are static NAT and dynamic NAT. Static NAT provides a one-to-one translation and is useful if an inside host needs to be accessed from the outside. Dynamic NAT maps a group of private IP addresses to a routable IP address from a pool of routable IP addresses dynamically.

Answer 15

Theoretically, 65,536 internal hosts can be translated by PAT using one routable IP address.

Question 16

As a network administrator, you have a router with its G0
interface connected to the Internet and G1 connected to your
internal network. Configure internal host 192.168.10.5/24 to be
statically translated to the external IP address 216.1.1.3/24.

Question 17

How do you configure PAT or overload NAT?

Question 18

How do you view the active NAT translations in the NAT table?

Answer 16

To configure static NAT, you need to define that address to translate and then configure NAT on the appropriate interfaces. The following example creates the static mapping and defines interface G0 as connecting to the outside network and interface G1 as connecting to the inside network:

```
RouterB(config)# ip nat inside source static 192.168.10.5 216.1.1.3
RouterB(config)# int g0
RouterB(config-if)# ip nat outside
RouterB(config-if)# int g1
RouterB(config-if)# ip nat inside
```

Answer 17

To configure PAT, you need to define an access list that permits the internal hosts to be translated. You then use the **ip nat inside source list** *access-list-number* interface *interface-type* **overload** global command followed by specifying the inside and outside interfaces. The following example enables PAT for internal host 192.168.10.0/24 using the external IP address on interface g0/1 and interface g0/0 as the inside interface:

```
RouterB(config)# access-list 20 permit 192.168.10.0 0.0.0.255
RouterB(config)# interface g0/0
    RouterB(config-if)# ip nat inside
    RouterB(config-if)# interface g0/1
    RouterB(config-if)# ip nat outside
RouterB(config)# ip nat inside source list 20 interface g0 overload
```

Answer 18

To view the active NAT mappings in the NAT table, use the **show ip nat translation** command, as follows:

```
RouterB# show ip nat translation
Pro Inside global   Inside local     Outside local    Outside global
--- 216.1.1.1       192.168.10.5     ---              ---
--- 216.1.1.2       192.168.10.16    ---              ---
```

Question 19

What Cisco command clears all the NAT mappings in the NAT table?

Question 20

When troubleshooting NAT, what Cisco IOS command displays every packet that is translated by the router?

Question 21

What does the show ip nat statistics **command display?**

Answer 19

The **clear ip nat translation** * command clears all the NAT translations in the NAT table. This command is useful for troubleshooting NAT.

NOTE   The NAT table is stored in memory and is cleared when the router is rebooted.

Answer 20

To troubleshoot NAT and view every packet that is translated by the router, use the **debug ip nat** command.

Answer 21

The **show ip nat statistics** command displays information about the total number of active translations, NAT configuration parameters, the number of addresses in the pool, and the number that have been allocated.

Section 8
Managing Network Device Security

Securing devices in today's networks is not an option. Internet and network threats can pose serious threats to a company's infrastructure that can cause tens of thousands of dollars or impact critical services. As such, it is paramount that network administrators take the proper steps to harden and secure access to network devices.

This section covers the fundamentals for securing Cisco network devices. This includes common threats facing network devices, the need to secure ports, how to monitor and secure unused services, securely connecting to Cisco devices, and the importance of a time server.

Further information on device security, such as access lists, can be found in Section 5, "Routing."

Question 1

What are five common threats network devices face?

Question 2

How do you mitigate remote access threats for network devices?

Question 3

What are some techniques used to mitigate local access and physical threats facing network devices?

Answer 1

Five common threats network devices face are

- **Remote access threats:** Include unauthorized remote access to network devices.
- **Local access and physical threats:** These threats include physical damage to network device hardware, password recovery by weak physical security, and theft.
- **Environmental threats:** Temperature extremes (heat or cold) or humidity extremes and storms.
- **Electrical threats:** Voltage spikes, brownouts, noise, and power loss.
- **Maintenance threats:** The improper handling of important electronic components, lack of critical spare parts, poor cabling and labeling, and poor change policies.

Answer 2

Mitigation of remote access threats includes configuration of strong authentication and encryption for remote access, configuration of a login banner, the use of ACLs, and VPN access.

Answer 3

Techniques used to mitigate local access and physical threats include locking wiring closets, providing physical access control, and blocking physical access through a dropped ceiling, raised floor, window, ductwork, or other points of entries. You can also monitor facilities with security cameras.

Question 4

What are techniques used to mitigate environmental threats?

Question 5

What can one do to mitigate electrical threats facing network devices?

Question 6

What are some ways to mitigate network device maintenance threats?

Answer 4

Mitigation techniques include creating a proper operating environment through temperature control, humidity control, airflow, remote environmental alarms, environment monitoring and recording, and policies/plans for environmental storms.

Answer 5

Mitigation of electrical threats includes using surge protectors, installing UPS systems and generators, providing redundant power supplies, following a preventive maintenance plan, and using remote monitoring.

Answer 6

Ways to mitigate network device maintenance threats include neat cabling runs, proper labeling of components, stocking critical spares, access by only authorized personnel, proper change management procedures, and ensuring that network documentation is accurate and up to date.

Question 7

On a Cisco router, how do you set a password to restrict access to privileged EXEC mode?

Question 8

When you view the configuration on Cisco routers, only the enable secret password is encrypted. How do you encrypt passwords that protect user mode access and the enable password?

Answer 7

The **enable password** and **enable secret** global configuration commands can set passwords to restrict access to privileged EXEC mode.

The **enable password** command restricts access to privileged EXEC mode but stores the password in the configuration unencrypted. The **enable secret** command creates an encrypted form of the enable password. The following example configures an encrypted password to privilege mode with ICND as the password:

```
RouterA(config)# enable secret ICND
```

NOTE   When the **enable secret** password is configured, it is used instead of **enable password**, rather than in addition to it. Also, you can use the **service password-encryption** global configuration mode command to encrypt passwords that are not encrypted by default. Finally, external authentication such as RADIUS or TACACS+ can be used to restrict access to privileged EXEC mode.

Answer 8

To encrypt passwords that protect user mode access and the enable password, use the **service password-encryption** global command, as follows:

```
RouterA(config)# service password-encryption
```

NOTE   Even though the enable password can be encrypted using this command, the encryption is weak and has been broken. Examples of passwords that would be encrypted using the **service password-encryption** command would include console line, vty line, and local username passwords.

Question 9

On a Cisco router, how do you add a password to the console line?

Question 10

How do you add a password to the VTY lines on a Cisco router?

Answer 9

To add a password to the console terminal, use the **line console 0** global configuration command, followed by the **login** and **password** *password* line subcommands, as follows:

```
RouterA(config)# line console 0
RouterA(config-line)# login
RouterA(config-line)# password ICND
```

The **login** subcommand forces the router to prompt for authentication. Without this command, the router does not authenticate the line password. The **password ICND** subcommand sets the console password to ICND. The password set is case sensitive.

NOTE   It is important to configure a password to the console line to prevent unauthorized access to the CLI from anyone who has physical access to the Cisco device.

Answer 10

The VTY lines provide access to telnet to a Cisco device. To add a password to the VTY lines, enter the **line vty 0 4** global configuration command, the **login** command, and finally the **password** line subcommand. The password is case sensitive. In the following example, the Telnet password is set to ciscopress:

```
RouterA(config)# line vty 0 4
RouterA(config-line)# login
RouterA(config-line)# password ciscopress
```

Question 11

What are the four steps to configure SSH on a Cisco router or switch?

Question 12

As a network administrator, you configure SSH on your Cisco device for remote access. What command will allow you to only permit SSH access and block Telnet access to the vty lines?

Question 13

What IOS command can you use to display whether SSH is configured on your Cisco device?

Answer 11

The four steps to configure SSH are

1. Use the **hostname** command to configure a host name of the device.
2. Configure the DNS domain with the **ip domain-name** command
3. Generate RSA keys with the **crypto key generate rsa** command.
4. Configure the user credentials to be used for authentication.

NOTE   An optional fifth and recommended step is to limit access to the device to only users that use SSH and block Telnet by using the **transport input ssh** vty line configuration mode command.

Answer 12

The vty line configuration mode command **transport input ssh** will limit access to the device through SSH while blocking Telnet.

Answer 13

Use the **show ip ssh** command.

This command will display the SSH version number and the configuration data for SSH on the Cisco device.

Question 14

Create an access list that permits only vty access from network 192.168.10.0 255.255.255.0 to connect to the Cisco router.

Question 15

What are the two most popular external authentication options for connecting to Cisco devices?

Question 16

What is AAA?

Answer 14

To create an access list that permits only vty access from network 192.168.10.0 255.255.255.0 to connect to the Cisco router, enter the following:

```
RouterA(config)# access list 10 permit 192.168.10.0 0.0.0.255
RouterA(config)# line vty 0 15
RouterA(config-if)# access-class 10 in
```

NOTE   The command to apply an access list to the router's lines (aux and vty) is **access-class**. The command to apply access lists to interfaces on the router is **ip access-group**.

Answer 15

The two most popular options are RADIUS and TACACS+.

RADIUS is an open standard with low use of CPU resources and memory.

TACACS+ is a security mechanism that enables modular authentication, authorization, and accounting services. It uses a TACACS+ daemon running on a security server.

NOTE   RADIUS and TACACS+ are both security protocols used for AAA.

Answer 16

Authentication, authorization, and accounting (AAA) is a security architecture for distributed systems that enables control over access to systems and determines which users are allowed access to particular services. AAA allows access to a device based on entering correct credentials, and any actions are accounted for (logged).

Question 17

What are some of the reasons a network administrator would want to secure unused device interfaces?

Question 18

How can you secure unused interfaces on a Cisco switch?

Question 19

How do you disable a switch interface?

Answer 17

Unused interfaces on a network device, such as a switch, can be a security risk. For example, an unauthorized user can plug into an unused port on a switch and gain access to the network.

Answer 18

You secure an unused switch interface by either disabling the port or putting the port in an unused nonroutable VLAN. Also, auto-trunking of ports should be disabled using the **switchport nonegotiate** interface command.

Answer 19

You disable a switch interface by issuing the **shutdown** interface command. To reenable the interface, issue the **no shutdown** command.

NOTE   To disable a range of interfaces, you can use the **interface range** global command.

Question 20

What is switch port security?

Question 21

What are the four ways port security related to MAC address associations can be configured on a switch port?

Question 22

As a network administrator, you want to restrict the laptops that are allowed to connect to a specific switch port. You want to restrict switch port access to the MAC addresses of these laptops. What are the four steps to limit and identify the MAC addresses of the laptops that are allowed access on the ports?

Answer 20

Switch port security allows you to restrict input to a port by limiting and/or identifying the MAC addresses of the devices allowed to access the port.

Answer 21

The four ways to implement port security related to MAC address associations are

- **Dynamic:** Secures the port by limiting the number of MAC addresses used on a port. Dynamic addresses are dynamically learned and can be configured to age out after a certain period.

- **Static:** Secures the port with a static configuration of specific MAC addresses that are permitted to use the port.

- **Combination:** Uses static MACs plus dynamic MACs.

- **Sticky learning:** Converts dynamically learned addresses to "sticky secure" addresses. In other words, dynamically learned MAC addresses are stored in the running configuration as if they were statically configured.

Answer 22

Port security limits the number of valid MAC addresses that are allowed on a port. When MAC addresses are assigned to a secure port, the port does not forward packets with source addresses outside the group of defined addresses.

The steps to configure port security are as follows:

1. Enable port security.
2. Set the MAC address limit.
3. Specify the allowable MAC addresses (optional).
4. Define the violation action.

Question 23

When enabling port security on a Catalyst switch, what is the default number of MAC addresses allowed and the default violation action?

Question 24

What commands enable port security on interface g0/1? Only allow two MAC addresses on the port, and let the switch dynamically learn the MAC addresses and store them in the running configuration. Restrict the port and drop illegal frames and log them to a server if a third MAC address is detected.

Question 25

Can you enable port security on a trunk port?

Answer 23

By default, port security is not enabled. When it is enabled, the default number of secure MAC addresses allowed on the interface is one and the default violation action is to shut down the port.

Answer 24

Use the following commands to enable port security on interface g0/1:

```
Cat2960(config)# int g0/1
Cat2960(config-if)# switchport mode access
Cat2960(config-if)# switchport port-security
Cat2960(config-if)# switchport port-security max 2
Cat2960(config-if)# switchport port-security mac-address sticky
Cat2960(config-if)# switchport port-sec violation restrict
```

Answer 25

Yes. Port security supports nonnegotiating trunks.

A trunk port is a port configured to trunk multiple VLANs and can be configured with port security as long as the trunk is configured as a nonnegotiating trunk.

NOTE   When enabling port security, the default number of secure MAC addresses is one and the default violation action is to shut down the port. Because trunk ports carry multiple VLANs, more than one MAC address traverses the link. It is recommended to configure the maximum number of secure MAC addresses on the port before you enable port security on a trunk.

Question 26

When configuring port security violation actions, what are the three modes that can be configured and what do these modes do when a security violation occurs?

Question 27

How can you tell whether port security is enabled on a switch?

Answer 26

The three port security violations modes and their operation are as follows:

- **Protect:** Drops packets with unknown source addresses until a sufficient number of secure MAC addresses are removed to drop below the maximum value.

- **Restrict:** Drops packets with unknown source addresses until a sufficient number of secure MAC addresses are removed to drop below the maximum value and causes the SecurityViolation counter to increment.

- **Shutdown:** Immediately puts the interface into the error-disabled state and sends an SNMP trap notification.

Answer 27

You determine whether port security is enabled on a switch by issuing the **show port-security** command, as follows:

```
Cat2960# show port-security
Secure Port  MaxSecureAddr  CurrentAddr  SecurityViolation  Security Action
             (Count)        (Count)      (Count)
---------------------------------------------------------------------------
Fa0/1            1              0             0              Restrict
---------------------------------------------------------------------------
Total Addresses in System (excluding one mac per port)     : 0
Max Addresses limit in System (excluding one mac per port) : 8320
```

NOTE   Port security is not enabled by default.

Question 28

How can you display the port security settings that are defined for an interface?

Question 29

How do you display the secure MAC address for all ports on a switch that has port security enabled?

Answer 28

The **show port-security interface** *interface-type interface-number* privileged EXEC command displays the port security settings configured for an interface. The output from this command displays the following:

- Whether port security is enabled
- The violation mode
- The maximum allowed number of secure MAC addresses for each interface
- The number of secure MAC addresses on the interface
- The number of security violations that have occurred

```
SwitchA# show port-security interface fastethernet 5/1
Port Security: Enabled
Port status: SecureUp
Violation mode: Shutdown
Maximum MAC Addresses: 11
Total MAC Addresses: 11
Configured MAC Addresses: 3
Aging time: 20 mins
Aging type: Inactivity
SecureStatic address aging: Enabled
Security Violation count: 0
```

Answer 29

The **show port-security address** privileged EXEC command displays the secure MAC addresses for all ports. Following is an example from the output of the **show port-security address** command:

```
SwitchA# show port-security address
          Secure Mac Address Table
-------------------------------------------------------------------
--
Vlan    Mac Address      Type              Ports    Remaining Age
                                                    (mins)
----    -----------      ----              -----    -------------
  1     0001.0001.0001   SecureDynamic     Fa5/1      15 (I)
  1     0001.0001.0002   SecureDynamic     Fa5/1      15 (I)
  1     0001.0001.1111   SecureConfigured  Fa5/1      16 (I)
  1     0001.0001.1112   SecureConfigured  Fa5/1      -
  1     0001.0001.1113   SecureConfigured  Fa5/1      -
  1     0005.0005.0001   SecureConfigured  Fa5/5      23
  1     0005.0005.0002   SecureConfigured  Fa5/5      23
  1     0005.0005.0003   SecureConfigured  Fa5/5      23
```

Question 30

What is the default mode of a Catalyst 2960 switch interface?

Question 31

As a network administrator, you enable port security on your switch ports. After a week, a user complains that he can no longer access the network. You issue the show interface status command and notice that the port the end user is connected to has err-disabled status. What has occurred?

Question 32

Port security is enabled on a switch with its default settings. When issuing the show interface status command, you notice that interface g0/1 is in the err-disabled state. How do you make the interface operational again?

Answer 30

The default mode of a Catalyst 2960 switch is dynamic auto. Because the default mode of a Catalyst 2960 switch interface is dynamic auto, the interface will try to negotiate to trunking if the other end of the link has a compatible setting. This setting can allow an unauthorized user to plug a device into an unused switch interface and gain access to the VLANs on the network. Cisco recommends securing unused switch interfaces.

Answer 31

In this example, the err-disabled status most likely indicates that a port security violation has occurred and the port was configured to shut down in the event of a violation, thus blocking network access for the end user.

Answer 32

When port security is enabled on a switch and an interface is in the err-disabled state, it means that a security violation has occurred and the interface was shut down. To make the interface operational, it will need to be enabled again with the **no shutdown** interface command.

In this example, the following commands would make interface g0/1 operational again:

```
SwitchA(config)# interface g0/1
SwitchA(config-if)# no shutdown
```

Question 33

Some services on Cisco devices might not be needed and can be disabled. What are two benefits for disabling these unused services?

Question 34

What Cisco IOS command displays open ports and services on your Cisco device?

Question 35

What are some general best practices for disabling unused services on a Cisco router?

Answer 33

Two benefits for disabling unused services on Cisco devices are

- Helps preserve system resources
- Eliminates the potential for security exploits on the unneeded services

Answer 34

The Cisco IOS command is **show control-plan host open-ports**.

This command shows all UDP and TCP ports the device is listening on to determine what services need to be disabled.

NOTE   Cisco provides the AutoSecure function to help disable unnecessary services and enable other security features.

Answer 35

Best practices for disabling unused services on a Cisco router are as follows:

- Unless needed, disable finger, identification (identd), and TCP and UDP small services.
- Disable CDP on interfaces where the service might represent a risk. Examples include external or Internet edge interfaces.
- Disable HTTP.

NOTE   In IOS 15.0 and later, finger, identd, TCP and UDP small services, and HTTP service are disabled by default.

Question 36

What is NTP and why is it important to configure on network devices?

Question 37

From what sources can an NTP device get the correct time?

Question 38

How do you configure a router to act as an NTP server?

Answer 36

Network Time Protocol is used to synchronize the clocks of network devices on a network to ensure that all devices are on the same time.

NTP is important to configure on network devices to allow correct tracking of events that transpire on a network, and clock synchronization is critical for digital certificates.

Answer 37

NTP clients can receive time from

- Local master clock
- Master clock on the Internet
- GPS or atomic clock

NOTE   A router can act as an NTP server and client.

Answer 38

The **ntp master** *stratum* global command configures a router as an NTP server. The *stratum* variable is a number from 1 to 15. A lower stratum value indicates higher NTP priority. The following configures a router as an NTP server with a stratum of 1:

```
RouterA(config)# ntp master 1
```

Question 39

How do you configure a router to synchronize its time from an NTP server?

Question 40

What banner is displayed before the username and password login prompts on a Catalyst switch?

Question 41

When is the message of the day (MOTD) banner displayed?

Answer 39

The **ntp server** *server-ip-address* global command configures a Cisco device to synchronize its time with an NTP server.

Answer 40

The login banner is displayed.

The login banner is configured using the **banner login** global command. For example:

```
Switch# config t
Enter configuration commands, one per line.   End with CNTL/Z.
Switch(config)# banner login #
Enter TEXT message.   End with the character '#'.
Notice! Only Authorized Personnel Are Allowed to Access This Device
#
```

Answer 41

The MOTD is displayed upon connection to the router or switch either by Telnet or by the console port.

If a login banner is also configured on the router or switch, the MOTD will display first, followed by the login banner.

Question 42

Why does Cisco recommend using SSH instead of Telnet for remote access of a Cisco device?

Question 43

By default, any IP address can connect to vty lines. How do you restrict access to vty lines, allowing only approved IP addresses to connect to the vty lines?

Answer 42

Cisco recommends using SSH because it encrypts communication between the Cisco device and the host. Telnet is unsecure, and all communication between the Cisco device and host is sent in clear text.

Answer 43

You restrict access to vty lines by using standard access lists.

Standard access lists allow you to permit or deny traffic based on the source IP address. To restrict access to vty lines, you would create a standard access list that permits each authorized IP address to connect to vty and apply the access list to the vty lines.

Section 9
Implementing VLANs and Trunks

Switches operate on Layer 2 of the OSI model and routers operate on Layer 3. Switches and routers increase the number of collision domains, decreasing the amount of collisions in a network; routers also increase the number of broadcast domains while reducing their size.

Prior to the introduction of VLANs, network designers segmented large Layer 2 networks with routers. A router would be installed between the two networks. All data communication between the two would pass through the router, and the broadcast domain was limited to the physical location of the network.

VLANs introduced a way to logically segment a broadcast domain within a switch. Additionally, VLANs are not bound to a physical location. For example, with VLANs, network traffic can be segmented based on department, division, function, or type of traffic, without regard to the physical location of end users. Any switch port can belong to a VLAN, and a unicast, broadcast, or multicast packet is forwarded or flooded to all end stations in the assigned VLAN. This segmentation not only reduces the size of broadcast domains but also increases the security on the network.

By default, each access port on a switch can belong to only one data VLAN. Trunks are point-to-point links between one or more switch interfaces and another networking device, such as another switch or router; trunks carry traffic of multiple VLANs over a single link.

This section covers the basics of VLANs and describes how to configure VLANs and trunk links on a Cisco Catalyst 2960 Series switch. Additionally, DHCP fundamentals are covered. Although all commands are specific to the Catalyst 2960 platform, because Cisco has moved all its Catalyst switches to the native IOS switching operating system, the commands here are universal to most Catalyst IOS switches.

Question 1

What are VLANs?

Question 2

What are the six characteristics of a typical VLAN setup?

Question 3

For VLANs to communicate with each other, what network component is needed?

Answer 1

VLANs are broadcast domains in a Layer 2 network.

Each VLAN is like a distinct virtual bridge within the switch. Each virtual bridge you create in a switch defines a broadcast domain. By default, traffic from one VLAN cannot pass to another VLAN. Each of the users in a VLAN would also be in the same IP subnet. By default, each access port can belong to only one data VLAN.

Answer 2

Six characteristics of a typical VLAN setup are as follows:

- Each logical VLAN is like a separate physical bridge.
- For different VLANs to communicate with each other, traffic must be forwarded through a router or Layer 3 switch.
- Each VLAN is considered to be a separate logical network.
- VLANs can span multiple switches.
- Each VLAN is a separate broadcast domain.
- VLANs can enhance security by logically segmenting a network.

NOTE   These are not the only characteristics of VLANs but are the most important ones to know for the exam.

Answer 3

A router or Layer 3 switch is needed for inter-VLAN communication. It is important to think of a VLAN as a distinct virtual bridge in a switch, with is its own IP subnet and broadcast domain. A network device cannot communicate from one IP subnet to another without a router. The same is true for a VLAN; you cannot communicate from one VLAN to another without a router-capable device.

Question 4

What is VLAN membership?

Question 5

What are the three ways that inter-VLAN communication can be established?

Question 6

What are two methods to assign a port to a VLAN?

Answer 4

VLAN membership describes which VLAN a port on a switch is assigned.

Answer 5

The three ways that inter-VLAN communication can be established are as follows:

- Router on a stick: Involves a single connection, called a trunk link, from the switch to a router. The trunk link uses a trunking protocol to differentiate between VLANs.
- Router with a separate interface in each VLAN.
- Layer 3 switch.

Answer 6

The two methods to assign a port to a VLAN are as follows:

- **Statically:** Statically assigning a port to a VLAN is a manual process performed by the administrator.
- **Dynamically:** VLAN Membership Policy Server (VMPS) allows you to define VLAN membership through the MAC address. Security products such as Cisco ISE allow you to set ports on VLANs based on the type of endpoint that connects to the port.

Question 7

What are trunk links?

Question 8

Describe 802.1Q tagging.

Question 9

In 802.1Q, what is the native VLAN?

Answer 7

Trunk links allow the switch to carry multiple VLANs across a single link.

By default, each port on a switch belongs to VLAN 1. For devices that are in a VLAN (that spans multiple switches) to talk to other devices in the same VLAN, you must use trunking or have a dedicated port for each VLAN.

Trunk links encapsulate frames using a Layer 2 protocol. This encapsulation contains information for a switch to distinguish traffic from different VLANs and to deliver frames to the proper VLANs. The Catalyst 2960 supports 802.1Q as its trunking protocol.

Answer 8

IEEE 802.1Q tagging provides an industry-standard method of identifying frames that belong to a particular VLAN. 802.1Q does this by using an internal tag that modifies the existing Ethernet frame with the VLAN identification.

Answer 9

The native VLAN is VLAN1 by default. 802.1Q does not tag the native VLAN across trunk links.

Question 10

What IOS commands assign interface g0/1 to VLAN 10 and interface g0/2 to VLAN 20?

Question 11

As a network administrator, you want to add gigabit interfaces 1 through 12 to VLAN 10 on your Catalyst 2960 switch. How do you statically assign these ports to VLAN 10?

Answer 10

From global configuration mode, the IOS commands that assign interface g0/1 to VLAN 10 and interface g0/2 to VLAN 20 are as follows:

```
Cat2960(config)# int g0/1
Cat2960(config-if)# switchport access vlan 10
Cat2960(config-if)# int g0/2
Cat2960(config-if)# switchport access vlan 20
```

The **switchport access vlan** *vlan-ID* interface command assigns an interface to a VLAN.

Answer 11

To configure a range of ports to a VLAN, enter the **range** command. The following commands from global configuration mode assign ports 1–12 to VLAN 10:

```
Cat2960(config)# interface range g 0/1 - 12
Cat2960(config-if-range)# switchport mode access
Cat2960(config-if-range)# switchport access vlan 10
```

You can assign one interface or a range of interfaces at a time to a VLAN. To assign a range of interfaces to a VLAN, first enter the interface range you want to configure. Then define the interfaces as access ports with the **switchport mode access** command. To finish, you will need to assign the range of ports to the desired VLAN with the **switchport access vlan** *vlan-id* interface command. When using the **interface range** command, take notice of the prompt change to config-if-range.

NOTE   When assigning interfaces to VLANs with the intention of being access ports, it is always recommended to explicitly configure the interfaces as access ports with the **switchport mode access** command. This is not a mandatory configuration but will prevent the interface from negotiating a trunk if a Cisco switch or a rogue device is connected into the interface.

Question 12

Configure a Catalyst 2960 switch with VLAN number 10 and name the VLAN "Accounting."

Question 13

As a network administrator, you want to create two VLANs, one named Admin and the other named Sales. What commands will create the two VLANs using VLAN ID 10 for the Admin VLAN and VLAN ID 20 for the Sales VLAN?

Answer 12

To configure a VLAN on a Catalyst 2960 switch, first ensure that the switch is in VTP server or transparent mode. When the switch is in one of these modes, the **vlan** *vlan-id* global configuration command adds a VLAN. The *vlan-id* can be a number from 2 to 1001 for normal-range VLANs and 1006 to 4094 for extended VLANs.

The following walks you through the solution configuration:

```
Switch(config)# vlan 10
Switch(config-vlan)# name Accounting
```

NOTE   When you create the VLAN, the prompt changes to Switch(config-vlan). This is config-vlan mode. Also, to configure VLANs, a switch must either be in VTP server or transparent mode. VTP is not covered in the ICND1 or CCNA exam, but it is a Cisco VLAN trunking protocol that helps propagate configured VLANs to other switches in a VTP domain. VTP has three modes: server, client, and transparent. In VTP server mode, the switch can create, modify, delete, and propagate VLANs to VTP clients participating in the VTP domain. In VTP client mode, the switch cannot create, modify, or delete VLANs. VTP transparent mode is the default mode of Cisco Catalyst switches and does not participate in VTP.

Answer 13

Issue the following commands from global configuration mode to create the two VLANs:

```
Cat2960(config)# vlan 10
Cat2960(config-vlan)# name Admin
Cat2960(config-vlan)# vlan 20
Cat2960(config-vlan)# name Sales
```

Question 14

What are normal-range VLANs?

Question 15

What are extended-range VLANs?

Question 16

What command allows you to view information that is specific to VLAN 10?

Answer 14

Normal-range VLANs are VLANs with VLAN IDs from 1 to 1005.

If the switch is in VTP server or transparent mode, you can add, modify, or remove configuration for VLANs 2 to 1001 in the VLAN database. VLAN IDs 1 and 1002–1005 are automatically created and cannot be removed. VLAN ID 1 is reserved as the default VLAN and VLAN IDs 1002–1005 are reserved for Token Ring and FDDI.

Answer 15

Extended-range VLANs are VLANs with VLAN IDs from 1006 to 4094. Extended-range VLANs can only be configured if the switch is in VTP transparent mode with the appropriate IOS licensing installed. Extended-range VLAN configurations are not stored in the VLAN database but are stored in the switch running the configuration file.

Answer 16

To view information that is specific to VLAN 10, enter the **show vlan id 10** privileged EXEC command, as follows:

```
Cat2960# show vlan id 10

VLAN Name                 Status    Ports
---------------------- --------- -------------------------------
10   sales                active    Fa0/1, Fa0/3, Fa0/4, Fa0/5
                                    Fa0/6, Fa0/7, Fa0/8, Fa0/9
                                    Fa0/10, Fa0/11, Fa0/12
<text omitted>
```

Question 17

What IOS commands display information on all configured VLANs?

Question 18

What are three ways to verify the ports assigned to VLANs?

Answer 17

The **show vlan** {**name** *vlan-name* | **id** *id*} command and the **show vlan brief** command display information on all configured VLANs.

In addition to displaying all information on configured VLANs, the **show vlan** and **show vlan brief** commands display the switch interfaces that are assigned to each VLAN.

Answer 18

To verify that a port is assigned to a VLAN, you could use the **show vlan** (and its applicable extensions), **show interface** *type number*, **show running-config** (and it applicable extensions), **show interface status**, and **show mac-address-table** commands. This list is not complete but does include some of the most common commands used by a CCNA candidate. Here is an example of the **show running-config** interface command for port g0/1 on the switch:

```
Cat2960# show running-config interface g0/1
Building configuration...
Current configuration : 84 bytes!
interface GigabitEthernet0/1
 switchport access vlan 10
 switchport mode access
```

Question 19

How do you verify the VLANs on a Catalyst switch and the ports assigned to each VLAN?

Question 20

How do you configure an interface for trunking on a Catalyst 2960 switch?

Answer 19

You can use two commands to verify the VLANs on a switch: the more detailed
show vlan {name *vlan-name* | **id** *id*} privileged EXEC command or the **show vlan
brief** privileged command, as follows:

```
Switch# show vlan brief
VLAN Name                        Status     Ports
---- -------------------- --------- ----------------------------
1    default              active    Gi0/2
10   InternetAccess       active
20   Operations           active    Fa0/1, Fa0/2,
30   Administration       active    Fa0/6, Fa0/7, Fa0/8, Fa0/9
40   Engineering          active    Fa0/3, Fa0/4,
                                    Fa0/5, Fa0/10, Fa0/11, Fa0/12,
                                    Fa0/13,Fa0/14, Fa0/15, Fa0/16,
                                    Fa0/17, Fa0/18, Fa0/19,Fa0/20
60   Public               active    Fa0/21, Fa0/22, Fa0/23, Fa0/24
!text-omitted!
```

Answer 20

To configure an interface for trunking, use the **switchport mode trunk** interface
command.

To enable an interface for trunking on a Catalyst 2960 switch, use the **switchport
mode [dynamic** {**auto** | **desirable**} | **trunk**] interface command. The following exam-
ples configure one interface for trunking and a second interface to trunk only if the
neighboring device is set to *trunk, desirable,* or *auto*:

```
Cat2960(config)# interface g0/1
Cat2960(config-if)# switchport mode trunk
Cat2960(config-if)# interface g0/2
Cat2960(config-if)# switchport mode dynamic desirable
```

NOTE   In addition to being configured on both ends, for trunk links to work, the
native VLAN on both ends of the link must match.

Question 21

What is DTP?

Question 22

When configuring trunking on a Catalyst 2960, what are the four Layer 2 interface modes supported?

Answer 21

Dynamic Trunking Protocol (DTP) is a Cisco-proprietary, point-to-point Layer 2 protocol that manages trunk negotiation. Switches from other vendors do not support DTP.

DTP is enabled by default on a switch port when certain trunking modes are configured on the switch port. DTP manages trunk negotiation only if the port on the other switch is configured in a trunk mode that supports DTP.

Answer 22

The four Layer 2 interface modes supported when configuring trunking on a Catalyst 2960 are as follows:

- **switchport mode access:** Makes the interface a nontrunking access port.

- **switchport mode dynamic auto:** Allows the interface to convert to a trunk link if the connecting neighbor interface is set to *trunk or desirable.*

- **switchport mode dynamic desirable:** Makes the interface attempt to convert the link to a trunk link. The link becomes a trunk if the neighbor interface is set to *trunk, desirable,* or *auto.*

- **switchport mode trunk:** Configures the port to permanent trunk mode and negotiates with the connected device if the other side can convert the link to trunk mode.

NOTE   Cisco recommends disabling autonegotiation. That is, do not use the dynamic auto and dynamic desirable switch port modes.

Question 23

What are the default Layer 2 Ethernet interface VLAN settings on a Catalyst 2960 switch?

Question 24

How do you display the trunking interfaces on a Catalyst 2960 switch?

Answer 23

The default Layer 2 Ethernet interface VLAN settings on a Catalyst 2960 switch are as follows:

- **Interface mode:** switchport mode dynamic auto
- **Trunking Encapsulation Type:** dot1q
- **Negotiation of Trunking:** On
- **Trunking VLANs:** All allowed
- **Default VLAN:** VLAN 1
- **VLAN pruning eligible range:** 2 to 1001
- **Native VLAN:** 1

The **switchport mode dynamic auto** command allows the interface to convert the interface from an access link to a trunk link. The interface becomes a trunk if the neighboring interface is set to *trunk* or *desirable*.

Answer 24

The **show interfaces trunk** privileged EXEC command shows the interfaces that are trunking on a switch and the trunk configuration, as follows:

```
Cat2960# show interfaces trunk
Port        Mode            Encapsulation  Status        Native vlan
Gi0/1       on              802.1q         trunking      1
Port        Vlans allowed on trunk
Gi0/1       1-4094
Port        Vlans allowed and active in management domain
Gi0/1       1-3,5,10,20,30,40,50,60
Port        Vlans in spanning tree forwarding state and not pruned
Gi0/1       1-3,5,40
```

NOTE   If you want to only see trunking information for a specific port, enter the interface number after **interfaces: show interfaces** *interface-id* **trunk**.

Question 25

Because VLANs are considered individual broadcast domains, for inter-VLAN communication to occur, a Layer 3 device is needed. What three things must occur for inter-VLAN routing?

Question 26

What are the three solutions for inter-VLAN routing?

Answer 25

Three requirements for inter-VLAN routing to occur are as follows:

- The router must know how to reach all VLANs.
- The routers must have a separate physical connection for each VLAN, or trunking must be enabled on a single physical connection.
- The use of a Layer 3 switch if no router is being used.

NOTE   Remember that each VLAN is a subnet and that a router is needed to route from one subnet to another.

Answer 26

The three solutions for inter-VLAN communication are

- Using a router with a separate interface for each VLAN
- A router on a stick
- A Layer 3 switch

NOTE   A router on a stick is a router with an interface connected to a switch with the interface being configured as a trunk interface.

Question 27

How do you enable routing between VLANs on a router on a stick?

Question 28

To enable inter-VLAN routing using a Layer 3 switch, what must be configured on the Layer 3 switch?

Answer 27

The **encapsulation dot1q** *vlan-id* subinterface command enables 802.1Q trunking on a Cisco router.

To configure trunking on a router, first create a subinterface and then configure the subinterface with the **encapsulation dot1q** *vlan-id* command, where the *vlan-id* is the VLAN number of the associated VLAN. The following example enables inter-VLAN routing for VLANs 1 (native VLAN), 10, and 20:

```
RouterB(config)# int g0/0
RouterB(config-if)# ip address 192.168.1.1 255.255.255.0
RouterB(config-if)# int g0/0.10
RouterB(config-if)# ip address 192.168.10.1 255.255.255.0
RouterB(config-if)# encapsulation dot1q 10
RouterB(config-if)# int g0/0.20
RouterB(config-if)# ip address 192.168.20.1 255.255.255.0
RouterB(config-if)# encapsulation dot1q 20
```

NOTE   Remember that in 802.1Q, the native VLAN is not encapsulated. In the previous example, the physical interface g0/0 was configured with the native VLAN, hence the reason for the missing **encapsulation dot1q** command. The subinterfaces g0/0.10 and g0/0.20 were configured for 802.1Q tagging.

Answer 28

To enable a Layer 3 switch to perform inter-VLAN routing, Switch Virtual Interfaces (SVI) on the switch need to be configured, IP routing must be enabled, VLANs must be configured on the switch, and at least one physical port must support the VLANs to be routed.

NOTE   Using a Layer 3 switch for inter-VLAN routing is more scalable than using a router on a stick.

Question 29

What is DHCP?

Question 30

When a DHCP-enabled client first boots up, what does the client broadcast?

Question 31

What is included in a DHCPOFFER message?

Answer 29

Dynamic Host Configuration Protocol (DHCP) allows a host to obtain an IP address automatically and to set TCP/IP stack configuration parameters such as subnet mask, default gateway, and DNS addresses from a DHCP server.

Answer 30

The client broadcasts a DHCPDISCOVER message on the local subnet. The destination address of DHCPDISCPOVER messages is 255.255.255.255.

Answer 31

In a DHCPOFFER message, initial IP configuration for the client, such as IP address, subnet mask, and default gateway, is included. A DHCPOFFER message originates from the DHCP server.

Question 32

Because a DHCPDISCOVER message is a broadcast, a router will not forward DHCPDISCOVER messages. If a client is on a different IP subnet than the DHCP server, how do you forward the DHCPDISCOVER message form the client to the DHCP server?

Answer 32

You forward the DHCPDISCOVER message by issuing the **ip helper-address** *dhcpserver-address* interface command on the remote router. The **ip helper-address** global configuration command is entered on the router that the remote host is directly connected to.

Section 10
WAN Technologies

Wide-area networks (WAN) connect local-area networks (LAN) that are separated over a geographic distance. WANs usually connect networks through a third-party carrier. These third-party companies are usually telephone or cable companies. The third-party carrier charges the company that connects the networks a monthly fee for the WAN connections.

Currently, several WAN implementations exist. These include point-to-point leased lines, packet-switched lines, and circuit-switched lines. Also, carriers are offering newer implementations such as Ethernet emulation. The ICND1 exam focuses on WAN connectivity over Ethernet emulation; serial connectivity is covered in ICND2.

This section will also introduce you to dynamic routing protocols and the concepts behind how they function.

Question 1

What is a WAN?

Question 2

WAN technologies operate at what layers of the OSI model?

Question 3

What are three major characteristics of WANs?

Answer 1

A wide-area network (WAN) is a data communications network that extends beyond the geographic scope of a LAN. WANs use service provider connections to interconnect LANs into one internetwork.

Answer 2

WAN technologies operate at the physical and data link layers of the OSI model.

A WAN interconnects LANs that are separated by a large geographical distance not supported by typical LAN media.

The physical layer defines the electrical, mechanical, and operational connections of WANs, in addition to the interface between the data terminal equipment (DTE) and data communications equipment (DCE).

The data link layer defines the WAN Layer 2 encapsulation, such as Frame Relay, ATM, HDLC, Ethernet emulation, and PPP.

NOTE   MPLS is considered a WAN technology but has some advanced features that operate above Layer 2 and many say operates at Layer 2.5.

Answer 3

Three major characteristics of WANs are

- They connect LANs that are located over wide geographical areas.
- They use service providers such as telephone companies, cable companies, satellite systems, and network providers for connections.
- They use various connection types to provide access to bandwidth over large geographical areas.

Question 4

What is the largest WAN in the world?

Question 5

What are three primary differences of WANs when compared to LANs?

Question 6

What roles do routers perform in a WAN?

Answer 4

The Internet is the largest WAN in the world. The Internet is the best example of a WAN. It is a collection of thousands of interconnected networks all over the world.

Answer 5

Three primary differences of WANs when compared to LANs are

- WANs span a wide geographic area. LANs are contained to a building or small geographic area.
- WAN links are owned by a service provider. LAN links are owned by the organization.
- WANs have recurring monthly costs for the use of the links. After they are installed, LANs do not have reoccurring monthly costs.

Answer 6

Routers perform several functions in a WAN. They provide a means to interconnect WAN links to LAN interfaces. They provide routing and perform certain functions needed for WANs such as clocking and encapsulation.

NOTE   Routers are not the only devices that provide clocking for WAN connections. Often CSU/DSUs and modems serve the clocking source for a circuit.

Question 7

What are the three types of interfaces typically found on routers?

Question 8

Define customer premises equipment (CPE), and give an example.

Question 9

What is the demarcation point (demarc)?

Answer 7

The three interfaces typically found on routers are

- **LAN interfaces:** copper or fiber
- **WAN interfaces:** copper or fiber
- **Management interfaces:** console, Ethernet, auxiliary

Answer 8

Typically, CPE is equipment that is located on the customer's (or subscriber's) premises. It is equipment owned by the customer or equipment leased by the service provider to the customer for the purpose of connecting to the service provider network. An example is a router.

Answer 9

The demarc is a point where the CPE ends and the local loop begins. It is the point between the wiring that comes in from the local service provider and the wiring installed to connect the customer's CPE to the service provider. It is the last responsibility of the service provider and is usually a network interface device (NID) located in the customer's telephone wiring closet. Think of the demarc as the boundary between the customer's wiring and the service provider's wiring.

Question 10

What is the local loop?

Question 11

Define the central office (CO).

Question 12

What are five available WAN connection types?

Answer 10

The local loop is the physical cable that extends from the demarc to the service provider's network.

Answer 11

The CO is the WAN service provider's office where the local loop terminates and in which circuit switching occurs. The CO is normally associated to a telco.

Answer 12

Five available WAN connection types are as follows:

- Dedicated connections (leased lines)
- Circuit-switching connections
- Packet-switching connections
- Cell-switching connections
- Broadband VPN connections

Question 13

What is WAN signaling?

Question 14

What are WAN data link layer protocols?

Question 15

What is a point-to-point communication link across a WAN?

Answer 13

WAN signaling is the process of sending a transmission signal over a physical medium for communication. WAN transmission facilities feature standardized signaling schemes that define transmission rates and media types. For example, the signaling standard for a T1 line in North America is DS1 with a transmission rate of 1.544 Mbps.

Answer 14

WAN data link layer protocols include High-Level Data Link Control (HDLC), PPP, ATM, Frame Relay, and so on.

Designed to operate over dedicated lines, multipoint services, and multiaccess-switched services such as Frame Relay, data link layer protocols provide the data link layer encapsulations associated with synchronous serial lines.

Answer 15

A point-to-point communication link across a WAN provides a single established WAN connection path from the customer premises through a service provider network to a remote network.

NOTE   Point-to-point WAN links can use either serial or Ethernet interfaces, depending on the technology used by the service provider (SP). Serial interfaces are used in traditional connections such as T1s, and T3s and require a DSU/CSU. Ethernet interfaces are becoming a more common option because of simplicity, cost, and flexibility. To provide Ethernet point-to-point connections, the service provider uses Ethernet emulation.

Question 16

What is the Point-to-Point Protocol (PPP)?

Question 17

How do you enable a point-to-point link on a router interface using Ethernet emulation?

Question 18

After configuring an interface for point-to-point WAN connectivity through a service provider network, how do you test end-to-end connectivity with the remote network?

Answer 16

PPP is an industry-standard protocol that provides router-to-router or router-to-host connections over synchronous and asynchronous links. It can be used to connect WAN links to other vendors' equipment. It is protocol independent; thus it works with several network layer protocols. PPP provides optional authentication through Password Authentication Protocol (PAP), Challenge Handshake Authentication Protocol (CHAP), or Microsoft CHAP (MS-CHAP).

Answer 17

Enabling a point-to-point link with Ethernet emulation is the same as configuring an IP address on an Ethernet interface and enabling the interface. The following example configures a router's Fast Ethernet interface 0/0 for Ethernet emulation using a /30 subnet mask:

```
RouterB(config-if)# interface f0/0
RouterB(config-if)# ip address 192.168.1.254 255.255.255.252
RouterB(config-if)# no shutdown
```

NOTE   Remember, if you are configuring the interface for the first time, you have to enable the interface with the **no shutdown** command. In the previous example, a /30 subnet mask is used to conserve IP addresses. /30 subnet masks are typically used on point-to-point Layer 3 links because they provide two usable IPs.

Answer 18

To test end-to-end connectivity, use ping, tracert, or traceroute to verify communications with the remote network.

NOTE   Checking the interface's state is not enough to ensure end-to-end WAN connectivity. This is because the local interface circuit can be enabled, but routing in the service provider's cloud could not be working or there could be a failure in the cloud. Verification of the interface would not show this.

Question 19

What are the purposes of routing protocols?

Question 20

What is administrative distance?

Question 21

What is the default administrative distance for each of the following?

- Directly connected interfaces
- Static route
- EIGRP
- OSPF
- IS-IS
- BGP
- RIP
- External EIGRP
- Unknown

Answer 19

The primary purposes of routing protocols are to

■ Discover remote networks

■ Maintain up-to-date routing information

■ Choose the best path to a destination network when multiple networks are learned from the same routing process

■ Find a new best path if the current path is no longer available

Answer 20

Administrative distance (AD) is an integer from 0 to 255 that rates the trustworthiness of the source of the IP routing information. It is only important when a router learns about a destination route from more than one source. The path with the lowest AD is the one given priority.

NOTE If a routing protocol has multiple paths within the same routing protocol to the same destination, the metric is used as the tiebreaker. The route with the lowest metric is the path taken.

Answer 21

The default ADs are as follows:

■ **Directly connected interface: 0**
■ **Static route: 1**
■ **EIGRP: 90**
■ **OSPF: 110**
■ **IS-IS: 115**
■ **RIP: 120**
■ **External EIGRP: 170**
■ **Unknown: 255**

Question 22

What is an autonomous system (AS)?

Question 23

What is the difference between interior gateway protocols (IGP) and exterior gateway protocols (EGP)?

Question 24

What is a routing protocol metric?

Answer 22

An AS is a collection of networks under common administrative control that share a common routing strategy.

Answer 23

IGPs exchange routing topology within an autonomous system (AS). EGPs exchange routing topology between autonomous systems. Examples of IGPs are RIPv2, EIGRP, IS-IS, and OSPF. BGP is an example of an EGP.

Answer 24

A routing protocol metric is a factor that determines the desirability of a route that has been sent within routing protocol data. A router uses the metric to determine the best or optimal path to which a same destination has been learned multiple times through the same routing protocol process. This value is evaluated after the administrative distance when building the routing table. Each routing protocol uses a unique metric.

Question 25

What are the most common metrics used by routing protocol algorithms?

Question 26

How do distance vector routing protocols function?

Answer 25

The most common metrics used by routing protocol algorithms are as follows:

- **Bandwidth:** The data capacity of a link
- **Delay:** The length of time required to move a packet from source to destination
- **Hop count:** The number of routers a packet must take to reach its destination
- **Cost:** A value assigned by the network administrator, usually based on bandwidth on the link

NOTE   Reliability and load are other metrics that can be used by routing protocols but are not used by default.

- **Load:** The amount of activity on the link or network resource
- **Reliability:** A reference to the error rate on each network link

Also, bandwidth and delay are not actual values but are configured values.

Answer 26

Distance vector routing protocols pass complete routing tables to neighboring routers. Neighboring routers then combine the received routing table with their own routing tables. Each router receives a routing table from its directly connected neighbor. RIPv2 is the most common distance vector protocol used in today's internetworks.

NOTE   As outlined in the split-horizon rule, distance vector protocols will not pass routing table updates to neighboring routers from which it learned routes.

Question 27

How do distance vector routing protocols keep track of changes to the internetwork?

Question 28

What are link-state routing protocols? List two common link-state routing protocols.

Question 29

Which of the following is an advanced distance vector routing protocol?

- RIPv2
- EIGRP
- DECnet
- OSPF

Answer 27

Distance vector routing protocols keep track of changes to the internetwork by periodically broadcasting updates out all active interfaces.

These broadcasts contain the entire routing table. This method is often called "routing by rumor."

Updates are not sent out interfaces where the router originally learned the update.

NOTE   RIPv2 is an update to the original version of RIP and is a distance vector protocol. An enhancement to RIPv2 is that it uses multicasts for routing updates instead of broadcasts and triggered updates.

Answer 28

Link-state routing protocols create a complete picture of the internetwork by determining the status of each interface (link) in the internetwork. When the interface goes down, link-state protocols send link-state advertisements (LSA) out all other interfaces, informing other routers of the downed link. Thus LSAs are only sent when there is a link change. Link-state protocols find the best paths to destinations by applying Dijkstra's algorithm against the link-state database.

OSPF and IS-IS are the most common link-state protocols used.

Answer 29

EIGRP is an advanced distance vector routing protocol.

EIGRP was developed by Cisco and is considered an advanced distance vector routing protocol because it combines the aspects of distance vector and link-state routing protocols.

Section 11
Implementing OSPF

Developed by the Internet Engineering Task Force (IETF) as a replacement to distance vector routing protocols, Open Shortest Path First (OSPF) was created to resolve the problems associated with Routing Information Protocol (RIP).

OSPF is an open standard interior gateway protocol (IGP). It is a link-state protocol that uses the shortest path first (SPF) algorithm. The SPF algorithm is sometimes called the Dijkstra SPF algorithm, after its inventor. OSPF is an open standard protocol, meaning that it is not proprietary to a vendor. As such, OSPF is the routing protocol of choice to route in a multivendor network. (Be prepared for questions on the ICND exam about which routing protocol to use in a multivendor network.)

OSPF's major advantage over RIP version 2 (RIPv2) and other distance vector protocols is its fast reconvergence and scalability. Reconvergence is the time required for routers to react to changes in the network, remove bad routes, and update routing tables with new or current routes.

OSPF can scale to support the largest IP networks. OSPF does this by segmenting networks into areas. Within each area, OSPF maintains a topology database of the entire network. An OSPF-enabled router does not maintain topology database information of routers not in its area. Instead, an OSPF router receives summary link-state advertisements about networks in other areas from an area border router. An area border router is a router running OSPF in two areas.

Question 1

What is the routing metric that OSPF is based on?

Question 2

What is the OSPF neighbor table?

Question 3

Provide four reasons why you would use OSPF instead of RIPv2.

Answer 1

Bandwidth is the routing metric that OSPF is based on.

OSPF's metric is a cost value based on bandwidth. The default formula used to calculate OSPF cost is as follows:

Cost = 100,000,000 / Bandwidth in bps

For example, OSPF assigns the cost of 10 to a 10-MB Ethernet line (100,000,000 / 10,000,000 = 10).

NOTE   For the exam, you might see multiple correct answers. If a question asks what the OSPF metric is based on, bandwidth is the correct answer. If the question asks what the OSPF metric is, the correct answer is cost.

Answer 2

The OSPF neighbor table is a list of all neighbors discovered by OSPF that an adjacency is formed with.

OSPF routers must have certain parameters matching before forming adjacencies and appearing in the neighbor table.

The **show ip ospf neighbor** command is used to display OSPF neighbors.

Answer 3

Four reasons why you would use OSPF instead of RIPv2 are as follows:

- Fast convergence.
- No reachability limitations.
- More efficient use of bandwidth.
- Path selection is based on bandwidth rather than hops.

Question 4

Before OSPF-enabled routers can exchange link-state information, what must be established?

Question 5

How do OSPF-enabled routers learn and recognize other OSPF-enabled routers?

Answer 4

Neighbor adjacencies must be established.

Before OSPF-enabled routers can exchange link-state information on directly connected routes, they must know about each other and form an adjacency with routers in their area.

Answer 5

OSPF-enabled routers learn and recognize other OSPF-enabled routers through Hello packets. OSPF-enabled routers send Hello packets out all OSPF-enabled interfaces to determine whether there are any neighbor routers on those links.

Question 6

What information does each Hello packet contain?

Question 7

What fields in Hello packets must match for OSPF-enabled routers to form adjacencies?

Answer 6

Each Hello packet contains the following information:

- Router ID of the originating router
- Area ID of the originating router interface
- IP address and mask of the originating router interface
- Authentication type and authentication password if required of the originating router interface
- HelloInterval
- DeadInterval
- Interface router priority
- Designated router (DR) and backup designated router (BDR)
- Neighbor field

Answer 7

Area ID, subnet mask and subnet number, Hello Interval, Dead Interval, and Authentication fields must match.

Question 8

How do OSPF-speaking routers build adjacencies and exchange advertisements?

Question 9

What are link-state advertisements?

Answer 8

OSPF-speaking routers build adjacencies based on OSPF network types and exchange link-state information by sending Hello packets out all OSPF-enabled interfaces.

If the routers share a common network type and agree on certain parameters set in their Hello packets, they become neighbors. If these parameters are different, they do not become neighbors and no adjacency is formed. OSPF routers can then form adjacencies with certain routers. The routers that OSPF-speaking routers build adjacencies with are determined by the data-link media type. After adjacencies have been formed, each router sends link-state advertisements (LSA) to all adjacent routers. These LSAs describe the state of each of the router's links. Because of the varying types of link-state information, OSPF defines multiple LSA types. Finally, a router receiving LSAs from its neighbors records the LSA in a link-state database and floods a copy of the LSA to all its other adjacent neighbors in most situations. When all databases are complete, each router uses the SPF algorithm to calculate a loop-free topology and builds its routing table based on this topology.

Answer 9

Link-state advertisements (LSA) are what OSPF-enabled routers send out all OSPF-enabled interfaces to describe the state of the routers' links. LSAs are also packets that OSPF uses to advertise changes in the condition of a specific link to other OSPF routers.

Question 10

How many LSAs exist in OSPF?

Question 11

What is the OSFP router ID, and how does an OSPF router derive its router ID?

Question 12

What IOS commands shows the router ID configured on an OSPF-enabled router?

Answer 10

Eleven distinct link-state packet formats are used in OSPF; each is used for a different purpose. However, Cisco only supports eight: Types 1–5 and 7–9.

The ICND1 exam will most likely test you on two LSA types: Type 1 and Type 2.

Type 1 LSAs are Router LSAs and are generated by each router for each area to which it belongs. These LSAs describe the states of the router's links to the area and are flooded within a single area.

Type 2 LSAs are Network LSAs and are generated by the DR and BDR. They describe the set of routers attached to a particular network. They are flooded within a single area.

Answer 11

For OSPF to initialize, it must be able to define a router ID for the entire OSPF process. A router ID is derived from the manual configuration through the **router-id** command and from the numerically highest IP address set on the loopback interface. The loopback interface is a logical interface that never goes down. If no loopback address is defined, an OSPF-enabled router selects the numerically highest IP address on all its interfaces as its router ID.

NOTE   The router ID is chosen when OSPF is initialized. Initialization occurs when a router loads its the OSPF routing process. If other interfaces later come online that have a higher IP address, the OSPF router ID does not change until the OSPF process is restarted.

Answer 12

The **show ip protocols, show ip ospf neighbor, show ip ospf**, and **show ip ospf interface** commands all display the router ID configured for OSPF.

Question 13

How do you enable OSPF on a Cisco router?

Question 14

What does the show ip protocols **command display?**

Answer 13

Basic OSPF is configured in two steps: Enable the OSPF routing process and then identify the networks that you want to advertise.

The **router ospf** *process-id* command enables the OSPF process, and the **network** *address wildcard-mask* **area** *area-id* command assigns networks to a specific OSPF area. Consider the following example:

```
RouterA(config)# router ospf 10
RouterA(config-router)# network 192.168.10.0 0.0.0.255 area 0
```

These commands enable OSPF process 10 and advertise any network assigned to any interface within 192.168.10.0/24 to possibly be part of area 0. Notice that you must specify the wildcard mask instead of the subnet mask.

NOTE   The process ID is locally significant to the router and is used to differentiate among different OSPF processes running on the router.

Answer 14

The **show ip protocols** command displays a summary of configured routing protocol information. It is useful for a quick verification of how routing protocols are configured. It allows you to verify which protocols are enabled and which networks they are routing to.

Question 15

What IOS commands display the OSPF neighbor information on a per-interface basis?

Question 16

What IOS command shows all the OSPF-learned routes?

Answer 15

The **show ip ospf neighbor** and **show ip ospf interface** *interface-type interface-number* commands display OSPF neighbor information on a per-interface basis.

```
RouterB# show ip ospf neighbor

Neighbor ID     Pri  State           Dead Time   Address      Interface
172.16.0.1       1   FULL/  -        00:00:31    10.1.1.1     Serial0
RouterB# show ip ospf interfaces
Serial00 is up, line protocol is up
  Internet Address 10.1.1.1, Area 0
  Process ID 1, Router ID 1.1.1.1, Network Type POINT_TO_POINT, Cost: 64
  Transmit Delay is 1 sec, State POINT_TO_POINT
  Timer intervals configured, Hello 10, Dead 40, Wait 40, Retransmit 5
    oob-resync timeout 40
    Hello due in 00:00:00
  Supports Link-local Signaling (LLS)
  Cisco NSF helper support enabled
  IETF NSF helper support enabled
  Index 1/1, flood queue length 0
  Next 0x0(0)/0x0(0)
  Last flood scan length is 1, maximum is 1
  Last flood scan time is 0 msec, maximum is 0 msec
  Neighbor Count is 1, Adjacent neighbor count is 1
    Adjacent with neighbor 172.16.0.1
  Suppress hello for 0 neighbor(s)
```

Answer 16

The **show ip route ospf** command shows all routes that the router learned through OSPF that are in the routing table.

Question 17

What command displays a router's OSPF neighbors?

Answer 17

The **show ip ospf neighbors** command displays a router's OSPF neighbors.

Section 12
Introducing IPv6

When the Internet was first created, no one envisioned that it would grow to its current size. At the time, a 32-bit address, yielding approximately 4.3 billion Internet addresses, seemed sufficient.

However, with the explosion of the Internet, experts in the 1990s predicted that all IP addresses would be exhausted in a few years. As a result of this prediction, IP version 6 (IPv6) was created to remedy the limited IP addresses.

Network Address Translation (NAT) and CIDR were used to slow the depletion of IPv4 addresses. However, although NAT and CIDR have successfully slowed the depletion of IPv4 addresses, the migration to IPv6 is still necessary. Newer technologies such as mobile IP and end-to-end security are not possible using NAT. Additionally, NAT breaks some applications and does not provide an end-to-end IP experience. As such, the move to IPv6 is under way.

IPv6 is the future of IP communications. It replaces IPv4 addresses with a 128-bit address, making more than 340 undecillion IP addresses. Additionally, IPv6 provides solutions to some problems found in IPv4.

Question 1

How many bits are in an IPv6 address?

Question 2

Besides a larger address space, what are some additional benefits of IPv6 when compared to IPv4?

Question 3

What are the three types of IPv6 addresses?

Answer 1

An IPv6 address is 128 bits long and is represented in eight 16-bit hexadecimal segments. An example of an IPv6 address is as follows:

2001:0D02:0000:0000:0000:C003:0001:F00D

Answer 2

Some additional benefits of IPv6 when compared to IPv4 are as follows:

- Simplified header
- Autoconfiguration
- Enhanced multicast support
- Extension headers
- Flow labels
- Security and mobility built in
- Improved address allocation
- Strict aggregation

Answer 3

The three types of IPv6 addresses are as follows:

- Unicast
- Anycast
- Multicast

Question 4

What is an IPv6 unicast address?

Question 5

What is a global unicast address?

Question 6

What is a link-local unicast address?

Answer 4

An IPv6 unicast address is an address that identifies a single device. It has a one-to-one mapping.

Unicast addresses include global, link local, loopback (::11), and unspecified (::).

Answer 5

A global unicast address is a unicast address that is globally unique and can be routed globally. RFC 4291 specifies 2000::/3 to be reserved as global unicast address space to be allocated by the IANA.

Answer 6

A link-local unicast address is an IPv6 address whose address is confined to a single physical link. Thus the address is not routable off the physical subnet. Link-local addresses typically begin with FE80. The next digits can be assigned manually. If the interface ID is not assigned manually, it can be based on the interface MAC address.

NOTE   An interface can have multiple link-local and global addresses.

Question 7

What is an IPv6 anycast address?

Question 8

What is an IPv6 multicast address?

Question 9

What is the address used for the IPv6 loopback address?

Answer 7

An IPv6 anycast address is an address that represents a group of devices that support a similar service. Each device will be assigned the same anycast address. Routers will deliver data to the nearest node that is used in the common anycast address. Anycast addresses have a one-to-nearest mapping.

To assign an anycast address to a router interface, configure a global unicast address with the keyword **anycast** appended to the end of the command line.

Answer 8

An IPv6 multicast address identifies a set of devices called a multicast group. It has a one-to-many mapping and also replaces IPv4 broadcast addresses. IPv6 multicast addresses use the reserved address space FF00::0/8.

Answer 9

The address used for the IPv6 loopback address is 0:0:0:0:0:0:0:1, which is normally expressed as ::1.

Question 10

What are the IPv6 addresses that are reserved by the IETF?

Question 11

What are the two rules for reducing the size of written IPv6 addresses?

Question 12

What is the EUI-64 standard?

Answer 10

The IETF reserved approximately 1/256 of all the total IPv6 address space. The reserved addresses are

■ The lowest address within each subnet prefix (the interface identifier set to all 0s) is reserved as the "subnet-router" anycast address.

■ Within each subnet, the highest 128 interface identifier values are reserved for the subnet anycast addresses.

Answer 11

The two rules for reducing the size of written IPv6 addresses are as follows:

■ **Rule 1:** The leading 0s in any fields do not have to be written. If a field has fewer than four hexadecimal digits, it is assumed that the missing digits are leading 0s. For example, 2001:0D02:0000:0000:0000:C003:0001:F00D can be written as follows:

2001:D02:0:0:0:C003:1:F00D

■ **Rule 2:** Any single, consecutive fields of all 0s can be represented with a double colon. For example, 2001:D02:0:0:0:C003:1:F00D can be further reduced to the following:

2001:D02::C003:1:F00D

NOTE The double colon can be used only once.

Answer 12

The EUI-64 standard explains how to stretch 802.3 MAC addresses from 48 to 64 bits by inserting the 16-bit 0xFFFE at the 24th bit of the MAC address to create a 64-bit unique identifier. Secondly, the universal/local (U/L) flag (bit 7) in the OUI portion of the address is flipped from 0 to 1 so that 1 now means universal. The EUI-64 standard is used to allow a host to automatically assign itself a unique 64-bit IPv6 address without the need for manual configuration or DHCP.

For example, MAC address 00-AA-11-17-FC-0F on the network 2001:0DB8:0:1::/64 becomes 02-AA-11-17-FC-0F. The resulting EUI-64 address on the network is 2001:0DB8:0:1:02AA:11FF:17FE:FC0F.

Question 13

What are the three ways that an IPv6 host can be assigned an address?

Question 14

Before you can forward IPv6 addresses on router interfaces, what must you enable?

Question 15

After enabling IPv6 on the router, how would you configure an IPv6 address to an interface?

Answer 13

An IPv6 host can be assigned an address statically, with stateless autoconfiguration, or by Dynamic Host Configuration Protocol version 6 (DHCPv6).

NOTE   Hosts use stateless autoconfiguration by waiting for a router to advertise the local prefix. If the end system has a 48-bit MAC address, the host inverts the global/local bit (bit 7) and inserts 0xFFFE in the middle of the MAC address. This is called the EUI-64 address, and it is joined to the prefix to form the IPv6 address.

Answer 14

You must enable IPv6 unicast routing.

By default, IPv6 is not enabled on a Cisco router. As such, before you can forward IPv6 addresses on router interfaces, you must enable IPv6 routing by issuing the **ipv6 unicast-routing** global command.

Answer 15

The **ipv6 address** *ipv6-address/ipv6-length* [*eui-64*] interface command configures an IPv6 address to a router interface.

Question 16

What IPv4 headers were removed in IPv6 headers and why?

Question 17

What are the eight fields contained in IPv6?

Answer 16

The following IPv4 headers were removed in IPv6:

- **Internet Header Length:** Removed because all IPv6 headers are a fixed 40-byte length, unlike IPv4.
- **Flags:** Used in fragmentation, and IPv6 routers no longer process fragmentation.
- **Fragmentation Offset:** IPv6 routers no longer process fragmentation.
- **Header Checksum:** Removed because most data link layer technologies already perform checksum and error control.
- **Identification:** No longer needed based on IPv6 implementations.
- **Padding:** Because the Options field was changed, the Padding field is no longer needed.

Answer 17

The eight fields in IPv6 are as follows:

- **Version:** 4-bit field; contains the number 6.
- **Traffic Class:** 8-bit field that is similar to the IPv4 ToS field.
- **Flow Label:** New 20-bit field used to mark individual traffic flows with unique values.
- **Payload Length:** Describes the length of the payload only.
- **Next Header:** Used to determine the type of information that follows the IPv6 header.
- **Hop Limit:** Specifies the maximum number of hops that an IP packet can traverse.
- **Source Address:** 128-bit (16 octets) identifying the source of the packet.
- **Destination Address:** 128-bit field identifying the destination of the packet.

Question 18

What are the functions of ICMPv6?

Question 19

What two message types does ICMPv6 use?

Question 20

How are ICMPv6 packets identified in the Next Header field?

Answer 18

The functions of ICMPv6 are

■ **Diagnostic tests:** Like ICMPv4, ICMPv6 provides diagnostic tests using echo and echo reply.

■ **Router discovery:** Router solicitation and router advertisements.

■ **Neighbor discovery:** Neighbor solicitation and neighbor advertisements.

Answer 19

The two message types that ICMPv6 implements are

■ **Error messages:** Examples include Destination Unreachable, Packet Too Big, or Time Exceeded

■ **Informational messages:** Echo Request and Echo Reply

Answer 20

ICMPv6 packets are identified as 58 in the Next Header field.

Question 21

In IPv6, what is neighbor discovery?

Question 22

In IPv6, what is stateless autoconfiguration?

Question 23

What is contained in the router solicitation message?

Answer 21

Neighbor discovery in IPv6 is used for router and neighbor solicitation and advertisements, and for redirection of nodes to the best gateway. It performs the same functions as ARP in IPv4. These functions include

■ Determining the link layer address of a neighbor

■ Finding neighbor routers on a link

■ Querying for duplicate addresses

NOTE   Neighbor discovery is performed using ICMPv6 with a multicast address.

Answer 22

Stateless autoconfiguration is a feature in IPv6 that uses neighbor discovery to find routers, and it will also dynamically create an IPv6 address based on a prefix found in the router advertisement and EUI-64 standard. When stateless autoconfiguration is enabled on the interface, additional addresses will also be assigned to the interface, one of these being a link-local unicast address.

Answer 23

The router solicitation messages contains the following:

■ ICMP type of 133

■ The source address is unspecified or ::

■ Destination address is the all-routers multicast address FF02::2

Question 24

What Cisco IOS command configures a router interface for stateless autoconfiguration?

Question 25

Because IPv6 uses a 128-bit address, routing protocols need to be modified to support IPv6. What routing protocols support IPv6?

Question 26

What is RIPng?

Answer 24

The **ipv6 address autoconfig** interface command configures a router's interface for stateless autoconfiguration.

Answer 25

The following routing protocols support IPv6:

- RIPng
- OSPFv3
- EIGRP for IPv6
- Intermediate System–to–Intermediate System (IS-IS) for IPv6
- Multiprotocol Border Gateway Protocol (MP-BGP)

NOTE   Although not a routing protocol, IPv6 also supports static routing.

Answer 26

RIPng is the IPv6 version of Routing Information Protocol (RIP), a distance vector protocol. RIPng is defined in RFC 2080 and is based on RIPv2. Thus RIPng uses hop count as its metric and has a maximum hop count of 15. However, some changes to RIPng are as follows:

- Uses IPv6 for transport.
- Uses multicast group FF02::09 to advertise routes every 30 seconds.
- Updates are sent on User Datagram Protocol (UDP) port 521.

Question 27

How do you configure IPv6 static routes?

Question 28

How do you configure an IPv6 default route on a Cisco router?

Question 29

What IOS command displays all IPv6 routes entered in the routing table?

Answer 27

Static routing with IPv6 is configured the same way as with IPv4. The **ipv6 route** *ipv6_network/ipv6_mask outgoing_interface/ipv6_next_hop* global command adds static routes to a router.

The following example configures a static route for network 2001:DB8:123::/48 to route traffic to interface serial 0/0:

```
Router(config)# ipv6 route 2001:DB8:123::/48  serial 0/0
```

Answer 28

To configure a default IPv6 route on a Cisco router, use the **ipv6 route** global configuration command with ::/0 specified as the *ipv6_network/mask*. The following example configures a default route to send all traffic to interface serial 2/0:

```
Router(config)# ipv6 route ::/0 serial 2/0
```

Answer 29

The **show ipv6 route** command displays all IPv6 routes entered in the routing table.

Question 30

What features does OSFPv3 add?

Question 31

Does OSPFv3 require an IPv4 address for the router ID?

Answer 30

Open Shortest Path First version 3 (OSPFv3) is based on the current version of OSPF for IPv4, which is version 2. Like version 2, OSPFv3 sends Hellos to neighbors, exchanges link-state advertisements (LSA), and exchanges database descriptor (DBD) packets. However, OSPFv3 runs directly over IPv6 and advertises using multicast groups FF02::5 and FF02::06, but uses its link-local address as the source address of its advertisements.

FF02::5 is the address listened to by "all OSPF routers," and FF02::06 is the address listened to by the OSPF DRs and BDR.

NOTE OSPFv3 does not include authentication because authentication in IPv6 is handled through IPsec.

Answer 31

No. OSPFv3 does not require an IPv4 address for the router ID; however, a 32-bit number must be set for the router ID.

When a router has not been configured with an IPv4 address to be used by OSPFv3 for purposes of the router ID, the OSPFv3 process will not immediately start. The required step to then start the OSPF process will be to manually configure the router ID using the **router-id** *router-id* command. The value entered into the **router-id** command will use the format of a normal IPv4 address. However, it is not actually an IPv4 address nor does it need to be configured on an interface of the device.

Question 32

How do you configure OSPFv3 on a Cisco router?

Answer 32

The commands to configure OSPFv3 on a Cisco router are as follows from global configuration mode:

- **ipv6 ospf** *process-id* **area** *area_id* interface command enables OSPFv3 routing on the interface.

- **ipv6 router ospf** *process_id* enables the OSPFv3 routing process and enters the routing process configuration mode.

- **router-id** *router-id* sets the OSPFv3 router ID with a 32-bit number.

The following example configures OSPF with process ID 10 and 0.0.0.2 as the router ID, and enables OSPF on gigabit interfaces g0/0 and g0/1, assigning them to area 0:

```
Router(config)# ipv6 router ospf 10
  Router(config-rtr)# router-id 0.0.0.1
  Router(config-rtr)# interface g0/0
    Router(config-if)# ipv6 ospf 10 area 0
    Router(config-if)# interface g0/0
    Router(config-if)# ipv6 ospf 10 area 0
```

Section 1

Exploring the Functions of Networking

A network is a collection of devices and end systems that share resources or can communicate with each other.

Networks consist of computers, servers, and network devices, such as switches and routers, that can communicate with each other.

Network locations consist of the main office and remote locations. Remote locations can be branch or home offices, and mobile users.

Physical Components of a Network

Figure 1-1 shows the four major categories of physical components on a network:

- **Endpoints:** Consist of personal computers, servers, laptops, tablets, and so on that send and receive data and are the endpoints of the network.

- **Interconnections:** Are the components that provide a means for data to travel across the network. This includes network interface cards (NIC), network media, and connectors.

- **Switches:** Provide network access for end-user nodes.

- **Routers:** Interconnect networks.

Figure 1-1 *Network Components*

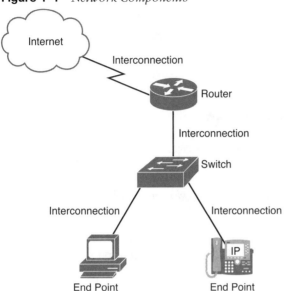

Networking Fundamentals

Networking has its own terminology and common terms. The following terms are used throughout the industry and appear many times in this study guide:

- **Network interface card (NIC):** Connects endpoints to a LAN.

- **Medium:** The physical transport used to carry data. Most of the time, this can be just a cable (twisted-pair or fiber), but it also includes air (for wireless transmission).

- **Protocol:** A set of communication rules used by computer or network devices.

- **Cisco IOS Software:** The most widely deployed network system software. Cisco IOS services include basic connectivity, security, network management, and other advanced services.

- **Client:** A computer or program that requests information from a server.

- **Server:** A computer or program that provides services of information to clients.

- **Network Operating System (NOS):** Refers to the operating system running on servers. This includes Windows 2003 Server, Novell NetWare, UNIX, and Linux.

- **Connectivity device:** Any device that connects cable segments, connects two or more small networks into a larger one, or divides a large network into small ones.

- **Local-area network (LAN):** A network confined to a small geographic area. This can be a room, building, or campus.

- **Wide-area network (WAN):** Interconnects LANs using leased carrier lines or satellite technology.

- **Physical topology:** A network's physical shape. These shapes include linear bus, ring, star, and mesh.

- **Logical topology:** The path that data takes from one computer to another.

Why Network Computers?

One of the primary functions of a network is to increase productivity by linking computers and computer networks. Corporate networks are typically divided into user groups, which are usually based on groups of employees. Remote-access locations such as branches, home offices, and mobile workers usually connect to the corporate LAN using a WAN service.

Resource-Sharing Functions and Benefits

Networks allow users to share resources and data. Major resources that are shared are

- **Data and applications:** Consist of computer data and network-aware applications like email.

- **Input and output devices:** Include resources such as camera and printers.

- **Network storage:** Consists of directly attached storage devices (physical storage that is directly attached to a computer and shared server), network attached storage, and storage-area networks.

- **Backup devices:** Devices that back up files and data from multiple computers.

Impact of User Applications on the Network

Networking applications are computer programs that run over networks.

Networking applications include

- Email

- Web browsers (this includes web applications or any application that uses HTTP/HTTPS)

- Instant messaging

- Video/collaboration

- Databases

Categories of Network Applications

Network applications are categorized as follows:

- **Batch applications:** Examples are FTP and TFTP. They are started by a person and complete with no other interaction. Bandwidth is important but not critical.

- **Interactive applications:** Include database updates and queries. A person requests data from a server and waits for a reply. Response time depends more on the server and storage than the network. Quality of service (QoS) can be used to give priority over batch applications.

- **Real-time applications:** Include VoIP and video. Network bandwidth is critical because these applications are time sensitive. QoS and sufficient network bandwidth are mandatory for these applications, requiring the highest priority when traversing the network.

Network Administration Applications

Network administration applications help manage a network. These applications are used to configure, monitor, and troubleshoot a network. Network administration applications fall into four general categories:

- **Protocol analyzers:** Capture network packets between network devices and decode the packets so that one can view what applications are being transmitted on a network.

- **Sniffers:** Work like a wiretap and allow one to observe network communication and view the data that is being transmitted.

- **Availability and performance programs:** Use protocols use as ICMP and SNMP to view availability of network devices and performance in real time.

- **Management applications:** Use software to manage and configure network devices.

Characteristics of a Network

Networks are characterized using the following terms:

- **Speed:** Also called data rate, speed is a measure of the data rate in bits per second of a given link on a network.

- **Cost:** The general expense for purchasing network components, installation, and maintenance.

- **Security:** Defines how protected the network and network data are.

- **Availability:** The measure of likelihood the network will be available for use when required. Assuming 24 hours a day, 7 days per week, and 365 days a year, availability percentage is calculated using the formula [(525600 − Minutes downtime) / 525600] * 100.

- **Scalability:** How well the network can accommodate more users and more data.
- **Reliability:** The dependability of the devices that make up the network—for example, switches, routers, PCs, and so on.
- **Topology:** Defines the design of the network. Physical topology defines the physical components of the network cables, network devices, and so on. Logical topology defines the data path of the network.

Physical Versus Logical Topologies

A topology refers to the way in which network devices are connected.

A physical topology refers to the physical layout of the devices and the connecting cables. There are four primary categories of physical topologies:

- Bus
- Ring
- Star
- Mesh

A logical topology refers to the path over which the data is transferred in a network. The logical paths are the paths data use to travel from one point in the network to another point in the network. The "physical" and "logical" topologies can be the same or different. An example of this is a network in which each endpoint is connected to every other endpoint (a meshed network), but the signal can flow only sequentially in a clockwise orientation (a ring network). The following sections discuss each of the topologies.

As showing in Figure 1-2, a bus or linear bus connects all devices with a single cable. The ends of the wire must be connected to a device or terminator, or signals will bounce back and cause errors. Only a single packet can be transmitted at a time on a bus, or the packets will collide and both will be destroyed (and must be resent).

Figure 1-2 *Bus Topology*

Figure 1-3 shows a ring topology. In a ring topology, a frame travels in a logical order around the ring, going from one end station to the next. If an end station wants to send data, it is added to the frame. The frame continues around the ring, and the data is removed at the intended destination. The frame, however, continues. In a single ring, data travels in a single direction. In a dual ring, each ring sends data in a different direction. Two rings create redundancy, or fault tolerance, which means that if one ring fails, the system can still operate. If parts of both rings fail, a "wrap" (a connection between the two rings) can heal the fault.

Figure 1-3 *Ring Topology*

Star topologies are the most commonly used physical topology in Ethernet LANs. As shown in Figure 1-4, stars have a central connection (hub, switch, or router) where all end devices meet. Stars cost more than other topologies but are more fault-tolerant because a cable failure usually affects only one end device, or host. The disadvantage of a star is that if the central device fails, the whole system fails.

Figure 1-4 *Star Topology*

In an extended star topology, the central networking device connects to other networking devices, which then connect to end stations. Figure 1-5 shows an extended star topology.

Figure 1-5 *Extended Star Topology*

In a full-mesh topology, all devices are connected to all other devices. There is great redundancy on full-mesh networks, but for networks with more than a few devices, it becomes overly expensive and complicated. Partial-mesh topologies, which have at least one device with multiple connections and one device without multiple connections, provide good redundancy without the expense of full meshes. Figure 1-6 shows a full-mesh topology.

Figure 1-6 *Full-Mesh Topology*

Understanding the Host-to-Host Communication Model

For different vendor networking devices and protocols to communicate with each other, a consistent model or standard is needed.

The OSI Reference Model

The OSI model is a standardized framework for network function and schemes. It breaks otherwise-complex network interaction into simple elements, which lets developers modularize design efforts. This method allows many independent developers to work on separate network functions, which can be applied on a "plug and play" manner.

The OSI model consists of seven layers, as outlined in Table 1-1.

Table 1-1   *OSI Model*

OSI MODEL	DESCRIPTION	Examples
Application (Layer 7)	Provides services to the user.	Telnet HTTP
Presentation (Layer 6)	Provides encryption and other processing.	ASCII/EBCDIC JPEG/MP3
Session (Layer 5)	Manages multiple applications.	Operating systems Scheduling
Transport (Layer 4)	Provides reliable or best-effort delivery and some error correction.	TCP UDP SPX
Network (Layer 3)	Provides logical addressing used by routers and the network hierarchy.	IP IPX
Data link (Layer 2)	Creates frames from bits of data. Uses MAC addresses to access endpoints. Provides error detection but no correction.	802.3 HDLC Frame Relay
Physical (Layer 1)	Specifies voltage, wire speed, and cable pin-outs.	EIA/TIA V.35

TCP/IP Reference Model

The TCP/IP suite of protocols is used to communicate across any set of inter-connected networks. These protocols, initially developed by Defense Advanced Research Projects Agency (DARPA), are well-suited for communication across both LANs and WANs. The protocol suite defines four layers:

- **Link layer:** Also called the network access layer, it consists of the physical and data-link OSI model layers.

- **Internet layer:** Provides routing of data from the source to a destination, and defines addressing schemes.

- **Transport layer:** The core of the TCP/IP suite, providing communication services directly to the application layer.

- **Application layer:** Provides specifications of applications such as email, file trans-fer, and network management.

TCP/IP Model Versus OSI Model

Figure 1-7 shows the TPC/IP model. The TCP/IP protocol stack closely follows the OSI reference model. All standard Layer 1 and 2 protocols are supported (called the Link layer in TCP/IP).

Figure 1-7 *OSI Versus TCP/IP Model*

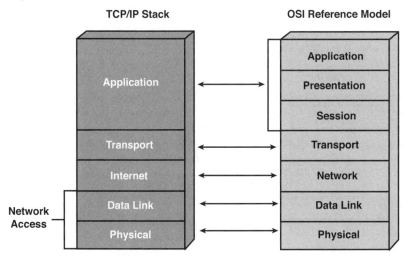

Encapsulation and Deencapsulation

Protocol data units (PDU) are used to communicate between layers. Encapsulation is the method of adding headers and trailers as the data moves down the communica-tion stack. When the receiving device gets the frame, it strips the headers moving up the stack. The header removed contains information for that layer (de-encapsulation).

A PDU can include different information as it goes up or down the OSI model. It is given a different name according to the information it is carrying (the layer it is at). When the transport layer receives upper-layer data, it adds a TCP header to the data; this is called a segment. The segment is then passed to the network layer, and an IP header is added; thus, the data becomes a packet. The packet is passed to the data link layer, thus becoming a frame. This frame is then converted into bits and is passed across the network medium. This is data encapsulation. For the ICND exam, you should know the following:

- Application layer: Data

- Transport layer: Segment

- Network layer: Packet

- Data link layer: Frame

- Physical layer: Bits

Peer-to-Peer Communication

For packets to travel from a source to a destination, each OSI layer of the source computer must communicate with its peer at the destination. As shown in Figure 1-8, each part of the message is encapsulated by the layer below it, and it is unwrapped at the destination for use by the corresponding layer.

Figure 1-8   *Data Encapsulation*

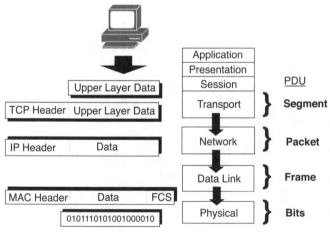

Section 2
Introducing Local-Area Networks

Local-Area Networks

Local-area networks (LAN) are high-speed, low-error data networks that cover a small geographic area.

LANs are usually located in a building or campus and do not cover a large distance. They are relatively inexpensive to develop and maintain. LANs connect computers, printers, terminals, and other devices in a single building or a limited area.

LANs consist of the following components:

- **Computers:** Such as PCs and servers.

- **Interconnections:** Provide a means for data to travel. Also include NICs and network media.

- **Network devices:** Hubs, routers, and switches.

- **Protocols:** Ethernet protocols, IP, ARP, and DHCP.

LAN Segments and Challenges

An Ethernet segment is a network connection made by a single unbroken network cable. Segments can only span a limited physical distance. Any transmission beyond the physical limitation will degrade the signal.

Extending a LAN Segment

Although Ethernet has segment distance limitations, one can extend the segment by adding repeaters, hubs, or switches.

Repeaters are Layer 1 devices that re-create a signal from one segment to another, extending the distance of the single.

Hubs, also called Ethernet concentrators or Ethernet repeaters, are self-contained Ethernet segments in a box. All devices connected to a hub compete for the same amount of bandwidth. Hubs let you add and remove computers without disabling the network but do not create additional collision domains. Hubs provide no filtering and forward all traffic out all ports regardless of where they are destined.

Switches are Layer 2 devices that extend the distance of a signal and use Layer 2 information to make intelligent forwarding decisions.

Collisions and Collision Domains

All stations on an Ethernet segment are connected to the same wire. Therefore, all devices receive all signals. Collisions occur when two or more end stations "listen" for traffic, hear nothing, and then transmit at the same time. The simultaneous transmissions collide, and all are destroyed and must be resent. Each end station resends after a random time (called a back-off algorithm). As the number of end stations increases, collisions increase to the point where the system is virtually unusable because collisions are constantly occurring. As networks grow, the chances that devices transmit at the same time increases, resulting in more collisions.

Repeaters and hubs amplify a signal and increase segment distance limitations; however, they cannot decrease collisions.

A collision domain is a group of LAN interfaces whose frames could collide with each other.

The Need for Switches

As networks grow and evolve, network congestion increases. The most common causes of network congestion are

- Increases in PC speed and network interface performance
- Increases in network data size
- Bandwidth-intensive applications

Bridges

Bridges were used as an early solution for network congestion. Bridges used the concept of segmentation to allow more end stations to be added to a LAN (called scaling). Segmentation is a method of breaking up collision domains. Bridges are more intelligent than hubs and can forward or block traffic based on the data frame's destination address (whereas hubs just send the frame to every port, except the interface it was received).

Figure 2-1 *Segmenting a Network Through Bridges*

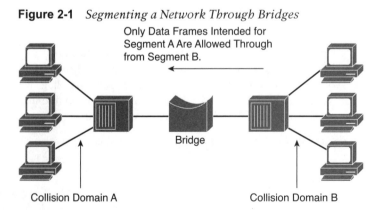

Only Data Frames Intended for
Segment A Are Allowed Through
from Segment B.

Bridge

Collision Domain A   Collision Domain B

Switches

Layer 2 switches are really just high-speed, multiport, very smart bridges. Unlike bridges that process frames using software, switches process frames in hardware through the use of application-specific integrated circuits (ASIC). Switches also have the following features:

- **High-speed backplane:** A circuit board that allows the switch to monitor multiple conversations, which increases the network's overall speed.

- **Large data buffering:** A buffer is memory storage. This function allows the switch to store frames and forward them to the correct port.

- **Higher port density:** Port density is the number of ports available on a single device. Depending on the model, a switch can have hundreds of ports.

- **High port speeds:** Switches can support a mixture of port speeds from 10 Mbps to 40 Gbps.

- **Lower latency:** Latency is the measure of the time it takes an incoming frame to come back out of a switch.

All these features (particularly port density) allow microsegmentation, which means that each end station has a dedicated switch port. This eliminates collisions, because each collision domain has only a single end station. Although these features can reduce some network congestion, faster PCs can flood a network with traffic. Broadcasts and multicasts also contribute to network congestion.

Switch Frame Transmission Modes

There are three primary frame-switching modes:

- **Cut-through:** The switch checks the destination address and immediately begins forwarding the frame. This can decrease latency but can also transmit frames containing errors.

- **Store-and-forward:** The switch waits to receive the entire frame before forwarding. The entire frame is read, and a cyclic redundancy check (CRC) is performed. If the CRC is calculated and identifies the frame as being bad, the frame is discarded. Increases latency.

- **Fragment-free (modified cut-through):** The switch reads the first 64 bytes before forwarding the frame. 64 bytes is the minimum number of bytes necessary to detect and filter out collision frames.

Operating Cisco IOS

Cisco IOS enables network services in switches and routers. It provides the following features:

■ Carries network protocols and functions

■ Connectivity for high-speed traffic between devices

■ Security to control access

■ Scalability to add interfaces and adjust to network growth

■ Reliability to ensure access to network resources

The Cisco IOS command-line interface (CLI) can be accessed through a console connection, modem connection, or Telnet/SSH sessions. These connections are called EXEC sessions.

Cisco IOS Command-Line Interface Functions

Cisco IOS uses a hierarchy of commands in its command-mode structure. For security, Cisco IOS separates EXEC sessions into these two access levels:

■ User EXEC mode

■ Privileged EXEC mode

User EXEC mode is the first mode you enter when you log in to the IOS. This mode is limited and is mostly used to view statistics. You cannot change a router's configuration in this mode. By default, the greater-than sign (>) indicates that you are in user mode. This is how the router prompt looks in user mode:

```
Router>
```

In privileged EXEC mode, you can view and change the configuration in a router; you have access to all the router's commands and the powerful **debug** commands.

To enter privileged mode, enter the **enable** command while in user mode. By default, the pound symbol (#) indicates that you are in privileged mode. This mode is usually protected with a password. Here is an example of how to enter privileged mode. You also see the output of the prompt:

```
Router> enable
Password:
Router#
```

Keyboard Help in the CLI

Several commands built into IOS provide help when you enter configuration commands:

- **?** displays a list of commonly used commands.

- **-More** appears at the bottom of the screen when additional information exists. Display the next available screen by pressing the spacebar. Display the next line by pressing Enter. Press any other key to return to the prompt.

- **s?** lists all commands that start with *s*.

- **show ?** lists all variants of the **show** command.

Enhanced Editing Commands

Enabled by default, enhanced editing commands allow shortcuts to speed the editing process. Table 2-1 shows the enhanced editing commands available in Cisco IOS Software.

Table 2-1   *Enhanced Editing Commands*

Command	Action
Ctrl-A	Moves the cursor to the beginning of the line
Ctrl-E	Moves the cursor to the end of the line
Esc-B	Moves the cursor back one word
Esc-F	Moves the cursor forward one word
Ctrl-B	Moves the cursor back one character
Ctrl-F	Moves the cursor forward one character
Ctrl-D	Deletes a single character
Backspace	Removes one character to the left of the cursor
Ctrl-R	Redisplays a line
Ctrl-U	Erases from the cursor to the beginning of the line
Ctrl-W	Erases a word
Ctrl-Z	Ends configuration mode and returns to the EXEC mode
Tab	Completes a partially entered (unambiguous) command
Ctrl-P or up arrow	Recalls commands in the history buffer, beginning with the most recent. Repeat the key sequence to recall successively older commands.
Ctrl-N or down arrow	Returns the most recent commands in the buffer after recalling older commands with Ctrl-P or the up arrow. Repeat the key sequence to recall successively more recent commands.

Command History

A command history is available to review previously entered commands. This buffer defaults to ten lines, but it can be configured to a maximum of 256 using the **terminal history size** command, as follows:

```
Switch# terminal history size number-of-lines        sets
   session command buffer size
Switch(config-line)# history size number-of-lines     sets the
   buffer size permanently
Switch# show history                                  shows
   command buffer
```

Console Error Messages

When you enter an incorrect command, you receive one of three messages detailed in Table 2-2.

Table 2-2 *Console Error Messages*

Error Message	Meaning	How to Get Help
% Ambiguous command: "show con"	Not enough characters were entered to define a specific command.	Reenter the command, followed by a question mark (?), with no space between the command and the question mark.
% Incomplete command.	Keywords or values are missing.	Reenter the command, followed by a question mark (?), with a space between the command and the question mark.
% Invalid input detected at '^' marker.	The command was entered incorrectly. The caret (^) marks the point of the error.	Enter a question mark (?) to display all the commands or parameters that are available in this mode.

Switch and Router Components

The major components of Cisco switches and routers are as follows:

- **RAM:** Random-access memory contains key software (IOS), the routing table, the fast switching cache, the running configuration, and so on.

- **ROM:** Read-only memory contains startup microcode used for troubleshooting.

- **NVRAM:** Nonvolatile RAM stores the startup configuration.

- **Interfaces:** The interface is the physical connection to the external devices. Physical connections can include Ethernet or Console.

- **Flash memory:** Flash contains the Cisco IOS Software image. Some routers run the IOS image directly from flash and do not need to transfer it to RAM.

ROM Functions

ROM contains the startup microcode and consists of the following three areas:

- **Bootstrap code:** Brings the router up during initialization. Reads the configuration register to determine how to boot.

- **POST:** Tests the basic function of the router hardware and determines the hardware present.

- **ROMMON:** A low-level operating system normally used for manufacturing, testing, troubleshooting, and password recovery.

How a Cisco Device Locates and Loads IOS Images

The bootstrap code locates and loads the Cisco IOS image. It does this by first looking at the configuration register. The default value for the configuration register is 0x2102. Changing the configuration register changes the location of the IOS load.

If the configuration register's fourth character is from 0x2 to 0xF, the bootstrap parses the startup config file in NVRAM for the **boot system** command that specifies the name and location of the Cisco IOS Software image to load.

After the IOS is loaded, the router must be configured. Configurations in NVRAM are executed. If one does not exist in NVRAM, the router initiates an auto-install or setup utility. The auto-install routine attempts to download a configuration file from a TFTP server.

The Configuration Register

The config register includes information that specifies where to locate the Cisco IOS Software image.

Before changing the configuration register, use the **show version** command to determine the current image. The last line contains the register value. Changing this value changes the location of the IOS load (and many other things). A **reload** command must be used for the new configuration to be set. The register value is checked only during the boot process.

Table 2-3 shows the configuration register values and meanings.

Table 2-3 *Configuration Register Values*

Configuration Register Boot Field Value	Meaning
0x0	Stays at the ROM monitor on reload or power cycle
0x1	Boots the first image in flash memory as a system image
0x2 to 0xF	Enables default booting from flash memory (0x2 is the default if router has flash)

The **show version** command verifies changes in the configuration register setting.

The **show flash** command displays contents in flash memory, including the image filenames and sizes.

The **show running-config** command shows the current running configuration in RAM and the IOS in use.

The **show startup-config** command shows the configuration file saved in NVRAM and the IOS in use. This is the configuration that will be loaded, if present when the router is rebooted.

Managing IOS Images

The Cisco IOS File System (IFS) feature provides an interface to the router file systems. The uniform resource locator (URL) convention allows you to specify files on network devices.

URL prefixes for Cisco network devices are as follows:

- **bootflash:** Boot flash memory
- **flash:** Available on all platforms
- **flh:** Flash load helper log files
- **ftp:** File Transfer Protocol (FTP) network server
- **nvram:** NVRAM
- **rcp:** Remote Copy Protocol (RCP) network server
- **slot0:** First PCMCIA flash memory card
- **slot1:** Second PCMCIA flash memory card
- **system:** Contains the system memory and the running configuration
- **tftp:** Trivial File Transfer Protocol (TFTP) network server

Backing Up and Upgrading IOS Images

When you copy to or from a TFTP server, you will need to specify the IP address or the host name of the remote host:

```
SwitchA# show flash
SwitchA# copy flash tftp
! backs up the IOS in flash to a TFTP server
SwitchA# copy tftp flash
! copies an IOS from a TFTP server to flash
```

Cisco IOS copy Command

As shown in Figure 2-2, the **copy** commands are used to duplicate files, duplicate configuration, or merge two configurations together from one component or device to another. The syntax is as follows:

```
copy source destination
```

For example:

```
copy running-config startup-config
```

Figure 2-2 *IOS copy Command*

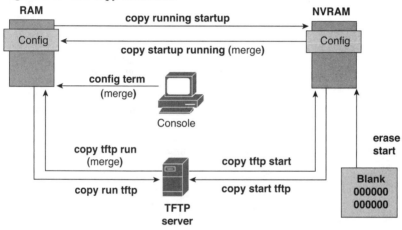

NOTE   When a configuration is copied into RAM, it merges with the existing configuration in RAM. It does not overwrite the existing configuration.

The **show running-config** and **show startup-config** commands are useful trouble-shooting aids. These commands allow you to view the current configuration in RAM or the startup configuration commands in NVRAM.

Starting a Switch

When a Catalyst switch is started for the first time, setup mode is loaded. Three main operations are performed during normal startup:

1. A power-on self-test (POST) checks the hardware.

2. A startup routine initiates the operating system.

3. Software configuration settings are loaded.

Initial startup procedure:

STEP 1.   Before you start the switch, verify the following:

- All network cable connections are secure.

- A terminal is connected to the console port.

- A terminal application is selected.

STEP 2.   Attach the switch to the power source to start the switch (there is no on/off switch).

STEP 3.   Observe the boot sequence.

LED Indicators

Figure 2-3 shows the LEDs on the front panel of the switch. These LEDs provide information on switch status during startup, normal operation, and fault conditions. The front of the switch has the following LEDs:

- **System LED:** Indicates whether the system is receiving power and functioning correctly.

- **Remote Power LED:** Indicates whether the remote power supply is in use.

- **Port Mode LEDs:** Indicate the current state of the Mode button. The modes are used to determine how the Port Status LEDs are interpreted.

- **Port Status LEDs:** Have different meanings depending on the current value of the Mode LED.

Pressing the Mode button toggles through the following LED display modes:

- Port status

- Port speed

- Full-duplex support

Figure 2-3   *Catalyst 2906S LEDs*

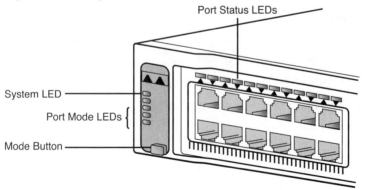

Table 2-4 details switch LED status on the Catalyst 2960x Series switches.

Table 2-4   *Catalyst 2960x Series LEDs*

LED	Status
System LED	Green: System powered and operational
	Amber: System malfunction; one or more POST errors
Redundant power supply (RPS)	Green: RPS operational
	Flashing green: RPS connected but is powering another device
	Amber: RPS installed but not operational
	Flashing amber: The internal power supply and RPS have power and are powering the switch
Port status (STAT)	Green: Link present
	Flashing green: Link present with traffic activity
	Alternating green and amber: Link fault
	Amber: Port not forwarding
Port speed	Off: Port is operating at 10 Mbps
	Green: Port is operating at 100 Mbps
	Blinking green: Port is operating at 1000 Mbps
Duplex (DUPLX)	Green: Ports are configured in full-duplex mode
	Off: Ports are half-duplex

External Configuration Sources

An IOS device can be configured from any of the following external sources:

- Console terminal
- Telnet
- TFTP
- Cisco Prime
- SSH

Console Connection

To establish a connection through a console port, you need a rollover cable to connect a console port to a PC. To set up the connection, follow these steps:

STEP 1.   Cable the device using a rollover cable. You might need an adapter for the PC.

STEP 2.   Configure the terminal emulation application with the following COM port settings: 9600 bps, 8 data bits, no parity, 1 stop bit, and no flow control.

Basic Switch Configuration from the Command Line

The following two configuration modes are available:

- **Global configuration:** Configures global parameters on a switch, such as host name and spanning-tree version
- **Interface configuration:** Configures parameters specific to a switch port

The IOS command to enter global configuration mode is **configure terminal**.

The IOS command to enter interface configuration mode is **interface** *interface-id*.

To enter interface mode, you first need to be in global configuration mode. The *interface-id* parameter identifies the type and number of the interface you want to configure, as follows:

```
switch(config)# interface g0
switch(config-if)#
```

The **interface range** command allows you to configure multiple interfaces at the same time. The following changes the mode to be able to configure gigabit interfaces g0/1–10:

```
switch(config)# interface range g0/ 1 - 10
switch(config-if-range)#
```

Configuring a Host Name

To give the switch a host name or identify it, use the **hostname** global IOS command, as follows:

```
switch(config)# hostname Admin-SW
Admin-SW(config)#
```

Configuring the Switch IP Address and Default Gateway

To assign an IP address on a Catalyst 2960x Series switch, follow these steps:

STEP 1. Enter the VLAN 1 interface. This is a logical interface used for management.

STEP 2. Assign the IP address and subnet masks.

STEP 3. Enable the interface by issuing the **no shutdown** command.

The following example shows the necessary command syntax for all three steps:

```
Admin-Sw(config)# interface vlan1
Admin-Sw(config-if)# ip address 192.168.0.10 255.255.255.0
Admin-Sw(config-if)# no shutdown
```

To configure the default gateway, use the **ip default-gateway** *ip-address* global con-figuration command, as follows:

```
Switch(config)# ip default-gateway 192.168.0.1
```

The default gateway is used to manage the switch from a remote network.

Verifying the Switch Initial Startup Status

To display the status of a switch, use one of the following commands:

- **show running-configuration** displays the currently active configuration in memo-ry, including any changes made in the session that have not yet been saved.

- **show startup-config** displays the last saved configuration.

- **show version** displays information about the system hardware and software.

- **show interfaces** displays interfaces—physical and SVIs.

Section 3
Understanding Ethernet and Switch Operations

Ethernet was developed in the 1970s by Digital Equipment Corporation (DEC), Intel, and Xerox. Later, the IEEE defined new standards for Ethernet called Ethernet 802.3. 802.3 is the standard that is in use today.

Ethernet

Ethernet is one of the most widely used LAN standards. As Figure 3-1 shows, Ethernet operates at Layers 1 and 2 of the OSI model.

Figure 3-1 *Physical and Data Link Layers*

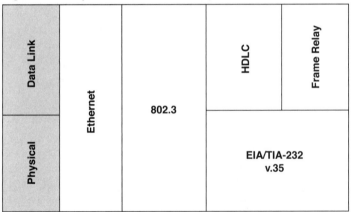

The physical layer (Layer 1) defines cabling, connection specifications, and topology.

The data link layer (Layer 2) has the following functions:

- Provides physical addressing

- Provides support for connection-oriented and connectionless services

- Provides frame sequencing and flow control

One sublayer performs data-link functions: the MAC sublayer. Figure 3-2 shows the Media Access Control (MAC) sublayer (802.3). The MAC sublayer is responsible for how data is sent over the wire. The MAC address is a 48-bit address expressed as 12 hex digits.

Figure 3-2 *MAC Sublayer*

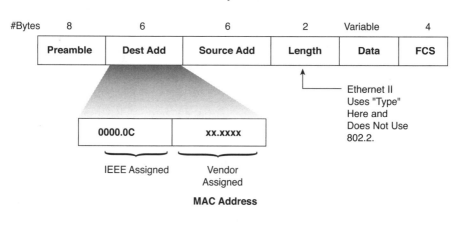

The MAC sublayer defines the following:

- Physical addressing
- Network topology
- Line discipline
- Error notification
- Orderly delivery of frames
- Optional flow control

Ethernet LAN Connection Media

The term *Ethernet* encompasses several LAN implementations. Physical layer implementations vary, and all support various cabling structures. The following four main categories of Ethernet exist:

- **Ethernet (DIX) and IEEE 802.3:** Operate at 10 Mbps over coaxial cable, unshielded twisted-pair (UTP) cable, or fiber. The standards are referred to as 10BASE2, 10BASE5, 10BASE-T, and 10BASE-F.
- **Fast Ethernet or 100-Mbps Ethernet:** Operates over UTP or fiber.
- **Gigabit Ethernet:** An 802.3 extension that operates over fiber and copper at 1000 Mbps, or 1 gigabit per second (Gbps).
- **10-Gigabit Ethernet:** Defined in 802.3ae, runs in full-duplex mode only, over fiber.

Network Media Types

Network media refers to the physical path that signals take across a network. The most common types of media are as follows:

- **Twisted-pair cable:** Used for telephony and most Ethernet networks. Each pair makes up a circuit that can transmit signals. The pairs are twisted to prevent interference (crosstalk). The two categories of twisted-pair cables are unshielded twisted-pair (UTP) and shielded twisted-pair (STP). UTP cable is usually connected to equipment with an RJ-45 connector. UTP (see Figure 3-3) has a small diameter that can be an advantage when space for cabling is at a minimum. It is prone to electrical noise and interference because of the lack of shielding. Examples of categories of UTP cable exist: CAT 1, CAT 2, CAT 3, CAT 4, CAT 5, CAT 5e, CAT 6, CAT 6a, CAT 7, and so on.

Figure 3-3   *UTP*

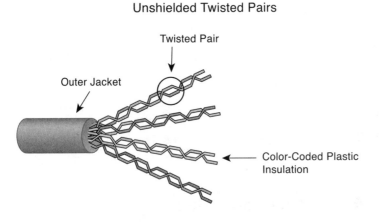

- **Fiber-optic cable:** Allows the transmission of light signals. This offers better support in bandwidth over other types of cables. The two types of fiber-optic cables are multimode and single-mode, defined as follows:

  - **Multimode:** With this type of fiber, several modes (or wavelengths) propagate down the fiber, each taking a slightly different path. Multimode fiber is used primarily in systems with transmission distances less than 2 km.

  - **Single-mode:** This type of fiber has only one mode in which light can propagate. Single-mode fiber is typically used for long-distance and high-bandwidth applications.

UTP Implementation

An RJ-45 connector is used with UTP cabling. Figure 3-4 shows an RJ-45 connector and its pin connections, following the T568B standards.

Figure 3-4 *RJ-45 Connector*

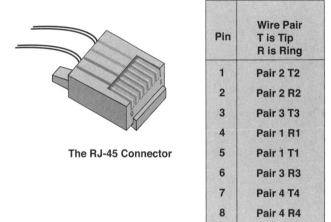

The RJ-45 Connector

Pin	Wire Pair T is Tip R is Ring
1	Pair 2 T2
2	Pair 2 R2
3	Pair 3 T3
4	Pair 1 R1
5	Pair 1 T1
6	Pair 3 R3
7	Pair 4 T4
8	Pair 4 R4

The two types of Ethernet cables are straight-through and crossover. Straight-through cables are typically used to connect different devices (data terminal equipment [DTE] to data communications equipment [DCE]), such as switch-to-router connections. Figure 3-5 shows the pins for a straight-through cable.

Figure 3-5 *Straight-Through Wiring*

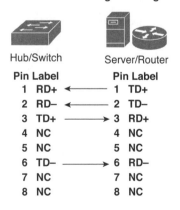

Cable 10 BASE TX
100BASE T Straight-Through

Hub/Switch   Server/Router

Pin Label		Pin Label
1 RD+	⟵	1 TD+
2 RD–	⟵	2 TD–
3 TD+	⟶	3 RD+
4 NC		4 NC
5 NC		5 NC
6 TD–	⟶	6 RD–
7 NC		7 NC
8 NC		8 NC

Crossover Ethernet cables are typically used to connect similar devices (DTE to DTE or DCE to DCE), such as switch-to-switch connections. Exceptions to this rule are switch-to-hub connections or router-to-PC connections, which use a crossover cable. Figure 3-6 shows the pins for a crossover cable.

Figure 3-6 *Crossover Wiring*

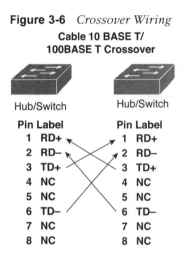

Cable 10 BASE T/
100BASE T Crossover

Hub/Switch   Hub/Switch

Pin Label		Pin Label
1 RD+		1 RD+
2 RD–		2 RD–
3 TD+		3 TD+
4 NC		4 NC
5 NC		5 NC
6 TD–		6 TD–
7 NC		7 NC
8 NC		8 NC

Role of CSMA/CD in Ethernet

All stations on an Ethernet segment are connected to the same media. Therefore, all devices receive all signals. When devices send signals at the same time, a collision occurs. A scheme is needed to detect and compensate for collisions. Ethernet uses a method called carrier sense multiple access collision detect (CSMA/CD) to detect and limit collisions.

In CSMA/CD, many stations can transmit on the Ethernet media, and no station has priority over any other. Before a station transmits, it listens to the network (carrier sense) to make sure that no other station is transmitting. If no other station is transmitting, the station transmits across the media. If a collision occurs, the transmitting stations detect the collision and run a backoff algorithm. The backoff algorithm computes a random time that each station waits before retransmitting.

Ethernet LAN Traffic

Three major types of network traffic exist on a LAN:

- **Unicasts:** The most common type of LAN traffic. A unicast frame is a frame intended for only one host.
- **Broadcasts:** Intended for all hosts. Stations view broadcast frames as public service announcements. All stations receive and process broadcast frames.
- **Multicasts:** Traffic in which one transmitter tries to reach only a subset, or group, of the entire segment.

Ethernet Addresses

The Ethernet address, or MAC address, is the Layer 2 address of the network adapter of the network device. Typically burned into the adapter, the MAC address is usually displayed in a hexadecimal format such as 00-0d-65-ac-50-7f.

As shown in Figure 3-7, the MAC address is 48 bits and consists of the following two components:

■ **Organizational Unique Identifier (OUI):** 24 bits. This is IEEE assigned and identifies the manufacturer of the card.

■ **Vendor-assigned:** 24 bits. Uniquely identifies the Ethernet hardware.

Figure 3-7   *MAC Addresses*

Switching Operation

Ethernet switches perform four major functions when processing packets: learning, forwarding, filtering, and flooding.

Switches perform these functions by the following methods:

■ **MAC address learning:** Switches learn the MAC addresses of all devices on the Layer 2 network. These addresses are stored in a MAC address table.

■ **Forwarding and filtering:** Switches determine which port a frame must be sent out to reach its destination. If the address is known, the frame is sent only on that port, filtering other ports from receiving the frame. If it's unknown, the frame is flooded to all ports except the one it originated from.

■ **Flooding:** Switches flood all unknown frames, broadcasts, and some multicasts to all ports on the switch except the one it originated from.

A switch uses its MAC address table when forwarding frames to devices. When a switch is first powered on, it has an empty MAC address table. With an empty MAC address table, the switch must learn the MAC addresses of attached devices. This learning process is outlined as follows using Figure 3-8:

   1. Initially, the switch MAC address table is empty.

Figure 3-8   *Frame Forwarding by a Switch*

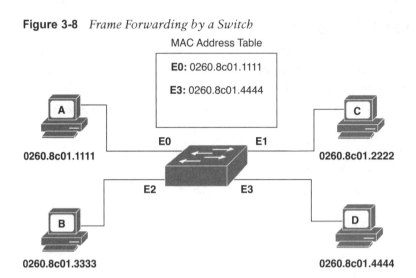

2. Station A with the MAC address 0260.8c01.1111 sends a frame to station C. When the switch receives this frame, it does the following:

   a.   Because the MAC table is empty, the switch must flood the frame to all other ports (except E0, the interface the frame was received).

   b.   The switch notes the source address of the originating device and associates it with port E0 in its MAC address table entry.

3. The switch continues to learn addresses in this manner, continually updating the table. As the MAC table becomes more complete, the switching becomes more efficient, because frames are forwarded to specific ports rather than being flooded out all ports.

Maximizing the Benefits of Switching

Microsegmentation

Microsegmentation is a network design (functionality) where each workstation or device on a network gets its own dedicated segment (collision domain) to the switch. Each network device gets the full bandwidth of the segment and does not have to share the segment with other devices. Microsegmentation reduces and can even eliminate collisions because each segment is its own collision domain.

Microsegmentation is implemented by installing LAN switches. Benefits of microsegmentation are as follows:

■ Collision-free domains from one larger collision domain

■ Efficient use of bandwidth by enabling full-duplex communication

■ Low latency and high frame-forwarding rates at each interface port

Duplex Communication

Duplexing is the mode of communication in which both ends can send and receive information. With full-duplex, bidirectional communication can occur at the same time. Half-duplex is also bidirectional communication, but signals can flow in only one direction at a time. Table 3-1 provides a comparative summary of full-duplex and half-duplex.

Table 3-1   *Full-Duplex and Half-Duplex*

Full-Duplex	Half-Duplex
Can send and receive data at the same time.	Can send and receive, but not simultaneously.
Collision-free.	The Ethernet segment is susceptible to collisions.
Point-to-point connection only.	Multipoint and point-to-point attachments.
Uses a dedicated switched port with separate circuits.	The medium is considered shared.
Efficiency is rated at 100 percent in both directions.	Efficiency is typically rated at 50 to 60 percent.
Both ends must be configured to run in full-duplex mode.	The duplex setting must match on devices sharing a segment.

Configuring and Verifying Port Duplex

The default port settings on a Catalyst 2960 switch are as follows:

- **Duplex:** auto
- **Speed:** auto

The default auto setting means that the switch will automatically try to negotiate the duplex and speed of connected interfaces.

To change the default settings, use the following commands:

```
Switch(config)# interface g0/1
Switch(config-if)# duplex {auto | full | half}
Switch(config-if)# speed {10 | 100 | 1000 | auto}
```

To view duplex and speed settings, use the **show interface** *interface-id* command, as follows:

```
Cat2960# show interface f0/1
FastEthernet0/1 is up, line protocol is up
  Hardware is Fast Ethernet, address is 0019.e81a.4801 (bia
    0019.e81a.4801)
  MTU 1500 bytes, BW 10000 Kbit, DLY 1000 usec,
     reliability 255/255, txload 1/255, rxload 1/255
  Encapsulation ARPA, loopback not set
  Keepalive set (10 sec)
  Auto-duplex, Auto-speed, media type is 10/100BaseTX
  input flow-control is off, output flow-control is unsupported
  ARP type: ARPA, ARP Timeout 04:00:00
```

Troubleshooting Common Switch Issues

When troubleshooting switch issues, remember the following:

- Switches operate at Layer 2 of the OSI model.
- Switches provide an interface to the physical media.
- Problems generally are seen at Layer 1 and Layer 2.
- Layer 3 issues could be regarding IP connectivity to the switch for management purposes.

Identifying and Resolving Media Issues

Common switch Layer 1 issues include the following:

- Bad wires or damaged wires.
- EMI is introduced.
- Malfunctioning equipment.

Bad wiring and EMI commonly show up as excessive collisions and noise. This is displayed by excessive collisions and runts when issuing the **show interface** command, as follows:

```
SwitchA# show interface g0/1
GigabitEthernet0/1 is up, line protocol is up (connected)
  Hardware is Gigabit Ethernet Port, address is 000d.65ac.5040
    (bia 000d.65ac.5040)
  MTU 1500 bytes, BW 1000000 Kbit, DLY 10 usec,
     reliability 255/255, txload 1/255, rxload 1/255
<Text-Ommited>
  5 minute output rate 10000 bits/sec, 7 packets/sec
```

```
1476671 packets input, 363178961 bytes, 0 no buffer
Received 20320 broadcasts (12683 multicast)
542 runts, 0 giants, 0 throttles
3 input errors, 3 CRC, 0 frame, 0 overrun, 0 ignored
0 input packets with dribble condition detected
1680749 packets output, 880704302 bytes, 0 underruns
8 output errors, 1874 collisions, 15 interface resets
0 babbles, 0 late collision, 0 deferred
0 lost carrier, 0 no carrier
0 output buffer failures, 0 output buffers swapped out
```

Identifying and Resolving Access Port Issues

Common port access issues are as follows:

- Media-related issues
- Duplex mismatch
- Speed mismatch

Media-Related Issues

Media-related issues might be reported as an access issue; for example, a user might say that she cannot access the network. Media issues should be isolated and identified as indicated in the previous topic.

Duplex Issues

The following items can create duplex issues:

- One end set to full-duplex and the other set to half-duplex results in a duplex mismatch.
- One end set to full-duplex and auto-negotiation on the other:
  - Auto-negotiation can fail, and the end reverts to half-duplex.
  - Results in a duplex mismatch.
- One end set to half-duplex and auto-negotiation on the other:
  - Auto-negotiation can fail, and the end reverts to half-duplex.
  - Both ends set to half-duplex causes no mismatch.

Speed Issues

The following items can create speed issues:

- One end set to one speed and the other set to another results in a mismatch.
- One end set to a higher speed and auto-negotiation on the other:
  - Auto-negotiation will fail, and the end will revert to a lower speed.
  - Results in a mismatch.

Section 4
Understanding TCP/IP

The TCP/IP suite of protocols is used to communicate across any set of interconnected networks. The protocols initially developed by DARPA are well suited for communication across both LANs and WANs.

Understanding the TCP/IP Internet Layer

The Internet Protocol (IP) is a connectionless protocol that provides best-effort delivery routing of packets.

IP has the following characteristics:

■ Operates at Layer 3 of the OSI (network) and Layer 2 of the TCP/IP (Internet) model

■ Is connectionless

■ Uses hierarchical addressing

■ Provides best-effort delivery of packets

■ Has no built-in data recovery

Figure 4-1 shows the IP header information.

Figure 4-1   *IP Header*

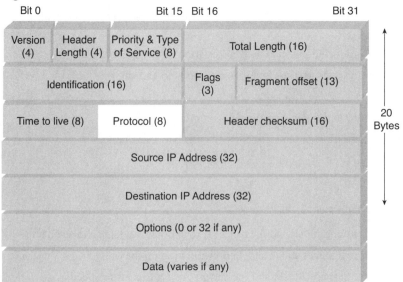

IP Addressing

In a TCP/IP environment, each node must have a unique 32-bit logical IP address. Each IP datagram includes the source and destination IP address in the header.

As shown in Figure 4-2, IP addresses consist of two parts: the network address portion (network ID) and the host address portion (host ID). A two-part addressing scheme allows the IP address to identify both the network and the host:

■ All the endpoints within a network share a common network number.

■ The remaining bits identify each host within that network.

Figure 4-2 *Two-Part IP Addresses*

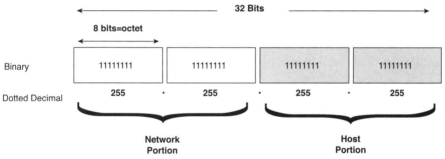

IP Address Classes

Five classes of IP addresses exist: Classes A through E. Classes A, B, and C are the most common. Class A has 8 network bits and 24 host bits. Class B has 16 network bits and 16 host bits. Class C addresses allow many more networks, each with fewer hosts (24 network bits and 8 host bits). Class D addresses are used for multicast purposes, and Class E addresses are used for research. Figure 4-3 shows the address range for Classes A–D.

Figure 4-3 *Class A Through D IP Addresses*

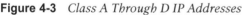

Reserved IP Addresses

Some IP addresses in TCP/IP are reserved for specific purposes. These addresses cannot be assigned to individual devices on a network. The reserved addresses are as follows:

- **Network address:** An IP address that has all binary 0s in the host bit portion of the address. For example, 172.16.0.0/16.

- **Directed broadcast address:** An IP address that has all binary 1s in the host bit portion of the address. Used to send data to all devices on the network. For example, 172.16.255.255/16.

- **Local broadcast address:** An address used if a device wants to communicate with all devices on the local network. The address is 255.255.255.255.

- **Loopback address:** Used by the TCP/IP stack to test TCP/IP by sending a message internally to itself. A typical address is 127.0.0.1.

- **All-zeros address:** Address 0.0.0.0 indicates the host in "this" network and is used only as a source address.

Private IP Addresses

RFC 1918 defines IP addresses that are reserved for use in private networks. The IP addresses are not routed on the Internet. Three blocks of IP addresses are reserved for private networks:

- 10.0.0.0 to 10.255.255.255
- 172.16.0.0 to 172.31.255.255
- 192.168.0.0 to 192.168.255.255

Networks using private addresses can still connect to the Internet if they use Network Address Translation (NAT).

Domain Name System

DNS converts domain names into IP addresses. Without DNS, users would have to remember IP addresses for websites. DNS functions in a client server model. A DNS server hosts the domain name–to–IP address mappings. A DNS client performs a DNS lookup by contacting a DNS server. Figure 4-4 demonstrates the DNS process:

1. The client requests the IP address of ciscopress.com from its DNS server.
2. The DNS server does not have the IP address of ciscopress.com in its database and forwards the request to another DNS server (can be a forwarding or root DNS server).
3. The secondary server responds with the IP address of ciscopress.com to the first DNS server.
4. The clients DNS server responds to the client with the IP address of ciscopress.com.
5. The client connects to IP address 172.16.0.32.

Figure 4-4 *DNS Process*

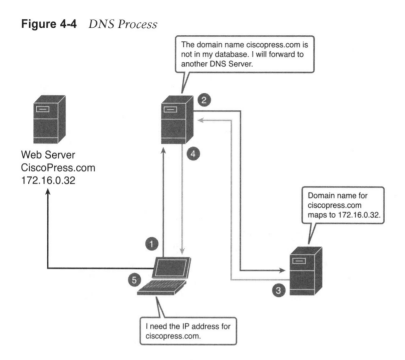

Verifying the IPv4 Address of a Host

The IPv4 address of a host is verified as follows:

- **Windows OS:** ipconfig is a command-line tool in Windows operating systems that finds the TCP/IP parameters assigned to a host.

- **UNIX/Linux:** ifconfig determines the TCP/IP information of a host.

Understanding Binary Basics

Computers use a numbering system based on only 1s and 0s. This type of system is called binary or base 2. This numbering system might seem awkward at first glance, but it uses the same logic as the base 10 system we use every day. As with base 10, binary counting starts with the "ones" column until all the numbers are exhausted, and then it rolls over to the next column, which is a power of the base. For example, base 10 has ten numbers (0 through 9). When counting, you start in the "ones" column and count until you reach the highest unit. Then you move to the "tens" column. This continues with successive powers (10^0, 10^1, 10^2, 10^3). The binary system's columns or placeholders are 2^0, 2^1, 2^2, 2^3, and so on. Table 4-1 shows the values for the first eight places.

Table 4-1 *Binary Basics*

Base 2 Numbering System								
Number of symbols	2							
Symbols	0, 1							
Base exponent	2^7	2^6	2^5	2^4	2^3	2^2	2^1	2^0
Place value	128	64	32	16	8	4	2	1
Example: Convert 47 to binary	0	0	1	0	1	1	1	1

Binary numbers are used extensively in networking. They are the basis of IP addressing. To convert between decimal and binary, it is best to build a simple table like the one just shown. To convert from binary to decimal, simply add up the "place values" of the digits that are 1s. In the preceding example, the placeholders for 1, 2, 4, 8, and 32 all contain 1s. Adding those values yields 47. (00101111 in binary is 47 in decimal.) To convert from decimal to binary, again build a table. Put a 1 in the highest one (1) value. (In this example, a 1 is placed in the column representing 32; 64 cannot be used, because it is greater than 47.) Now subtract the place value from the decimal number (47 – 32 = 15). The next value (16) is too large, so a 0 is placed in that column. A 1 is then placed in the 8 column, and the subtraction is performed again (15 – 8 = 7). Repeat the process until the value of the subtraction equals 0.

Subnets

Without subnets, an organization operates as a single network. These flat topologies result in short routing tables, but as the network grows, the use of bandwidth becomes very inefficient (all systems on the network receive all the broadcasts on the network). Figure 4-5 shows a flat network with all hosts in the same broadcast domain.

Figure 4-5 *Flat Network Address*

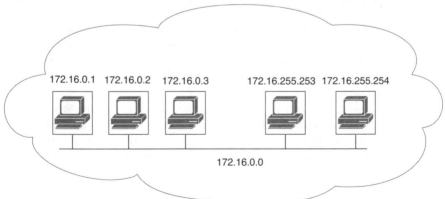

Network addressing can be made more efficient by breaking the addresses into smaller segments, or subnets. Subnetting provides additional structure to an addressing scheme without altering the addresses.

In Figure 4-6, the network address 172.16.0.0 is subdivided into four subnets: 172.16.1.0, 172.16.2.0, 172.16.3.0, and 172.16.4.0. If traffic were evenly distributed to each end station, the use of subnetting would reduce the overall traffic seen by each end station by 75 percent.

Figure 4-6   *Subnetted Address Scheme*

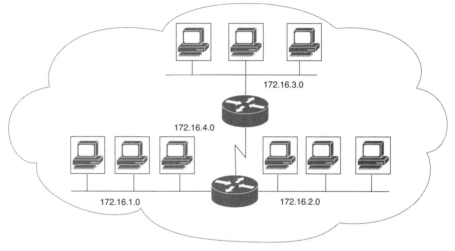

Subnet Mask

As shown in Figure 4-7, a subnet mask is a 32-bit value written as four octets. In the subnet mask, each bit is used to determine how the corresponding bit in the IP address should be interpreted (network, subnet, or host). The subnet mask bits are coded as follows:

- Binary 1 for the network bits
- Binary 1 for the subnet bits
- Binary 0 for the host bits

Figure 4-7 *IP Address and Subnet Mask*

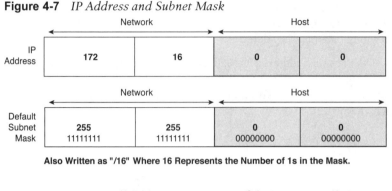

Also Written as "/16" Where 16 Represents the Number of 1s in the Mask.

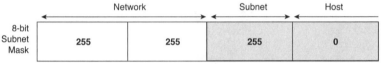

Also Written as "/24" Where 24 Represents the Number of 1s in the Mask.

Although dotted-decimal (bit count) is most common, the subnet can be represented in several ways:

- **Bit count:** 172.16.0.0 255.255.0.0

- **Decimal:** 172.16.0.0/16

- **Hexadecimal:** 172.16.0.0 0xFFFF0000

The **term ip netmask-format** command can specify the display format of network masks for the router. Dotted-decimal is the default.

Default Subnet Mask

Each address class has a default subnet mask. The default subnet masks only the network portion of the address, the effect of which is no subnetting. With each bit of subnetting beyond the default, you can create 2^n subnets. Figure 4-8 and Table 4-2 show the effect of increasing the number of subnet bits.

Figure 4-8   *Default Subnet Masks*

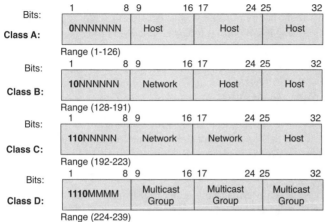

Table 4-2   *Subnetting*

Address	Subnet Address	Number of Subnets	Comments
10.5.22.5/8	255.0.0.0	0	This is the default Class A subnet address. The mask includes only the network portion of the address and provides no additional subnets.
10.5.22.5/16	255.255.0.0	254	This Class A subnet address has a 16-bit subnet mask, but only the bits in the second octet (those beyond the default) contribute to the subnetting.
155.13.22.11/16	255.255.0.0	0	In this case, 16 bits are used for the subnet mask, but because the default for a Class B address is 16 bits, no additional subnets are created.
155.13.10.11/26	255.255.255.192	1024	This case has a total of 26 bits for the subnet mask, but the Class B address can use only 10 of them to create subnets. The result creates 1024 subnets.

Default Gateway

By default, hosts are only able to communicate with other hosts directly on their local network when a default gateway is not configured. If a host wants to communicate with a host on a different network, the sending host must send the data to a default gateway. A default gateway is needed to send a packet out of the local network.

How Routers Use Subnet Masks

To determine the subnet of the address, a router performs a logical AND operation with the IP address and subnet mask. Recall that the host portion of the subnet mask is all 0s. The result of this operation is that the host portion of the address is removed, and the router bases its decision only on the network portion of the address.

In Figure 4-9, the host bits are removed, and the network portion of the address is revealed. In this case, a 10-bit subnet address is used, and the network (subnet) number 172.16.2.128 is extracted.

Figure 4-9   *Identifying Network Portion of Address*

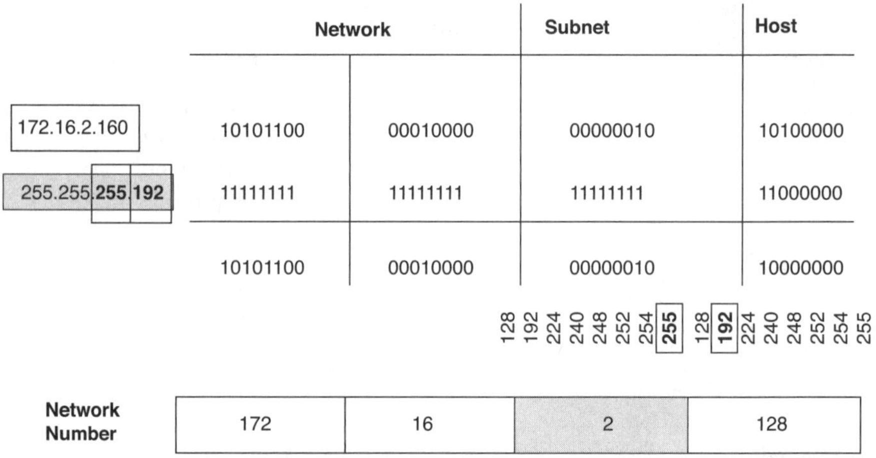

Identifying Subnet Addresses

Given an IP address and subnet mask, you can identify the subnet address, broadcast address, first usable address, and last usable address using the following method, which is displayed in Figure 4-10:

STEP 1.   Write the 32-bit address, and write the subnet mask below that.

STEP 2.   Draw a vertical line just after the last 1 bit in the subnet mask.

STEP 3.   Copy the portion of the IP address to the left of the line. Place all 0s for the remaining free spaces to the right. This is the subnet number.

STEP 4.   Copy the portion of the IP address to the left of the line. Place all 1s for the remaining free spaces to the right. This is the broadcast address.

STEP 5.   Copy the portion of the IP address to the left of the line. Place all 0s in the remaining free spaces until you reach the last free space. Place a 1 in that free space. This is your first usable address.

STEP 6.   Copy the portion of the IP address to the left of the line. Place all 1s in the remaining free spaces until you reach the last free space. Place a 0 in that free space. This is your last usable address.

Figure 4-10   *Identifying Subnet Addresses*

	174	24	4	176	
174.24.4.176	10101110	00011000	00000100	10110000	Host
255.255.255.192	11111111	11111111	11111111	11000000	Mask
174.24.4.128	10101110	00011000	00000100	10000000	Subnet
174.24.4.191	10101110	00011000	00000100	10111111	Broadcast
174.24.4.129	10101110	00011000	00000100	10000001	First
174.24.4.190	10101110	00011000	00000100	10111110	Last

Broadcast Addresses

Broadcast messages are sent to every host on the network. Two kinds of broadcasts exist:

- Directed broadcasts can broadcast to all hosts within a subnet and to all subnets within a network. (170.34.2.255 sends a broadcast to all hosts in the 170.34.2.0 subnet.)
- The local broadcasts (255.255.255.255) are flooded within a subnet.

How to Implement Subnet Planning

Subnetting decisions should typically be based on growth estimates rather than current needs.

To plan a subnet, follow these steps:

STEP 1.   Determine the number of subnets and hosts per subnet required.

STEP 2.   The address class you are assigned, and the number of subnets required, determine the number of subnetting bits used. For example, with a Class C address and a need for 20 subnets, you have a 29-bit mask (255.255.255.248). This allows the Class C default 24-bit mask and 5 bits required for 20 subnets. (The formula 2^n yields only 16 subnets for 4 bits, so 5 bits must be used.)

STEP 3.   The remaining bits in the last octet are used for the host field. In this case, each subnet has $2^3 - 2$, or 6, hosts.

STEP 4.   The final host addresses are a combination of the network/subnet plus each host value. In Figure 4-11, the hosts on the 192.168.5.32 subnet would be addressed as 192.168.5.33, 192.168.5.34, 192.168.5.35, and so forth.

Figure 4-11   *Subnetting a Network*

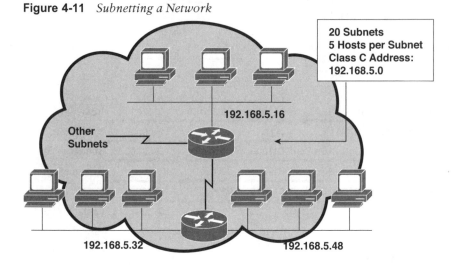

20 Subnets
5 Hosts per Subnet
Class C Address:
192.168.5.0

192.168.5.16

Other Subnets

192.168.5.32

192.168.5.48

Variable-Length Subnet Mask (VLSM)

VLSMs were developed to allow multiple levels of subnetting in an IP network. VLSM occurs when an internetwork uses more than one mask for different subnets of a single Class A, B, or C network.

The primary benefit of VLSMs is more efficient use of IP addresses.

Figure 4-12 shows an example of VLSM used in Class A network 10.0.0.0 with mask /24 and /30.

Figure 4-12   *VLSM in Network 10.0.0.0*

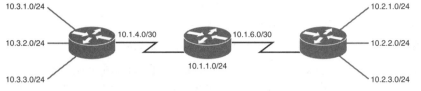

10.3.1.0/24

10.3.2.0/24   10.1.4.0/30   10.1.6.0/30

10.1.1.0/24

10.3.3.0/24

10.2.1.0/24

10.2.2.0/24

10.2.3.0/24

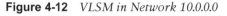

In the figure, /30 prefixes are being used on point-to-point links and /24 prefixes for LAN subnets.

Understanding the TCP/IP Transport Layer

The TCP/IP model transport layer is responsible for the following:

- Session multiplexing
- Segmentation
- Flow control
- Connection-oriented or connectionless transport
- Reliable or unreliable data transport

Two protocols function at the transport layer: UDP and TCP. UDP is a connectionless, best-effort delivery protocol. TCP is a connection-oriented, reliable protocol.

UDP

UDP is a connectionless, best-effort protocol used for applications that provide their own error-recovery process. It trades reliability for speed. UDP is simple and efficient but unreliable. UDP does not check for segment delivery. Figure 4-13 shows the UDP header.

Figure 4-13   *UDP Header*

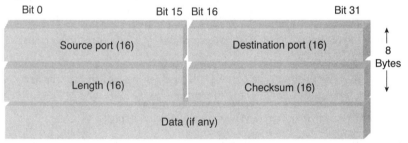

TCP

TCP is a connection-oriented, reliable protocol that is responsible for breaking messages into segments and reassembling them at the destination (resending anything not received). TCP also provides virtual circuits between applications. Figure 4-14 shows the TCP header.

Figure 4-14   *TCP Header*

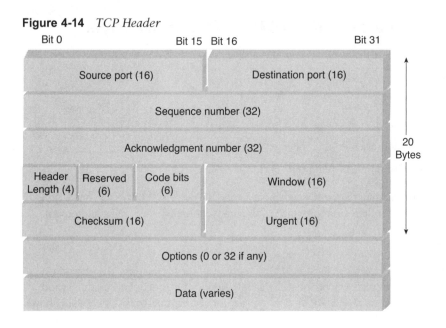

TCP/IP Applications

Some of the most common TCP/IP applications are as follows:

- **File Transfer Protocol (FTP):** A TCP-based protocol that supports bidirectional binary and ASCII file transfers

- **Trivial File Transfer Protocol (TFTP):** A UDP-based protocol that can transfer configuration files and Cisco IOS Software images between systems

- **Simple Mail Transfer Protocol (SMTP):** An email delivery protocol

- **Terminal Emulation (Telnet):** Allows remote command-line access to another computer

- **Simple Network Management Protocol (SNMP):** Provides the means to monitor and control network devices

- **Dynamic Host Configuration Protocol (DHCP):** Assigns IP addresses and other TCP/IP parameters such as subnet mask, DNS/WINS server addresses, and default gateways automatically to hosts

- **Domain Name System (DNS):** Translates domain names into IP addresses

NOTE   Other examples include HTTP, HTTPS, and SSH.

Port Numbers

Both TCP and UDP can send data from multiple upper-layer applications at the same time. Port (or socket) numbers keep track of different conversations crossing the network at any given time. Well-known port numbers are controlled by the Internet Assigned Numbers Authority (IANA). Applications that do not use well-known port numbers have them randomly assigned from a specific range. Figure 4-15 shows the TCP/UDP port numbers from common applications.

Figure 4-15 *Port Numbers*

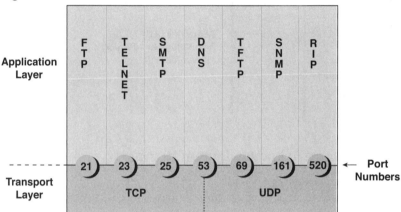

Port number ranges are as follows:

- Numbers 1 through 1023 are considered well-known ports.

- Numbers 1024 through 49151 are registered.

- Numbers 49152 through 65535 are private vendor assigned and are dynamic.

Establishing a TCP Connection

Each TCP segment contains the source and destination port number to identify the sending and receiving application. These two values, along with the source and destination IP addresses in the IP header, uniquely identify each connection.

Three-Way Handshake

The synchronization requires each side to send its own initial sequence number and to receive a confirmation of it in acknowledgment (ACK) from the other side. Figure 4-16 outlines the steps in the TCP three-way handshake, which are further defined in the following list:

STEP 1.   Host A sends a SYN segment with sequence number 100.

STEP 2.   Host B sends an ACK and confirms that the SYN it received. Host B also sends a SYN. Note that the ACK field in host B is now expecting to hear sequence 101.

STEP 3.   In the next segment, host A sends data. Note that the sequence number in this step is the same as the ACK in Step 2.

Figure 4-16   *TCP Three-Way Handshake*

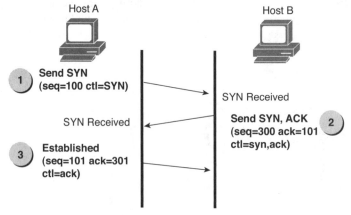

TCP Sequence and Acknowledgment Numbers

In TCP, each segment is numbered so that at the receiving end, TCP reassembles the segments into a complete message. If a segment is not acknowledged within a given period, it is resent.

TCP Flow Control

Flow control provides a mechanism for the receiver to control the transmission speed.

TCP implements flow control by using the SYN and ACK fields in the TCP header, along with the Window field. The Window field is a number that indicates the maximum number of unacknowledged bytes allowed to be outstanding at any time.

TCP Windowing

Windowing ensures that one side of a connection is not overwhelmed with data it cannot process. The window size from one end station tells the other side of the connection how much it can accept at one time. With a window size of 1, each segment must be acknowledged before another segment is sent. This is the least-efficient use of bandwidth. Figure 4-17 shows the windowing process as outlined here:

STEP 1.   The sender sends 3 bytes before expecting an ACK.

STEP 2.   The receiver can handle a window size of only 2, so it drops byte 3 and then specifies 3 as the acknowledgment. This indicates that the receiver is ready to receive that sequence (3 will need to be retransmitted), and also specifies an acceptable receiving window size of 2.

STEP 3.   The sender sends the next 2 bytes and specifies its own acceptable window size of 3.

STEP 4. The receiver replies by requesting byte 5 and specifying again an acceptable window size of 2.

Figure 4-17 *TCP Windowing Example*

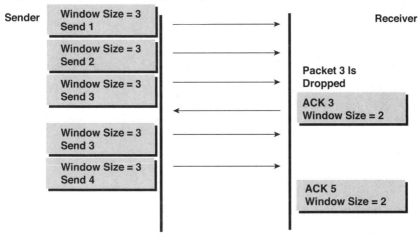

A TCP/IP session can have different window sizes for each node.

Section 5

Routing

Exploring the Functions of Routing

Routing is the act of finding a path to a destination and moving data across this path from source to destination. The routing process uses network routing tables, protocols, and algorithms to determine the most efficient path for forwarding the IP packet.

Role of a Router

Routers are required to reach hosts that are not in the local LAN.

Router Characteristics

The major router components are as follows:

- **CPU:** Processor chip installed on the motherboard that carries out the instructions of a computer program.

- **Motherboard:** Central circuit board that connects all peripherals and interfaces.

- **RAM:** Random-access memory contains key software (IOS).

- **ROM:** Read-only memory contains startup microcode.

- **NVRAM:** Nonvolatile RAM stores the configuration.

- **Configuration register:** Controls the bootup method.

- **Interfaces:** The interface is the physical connection to the external devices.

- **Flash memory:** Flash contains the Cisco IOS Software image.

Router Function

Routers have the following two key functions:

- **Path determination:** The process of routing includes determining the sources of routing information, identifying the optimum path through the network, and maintaining and verifying routing information. Routers do this by using a routing protocol to communicate the network information from the router's own routing table with neighboring router's.

- **Packet forwarding:** After the path is determined, a router forwards the packets through its network interface toward the destination.

Routers support three packet-forwarding mechanisms:

- **Process switching:** Every packet requires a full lookup in the routing table. Very slow.

- **Fast switching:** Uses the cache to increase the switching process. The first packet is process switched. An entry in the cache is created, and each additional packet is switched in the cache.

- **Cisco Express Forwarding:** The default mode on Cisco routers. Cisco Express Forwarding (CEF) is the preferred Cisco IOS packet-forwarding mechanism. CEF consists of two key components: the Forwarding Information Base (FIB) and adjacencies. The FIB is similar to the routing table created by the router but maintains only the next-hop address for a particular route. The adjacency table maintains Layer 2 information linked to a particular FIB entry, avoiding the need to do an ARP request for each table lookup.

Key Information a Router Needs

In Figure 5-1, for hosts in network 10.120.2.0 to communicate with hosts in network 172.16.1.0, a router needs the following key information:

- **Destination address:** The destination (typically an IP address) of the information being sent.

- **Sources of information:** Where the information came from (typically an IP address of the router sending the route). Can also be a routing protocol or directly connected route.

- **Possible routes:** The likely routes to get from source to destination.

- **Best route:** The best path selected by the router to reach the intended destination.

- **Status of routes:** The known paths to the destination.

Figure 5-1   *Routing Tables*

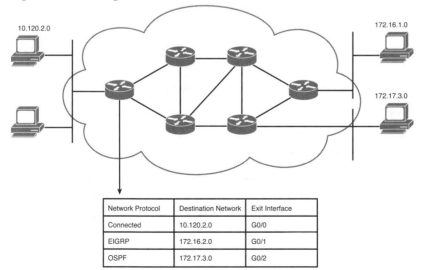

Network Protocol	Destination Network	Exit Interface
Connected	10.120.2.0	G0/0
EIGRP	172.16.2.0	G0/1
OSPF	172.17.3.0	G0/2

Routing Versus Routed

Network layer protocols are either routed protocols or routing protocols. These are defined as follows:

- A routed protocol
    - Is any network layer protocol that provides enough information within its address to allow the packet to direct user traffic.
    - Defines the address format and use of fields within the packet.
    - Routed protocols include IPv4, IPv6, AppleTalk, and others.
- Routing protocols determine how routed protocols are used by
    - Providing mechanisms finding routes in an internetwork and maintaining route awareness.
    - Allowing routers to update each other about network changes.
    - Routing Information Protocol v2 (RIPv2), Enhanced IGRP (EIGRP), Open Shortest Path First (OSPF), and Border Gateway Protocol (BGP) are examples of routing protocols.

Path Determination

Routing tables and network addresses transmit packets through the network. The process of routing includes determining the optimum path through the network and then moving the packets along the path.

Routing Table

A router is connected, is configured, or learns about routes in the network and stores this information in its routing table. The router uses its table to make forwarding decisions.

A router can use the following types of entries in the routing table to select the best path:

- **Directly connected:** Networks that the router has a directly connected interface to
- **Static routes:** Manually entered routes in the routing table
- **Dynamic routes:** Routes dynamically learned from a routing protocol
- **Default routes:** A static or dynamic route that tells the router where to route packets not explicitly in the router's routing table

Information stored in a routing table includes destination network/subnetwork, forwarding interfaces, and routing sources. You may also see Administrative Distance, routing metrics, next-hop IP addresses, and timer information.

Dynamic Routing Protocols

Routing protocols use their own rules and metrics to build and update routing tables automatically. Routing metrics are values used by routing protocols to determine whether one particular route should be chosen over another. Different protocols use different metrics. Some common metrics are as follows:

- **Bandwidth:** The link's data capacity.

- **Delay:** The time required to move the packet from the current router to the destination. This depends on the bandwidth of intermediate links, port delays at each router, congestion, and distance.

- **Load:** The amount of activity on the network.

- **Reliability:** The error rate of each network link.

- **Hop count:** The number of routers the packet must travel through before reaching the destination.

- **Cost:** An arbitrary value based on bandwidth and other metrics assigned by the administrator.

Configuring a Cisco Router

Initial Router Startup

When a router is booted up, it goes through the following sequence:

1. The router checks its hardware with a power-on self-test (POST). Diagnostics are performed to verify the basic operation of CPU, memory, and interface circuitry.

2. The router loads a bootstrap code.

3. The Cisco IOS Software is located and loaded using the information in the bootstrap code.

4. The configuration is located and loaded.

After this sequence completes, the router is ready for normal operation.

When the router is started for the first time, it does not have an initial configuration. The IOS will execute a question-derived initial configuration routine called setup mode. You can enter setup mode at any time by entering the **setup** privileged EXEC command. Setup mode configures the following:

- Initial global parameters, such as host name, enable secret password, and VTY passwords

- Interfaces

When the setup mode configuration process is completed, the **setup** command gives you the following options:

- **[0]:** Go to the IOS command prompt without saving this config.
- **[1]:** Go back to the setup without saving this config.
- **[2]:** Save this configuration to NVRAM and exit.

Default answers appear in square brackets ([ ]). Pressing Enter accepts the defaults. At the first setup prompt, you can enter **No** to discontinue the setup. The setup process can be aborted at any time by pressing Ctrl-C.

Router Configuration

From privileged EXEC mode, the **configure terminal** command provides access to global configuration mode. From global configuration mode, you can access some of these configuration modes:

- **Interface:** Configures operations on a per-interface basis
- **Subinterface:** Configures multiple virtual interfaces
- **Line:** Configures the operation of a terminal line
- **Router:** Configures IP routing protocols

Assigning a Router Name Example

The **hostname** command, as follows, names a router (or a switch):

```
Router> enable
Router# configure terminal
Router(config)# hostname Dallas
Dallas(config)#
```

Configuring Router Interfaces

The following commands configure a router interface with an IP address and a description:

```
Router# configure terminal
Router(config)# interface g0/0
Router(config-if)#ip address 192.168.1.1 255.255.255.0
Router(config-if)#no shutdown
Router(config-if)#description Internet Link
```

Verifying Interface Configuration

Some of the things you can see from the **show interface** command are as follows:

- Whether the interface is administratively down

- Whether the line protocol is up or down

- An Internet address (if one is configured)

- Maximum transmission unit (MTU) and bandwidth

- Traffic statistics on the interface

- Interface encapsulation type

One of the most important elements of the **show interface** command is the display of the interface and line protocol status.

Table 5-1 displays the interface and line protocol status of router interfaces and describes the interface status.

Table 5-1   *Interface and Line Protocol Status*

Meaning	Status
Operational	`FastEthernet0/0 is up, line protocol is up`
Connection problem (Layer 2)	`FastEthernet0/0 is up, line protocol is down`
Interface problem (Layer 1)	`FastEthernet0/0 is down, line protocol is down`
Disabled	`FastEthernet0/0 is administratively down, line protocol is down`

Exploring Connected Devices

Cisco Discovery Protocol

Cisco Discovery Protocol (CDP) is a proprietary tool that provides protocol and address information on directly connected devices. CDP runs over the data link layer, allowing devices running different network layer protocols to learn about each other. CDP summary information includes device identifiers, the Layer 3 address of the directly connected interface, port identifiers, and platform. See Figure 5-2.

Figure 5-2   *CDP*

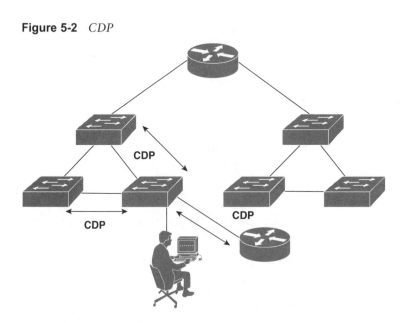

CDP runs over all LANs, Frame Relay (disabled by default), ATM, and other WANs employing Subnetwork Access Protocol (SNAP) encapsulation. CDP starts by default on bootup and sends updates every 60 seconds.

Implementation of CDP

The following commands are relevant to implementing CDP:

- **cdp enable** enables CDP on an interface.
- **no cdp enable** disables CDP on an interface.
- **cdp run** allows other CDP devices to get information about your device.
- **no cdp run** disables CDP on a device.
- **show cdp** displays the CDP output.
- **show cdp neighbors** displays the CDP updates received on the local interfaces and information about CDP neighbors. For each CDP neighbor, the following is displayed:
  - Neighbor device ID
  - Local interface
  - Holdtime value in seconds
  - Neighbor device capability code (router, switch)
  - Neighbor hardware platform
  - Neighbor remote port ID

- **show cdp neighbors detail** displays updates received on the local interfaces. This command displays the same information as the **show cdp entry *** command. The **show cdp neighbors detail** command shows the same information as **sh cdp neighbors,** in addition to the network layer address of the CDP neighbor.

- **show cdp entry** displays the following information about neighboring devices:

  - Neighbor device ID

  - Layer 3 address of directly connected interface

  - Device platform

  - Device capabilities

  - Local interface type and outgoing remote port ID

  - Holdtime value in seconds

  - Cisco IOS Software type and release

- **show cdp traffic** displays information about interface traffic.

- **show cdp interface** displays interface status and configuration information.

Exploring the Packet Delivery Process

For hosts on an IP network to communicate with each other, they need a Layer 2 address (MAC address) and an IP address.

IP-enabled hosts use ARP to map the MAC address to the IP address when communicating with hosts on a local segment. Each host maintains an ARP table that contains the IP-to-MAC address mappings (see Figure 5-3).

Figure 5-3   *Host-to-Host Packet Delivery*

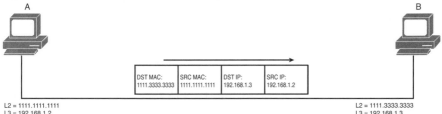

When an IP host wants to communicate with a host on a remote network, the local host will send an ARP request to find the MAC address of the host's default gateway. Because the remote host is on a remote network, the router will respond with its local MAC address and the IP address of the remote host. In Figure 5-4, host A wants to communicate with host B. Host A sends a packet with the destination MAC address of the router's Ethernet interface and the IP address of host B. The source MAC address and IP will be that of host A. When the router receives the packet, the router will take the packet, strip off the MAC address information, and rewrite the

MAC address with the source MAC address of the router's exiting Ethernet interface
and the destination MAC address of host B. The IP information does not change.

Figure 5-4   *Host-to-Host Packet Delivery Through a Router*

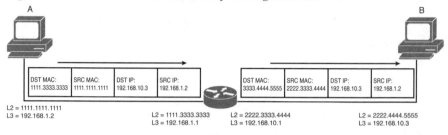

Enabling Static Routing

There are two ways to tell the router where to forward packets to the networks that
are not directly connected:

- Static routes
- **Dynamic** routes

Static routes are used in small networks with limited destinations, in hub-and-spoke
networks, and for troubleshooting.

Dynamic routes are used for larger networks or when the network is expected to grow.

Static Route Configuration

To configure a static route on a Cisco router, enter the following global command:

```
ip route destination-network mask {next-hop-address | outbound-
   interface} [distance] [permanent]
```

Here's an example:

```
RouterB(config)# ip route 172.17.0.0 255.255.0.0 172.16.0.1
```

This example instructs the router to route to 172.16.0.1 any packets that have a destination of 172.17.0.0 to 172.17.255.255.

The *distance* parameter defines the administrative distance or the route. The value
for *distance* is a number from 1 to 255 (1 is the default if not defined) that changes
the administrative distance of the route. Using this option could allow a dynamic
routing protocol to be preferred over a static route. For example, if you are running
EIGRP on a router and configure a static route with a distance of 110, the EIGRP
route will be preferred over the static route.

The **permanent** statement specifies that the route will not be removed even if the router interface shuts down.

Default Route

A default route is a special type of route with an all-0s network and network mask. The default route directs any packets for which a next hop is not specifically listed in the routing table. By default, if a router receives a packet to a destination network that is not in its routing table, it drops the packet. When a default route is specified, the router does not drop the packet. Instead, it forwards the packet to the IP address specified in the default route.

To configure a static default route on a Cisco router, enter the following global configuration command:

```
ip route 0.0.0.0 0.0.0.0 [ip-address-of-the-next-hop-router |
    outbound-interface]
```

For example, the following command configures the router to route all packets with destinations not in its routing table to IP 172.16.0.2:

```
RouterB(config)# ip route 0.0.0.0 0.0.0.0 172.16.0.2
```

Verifying Routing

The **show ip route** command, as follows, verifies routing tables:

```
RouterA# show ip route
Codes: C - connected, S - static, R - RIP, M - mobile, B - BGP
       D - EIGRP, EX - EIGRP external, O - OSPF, IA - OSPF inter
          area
       N1 - OSPF NSSA external type 1, N2 - OSPF NSSA external
          type 2
       E1 - OSPF external type 1, E2 - OSPF external type 2
       i - IS-IS, su - IS-IS summary, L1 - IS-IS level-1, L2 -
          IS-IS level-2
       ia - IS-IS inter area, * - candidate default, U - per-user
          static route
       o - ODR, P - periodic downloaded static route

Gateway of last resort is 10.1.10.1 to network 0.0.0.0

     10.0.0.0/8 is variably subnetted, 9 subnets, 2 masks
D       10.1.10.0/24 [90/28416] via 10.1.10.254, 2w0d,
   FastEthernet0/0
D       10.1.20.0/24 [90/28416] via 10.1.10.254, 2w0d,
   FastEthernet0/0
```

```
C          10.1.10.0/24 is directly connected, FastEthernet0/0
S          10.0.0.0/8 [1/0] via 10.1.10.0
D          10.1.60.0/24 [90/28416] via 10.1.10.254, 2w0d,
  FastEthernet0/0
D          10.1.50.0/24 [90/28416] via 10.1.10.254, 2w0d,
  FastEthernet0/0
D          10.1.40.0/24 [90/28416] via 10.1.10.254, 2w0d,
  FastEthernet0/0
D          10.1.100.0/24 [90/28416] via 10.1.10.254, 2w0d,
  FastEthernet0/0
D          10.1.254.0/24 [90/28416] via 10.1.10.254, 2w0d,
  FastEthernet0/0
D       192.168.0.0/24 [90/2172416] via 192.168.1.2, 1w6d,
  Serial0/0/0
        192.168.1.0/24 is variably subnetted, 2 subnets, 2 masks
C          192.168.1.0/30 is directly connected, Serial0/0/0
D          192.168.1.0/24 is a summary, 1w6d, Null0
S*      0.0.0.0/0 [1/0] via 10.1.10.1
```

Section 6
Managing Traffic Using Access Lists

Understanding ACLs

As a network grows, it becomes more important to manage the increased traffic going across the network. Access lists help limit traffic by filtering based on packet characteristics. Access lists define a set of rules that routers use to identify particular types of traffic. Access lists can be used to filter both incoming and outgoing traffic on a router's interface. An access list applied to a router interface specifies only rules for traffic going to or through the router. Traffic originating from a router is not affected by that router's access lists. (It is subject to access lists within other routers as it passes through them.)

Access lists are used for many reasons. Cisco security devices like firewalls use access lists to define access to the network. Access lists are used to define the traffic that will be encrypted through a VPN. Cisco routers also use access lists for quality of service (QoS), route filters, and Network Address Translation.

Packet Filtering

Access lists can be configured to permit or deny incoming and outgoing packets through an interface. By following a set of conventions, the network administrator can exercise greater control over network traffic by restricting network use by certain users or devices.

Access List Operations

Access list statements are operated on one at a time from top to bottom. Figure 6-1 shows the process of ACLs.

Figure 6-1   *ACL Process*

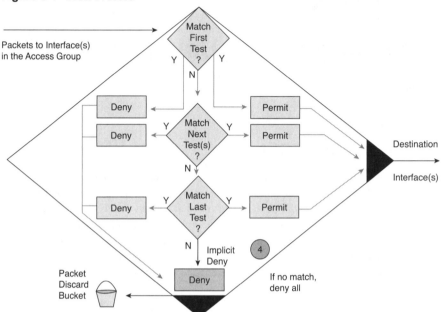

As soon as a match is found, the packet is analyzed and either permitted or denied; the rest of the statements are skipped.

If no match is found, the packet is tested against the next statement until a match is found or the end of the list is reached. An implicit deny statement is present at the end of the list, and all remaining packets are dropped. Unless at least one permit statement exists in an access list, all traffic is blocked.

Access List Process Options

The inbound/outbound access list process options are described as follows:

- **Inbound access lists:** Incoming packets to an interface are processed before they are sent to the outbound interface. If the packet is to be discarded, this method reduces overhead (no routing table lookups). If the packet is permitted, it is processed in the normal way.

- **Outbound access lists:** Outgoing packets are processed by the router first before going to the outbound interface and then are tested against the access list criteria.

Access List Identifiers

The access list number entered by the administrator determines how the router handles the access list. The arguments in the statement follow the number. The types of conditions allowed depend on the type of list (defined by the access list number). Conditions for an access list vary by protocol. You can have several different access lists for any given protocol, but only one protocol, per direction, per interface is allowed.

Wildcard Masking

It is not always necessary to check every bit within an address. Wildcard masking identifies which bits should be checked or ignored (see Figure 6-2). Administrators can use this tool to select one or more IP addresses for filtering. Wildcard mask bits are defined as follows:

- A wildcard mask bit of 0 means to check the corresponding bit value.

- A wildcard mask bit of 1 means do not check (ignore) that corresponding bit value.

Figure 6-2   *Wildcard Masking*

To specify an IP host address within a permit or deny statement, enter the full address followed by a mask of all binary 0s (0.0.0.0).

To specify that all destination addresses are permitted in an access list, enter 0.0.0.0 as the address, followed by a mask of all binary 1s (255.255.255.255).

A shortcut to find the wildcard mask is to subtract the subnet mask from 255.255.255.255. For example, 172.16.0.0/22 has the following subnet mask: 255.255.252.0. If you subtract this subnet mask from 255.255.255.255 you get the wildcard mask to use:

$$255.255.255.255$$
$$- 255.255.252.0$$
$$0.\ \ 0.\ \ 03.255$$

Abbreviations can be used instead of entering an entire wildcard mask.

- **Check all addresses:** To match a specific address, use the word *host*: 172.30.16.29 0.0.0.0 can be written as **host 172.30.16.29**.

- **Ignore all addresses:** Use the word *any* to specify all addresses: 0.0.0.0 255.255.255.255 can be written as **any**.

Testing Against Access List Statements

For TCP/IP packets, access lists check the packet and segment for different items (depending on the type of access list [standard or extended]).

Standard IP access lists are assigned the range of numbers 1 to 99 and 1300 to 1999. Extended IP access lists use the range 100 to 199 and 2000 to 2699. After a packet is checked for a match with the access list statement, it is either permitted or discarded.

IP Access List Entry Sequence Numbering

IP access list entry sequence numbering allows you to edit the order of ACL statements using sequence numbers. Prior to IP access list entry sequence numbering, if you wanted to edit one line in an access list, the entire access list had to be removed and replaced with the new updated access list.

IP access list entry sequence numbering requires Cisco IOS Software Release 12.2 and allows you to add access-list entry sequence numbers to the beginning standard and extended access-list statements to allow you to make additions and changes to individual statements in the access list.

Guidelines for Placing Access Lists

When applying access lists to an interface, the follow guidelines are recommended:

- Extended IP access lists filter based on destination, source, and protocol number. They should be placed as close as possible to the source you want to deny.

- Standard IP access lists filter traffic based on the source address and should be placed as close as possible to the destination of the traffic that you want to deny.

Types of ACLs

The following two methods identify access control lists (ACL):

- **Numbered ACLs:** Use a number for identification

- **Named ACLs:** Use a descriptive name or number for identification

Numbered and named ACLs can be categorized further into the following types of ACLs:

- **Standard access lists** check packets' source addresses. Standard IP access lists permit or deny output for an entire protocol suite based on the source network/subnet/host IP address. When applied to an interface, standard ACLs should be placed as close to the destination as possible. Figure 6-3 shows the standard access list processes.

Figure 6-3 *Standard Access List Processes*

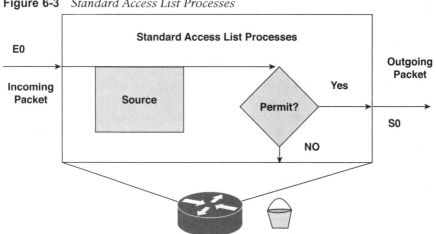

- **Extended access lists** check both source and destination packet addresses. Extended lists specify protocols, possible port numbers, and other possible parameters, allowing admins more flexibility and control. When applied to an interface, extended ACLs should be placed as close to the source as possible.

Table 6-1 shows the difference between standard and extended access lists.

Table 6-1 *Types of Access Lists*

Standard	Extended
Filter based on source	Filter based on source, destination, and protocol of the suite.
Permit or deny the entire TCP/IP protocol suite	A specific protocol of the suite can be used for filtering. Depending on the protocol specified, more options may become available, such as port numbers for TCP and UDP.
Range: 1 to 99, 1300 to 1999	Range: 100 to 199, 2000 to 2699

Additional Types of ACLs

Standard and extended ACLs can become the basis for other types of ACLs that provide additional functionality. These other types of ACLS include the following:

- Dynamic ACLs (lock-and-key)
- Reflexive ACLs
- Time-based ACLs

Dynamic ACLs

Dynamic ACLs (lock-and-key) dynamically create access-list entries in an existing ACL of the router to allow a user that has authenticated to the router through Telnet to access resources that are blocked behind the router.

Dynamic ACLs depend on the user authenticating to the router and an extended access list. Considered lock-and-key, the configuration starts with an extended ACL that blocks traffic through the router. A user who wants to traverse through the router is blocked by the extended ACL until he authenticates to the router through Telnet with a username and password. After being authenticated, the Telnet connection is dropped and a single-entry dynamic ACL entry is added to the extended ACL to permit the user to traverse through the router.

Reflexive ACLs

Reflexive ACLs allow IP packets to be filtered based on upper-layer session information. They are used to allow outbound traffic, and they limit inbound traffic in response to sessions that originate from a network inside the router.

Reflexive ACLs contain only temporary entries that are created when a new IP session begins and are removed when the session ends. Reflective ACLs are *not* applied directly to an interface, but are "nested" within an extended named IP ACL that is applied to an interface.

Time-Based ACLs

Time-based ACLs are similar to extended access lists, except they control access based on time.

Implementing a Traffic Filter with ACLs

Access lists are processed from top to bottom, making statement ordering critical to efficient operation. Always place specific and frequent statements at the beginning of an access list. Named access lists and ACLs using extended sequence entries allow the addition and removal of individual statements. Remember that all access lists end with an implicit deny any statement.

Configuring Standard IPv4 ACLs

The command syntax to create a standard IP access list is as follows:

```
access-list access-list-number {permit | deny} source-address
[wildcard-mask]
```

where *access-list-number* is a number from 1 to 99 or 1300 to 1999.

For example, the following commands create access list number 10, which denies any source IP address between 192.168.0.1 and 192.168.255.255:

```
RouterA(config)# access-list 10 deny 192.168.0.0 0.0.255.255
RouterA(config)# access-list 10 permit any
```

Configuring Extended IPv4 ACLs

The Cisco IOS command syntax to create an extended access list is as follows:

```
access-list access-list-number {permit | deny} protocol source-
  address
  source-wildcard [operator port] destination-address
    destination-wildcard
  [operator port]
```

where:

■ *protocol* examples include IP, TCP, User Datagram Protocol (UDP), Internet Control Message Protocol (ICMP), and generic routing encapsulation (GRE).

■ *operator port* is used when TCP and UDP protocols are selected. Can be **lt** (less than), **gt** (greater than), **eq** (equal to), or **neq** (not equal to) and a protocol port number or port number range.

The following example creates an extended access list that blocks FTP traffic from network 172.16.4.0/24 to network 172.16.3.0/24 and applies the ACL to interface G0/0:

```
RouterA> enable
RouterA# config term
RouterA(config)# access-list 101 deny tcp 172.16.4.0 0.0.0.255
  172.16.3.0 0.0.0.255 eq 21
RouterA(config)# access-list 101 permit ip any any
RouterA(config)# interface g 0/0
RouterA(config-if)# access group 101 in
```

Using IP Access List Entry Sequence Numbers

To use entry sequence numbers, you first create the access list. Then you add the access list rules by first defining the entry sequence where you want the rule to be added in the access list. The following example creates an extended ACL, using entry sequence numbers, that permits HTTP and FTP traffic from network 192.168.1.0/24 to network 172.16.0.0/16:

```
RouterA(config)# ip access-list extended 100
RouterA(config-ext-nacl)# 1 permit tcp 192.168.1.0 0.0.0.255
  172.16.0.0 0.0.255.255 eq www
RouterA(config-ext-nacl)# 10 permit tcp 192.168.1.0 0.0.0.255
  172.16.0.0 0.0.255.255 eq ftp
```

In the preceding example, if you want to add a rule in between rule 1 and 10, you give it a sequence number between 1 and 10. If you want to add or delete only one line in the ACL, you would enter the ACL you want to add or delete and then use the sequence number to identify which line you want to edit.

Configuring Named ACLs

When you create a named access list, you use the **ip access-list extended** *name* global command, where *name* is the name of the access list. Issuing this command places you in named IP access list subcommand mode, which then allows you to enter the access list parameters.

The following creates a named access list that blocks ping from networks 172.160.0.0/22 to host 192.168.0.101:

```
RouterA(config)# ip access-list extended block-ping
RouterA(config-ext-nacl)# deny icmp 172.160.0.0 0.0.3.255 host
 192.168.0.101 echo
RouterA(config-ext-nacl)# permit ip any any
```

Applying Access Lists

To apply an access list to an interface on a Cisco router, use the **ip access-group** interface command, as follows:

```
ip access-group access-list-number {in | out}
```

For example, the following applies access list 10 to serial interface 0 as an inbound access list:

```
RouterA(config)# int s0
RouterA(config-if)# ip access-group 10 in
```

To remove an access list from a router, first remove it from the interface by entering the **no ip access-group** *access-list-number direction* command. Then remove the access list by entering the **no access-list** *access-list-number* global command.

ACL Configuration Guidelines

Some useful guidelines for configuring an ACL are as follows:

- Be sure to use the correct numbers for the type of list and protocols you want to be filtered.

- You can use only one access list per protocol, per direction, per interface. Multiple ACLs are permitted per interface, but each must be for a different protocol or direction.

- Put more-specific statements before more-general ones. Frequently occurring conditions should be placed before less-frequent conditions.

- Without an explicit permit, the implicit deny at the end of every list causes all packets to be denied. Every access list should include at least one permit statement.

- An interface with an empty access list applied to it allows (permits) all traffic. Create your statements before applying the list to an interface.

- Access lists filter only traffic going through the router or traffic to and from the router, depending on how it is applied.

Verifying ACLs

The **show ip interface** *interface-type interface-number* command displays whether an IP access list is applied to an interface.

The **show running-config** and **show access-list** commands display all access lists configured on a router.

Troubleshooting ACLs

Access lists are processed from the top down. Most access list errors are due to an incorrect statement entry that denies or permits traffic.

To troubleshoot access lists, verify that the statements are correct and applied to the proper interface and direction. Also, remember that at the end of each access list is an implicit deny any statement.

Section 7
Enabling Internet Connectivity

Internet WAN Terminology

Typical Internet WAN terminology is as follows:

- **Customer premises equipment (CPE):** Equipment located on the subscriber's premises and includes both equipment owned by the subscriber and devices leased by the service provider.

- **Demarcation (or demarc):** Marks the point where the CPE ends and the local loop begins. It is usually located in the telecommunications closet. The demarcation point is different from country to country.

Configuring Public IP Addresses

The two options for configuring public IP addresses are

- Statically
- Dynamically through DHCP

Configuring a Static Public IP Address

The steps for configuring a static assigned public IP address are

STEP 1. Use the **ip address** interface command to assign an IP address to the interface connecting to the Internet.

STEP 2. Enter a default route pointing to the ISP next-hop router to allow access to the Internet.

The following configures a static public IP address to a router interface and assigns a default router to go out interface g0/0:

```
Router# configure terminal
Router(config)# interface g0/0
Router(config-if)# ip address 201.54.1.5 255.255.255.0
Router(config-if)# no shutdown
Router(config-if)# exit
Router(config)# ip route 0.0.0.0 0.0.0.0 g0/0
```

Configuring Dynamic IP Addresses

If your ISP allocates your IP address dynamically, the Internet router needs to be configured as a DHCP client. The **ip address dhcp** interface command configures a router interface to receive its IP address from a DHCP server.

```
Router# configure terminal
Router(config-if)# interface g0/0
Router(config-if)# ip address dhcp
```

If the router received the optional DHCP parameter called default gateway with its assigned IP address, the default route will get injected into the routing table. If not, it will need to be statically configured.

Public Versus Private IPv4 Addresses

Public IPv4 addresses are Internet addresses that are routable on the Internet. RFC 1918 defines IP addresses that are reserved for use in private networks. The IP addresses are not routed on the Internet. Three blocks of IP addresses are reserved for private networks:

- 10.0.0.0 to 10.255.255.255
- 172.16.0.0 to 172.31.255.255
- 192.168.0.0 to 192.168.255.255

Networks using private addresses can still connect to the Internet if they use Network Address Translation (NAT).

Introducing NAT and PAT

Network Address Translation (NAT) provides address translation and was initially developed as an answer to the diminishing number of IP addresses. When the IP address scheme was originally developed, it was believed that the address space would not run out. The combination of the PC explosion and the emergence of other network-ready devices quickly consumed many of the available addresses.

An additional (and equally important) benefit of NAT is that it hides private addresses from public networks, making communication more secure from hackers. Figure 7-1 shows how NAT translates the inside source address (SA) of 10.0.0.1 to the outside source address 172.2.34.21. Properties of NAT are as follows:

Figure 7-1 *NAT*

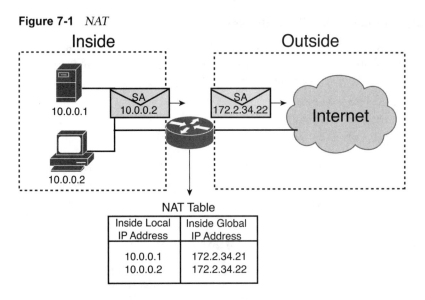

NAT Table

Inside Local IP Address	Inside Global IP Address
10.0.0.1 10.0.0.2	172.2.34.21 172.2.34.22

- NAT is configured on a router, firewall, or other network device.

- Static NAT uses one-to-one, private-to-public address translation.

- Dynamic NAT matches private addresses to a pool of public addresses on an as-needed basis. The address translation is many-to-many.

Port Address Translation (PAT) is a form of dynamic network address translation that uses many (private addresses) to a few or one (public address). This is called overloading and is accomplished by inspecting port numbers to identify unique traffic flows, as shown in Figure 7-2.

Figure 7-2 *PAT*

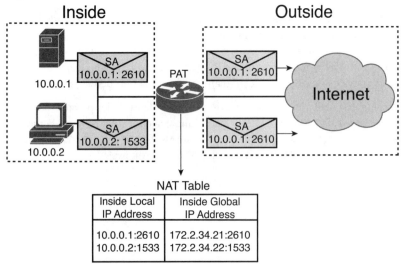

NAT Table

Inside Local IP Address	Inside Global IP Address
10.0.0.1:2610	172.2.34.21:2610
10.0.0.2:1533	172.2.34.22:1533

Details of PAT are as follows:

- Because the port number is 16 bits, PAT can theoretically map 65,536 sessions to a single public address.

- PAT continues to look for available port numbers. If one is not found, PAT increments the IP address (if available).

NAT Terminology

Table 7-1 lists the Cisco NAT terminology.

Table 7-1   *NAT Terminology*

Name	Description
Inside local address	The IP address assigned to a host on the inside, private network. Usually a private IP address.
Inside global address	A legal routable IP address that represents one or more inside local IP addresses to the outside world.
Outside local address	The IP address of an outside host as it appears to the inside, private network. Not necessarily legitimate, the outside local address is allocated from routable address space on the inside.
Outside global address	The IP address assigned to a host on the outside network by the host's owner. Usually a routable IP address.

Configuring Static NAT

To configure static NAT, you must create the static mapping table and define which interfaces on your router connect to the inside network and the outside network. The following example creates the static mapping and defines interface g0 as connecting to the outside network and interface g1 as connecting to the inside network:

```
RouterB(config)# ip nat inside source static 192.168.10.5
  216.1.1.3
RouterB(config)# int g0
RouterB(config-if)# ip nat outside
RouterB(config-if)# int g1
RouterB(config-if)# ip nat inside
```

Configuring Dynamic NAT

To configure dynamic NAT, you create a NAT pool of external IP addresses that internal hosts can draw from, create an access list that defines the internal hosts to be translated, and enable the translation to occur. As with static NAT, you have to define which interface is internal and which interface is external:

```
RouterB(config)# ip nat pool cisco 216.1.1.1 216.1.1.14 netmask
  255.255.255.240 (creates a NAT pool called cisco)
RouterB(config)# access-list 10 permit 192.168.10.0 0.0.0.15
  (defines the IP addresses that will be translated)
RouterB(config)# ip nat inside source list 10 pool cisco (estab-
  lishes dynamic translation of access list 10 with the NAT pool
  named cisco)
RouterB(config)# int g0
RouterB(config-if)# ip nat outside
RouterB(config-if)# int g1
RouterB(config-if)# ip nat inside
```

Configuring PAT

To configure PAT, you define an access list that permits the internal hosts to be translated and use the **ip nat inside source list** *access-list-number* **interface** *interface-type* **overload** global command, as follows:

```
RouterA> enable
RouterA# config term
RouterA(config)# access-list 99 permit 10.0.0.1
RouterA(config)# ip nat inside source list 99 interface g0/1
  overload
RouterA(config)# interface g0/0
RouterA(config-if)# ip nat inside
RouterA(config-if)# exit
RouterA(config)# interface g0/1
RouterA(config-if)# ip nat outside
RouterA(config-if)# exit
RouterA(config)# exit
```

Verifying NAT and Resolving Translation Table Issues

The **clear ip nat translation** * command clears all dynamic translation tables.

The **clear ip nat translation inside** *global-ip local-ip* command clears a specific entry from a dynamic translation table.

The **clear ip nat translation outside** *local-ip global-ip* command clears a specific outside translation address.

The **show ip nat translations** command lists all active translations.

The **show ip nat statistics** command shows all translation statistics.

The **debug ip nat** command for use in troubleshooting address translations.

Section 8
Managing Network Device Security

Network Device Security Overview

Five common threats network devices faces are

- **Remote access threats:** Include unauthorized remote access to network devices.

- **Local access and physical threats:** These threats include physical damage to network device hardware, password recovery by weak physical security, and theft.

- **Environmental threats:** Temperature extremes (heat or cold) or humidity extremes.

- **Electrical threats:** Voltage spikes, brownouts, noise, and power loss.

- **Maintenance threats:** The improper handling of important electronic components, lack of critical spare parts, poor cabling and labeling, and poor change policies.

Mitigation of remote access threats includes configuration of strong authentication and encryption for remote access, configuration of a login banner, the use of ACLs, and VPN access.

Techniques to mitigate local access and physical threats include locking wiring closets, physical access control, and blocking physical access through a dropped ceiling, raised floor, window, ductwork, or other points of entries. You can also monitor facilities with security cameras.

Mitigation of environmental threats includes creating a proper operating environment through temperature control, humidity control, airflow, remote environmental alarms, and environment monitoring and recording.

Mitigation of electrical threats includes using surge protectors, installing UPS systems and generators, using redundant power supplies, following a preventive maintenance plan, and using remote monitoring.

Mitigation of network device maintenance threats include neat cabling runs, proper labeling of components, stocking critical spares, access by only authorized personnel, and proper change management procedures.

Securing Access to Privileged Mode

Securing access to privileged mode is done by configuring enable passwords.

The following configures an enable password of apu and an enable secret password of flanders:

```
Router(config)# enable password apu
Router(config)# enable secret flanders
```

The **no enable password** command disables the privileged EXEC mode password.

The **no enable secret** command disables the encrypted password.

NOTE   When the enable secret password is set, it is used instead of the enable password.

The console, VTY, and enable passwords are displayed unencrypted in the configuration file. The **service password-encryption** global command can be used to instruct the router to store these passwords in an encrypted format as follows:

```
Router(config)# service password-encryption
```

Securing Console and Remote Access

The following example configures passwords on the console and vty lines of a router to homer and bart:

```
Router(config)# line console 0
Router(config-line)# login
Router(config-line)# password homer
Router(config-line)# exec-timeout 15
Router(config-line)# line vty 0 4
Router(config-line)# login
Router(config-line)# password bart
```

The numbers 0 through 4 in the **line vty** command specify the number of Telnet sessions allowed in the router. You can also set up a different password for each line by using the **line vty** *line number* command.

The **exec-timeout** command prevents users from remaining logged on to a console port when no activity is detected. The previous example will log the user out when no activity is detected for 15 minutes.

Cisco recommends using SSH to encrypt communication between the Cisco device and the host. Telnet is unsecure, and all communication between the Cisco device and host is sent in clear text. Use the following steps to configure SSH access:

STEP 1. Create a local username and password on the device.

STEP 2. Assign a domain name to the device with the **ip domain-name** command.

STEP 3. Generate an RSA security key with the **crypto key generate rsa** command.

STEP 4. Enable SSH.

STEP 5. Configure vty ports to authenticate using SSH.

```
Router(config)# username eric password 0 ciscopress
Router(config)# ip domain-name cisco.com
Router(config)# crypto key generate rsa
The name for the keys will be: router.cisco.com
Choose the size of the key modulus in the range of 360 to 2048
  for your General Purpose Keys. Choosing a key modulus greater
  than 512 may take a few minutes.
How many bits in the modulus [1024]:
% Generating 1024 bit RSA keys ...[OK]
Router(config)# ip ssh ver 2
Router(config)# line vty 0 15
Router(config-line)# login local
Router(config-line)# transport input ssh
```

Limiting Remote Access with ACLs

By default, after a vty password has been applied, any IP address can connect to vty ports. You should restrict access to vty ports to only specific IP addresses or management subnets. This is done through access lists. Common practice is to use standard access lists.

Standard access lists allow you to permit or deny traffic based on the source IP address. To restrict access to vty ports, you would create a standard access list that permits each authorized IP address to connect to vty and apply the access list to the vty ports.

At the end of each access list is an implicit deny any statement. So, if a host is not specifically permitted, it will be denied.

The command syntax to create a standard IP access list is as follows:

```
access-list access-list-number {permit | deny} source-address
  [wildcard-mask]
```

The *access-list-number* parameter is a number from 1 to 99 or 1300 to 1999.

```
Router(config)# access list 10 permit ip 192.168.10.0 0.0.0.255
Router(config)# line vty 0 15
Router(config-line)# access-class 10 in  This applies the access
  list to vty lines
```

External Authentication Options

RADIUS and TACACS+ provide external authentication options for connecting and authenticating to Cisco devices.

RADIUS is an open standard with low CPU and memory use.

TACACS+ enables modular authentication, authorization, and accounting services.

Configuring the Login Banner

The login banner is displayed before the username and password login prompts on a Cisco router. The login banner is configured using the **banner login** global command, as follows:

```
Router# config t
Enter configuration commands, one per line.  End with CNTL/Z.
Router(config)# banner login #
Enter TEXT message.  End with the character '#'.
Notice! Only Authorized Personnel Are Allowed to Access This
  Device
#
```

The MOTD is displayed before the login banner (except with SSH). It is displayed to anyone connecting to the router through Telnet, the console port, or the auxiliary port. Use the **banner motd #** *text* **#** global configuration command to configure the MOTD, as follows:

```
Router(config)# banner motd #
Enter TEXT message.  End with the character '#'.
Warning only authorized users many access this switch.
#
Router(config)#
```

Implementing Device Hardening

Some basic security suggestions for network devices are as follows:

- Use complex passwords for all devices.
- Limit Telnet access using access lists.
- Use SSH instead of Telnet.
- Physically secure access to the switch.
- Use banners to warn against unauthorized access.
- Set up and monitor syslog.
- Configure port security.
- Disable unused ports.

Securing Unused Ports

Securing a switch includes physical, environmental, and access security.

To secure unused ports, either disable the port or place the port in an unused VLAN.

A switch port is disabled by issuing the **shutdown** interface command.

Port Security

Port security limits the number of MAC address allowed per port and can also limit which MAC addresses are allowed. Allowed MAC addresses can be manually configured, dynamically learned by the switch, a combination of both, or by sticky learning as detailed here:

- **Static:** Secures the port with a static configuration of specific MAC addresses that are permitted to use the port.

- **Dynamic:** Secures the port by limiting the number of MAC addresses used on a port. These addresses are dynamically learned and aged out after a certain period.

- **Combination:** Uses static MACs plus dynamic MACs.

- **Sticky learning:** Converts dynamically learned addresses to "sticky secure" addresses. In other words, dynamically learned MAC addresses are stored in the running configuration as if they were statically configured.

The interface command to configure port security is as follows:

```
switchport port-security [mac-address mac-address | mac-address
    sticky [mac-address] | maximum value | violation {restrict |
    shutdown}
```

- switchport port-security mac-address *mac-address*: Manually configures the port to accept a specific MAC address.

- switchport port-security mac-address sticky: Configures the switch to dynamically learn the MAC address of the device(s) attached to the port.

- switchport port-security maximum *value*: Configures the maximum number of MAC addresses allowed on the port. The default value is 1.

- switchport port-security violation {protect | restrict | shutdown}: Configures the action to be taken when the maximum number of MAC addresses is reached and when MAC addresses not associated with the port try to access the port. The **protect** keyword drops all the packets from the insecure hosts at the port-security process level but does not increment the security-violation count. The **restrict** keyword tells the switch to restrict access to learned MAC addresses that are above the maximum defined addresses and increments the security-violation count. The **shutdown** keyword tells the switch to shut down all access to the port if a violation occurs.

The following example demonstrates how to configure port security:

```
Cat2960(config)# int f0/1
Cat2960(config-if)# switchport mode access
Cat2960(config-if)# switchport port-security
Cat2960(config-if)# switchport port-security max 1
Cat2960(config-if)# switchport port-security mac-address sticky
Cat2960(config-if)# switchport port-sec violation restrict
```

To verify port security, use the **show port-security** command, as follows:

```
Cat2960# show port-security
```

Secure Port	MaxSecureAddr (Count)	CurrentAddr (Count)	SecurityViolation (Count)	Security Action
Fa0/1	1	0	0	Restrict

```
Total Addresses in System (excluding one mac per port)   : 0
Max Addresses limit in System (excluding one mac per port) : 8320
```

Disabling Unused Services

Best practices for disabling unused services on a Cisco router are as follows:

- Unless needed, finger, identification (identd), and TCP and UDP small services should remain disabled.
- Disable CDP on interfaces where the service may represent a risk. Examples include external or Internet edge interfaces.
- Disable HTTP.

NOTE In IOS 15.0 and later, finger, identd, TCP and UDP small services, and HTTP service are disabled by default.

The **no cdp run** global command disables CDP globally on a Cisco device. The **no cdp enable** command disables CDP only on an interface.

The **no ip http server** global command disables HTTP.

Network Time Protocol

Network Time Protocol is used to synchronize the clocks of network devices on a network to ensure that all devices are on the same time.

NTP is important to configure on network devices to allow correct tracking of events that transpire on a network, and clock synchronization is critical for digital certificates.

NTP functions in a client server mode.

NTP clients can receive time from a local master clock, master clock on the Internet, or GPS or atomic clock. A Cisco device can act as an NTP server or client.

The **ntp server** *server-ip-address* global command configures a Cisco device to synchronize its time with an NTP server.

The **show ntp associations** command displays the associated device that the device is connected to.

The **show ntp status** command displays the status of NTP configured.

Section 9
Implementing VLANs and Trunks

Issues in a Poorly Designed Network

Poorly designed networks have many issues that can impact performance. Issues typically found in a poorly designed networking include

- Unbound failure domains
- Large broadcast domains
- Large amounts of unknown MAC unicast traffic
- Difficult management and support
- Security vulnerabilities

VLAN Overview

Users of shared LANs are usually grouped based on where people are located rather than how they use the network (physical rather than logical). Shared LANs have little embedded security, because all traffic can be seen by all end stations. It is also expensive to make moves or changes in the network setup. Virtual LANs solve these problems.

The virtual LAN (VLAN) organizes physically separate users into the same broadcast domain. The use of VLANs improves performance, security, and flexibility. The use of VLANs also decreases the cost of arranging users, because no extra cabling is required.

VLAN Characteristics

VLANs are logical broadcast domains that can span multiple physical LAN segments.

VLANs allow logically defined user groups rather than user groups defined by their physical locations. For example, you can arrange user groups such as accounting, engineering, and finance, rather than everyone on the first floor, everyone on the second floor, and so on.

VLANs are characterized as follows:

- VLANs define broadcast domains that can span multiple LAN segments.
- VLANs improve segmentation, flexibility, and security.
- VLAN segmentation is not bound by the physical location of users.

- Only ports assigned to a specific VLAN share broadcasts; other VLANs do not see other VLANs' broadcasts.

- A VLAN can exist on one or several switches.

Figure 9-1 shows a typical VLAN design.

Figure 9-1   *VLAN Design*

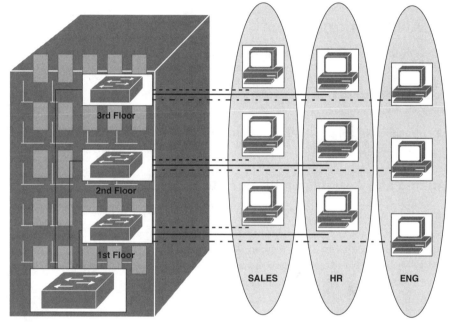

VLAN Operation

Each VLAN on a switch behaves as if it were a separate physical bridge. The switch forwards packets (including unicasts, multicasts, and broadcasts) only to ports assigned to the same VLAN from which they originated. This drastically reduces network traffic.

VLANs require a trunk or physical connection for each VLAN to span multiple switches. Each trunk can carry traffic for multiple VLANs.

Trunking with 802.1Q

The IEEE 802.1Q is a standard that defines a system of VLAN tagging for Ethernet frames and the procedures to be used by bridges and switches in handling such frames. 802.1Q tagging provides a standard method of identifying frames that belong to a particular VLAN by using an internal tag that modifies the existing Ethernet frame with the VLAN identification.

Cisco supports 802.1Q trunking over Fast Ethernet and above links. 802.1Q defines how to carry traffic from multiple VLANs over a single point-to-point link. By default, all VLANs are carried over a trunk interface.

VLAN IDs are added to Ethernet frames via an 802.1Q header. 802.1Q uses an internal tagging mechanism that inserts a 4-byte tag filed into the original Ethernet frame between the Source address and Type of Length Fields.

An 802.1Q trunk and associated trunk ports have a native VLAN value. The native VLAN must match between interfaces participating in the 802.1Q trunk. Frames on the native VLAN are not tagged. The default native VLAN is VLAN 1.

VLAN Configuration

A port can be assigned (configured) to a given VLAN. VLAN membership can be either static or dynamic:

- **Static assignment:** The switch port is statically configured by an administrator to a VLAN.

- **Dynamic assignment:** Assigned to a port based on the MAC address of the device plugged into a port. Requires a VLAN Membership Policy Server.

Adding and Assigning Interfaces to VLANS

The **vlan** *vlan-id* global command adds a VLAN to a Catalyst switch as demonstrated here:

```
Cat2960(Cat2960(config)# vlan 10
Cat2960(config-vlan)# name Admin
Cat2960(config-vlan)# vlan 20
Cat2960(config-vlan)# name Sales
```

The **switchport access vlan** *vlan-id* interface command assigns a port to a specific VLAN as demonstrated here:

```
Cat2960(config)# int f0/1
Cat2960(config-if)# switchport access vlan 10
Cat2960(config-if)# int f0/2
Cat2960(config-if)# switchport access vlan 20
```

Verifying VLANs

The commands to verify VLAN configurations are as follows:

- **show vlan id** *vlan#*: Displays information about a specific VLAN

- **show vlan brief:** Displays one line for each VLAN that displays the VLAN name, the status, and the switch ports assigned to that VLAN

- **show vlan:** Displays information on all configured VLANs

Configuring an 802.1Q Trunk

Cisco switches use DTP (Dynamic Trunking Protocol) to negotiate a trunk link. The **switchport trunk** command sets Fast Ethernet or higher ports to trunk mode.

`switchport mode [dynamic {auto | desirable} | trunk]`

- **mode dynamic auto** allows the interface to convert to a trunk link if the connecting neighbor interface is set to **trunk** or **desirable**.

- **mode dynamic desirable** allows the interface to actively attempt to convert the link to a trunk link. The link becomes a trunk if the neighbor interface is set to **trunk, desirable,** or **auto**.

- **trunk** sets the interface to trunking on.

```
Cat2960(config)# interface g0/1
Cat2960(config-if)# switchport mode trunk
Cat2960(config-if)# interface g0/2
Cat2960(config-if)# switchport mode dynamic desirable
```

By default, all VLANs (1–4094) are allowed to propagate on all trunk links. To limit a trunk to allow only specified VLANs, use the following command:

`switchport trunk allowed vlan {add | all | except | remove}`
`   vlan-list`

The following command allows only VLANs 10–50 on a trunk link:

`Cat2960(config-if)# switchport trunk allowed vlan 10-50`

VLAN Design Considerations

VLAN design best practices include

- Limiting the VLAN number on switches because the maximum number of VLANs is switch dependent.

- VLAN 1 is the default native VLAN.

- The Cisco switch IP address should be in the management VLAN.

- Management traffic should be kept in a separate VLAN.

- Change the native VLAN to another value than VLAN 1.

- Make sure that the native VLAN is the same on both ends of an 802.1Q trunk link.

- Remember that DTP manages trunk negotiations between Cisco switches and needs to be set to approved values.

Physical Redundancy in a LAN

A redundant topology has multiple connections to switches or other devices. Redundancy ensures that a single point of failure does not cause the entire switched network to fail. Layer 2 redundancy, however, can cause problems in a network, including broadcast storms, multiple copies of frames, and MAC address table instability. Figure 9-2 depicts a redundant topology.

Figure 9-2 *Redundant Topology*

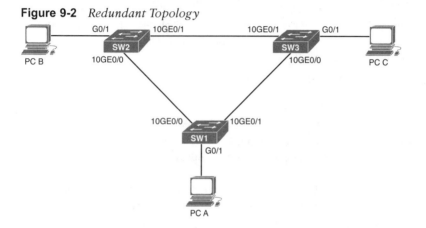

The solution to problems caused in a redundant switched network is the Spanning Tree Protocol (STP). STP is a Layer 2 protocol that prevents looping traffic in a redundant switched network by blocking traffic on the redundant links. If the main link goes down, STP activates the standby path.

Routing Between VLANs

VLANs create a logical segmentation of Layer 3, performed at Layer 2. End stations in different networks (broadcast domains) cannot communicate with each other without the use of a Layer 3 device such as a router. InterVLAN routing is handled by either a router or a Layer 3 switch. For interVLAN routing with a router, each VLAN must have a separate physical connection on the router, or trunking must be configured on a router interface and the switch interface connecting to the router.

Understanding InterVLAN Routing

Figure 9-3 shows a router attached to a switch. The end stations in the two VLANs communicate with each other by sending packets to the router, which forwards them to the other VLAN. This setup is called "router on a stick."

Figure 9-3 *Router on a Stick*

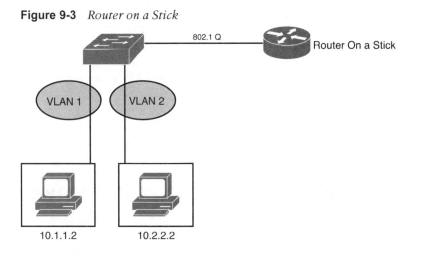

InterVLAN routing using router on a stick requires the use of subinterfaces. A sub-interface is a logical, addressable interface on the router's physical port. A single port can have many subinterfaces. Router on a stick requires a Fast Ethernet or faster interface, with one subinterface configured per VLAN.

In Figure 9-4, the FastEthernet 0/0 interface is divided into multiple subinterfaces (FastEthernet 0.1, FastEthernet 0.2, and so on).

Figure 9-4 *Using Subinterfaces*

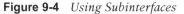
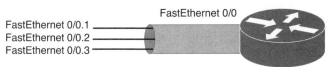

Configuring InterVLAN Routing

To configure interVLAN routing on a router, first create a subinterface and then configure the subinterface with the **encapsulation dot1q** *vlan-id* command, where the *vlan-id* is the VLAN number of the associated VLAN. The following example enables interVLAN routing for VLANs 1, 10, and 20:

```
RouterB(config)# int f0/0
RouterB(config-if)# ip address 192.168.1.1 255.255.255.0
RouterB(config-if)# int f0/0.10
RouterB(config-if)# ip address 192.168.10.1 255.255.255.0
RouterB(config-if)# encapsulation dot1q 10
RouterB(config-if)# int f0/0.20
RouterB(config-if)# ip address 192.168.20.1 255.255.255.0
RouterB(config-if)# encapsulation dot1q 20
```

Remember that in 802.1Q, the native VLAN is not encapsulated. In the previous example, the physical interface f0/0 is in the native VLAN because the **encapsulation dot1q** command is not configured. VLAN 1 is the default native VLAN if not otherwise specified with the **dot1q** *vlan-id* **native** command. The subinterfaces f0/0.10 and f0/0.20 were configured for 802.1Q tagging and are therefore in VLANs 10 and 20, respectively.

By using subinterfaces for interVLAN communication, all traffic must go through the router's interface. For large networks, this can cause a bottleneck. To prevent a bottleneck, use a Layer 3 switch to perform interVLAN routing.

Using a Cisco Network Device as a DHCP Server

DHCP is a protocol that leases IP addresses to IP hosts. DHCP is built on a client-server model. The DHCP server hosts allocated network addresses and other IP configuration parameters. The DHCP client is a host that requests initialization parameters from a DHCP server.

DHCP supports the following three mechanisms for IP address allocation:

- **Automatic allocation:** Assigns a permanent IP address to a client
- **Dynamic allocation:** Assigns an IP address to a client for a set period of time
- **Manual allocation:** Assigns a specific IP address to a client as defined by the administrator using the client's MAC address

Understanding DHCP

Figure 9-5 shows the DHCP process as outlined here:

1. When a client boots up, it broadcasts a DHCPDISCOVER message on its local physical segment using IP address 255.255.255.255.

2. A DHCP server receives the DHCPDISCOVER message and responds with a DHCPOFFER message. This message contains IP configuration information such as DNS and default gateway.

3. After the client receives the DHCPOFFER, it responds with a DHCPREQUEST, indicating that it accepted the DHCPOFFER.

4. The server receives the DHCPREQUEST and sends a DHCPACK, acknowledging the process.

Figure 9-5   *DHCP Process*

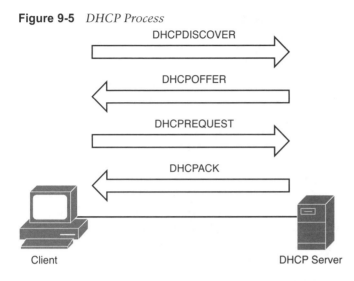

Configuring a DHCP Server

The steps to configure a Cisco device as a DHCP server are as follows:

STEP 1.   Enter DHCP pool configuration mode.

STEP 2.   Assign DHCP parameters to the DHCP pool.

STEP 3.   Exclude IP addresses from DHCP assignment.

The **ip dhcp pool** global command enters the DHCP pool configuration. The following example creates a DHCP pool named CiscoPress for the network 192.168.1.0/24, assigns the default gateway as 192.168.1.1, assigns the DNS server as 192.168.1.10, sets the domain name to ciscopress.com, sets the DHCP lease to 30 days, and excludes IP addresses 192.168.1.1–192.168.1.50 from being assigned by the DHCP server:

```
Router(config)# ip dhcp pool CiscoPress
Router(dhcp-config)# network 192.168.1.0 /24
Router(dhcp-config)# default-router 192.168.1.1
Router(dhcp-config)# dns-server 192.168.1.10
Router(dhcp-config)# domain-name ciscopress.com
Router(dhcp-config)# lease 30 0
Router(dhcp-config)# exit
Router(config)# ip dhcp excluded-address 192.168.1.1 192.168.1.50
```

Monitoring DHCP Server Functions

show ip dhcp pool privileged EXEC mode command displays the total number of available addresses, configured address range, and number of leased addresses.

show ip dhcp binding displays all IP address–to–MAC address bindings that have been provided by the DHCP server.

show ip dhcp conflict displays address conflicts found by the DHCP server.

DHCP Relay Agent

When a DHCP-enabled client requests an IP address through a DHCPDISCOVER message, this message is broadcast to the local segment. By default, routers do not forward broadcasts. If the DHCP server is on a different segment than the DHCP client, the DHCP server will not see the DHCPDISCOVER messages from clients. The router needs to be configured to forward the DHCPDISCOVER broadcasts to the DHCP server. This is done through the following interface command:

```
ip helper-address [global] address
```

The *address* parameter is the IP address of the DHCP server.

The **ip helper-address** command enables forwarding of UDP broadcasts received on the configured interface to a specific IP address, as follows:

```
Router(config)# int f0/0
Router(config-if)# ip helper-address 192.168.11.200
```

Section 10
WAN Technologies

Introducing WAN Technologies

WANs connect networks, users, and services across a broad geographic area. Figure 10-1 shows that companies use the WAN to connect company sites and mobile users for information exchange.

Figure 10-1 *WAN Connections*

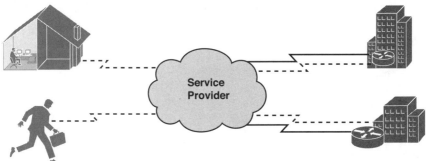

WANs Versus LANs

LANs connect computers, peripherals, and other devices in a building or small geographic area. WANs connect LANs across a wide geographic area. LANs and all devices in the LAN are usually owned by the local organization. Outside service providers own the WAN and WAN devices. LAN costs are fixed, and WAN costs are recurring.

WAN Access and the OSI Model

WANs and their protocols function at Layers 1 and 2 of the OSI reference model.

The physical components of WANs define electrical, mechanical, and operational connections.

The data link layer defines WAN protocols that define how data is encapsulated for transmission across the WAN. Examples of these protocols are Frame Relay, ATM, High-Level Data Link Control (HDLC), and PPP.

WAN Review

Figure 10-2 shows the typical WAN terminology and the list that follows provides more detailed definitions:

- **Customer premises equipment (CPE):** Located on the subscriber's premises and includes both equipment owned by the subscriber and devices leased by the service provider.

- **Demarcation (or demarc):** Marks the point where the CPE ends and the local loop begins. It is usually located in the telecommunications closet.

- **Local loop (or last mile):** The cabling from the demarc into the WAN service provider's central office.

- **Central office (CO):** A switching facility that provides a point of presence for WAN service. The central office is the entry point to the WAN cloud, the exit point from the WAN for called devices, and a switching point for calls.

- **Toll network:** A collection of trunks inside the WAN cloud.

Figure 10-2 *WAN Terminology*

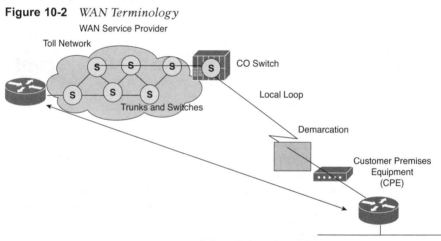

WAN Devices

The following devices are used for WAN services:

- **Routers:** Connect the LAN to the WAN. Routers provide network layer services; they route data from one network to another.

- **Modems or DSU/CSUs:** In analog lines, modems convert analog to digital. Modems modulate and demodulate a signal, enabling data to be transmitted over telephone lines. In digital lines, data service units/channel service units (DSU/CSU) convert one form of digital format to another digital format.

■ **WAN networking devices:** Used in the WAN network, they are multiport devices that switch MPLS, X.25, or ATM traffic. They operate at the data link layer of the OSI model.

Roles of Routers in a WAN

Routers connect WANs to LANs and vice versa. Routers have LAN and WAN interfaces. The LAN interfaces allow the router to connect to the LAN media such as Ethernet. WAN interfaces are used to make WAN connections. These may be serial WAN interfaces or an Ethernet interface using Ethernet emulation. Some WAN interfaces require an external device such as a DSU/CSU to connect a router to a service provider.

WAN Communication Link Options

WAN services are generally leased from service providers on a subscription basis. The following three main types of WAN connections (services) exist:

■ **Dedicated leased line:** A leased line (or point-to-point dedicated connection) provides a preestablished connection through the service provider's network (WAN) to a remote network. Leased lines provide a reserved connection for the client but are costly. Leased-line connections are typically synchronous serial connections. Figure 10-3 shows an example of a leased-line WAN topology.

Figure 10-3   *Dedicated Leased-Line WAN Topology*

Synchronous Serial

■ **Packet-switched:** With packet switching, devices transport packets using virtual circuits (VC) that provide end-to-end connectivity. Programmed switching devices provide physical connections. Packet headers identify the destination; the data is transmitted in labeled cells, frames, or packets over a common infrastructure. Packet switching offers leased line–type services over shared lines, but at a much lower cost. Figure 10-4 shows an example of a packet-switched WAN topology.

Figure 10-4   *Packet-Switched WAN Topology*

Service Provider

Synchronous Serial

■ **Internet:** Public connections use the global Internet infrastructure. Connections are made through DSL, cable, and other broadband technologies. VPN technology is used to provide private connections to the corporation.

Point-to-Point Connectivity

A point-to-point WAN link provides a single established WAN connection path from the customer premises through a service provider network, to a remote network.

Point-to-point WAN links can use either serial or Ethernet interfaces, depending on the technology used by the service provider (SP). Serial interfaces are used in traditional connections such as T1s and T3s and require a DSU/CSU. Ethernet interfaces are becoming a more common option due to simplicity, cost, and flexibility. To provide Ethernet point-to-point connections, the service provider uses Ethernet emulation.

Configuring a Point-to-Point Link Using Ethernet Emulation

Configuring a point-to-point WAN link using Ethernet emulation consists of configuring the Ethernet interface with an IP address and enabling the interface:

```
RouterB(config)# interface g0/0
RouterB(config-if)# ip address 192.168.1.254 255.255.255.252
RouterB(config-if)# no shutdown
```

Introducing Dynamic Routing Protocols

Routing is the act of finding a path to a destination and moving data across this path from source to destination. The routing process uses network routing tables, protocols, and algorithms to determine the most efficient path for forwarding the IP packet.

Dynamic Routing Protocols

Routing protocols allow communication between routers to discover paths to different destination networks. If a routing protocol learns multiple paths to the same destination, it will choose the best path to that destination. If a path is lost to a destination network, when possible, the routing protocol may find a new best path. As the topology of the network changes, routing protocols help maintain up-to-date information in the routing table.

The primary purposes of routing protocols are to

- Discover remote networks
- Maintain up-to-date routing information
- Choose the best path to destination networks
- Find a new best path if the current path is no longer available

Routing protocols use their own rules and metrics to build and update routing tables automatically. Routing metrics are measures of path desirability. Different protocols use different metrics. Some common metrics are as follows:

- **Bandwidth:** The link's data capacity.

- **Delay:** The time required to move the packet from the current router to the destination. This depends on the bandwidth of intermediate links, port delays at each router, congestion, and distance.

- **Load:** The amount of activity on the network.

- **Reliability:** The error rate of each network link.

- **Hop count:** The number of routers the packet must travel through before reaching the destination.

- **Cost:** An arbitrary value based on bandwidth and other metrics assigned by the administrator.

IGP and EGP

Routing protocols are divided into two classes based on how they interact with other autonomous systems: exterior gateway protocols (EGP) and interior gateway protocols (IGP), as illustrated in Figure 10-5.

An autonomous system (AS) refers to a group of networks under a common administrative domain.

IGPs exchange information within an AS. Examples include RIP, EIGRP, OSPF, and IS-IS.

EGPs exchange information between autonomous systems. BGP is an example of an EGP.

Figure 10-5 *IGPs and EGPs*

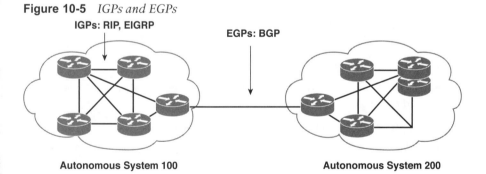

Distance Vector and Link-State Routing Protocols

Routing protocols are designed around one of the following routing methods:

- **Distance vector routing:** Routers using distance vector–based routing share routing table information with each other. This method of updating is called "routing by rumor." Each router receives updates from its direct neighbor. In Figure 10-6, Router B shares information with Routers A and C. Router C shares routing information with Routers B and D. In this case, the routing information is distance vector metrics (such as the number of hops). Each router increments the metrics as they are passed on (incrementing hop count, for example). Distance accumulation keeps track of the routing distance between any two points in the network, but the routers do not know the exact topology of an internetwork. RIPv2 is an example of a distance vector routing protocol.

Figure 10-6   *Distance Vector Routing Protocols*

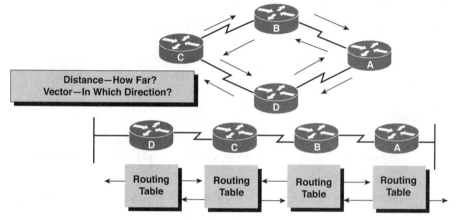

- **Link-state routing:** The link-state–based routing algorithm (also known as shortest path first [SPF]) maintains a database of topology information. Unlike the distance vector algorithm, link-state routing maintains full knowledge of distant routers and how they interconnect. Network information is shared in the form of link-state advertisements (LSA). See Figure 10-7. Link-state routing provides better scaling than distance vector routing for the following reasons:

  - Link-state sends only topology changes. Distance vector sends complete routing tables.

  - Link-state updates are sent only when the topology changes.

  - Link-state uses a two-tier hierarchy (backbone area and other areas), which limits the scope of route changes.

  - Link-state supports classless addressing and summarization.

  - Link-state routing converges fast and is robust against routing loops, but it requires a great deal of memory and strict network designs.

OSPF and Intermediate System–to–Intermediate System (IS-IS) are examples of link-state routing protocols.

Figure 10-7 *Link-State Routing*

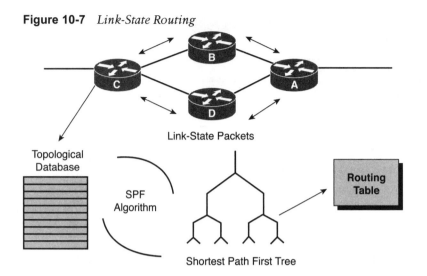

- **Advanced distance vector (hybrid):** Combines aspects of both distance vector and link-state protocols. Advanced distance vector routing uses distance vectors with more accurate metrics, but unlike distance vector routing protocols, it updates only when there is a topology change. Advanced distance vector routing provides faster convergence while limiting the use of resources such as bandwidth, memory, and processor overhead. Cisco Enhanced IGRP (EIGRP) is an example of a advanced distance vector protocol.

Administrative Distance

Several routing protocols can be used at the same time in the same network. When more than a single source of routing information exists for the same destination prefix, the source with the lowest administrative distance value is preferred.

Table 10-1 shows the default administrative distance of learned routes.

Table 10-1 *Administrative Distance*

Route Source	Default Distance Values
Connected interface	0
Static route	1
EIGRP	5
External BGP	20
Internal EIGRP	90
IGRP	100
IS-IS	115
OSPF	110

Route Source	Default Distance Values
RIPv2	120
EGP	140
ODR	160
External EIGRP	170
Internal BGP	200
Unknown	255

Section 11
Implementing OSPF

OSPF is an interior gateway protocol based on link state rather than distance vectors. OSPF uses Dijkstra's shortest path first (SPF) algorithm to determine the best path to each network. OSPF was developed in the 1980s as an answer to RIP's inability to scale well in large IP networks.

OSPF is an open-standard, classless protocol that converges quickly and uses costs as a metric. Cisco IOS automatically calculates cost based on the interface bandwidth.

When a router is configured for OSPF, the first thing the router does is create a topology table of the network. OSPF does this by sending Hellos out each OSPF interface, while listening for Hellos from other routers. If the routers share a common data link and agree on certain parameters set in their Hello packets, they become neighbors. If these parameters are different, they do not become neighbors and communication stops. OSPF routers can form adjacencies with certain neighbor routers. The routers that OSPF routers build adjacencies with are determined by the OSPF network type and area ID.

After adjacencies have been formed, each router sends link-state advertisements (LSA) to all adjacent routers. These LSAs describe the state of each of the router's links. Because of the varying types of link-state information, OSPF defines multiple LSA types.

Finally, routers receiving an LSA from neighbors record the LSA in a link-state database and flood a copy of the LSA to all adjacent neighbors. When all databases are complete, each router uses the SPF algorithm to calculate a loop-free, best-path topology and builds its routing table based on this topology.

OSPF Adjacencies

OSPF routers must recognize each other on the network before they can share routing tables. OSPF depends on the status of the link between two routers. OSPF-enabled routers recognize neighbors by using the Hello protocols. OSPF-enabled routers send hello packets out all OSPF-enabled interfaces to find neighbors on directly connected links. An OSPF neighbor relationship, or adjacency, is formed between two routers if they both have the same area ID, hello and dead interval timers, and authentication.

OSPF Terminology

When learning about OSPF, you might encounter different terminology for the OSPF tables. Following is list of common terminology used in OSPF:

■ OSPF neighbor table = Adjacency database

■ OSPF topology table = OSPF topology database (link-state database [LSDB])

■ Routing table = Forwarding database

Hello Packet

The Hello protocol ensures that communication between OSPF routers is bidirectional. It is the means by which neighbors are discovered and acts as keepalives between neighbors. It also establishes and maintains neighbor relationships and elects the designated router (DR) and the backup designated router (BDR) to represent the segment on broadcast multiaccess and nonbroadcast multiaccess (NBMA) networks.

Each Hello packets contains the following:

■ Router ID of the originating router

■ Area ID of the originating router interface

■ IP address and mask of the originating router interface

■ Authentication type and authentication password if required of the originating router interface

■ HelloInterval

■ DeadInterval

■ Interface router priority

■ Designated router (DR) and backup designated router (BDR)

■ Neighbor field

Hello packets are periodically sent out each interface using IP multicast address 224.0.0.5 (AllSPFRouters). The HelloInterval each router uses to send out the Hello protocol is based on the media type. The default HelloInterval of broadcast, point-to-point, and point-to-multipoint networks is 10 seconds. On NBMA networks, the default HelloInterval is 30 seconds. The dead timer intervals are four times the HelloInterval.

For OSPF-enabled routers to become neighbors, certain parameters in the Hello packet must match. These parameters are as follows:

■ IP subnet

■ Authentication

■ HelloInterval

■ DeadInterval

■ OSPF area ID

SPF Algorithm

The SPF algorithm places each router at the root of a tree and calculates the shortest path to each node. This is done using Dijkstra's algorithm, and it is based on the cumulative cost to reach a destination.

OSFP using path cost as a metric. A lower cost to a destination is preferred over a higher cost.

By default, cost is calculated on the interface bandwidth. For example, an Ethernet line with 1 Gbps will have a lower cost than a line with 10 Mbps.

The formula to calculate OSPF cost is as follows:

Cost = Reference bandwidth / Interface bandwidth (in bits per second)

The default reference bandwidth is 100,000,000 of 100 Mbps.

Router ID

For OSPF to initialize, it must be able to define a router ID for the entire OSPF process. A router can receive its router ID from several sources. First, it can be assigned manually through the **router-id** command. Second, it is the numerically highest IP address set on a loopback interface. The loopback interface is a logical interface that never goes down. If no loopback address is defined, an OSPF-enabled router will select the numerically highest IP address on any of its OSPF-configured interfaces as its router ID.

The router ID is chosen when OSPF is initialized. Initialization occurs when a router loads its OSPF configuration, whether at startup or when OSPF is first configured or reloaded. If other interfaces later come online that have a higher IP address, the OSPF router ID does not change until the OSPF process is restarted.

LSAs

After OSPF-enabled routers form full adjacencies, the next step is for routers to exchange link-state information. This is done through LSAs. LSAs report the state of routers' links. LSAs are also packets that OSPF uses to advertise changes in the condition of links to other OSPF routers in the form of a link-state update.

LSAs have the following characteristics:

- LSAs are reliable.
- LSAs are flooded throughout the OSPF area.
- LSAs have a sequence number and an age. The sequence number and age ensure that each router has the most current LSA.
- LSAs are refreshed every 30 minutes.

Eleven different and distinct link-state packet formats are used in OSPF, and each is used for a different purpose. Cisco only supports eight LSA types: Types 1–5 and 7–9. The ICND1 exam will only test you on two LSA types, Type 1 and Type 2.

Type 1 LSAs are Router LSAs and are generated by each router for each area to which it belongs. These LSAs describe the states of the router's links to the area and are flooded within a single area.

Type 2 LSAs are Network LSAs and are generated by the DR and BDR. They describe the set of routers attached to a particular network. They are flooded within a single area.

Configuring OSPF

The **router ospf** *process-id* command enables the OSPF process, and the **network** *address wildcard-mask* **area** *area-id* command assigns interfaces to a specific OSPF area. For example, the following configuration enables OSPF process 10 and activates OSPF on all interfaces that have interface addresses that match the address and wildcard mask combination for area 0. If the router has two interfaces configured with IP addresses 192.168.10.1/27 and 192.168.10.33/27, OSPF will be enabled on both interfaces. Notice that you must specify the wildcard mask instead of the subnet mask.

```
RouterA(config)# router ospf 10
RouterA(config-router)# network 192.168.10.0 0.0.0.255 area 0
```

The process ID is locally significant to the router and is used to differentiate between different OSPF processes running on the router; this value (unlike the autonomous system value in EIGRP) does not need to match between routers.

Verifying OSPF

The **show ip protocols** command verifies that OSPF is configured.

The **show ip route** command displays best, current, and used routes to a destination.

The **show ip ospf interface** command lists the area in which the router interface resides and the neighbors of the interface. Additionally, it lists the interface state, process ID, router ID, network type, cost, priority, DR and BDR, timer intervals, and authentication if it is configured. Here is an example of the **show ip ospf interface** command:

```
RouterB# show ip ospf interface ethernet 0
Ethernet0 is up, line protocol is up
   Internet Address 10.1.1.1/24, Area 0
   Process ID 1, Router ID 172.16.0.2, Network Type BROADCAST,
   Cost: 10
   Transmit Delay is 1 sec, State BDR, Priority 1
   Designated Router (ID) 172.16.0.1, Interface address 10.1.1.2
```

```
 Backup Designated router (ID) 172.16.0.2, Interface address
 10.1.1.1
 Timer intervals configured, Hello 10, Dead 40, Wait 40,
 Retransmit 5
    Hello due in 00:00:06
 Index 1/1, flood queue length 0
 Next 0x0(0)/0x0(0)
 Last flood scan length is 2, maximum is 2
 Last flood scan time is 0 msec, maximum is 4 msec
 Neighbor Count is 1, Adjacent neighbor count is 1
    Adjacent with neighbor 172.16.0.1  (Designated Router)
 Suppress hello for 0 neighbor(s)
```

To analyze the OSPF events, use the **debug ip ospf events** command.

Section 12
Introducing IPv6

Issues with IPv4

To extend the IPv4 addresses and to circumvent address shortage, several techniques were created:

- **Classless interdomain routing (CIDR):** Allowed IP addresses to be divided into smaller blocks

- **Variable-length subnet masks (VLSM):** Allowed more efficient use of IP addresses

- **Network Address Translation:** Allowed private nonroutable IPs as defined in RFC 1918 to be translated to public routable IP addresses

- **Dynamic Host Configuration Protocol:** Allowed a client to receive a dynamic temporary address instead of a permanent static one

Problems with some of these IPv4 work-arounds are

- NAT breaks the end-to-end model of IP. Underlying IP layers do not process the connection; only the endpoints do.

- NAT inhibits end-to-end network security. The IP header cannot be changed by some cryptographic functions due to integrity checks. Any translation of the IP header will break the integrity check.

- Some applications do not support NAT.

- Merging of private networks is difficult if the same IP address ranges are used.

IPv6 Features

IPv6 is an updated version of IP with the following features:

- Larger address space (128 bits)
- Simplified header
- Autoconfiguration
- Enhanced multicast support
- Extensions headers
- Flow labels
- Improved address allocation

- Security and mobility built in

- Strict aggregation

Although IPv6 has many advanced features, the primary reason for the move to IPv6 is because of the depletion of IPv4 addresses.

IPv6 Addresses

IPv6 addresses are 128 bits long and are represented in eight 16-bit hexadecimal segments. An example of an IPv6 address is as follows:

2001:0D02:0000:0000:0000:C003:0001:F00D

Figure 12-1 shows the IPv6 address structure.

Figure 12-1　*IPv6 Address Structure*

48 bits	16 bits	64 bits
Prefix (Provider-assigned)	Subnet	Interface ID

Two rules for reducing the size of written IPv6 address are as follows:

- **Rule 1:** The leading 0s in any fields do not have to be written. If any fields have fewer than four hexadecimal digits, it is assumed that the missing digits are leading 0s. For example,

  2001:0D02:0000:0000:0000:C003:0001:F00D

  can be written as

  2001:D02:0:0:0:C003:1:F00D

- **Rule 2:** Any single, consecutive fields of all 0s can be represented with a double colon (::). For example, 2001:D02:0:0:0:C003:1:F00D can be further reduced to

  2001:D02::C003:1:F00D

  The double colon can only be used once.

IPv6 Address Types

The three types of IPv6 addresses are as follows:

- **Unicast:** A global unicast address is an address that is globally unique and can be routed globally. Link-local unicast addresses are addresses that are confined to a single link.

- **Anycast:** An address that represents a group of devices that support a similar service. Each device will be assigned the same anycast address. Routers will deliver data to the nearest node that is using the common anycast address. Anycast addresses have a one-to-nearest mapping.

- **Multicast:** An address that identifies a set of devices called a multicast group. It has a one-to-many mapping and also replaces IPv4 broadcast addresses. IPv6 multicast addresses use the reserved address space FF00::0/8.

IPv6 Unicast Address

Five types of IPv6 unicast addresses are as follows:

- **Global:** Defined in RFC 4291. A unicast address that is globally unique and can be routed globally. Specifies 2000::/3 as global unicast address spaces that the IANA can allocate.

- **Link-local:** Address confined to a single physical link. Thus the address is not routable off the physical subnet. Link-local addresses typically begin with FE80. The next digits can be assigned manually. If the interface ID is not assigned manually, it may be based on the interface MAC address.

- **Loopback:** Used for testing. Defined as ::1.

- **Unspecified:** Defined as :: or all 0s and is used when the host does not know its own address.

- **Reserved:** For use by the IETF. These represent 1/256 of the total IPv6 address space and are as follows:

  - The lowest address within each subnet prefix is the subnet-router anycast address.

  - Within each subnet, the highest 128 interface identifier values are reserved as the subnet anycast address.

IPv6 Address Allocation

IPv6 addresses can be assigned in one of the following ways:

- Statically.

- Stateless autoconfiguration.

- DHCPv6.

- In static assignment, the network administrator assigns an IPv6 address to a host.

Hosts use stateless autoconfiguration by waiting for a router to advertise the local prefix. If the end system has a 48-bit MAC address, the host inverts the global/local bit (bit 7) and inserts 0xFFFE in the middle of the MAC address. This is called the EUI-64 address and it is joined to the prefix to form the IPv6 address.

DHCPv6 works that same way that DHCPv4 works.

Basic IPv6 Connectivity

IPv6 is not enabled by default on Cisco routers. The **ipv6 unicast-routing** global command enables IPv6 forwarding on the router. The **ipv6 address** *ipv6-address/ipv6-length* [*eui-64*] interface command configures an IPv6 address to a router interface.

The following commands enable IPv6 on a Cisco router and configure the gigabit interface 0/0 with the IPv6 address of 2001:0d02::20100/64:

```
RouterA# config term
RouterA(config)# ipv6 unicast-routing
RouterA(config)# interface g 0/0
RouterA(config-if)# ipv6 address 2001:0d02::2:0100/64
```

The **show ipv6 interface** *interface-id* privileged EXEC command displays the status of IPv6 on an interface.

Understanding IPv6

IPv6 not only increased the address bits from 32 to 128, but it also includes enhancements to

- The IPv6 header

- ICMP

- The neighbor discovery process

- Autoconfiguration

IPv6 Header Format

Figure 12-2 shows the IPv4 header.

Figure 12-2 *IPv4 Header*

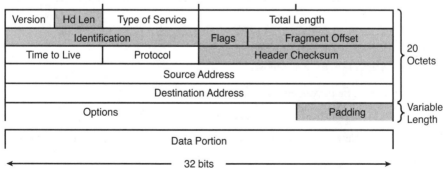

The IPv4 header contains 12 fields. Of these 12 header fields, six are removed in IPv6. The reason these header fields were removed are as follows:

- **Internet Header Length:** Removed because all IPv6 headers are a fixed 40-byte length, unlike IPv4.

- **Flags:** Used in fragmentation and IPv6 routers no longer process fragmentation.

- **Fragmentation Offset:** IPv6 routers no longer process fragmentation.

- **Header Checksum:** Removed because most data link layer technologies already perform checksum and error control.

- **Identification:** No longer needed based on IPv6 implementations.

- **Padding:** Because the Options field was changed, the Padding field is no longer needed.

Figure 12-3 shows the IPv6 header. The IPv6 header has 40 octets and fewer fields than the IPv4 header.

Figure 12-3 *IPv6 Header*

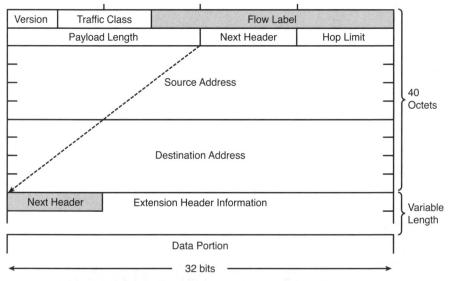

The eight fields in IPv6 are as follows:

- **Version:** 4-bit field; contains the number 6.

- **Traffic Class:** 8-bit field that is similar to the IPv4 ToS field.

- **Flow Label:** New 20-bit field used to mark individual traffic flows with unique values.

- **Payload Length:** Describes the length of the payload only.

- **Next Header:** Used to determine the type of information that follows the IPv6 header.

- **Hop Limit:** Specifies the maximum number of hops that an IP packet can traverse.

- **Source Address:** 128-bit field (16 octets) identifying the source of the packet.

- **Destination Address:** 128-bit field identifying the destination of the packet.

ICMPv6

Figure 12-4 displays the ICMPv6 packet format.

Figure 12-4   *ICMPv6 Packet*

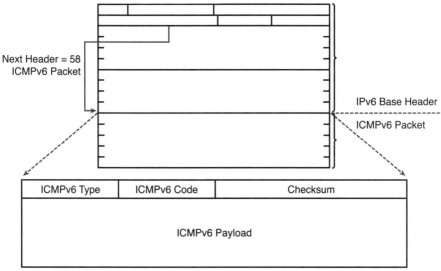

ICMPv6 packets are identified as 58 in the Next Header field. ICMPv6 is like ICMPv4. The functions of ICMPv6 are

- **Diagnostic Tests:** Like ICMPv4, ICMPv6 provides diagnostic testing using echo and echo reply.

- **Router Discovery:** Router solicitation and router advertisements.

- **Neighbor Discovery:** Neighbor solicitation and neighbor advertisements.

ICMPv6 has two error message types:

- **Error Messages:** Examples include Destination Unreachable, Packet Too Big, or Time Exceeded

- **Informational Messages:** Echo Request and Echo Reply

Neighbor Discovery

Neighbor discovery in IPv6 is used for router and neighbor solicitation and advertisements, and for redirection of nodes to the best gateway. It performs the same functions as ARP in IPv4. These functions include

- Determines the data link layer address of a neighbor
- Finds neighbor routers on a data link
- Queries for duplicate addresses

Neighbor discovery is performed using ICMPv6 with a multicast address.

Stateless Autoconfiguration

Stateless autoconfiguration is a feature in IPv6 that uses neighbor discovery to find routers, and it will also dynamically create an IPv6 address based on a prefix found in the router advertisement and EUI-64 standard. When stateless autoconfiguration is enabled on the interface, additional addresses will also be assigned to the interface, one being a link-local unicast address.

IPv6-enabled routers periodically send router advertisements to the all-nodes multicast address. These advertisements include the router prefix, which enables autoconfiguration of hosts.

Router advertisements are typically sent immediately following a router solicitation. Router solicitations are sent by hosts at boot time, to ask routers to send a router advertisement on the local link so that the host can receive the autoconfiguration information.

Stateless autoconfiguration is enabled on a router interface using the **ipv6 address autoconfig** interface command:

```
Router(config)# interface g 0/0
Router(config-if)# ipv6 address autoconfig
```

Configuring IPv6 Routing

Because IPv6 uses a 128-bit address, dynamic routing protocols need to be modified to support IPv6. The following routing protocols support IPv6:

- RIPng
- OSPFv3
- EIGRP for IPv6
- Intermediate System–to–Intermediate System (IS-IS) for IPv6
- Multiprotocol Border Gateway Protocol (MP-BGP)

RIPng

RIPng is the IPv6 version of Routing Information Protocol (RIP), a distance vector protocol. RIPng is defined in RFC 2080 and is based on RIPv2. Thus RIPng uses hop count as its metric and has a maximum hop count of 15. However, some changes to RIPng are as follows:

- Uses IPv6 for transport.
- Uses multicast group FF02::09 to advertise routes every 30 seconds.
- Updates are sent on User Datagram Protocol (UDP) port 521.

Static Routing

Static routing with IPv6 is configured the same way as with IPv4. The **ipv6 route** *ipv6_network/ipv6_mask outgoing_interface/ipv6_next_hop* global command adds static routes to a router.

The following configures the route to network 2001:DB8:A01::/48 out interface G0/0:

```
Router(config)# ipv6 route 2001:DB8:A01::/48 g0/0
```

The following configures the default route out interface G0/0:

```
Router(config)# ipv6 route ::/0 g0/0
```

The **show ipv6 route** command displays the IPv6 routing table.

OSPFv3

OSPFv3 is based on the current version of OSPF for IPv4, which is version 2. Like version 2, OSPFv3 sends Hellos to neighbors and exchanges LSAs and database descriptors (DBD). However, OSPFv3 runs directly over IPv6 and advertises using multicast groups FF02::5 and FF02::06, but uses its link-local address as the source address of its advertisements.

FF02::5 is the address listened to by "all OSPF routers," and FF02::06 is the address listened to by the OSPF DRs and BDR.

OSPFv3 does not include authentication because authentication in IPv6 is handled through IPsec.

The following example configures OSPFv3 using process id 10 with a router ID of 1.1.1.1, and configures interface g0/0 and g0/1 in area 0:

```
Router(config)# ipv6 router ospf 10
Router(config-rtr)# router-id 1.1.1.1
Router(config-rtf)# interface g0/0
Router(config-if)# ipv6 ospf 1 area 0
Router(config-if)# interface g0/1
Router(config-if)# ipv6 ospf 1 area 0
```

The **show ipv6 route ospf** EXEC command displays the IPv6 OSPFv3 entries in the routing table.

The **show ipv6 ospf neighbor** EXEC command shows OSPF neighbors that the router is exchanging routing tables with.

The **show ipv6 ospf** EXEC command shows the OSPFv3 setting such as process ID, router ID, and number of areas configured.

PART II   ICND2

Section 1
VLANs and Trunk Links

ICND1 introduced the basics of VLANs and inter-VLAN routing through a router on a stick. As previously written, switches operate on Layer 2 of the OSI model and routers operate on Layer 3. Switches increase the number of collision domains, which in turn decreases the amount of collisions in a network; routers increase the number of broadcast domains, while reducing their size.

Prior to the introduction of VLANs, network designers segmented large Layer 2 networks with routers. A router would be installed between the two networks. All data communication between the two would pass through the router, and the broadcast domain was limited to the physical location of the network.

VLANs introduced a way to logically segment a broadcast domain within a switch. Additionally, VLANs are not bound to a physical location. For example, with VLANs, network traffic can be segmented based on department, division, function, or type of traffic, without regard to the physical location of end users. Any switch port can belong to a VLAN, and a unicast, broadcast, or some multicast packets are forwarded or flooded to all end stations in the assigned VLAN. This segmentation not only reduces the size of broadcast domains but also increases the security on the network.

By default, each interface on a switch can belong to only one data VLAN. Trunks are point-to-point links between one or more switch interfaces and another networking device, such as another switch or router; trunks carry traffic of multiple VLANs over a single link.

This section provides an overview of VLANs and Dynamic Trunking Protocol (DTP).

Question 1

What are VLANs?

Question 2

Implementing VLANs addresses what three items?

Question 3

What Cisco IOS commands would configure a Catalyst 2960s switch with VLAN number 10 with the name "Accounting"?

Answer 1

VLANs are broadcast domains in a Layer 2 network.

A VLAN is an independent LAN network. Each broadcast domain is like a distinct virtual bridge within the switch. Each virtual bridge created in a switch defines a broadcast domain. By default, traffic from one VLAN cannot pass to another VLAN. Each user in a VLAN is also in the same IP subnet. Each switch port can belong to only one data VLAN. The exception to this is if the port is a trunk port.

NOTE　For the exam, remember:
- VLAN = Broadcast domain
- VLAN = Logical network (subnet)

Answer 2

The three items that VLAN implementation addresses are as follows:

- Segmentation
- Security
- Network flexibility

Answer 3

To configure a VLAN on a Catalyst 2960 switch, first ensure that the switch is in VTP server or transparent mode. When the switch is in one of these modes, the **vlan** *vlan-id* global configuration command adds a VLAN. The *vlan-id* can be a number from 2 to 1001 for normal-range VLANs, as follows:

```
Switch(config)# vlan 10
Switch(config-vlan)# name Accounting
```

NOTE　When you create a VLAN, the prompt changes to Switch(config-vlan). This is config-vlan mode.

Question 4

As a network administrator, you want to add interfaces 1 through 12 to VLAN 30 on your Catalyst 2960s switch. How do you statically assign these interfaces to the switch?

Question 5

As a network administrator, you added a new VLAN (VLAN 10) on a switch and called it "Accounting." However, you later find that VLAN 10 is to be assigned to Sales. How do you modify the VLAN name?

Question 6

How do you delete a VLAN from a Catalyst switch?

Answer 4

You assign one interface or range of interfaces at a time to a VLAN. To assign a range of interfaces to a VLAN, first enter the interface range you want to configure. Then define the interfaces as access ports with the **switchport mode access** command. To finish, you will need to assign the range of ports to the desired VLAN with the **switchport access vlan** *vlan-id* interface command. When using the **interface range** command, take notice of the prompt change to config-if-range.

To configure a range of interfaces to a VLAN, enter the **range** command. The following commands assign ports 1–12 to VLAN 30:

```
Cat2960(config)# interface range fastethernet 0/1 - 12
Cat2960(config-if-range)# switchport mode access
Cat2960(config-if-range)# switchport access vlan 30
```

Answer 5

To modify a VLAN name, you need to enter config-vlan mode for the VLAN you want to modify and rename the VLAN, as follows:

```
Switch(config)# vlan 10
Switch(config-vlan)# name Sales
Switch(config-vlan)# exit
```

Answer 6

Enter the **no vlan** *vlan-id* global command for the VLAN you want to delete, as follows:

```
Switch(config)# no vlan 10
```

Question 7

What IOS commands allow you to verify the VLANs on a Catalyst switch and the interfaces assigned to each VLAN?

Question 8

How do you carry multiple VLANs across a single link?

Answer 7

The **show vlan name** *vlan-name* privileged EXEC command and the **show vlan brief** privileged command allow you to verify the VLANs on a Catalyst switch and the interfaces assigned to each VLAN.

You can use two commands to verify the VLANs on a switch: the more detailed **show vlan** {name *vlan-name* | id *id*} command or the **show vlan brief** command, as follows:

```
Switch# show vlan brief
VLAN Name                          Status    Ports
---- -------------------------- --------- ------------------------------
1    default                    active    Gi0/2
10   InternetAccess             active
20   Operations                 active    Fa0/1, Fa0/2,
30   Administration             active    Fa0/6, Fa0/7,
                                           Fa0/8, Fa0/9
40   Engineering                active    Fa0/3, Fa0/4,
                                           Fa0/5, Fa0/10, Fa0/11, Fa0/12,
                                           Fa0/13,Fa0/14, Fa0/15, Fa0/16,
                                           Fa0/17, Fa0/18, Fa0/19,Fa0/20
60   Public                     active    Fa0/21, Fa0/22, Fa0/23, Fa0/24
!text-omitted!
```

Answer 8

You carry multiple VLANs across a single link by using trunk links.

Trunk links allow the switch to carry multiple VLANs across a single link.

By default, each port on a switch can belong to only one data VLAN. For devices that are in a VLAN (that spans multiple switches) to talk to other devices in the same VLAN, you must use trunking or have a dedicated port for each VLAN.

Trunk links encapsulate frames using a Layer 2 protocol. This encapsulation contains information for a switch to distinguish traffic from different VLANs and to deliver frames to the proper VLANs. The Catalyst 2960 Series switches support 802.1Q as their trunking protocol.

Question 9

What tagging mechanism allows multiple VLANs to be carried across a single link?

Question 10

Define the 802.1Q native VLAN.

Question 11

How do you set an interface for trunking on a Catalyst series switch?

Answer 9

802.1Q tagging allows multiple VLANs to be carried across a single link.

IEEE 802.1Q tagging provides an industry-standard method of identifying frames that belong to a particular VLAN. 802.1Q does this by using an internal tag that modifies the existing Ethernet frame with the VLAN identification. 802.1Q uses an internal tagging mechanism that inserts a 4-byte tag field in the original Ethernet frame between the Source Address and Type or Length fields.

Answer 10

The native VLAN is VLAN1 by default. 802.1Q does not tag the native VLAN across trunk links.

Answer 11

To configure an interface for trunking, use the **switchport mode trunk** interface command.

To enable an interface for trunking on a Catalyst 2960 switch, use the **switchport mode [dynamic {auto | desirable} | trunk]** interface command. The following examples configure one interface for trunking and a second interface to trunk only if the neighboring device is set to *trunk, desirable,* or *auto*:

```
Cat2960(config)# interface g0/1
Cat2960(config-if)# switchport mode trunk
Cat2960(config-if)# interface g0/2
Cat2960(config-if)# switchport mode dynamic desirable
```

Question 12

How do you display the trunked interfaces on a Catalyst series switch?

Question 13

Define Dynamic Trunking Protocol (DTP).

Answer 12

The **show interfaces trunk** privileged EXEC command shows the interfaces that are trunking on a switch and the trunk configuration, as follows:

```
Cat2960# show interfaces trunk
Port        Mode            Encapsulation   Status          Native vlan
Gi0/1       on              802.1q          trunking        1
Port        Vlans allowed on trunk
Gi0/1       1-4094
Port        Vlans allowed and active in management domain
Gi0/1       1-3,5,10,20,30,40,50,60
Port        Vlans in spanning tree forwarding state and not pruned
Gi0/1       1-3,5,40
```

Answer 13

Dynamic Trunking Protocol (DTP) is a Cisco-proprietary, point-to-point Layer 2 protocol that sets up and manages trunk link formation.

Question 14

What are the five DTP switch port interface modes?

Question 15

How do you determine the default DTP mode of a Catalyst switch?

Answer 14

The five DTP switch port interface modes supported are as follows:

- **switchport mode access:** Makes the interface a nontrunking access port regardless of any DTP request sent from the neighboring switch.

- **switchport mode dynamic auto:** Allows the interface to convert to a trunk link if the connecting neighbor interface is set to *trunk* or *desirable*.

- **switchport mode dynamic desirable:** Makes the interface attempt to convert the link to a trunk link. The link becomes a trunk if the neighbor interface is set to *trunk*, *desirable*, or *auto*.

- **switchport mode trunk:** Configures the port to permanent trunk mode and negotiates with the connected device if the other side can convert the link to trunk mode.

- **switchport nonegotiate:** Prevents the interface from generating DTP frames. The neighboring interface must be manually configured as a trunk link.

Answer 15

The default DTP mode is dependent on the Cisco IOS Software version and the platform. To determine the DTP mode, issue the **show dtp interface** command.

Question 16

By default, VLANs 1–4094 are allowed to propagate on all trunk links. How do you limit a trunk to allow only VLANs 10–50 on a trunk link?

Answer 16

To limit the VLANs on a trunk link, enter the **switchport trunk allowed vlan** {**add** | **all** | **except** | **remove**} *vlan-list* interface command. To allow only VLANs 1–50 on a trunk link, you would enter the following:

```
Switch(config-if)# switchport trunk allowed vlan 1-50
```

NOTE To verify the VLANs allowed on the trunk link, use the **show interfaces** *interface-id* **switchport** privileged EXEC command.

Section 2
Building Redundant Switched Topologies

The network has become the critical foundation for all of today's communications. The Internet and cloud technologies all require the network to have little to no downtime. As such, network redundancy is critical.

This increased demand on switched networks has made it a priority to design redundant and scalable switched and routed networks. Redundant switched networks have multiple uplinks to each other to help eliminate a single source of failure. However, because of the nature of switching, redundant links in a switched environment can cause broadcast storms through the redundant links. To prevent this, the Spanning Tree Protocol (STP) was created to maintain a dynamic, loop-free, switched environment. Spanning Tree did this by assigning one switch as the root. Any switch that is not the root switch and has redundant links would place one of the links in the forwarding state and the redundant link in the blocking state.

Although Spanning Tree worked fine for many years, it had some drawbacks. For example, if a link failed, it would take Spanning Tree 50 seconds to activate the redundant link. In today's fast computing world, 50 seconds is an eternity. Because of Spanning Tree's limitations, Cisco introduced some proprietary features, such as PortFast and UplinkFast, to help shorten the spanning-tree time to transition from blocking to forwarding.

Since then, the IEEE has released an update to Spanning Tree called the Rapid Spanning Tree Protocol (RSTP). RSTP (802.1w) is standards based. It drastically reduces the time for a port to move to the forwarding state and helps make Spanning Tree more scalable.

This section covers the topics on the exam for Spanning Tree and RSTP and other high-available technologies such as EtherChannel and gateway redundancy using HSRP and GLBP.

Question 1

What is the Spanning Tree Protocol (STP)?

Question 2

What steps does STP use to create a loop-free Layer 2 network?

Question 3

What two key concepts does the STP calculation use to create a loop-free topology?

Answer 1

STP, or 802.1D, is a Layer 2 loop-prevention, bridge-to-bridge protocol. Its main purpose is to dynamically maintain a loop-free Layer 2 network. STP does this by sending out bridge protocol data units (BPDU), discovering any loops in the topology and blocking one or more redundant links.

Answer 2

STP maintains a loop-free network by doing the following:

- Electing a root bridge
- Electing a root port on each nonroot bridge
- Electing designated ports on each segment
- Blocking any redundant port that is not a root port or a designated port

Answer 3

The two key concepts that the STP calculation uses to create a loop-free topology are as follows:

- Bridge ID (BID)
- Path cost

Question 4

In Spanning Tree, what is the bridge ID (BID)?

Question 5

What is the default bridge priority in a BID for all Cisco switches?

Question 6

In Spanning Tree, what is path cost?

Answer 4

A BID is an 8-byte field that is comprised of a 2-byte bridge priority and the bridge's 6-byte MAC address.

Answer 5

32,768 is the default bridge priority.

Answer 6

Path cost is a calculation based on the link's bandwidth. It is a value assigned to each port that is based on the port's speed.

Question 7

Determine the Spanning Tree path cost for each of the following:

- 10 Mbps
- 100 Mbps
- 1 Gbps
- 10 Gbps

Question 8

When calculating a loop-free environment, Spanning Tree uses a four-step decision sequence to determine which switch will be the root bridge and which ports will be in the forwarding or blocking state. What are these four steps?

Question 9

How do switches pass Spanning Tree information between them?

Answer 7

The path costs are as follows:

- 10 Mbps: 100
- 100 Mbps: 19
- 1 Gbps: 4
- 10 Gbps: 2

Answer 8

The four-step decision sequence that Spanning Tree uses to determine the root bridge and which ports will be in the forwarding or blocking state is as follows:

Step 1.   Elect a root bridge. The root bridge is the switch with the lowest BID.

Step 2.   Elect a root port for each nonroot switch, based on the lowest root path cost.

Step 3.   Elect a designated port for each segment based on the lowest root path cost.

Step 4.   Root ports and designated ports transition to the forwarding state; all other ports stay in the blocking state.

Answer 9

Switches pass STP information using special frames called bridge protocol data units (BPDU).

Every time a switch receives a BPDU, it compares it with all received BPDUs as well as with the BPDU that would be sent on the port. The switch checks the BPDU against the four-step Spanning Tree root bridge sequence to see whether it has a lower value than the existing BPDU saved for that interface.

Question 10

How often do switches send BPDUs out active ports in 802.1D Spanning Tree?

Question 11

What are the four STP port roles?

Question 12

What is the STP root port?

Answer 10

Switches send BPDUs out active ports every two seconds by default.

NOTE   In 802.1D, only the root bridge generates BPDUs; all other switches forward them. All interfaces on a switch listen for BPDUs in case a topology change occurs.

Answer 11

The four STP port roles are

- Root port
- Designated port
- Nondesignated port
- Disabled port

Answer 12

The root port exists on switches that are not the root bridge/switch and is the port that has the lowest cost to the root bridge. Only one root port is allowed per bridge.

NOTE   In the case where there are multiple ports that have the same cost to a root bridge, port priority and port number will be considered in succession as the tie-breakers.

Question 13

What is the STP designated port?

Question 14

What is the STP nondesignated port?

Question 15

In STP, how is a root bridge elected?

Answer 13

The designated port exists on root and nonroot bridges. For root bridges, all ports are designated ports. For nonroot bridges, the designated port is the switch port that receives and forwards frames to the root bridge as needed. Only one designated port is allowed per segment.

Answer 14

Nondesignated ports are switch ports that are blocking data frames and will not populate the MAC address table when a frame is received.

Answer 15

The switch with the lowest BID is elected the root bridge.

All ports on the root bridge are placed in the forwarding state and are called designated ports.

The BID is 8 bytes and is comprised of two fields: the default priority of 32,768 (2 bytes) and a MAC address (6 bytes). By default, all Cisco switches use the default priority, and the switch with the lowest MAC address is elected the root bridge, unless the default priority is changed to a lower value.

NOTE For the exam, remember that lower always wins in Spanning Tree.

Question 16

After bridges elect a root bridge, what is the next step in the spanning-tree process?

Question 17

How do nonroot bridges decide which port they will elect as a root port?

Question 18

What is the difference between path cost and root path cost?

Answer 16

The next step is to elect root ports. After electing the root bridge, switches elect root ports. A root port is the port on nonroot bridges that has the lowest cost to the root bridge. If two ports have an equal path cost to the root, the switch looks at the BID values as the tiebreaker. If the BID values in the BPDUs are the same, the port ID is used as the tiebreaker.

Every nonroot bridge must select one root port.

Answer 17

Nonroot bridges use root path cost to determine which port will be the root port. Root path cost is the cumulative cost of all links to the root bridge. The port with the lowest root path cost is elected the bridge's root port and is placed in the forwarding state. If two ports have an equal path cost to the root, the switch looks at the BID values as the tiebreaker. The port with the lower BID will become the root port. If the BID values in the BPDUs are the same, the port ID is used as the tiebreaker.

Answer 18

Path cost is the value assigned to each port. It is added to the BPDUs received on that port to calculate the root path cost.

When a switch starts, all ports are in the blocking state. This is to prevent any loops in the network. If there is a better path to the root bridge, the port remains in the blocking state. Ports in the blocking state cannot send or receive traffic, but they can receive BPDUs.

Root path cost is defined as the cumulative cost to the root bridge. In a BPDU, this is the value transmitted in the cost field. In a bridge, this value is calculated by adding the receiving port's path cost to the value contained in the BPDU.

Question 19

If a nonroot bridge has two redundant ports with the same root path cost, how does the bridge choose which port will be the root port?

Question 20

After the root bridge and root ports are selected, the last step in the Spanning Tree process is to elect designated ports. How do bridges elect designated ports?

Question 21

If a bridge is faced with a tie in electing designated ports, how does it decide which port will be the designated port?

Answer 19

The port with the lowest port ID becomes the root port.

If a nonroot bridge has redundant ports with the same root path cost, the deciding factor is the port that receives the lowest BID from the upstream switch. If there are two links connected to the same switch, the lowest port ID is selected as the root port.

Answer 20

Bridges elect designated ports by choosing the lowest value based on the cumulative root path cost to the root bridge.

In Spanning Tree, each segment in a bridged network has one designated port. This port is a single port on every switched segment that both sends and receives traffic to and from that segment. All other ports are placed in a blocking state. This ensures that only one port on any segment can send and receive traffic to and from the root bridge, ensuring a loop-free topology. The bridge that contains the designated port for a segment is called the designated bridge for that segment. Designated ports are chosen based on the cumulative root path cost to the root bridge.

NOTE   Every active port on the root bridge becomes a designated port.

Answer 21

In the event of a tie, STP uses the four-step decision process. It first looks for the BPDU with the lowest BID; this is always the root bridge. If the switch is not the root bridge, it moves to the next step: the BPDU with the lowest path cost to the root bridge. If both paths are equal, STP looks for the BPDU with the lowest sender BID. If these are equal, STP uses the link with the lowest port ID as the final tie-breaker.

Question 22

What are the five Spanning Tree port states?

Question 23

What is the STP blocking state?

Question 24

What is the STP listening state?

Answer 22

The five Spanning Tree port states are as follows:

- Blocking
- Listening
- Learning
- Forwarding
- Disabled

Answer 23

When a switch starts, all ports are in the blocking state. This is to prevent any loops in the network. If a better path to the root bridge exists, the port remains in the blocking state. Ports in the blocking state cannot send or receive traffic; however, they can receive BPDUs.

Answer 24

Ports transition from a blocking state to a listening state. In this state, no user data is passed. The port sends and receives BPDUs. After listening for 15 seconds (if the bridge does not find a better path), the port moves to the next state, a learning state.

Question 25

What is the STP learning state?

Question 26

What is the STP forwarding state?

Question 27

Define the following STP terms:

- Forward delay timer
- Hello time
- Max age timer

Answer 25

In the STP learning state, no user data is passed but the switch still sends and receives BPDUs. The switch builds its bridging table. The default time in the learning state is 15 seconds.

Answer 26

After the default time in the learning state is up, the port moves to the forwarding state. In the forwarding state, the port sends and receives data, collects MAC addresses in its address table, and sends and receives BPDUs.

Answer 27

These STP terms are defined as follows:

- **Forward delay timer:** The time it takes a port to move from listening to learning or from learning to forwarding. The default time is 15 seconds. For a port to transition from listening to forwarding, it will go through two forward delay timers: 15 seconds to transition to listening and 15 seconds to transition to learning.

- **Hello time:** The time interval between the sending of BPDUs. The default time is 2 seconds.

- **Max age timer:** How long a bridge stores a BPDU before discarding it. The default time is 20 seconds (10 missed hello intervals).

Question 28

What is the default amount of time a port takes to transition from blocking to forwarding in STP?

Question 29

What are four types of spanning-tree implementations?

Question 30

What are the RSTP port states?

Answer 28

The default time is 50 seconds.

It takes 20 seconds for the max age to expire, 15 seconds for listening, and 15 seconds for learning.

Answer 29

Four types of spanning-tree implementations are

- **802.1D:** The legacy standard for bridging and STP.
- **PVST+:** A Cisco enhancement that provides a separate 802.1D spanning-tree instance for each VLAN.
- **802.1w (RSTP):** Provides faster convergence of 802.1D by adding roles to ports and enhancing BPDU exchanges.
- **Rapid PVST+:** A Cisco enhancement that provides a separate instance of 802.1w per VLAN.

Answer 30

The RSTP port states are as follows:

- Discarding
- Learning
- Forwarding

Discarding is the equivalent to disabled, blocking, and listening STP port states.

Question 31

What are the five different port roles in RSTP?

Question 32

How does RSTP handle BPDUs?

Question 33

In RSTP, when does a bridge consider it has lost connectivity to a direct neighbor?

Answer 31

The five different port roles in RSTP are as follows:

- **Root port:** The best path to the root (the same as in STP).
- **Designated port:** The port on the network that has the best root path cost to a root (the same as in STP).
- **Alternate port:** A port that has an alternative path to the root, different than the path the root port takes.
- **Backup port:** A port that provides a redundant, but less desirable, connection to a segment where another switch port already connects.
- **Disabled port:** A port with no role in Spanning Tree.

Answer 32

In 802.1D (Spanning Tree), BPDUs originate from the root bridge and are relayed by all switches. In RSTP (802.1w), a bridge sends a BPDU every two seconds by default, even if it does not receive any from the root bridge.

Answer 33

In RSTP, a bridge considers that it has lost connectivity to a directly connected neighbor if it misses three BPDUs in a row (six seconds). In RSTP, BPDUs act as keepalive mechanisms between bridges. If a bridge does not receive a BPDU from a neighbor, the switch is certain that the connection to the neighbor has failed.

NOTE Backup and alternate ports can transition to forwarding when no BPDUs are received from a neighbor switch.

Question 34

In RSTP, what is an edge port?

Question 35

How are link types derived in RSTP?

Question 36

What is the default spanning-tree configuration for Cisco Catalyst switches?

Answer 34

An edge port is a port that is directly connected to end stations.

Because directly connected end stations cannot create bridging loops in the network, an edge port directly transitions to the forwarding state, skipping the listening and learning states.

Edge ports are configured using the **spanning-tree portfast** interface command.

Answer 35

In RSTP, a link can only rapidly transition to a forwarding state on edge ports and on point-to-point links. A point-to-point link is a link that directly connects two switches. In RSTP, the link type is automatically derived from the duplex mode of a port. Full-duplex is assumed to be point-to-point, and a half-duplex link is considered a shared point.

Answer 36

The default spanning-tree configuration for Cisco Catalyst switches is

- PVST+
- Spanning-tree enabled on all ports

Question 37

What are Per-VLAN Spanning Tree (PVST) and PVST+?

Question 38

PVST+ requires that a separate instance of Spanning Tree run in each VLAN. As such, the Bridge ID (BID) must carry VLAN ID (VID) information. How is this accomplished?

Question 39

What three types of STP are supported on Cisco switches?

Answer 37

In PVST, a different 802.1D spanning-tree instance exists for each VLAN on a switch. So, each VLAN has its own root bridge, root port, designated port, and nondesignated port. PVST is Cisco proprietary.

PVST+ is based on PVST but also includes Cisco-proprietary features such as UplinkFast, BackboneFast, BPDU Guard, BPDU Filter, Root Guard, and Loop Guard.

Answer 38

To carry the VID for each VLAN, the 2-byte Bridge Priority field in the BPDU is split: 4 bits are used for the bridge priority and 12 bits are used for the Extended System ID. The VID is carried in the Extended System ID.

Answer 39

The three types of STP supported on Cisco switches are as follows:

- **PVST+:** PVST+ is Cisco proprietary. It is based on the 802.1D standard that has one 802.1D STP instance per VLAN.

- **PVRST+:** PVRST+ (Per-VLAN Rapid Spanning Tree Plus) is a Cisco-proprietary enhancement to RSTP that provides a separate 802.1w spanning-tree instance for every VLAN.

- **MSTP:** Defined in 802.1s and maps one or more VLANs to a single STP instance. Up to 16 instances are allowed.

Question 40

Why would you want to change the default BID on a switch and how do you do so?

Question 41

What commands can you use to verify and troubleshoot the STP topology in your network?

Question 42

What are the two types of failures that occur in STP?

Answer 40

In Spanning Tree, the bridge with the lowest bridge ID (BID) is elected as the root port. The BID is 8 bytes and is comprised of two fields: the default priority of 32,768 (2 bytes) and a MAC address (6 bytes). Thus, the switch with the lowest MAC address becomes the root bridge. Typically, this means that the oldest switch has the lowest bridge ID, and this is not ideal.

Best practice is to manually configure your root bridge. This is done by lowering the default priority on a switch to ensure that it will always have the lowest priority on the network. This is done by using the **spanning-tree vlan** *vlan-number* **root primary** global command.

Answer 41

Although many commands are available to troubleshoot Spanning Tree, the ones required to know for the ICND2 exam are as follows:

- **show spanning-tree:** Displays the root ID, bridge ID, priority, and timers for all VLANs in STP

- **show spanning-tree vlan** *vlan-id*: Displays STP information for a specific VLAN

- **debug spanning-tree all:** Verifies receipt of BPDUs and troubleshoots other spanning-tree errors

Answer 42

The two possible types of STP failure are as follows:

- STP erroneously decides to block ports that should be forwarding.
- STP moves blocked ports into the forwarding state.

Question 43

What happens if STP erroneously moves blocked redundant ports to a forwarding state?

Question 44

What is PortFast?

Question 45

What is BPDU Guard?

Answer 43

A bridging loop will occur and any flooded frames passing through the switch will continue to be forwarded through the switches indefinitely. If this occurs, the load on all links in the LAN increases and the CPU load of the switch increases drastically, often causing the switch to become unreachable.

Answer 44

PortFast is a Cisco-proprietary technology that enables a port to transition immediately from the blocking state to the forwarding state, bypassing the typical STP listening and learning states.

Because PortFast transitions immediately to the forwarding state, it should be enabled only on ports that are connected to a single workstation or server. PortFast should not be implemented on interfaces that are trunking between switches.

Answer 45

BPDU Guard is a Cisco technology that is used in combination with PortFast. If a BPDU is received on a PortFast port configured with BPDU Guard, the port in the error-disabled state to prevent a Layer 2 loop.

Question 46

How do you configure PortFast on an access port on a Cisco switch?

Question 47

How do you enable BPDU Guard on a port on a Cisco switch?

Question 48

What is EtherChannel?

Answer 46

PortFast is configured using the **spanning-tree portfast** interface command. The following commands configure PortFast for interface G0/1:

```
Switch(config)# interface G0/1
Switch(config-if)# spanning-tree portfast
```

NOTE   PortFast can be configured globally on all nontrunking interfaces by using the **spanning-tree portfast default** global command.

Answer 47

BPDU Guard is configured using the **spanning-tree bpduguard enable** interface command.

BPDU Guard can be enabled globally on all PortFast-enabled ports by using the **spanning-tree portfast bpduguard default** global command.

Answer 48

EtherChannel is a feature that allows you to combine several physical links (up to eight) into one logical connection for increased bandwidth. Data between the links is load shared, and Spanning Tree sees the logical link as one link; thus all physical ports are forwarding. Fast Ethernet, Gigabit Ethernet, and 10 Gigabit Ethernet links can be configured for EtherChannel. For example, two 1-Gigabit links can be configured for EtherChannel, providing, in theory, 2 Gbps of available bandwidth.

Question 49

What are five advantages of EtherChannel?

Question 50

What is PAgP?

Question 51

When PAgP is enabled, how often are PAgP packets sent out EtherChannel interfaces?

Answer 49

Five advantages of using EtherChannel technology are as follows:

- Logical aggregation of links between switches.
- The logical aggregation of links provides higher bandwidth than with single links alone.
- Load sharing across EtherChannel-configured links.
- EtherChannel-configured interfaces are viewed as one logical port to STP; thus all ports are forwarding (unless there are multiple EtherChannels) without causing a Layer 2 loop.
- Redundancy. Because all EtherChannel-configured links are seen as one logical port, the failure of a single physical port in an EtherChannel will not cause a change in STP topology.

Answer 50

Port Aggregation Group Protocol (PAgP) is a Cisco-proprietary protocol that helps with the automatic creation of EtherChannel links.

PAgP works by sending packets between EtherChannel-capable ports to negotiate the forming of the EtherChannel. PAgP also manages the EtherChannel by checking for configuration consistency and manages link additions and failures between two switches.

Answer 51

PAgP packets are sent every 30 seconds.

Question 52

What is LACP?

Question 53

What are the three PAgP modes?

Question 54

What are the three LACP modes?

Answer 52

Link Aggregation Control Protocol (LACP) is an IEEE 802.3ad standard that functions similarly to the Cisco PAgP in enabling the automatic creation of EtherChannel links.

NOTE Because LACP is an IEEE standard, it can be used to configure EtherChannels in multivendor environments.

Answer 53

The three PAgP modes are

- **On:** Forces the interface to be an EtherChannel without PAgP.

- **Desirable:** Places an interface in an active negotiation state, asking whether the other side can or will participate in the EtherChannel. Will form an EtherChannel if the other end of the link is configured as Desirable or Auto.

- **Auto:** Places an interface in a passive negotiation state, waiting for the other end of the link to form the EtherChannel. Will form an EtherChannel only if the other end of the link is configured as Desirable.

Answer 54

The three LACP modes are

- **On:** Forces the interface to participate in an EtherChannel without LACP.

- **Active:** Places a port in an active negotiation state. Will form an EtherChannel if the other end of the link is configured as either Active or Passive.

- **Passive:** Places a port in a passive negotiation state. Will form an EtherChannel if the other end of the link is configured as Active.

Question 55

To successfully create an EtherChannel, what configuration must be the same between participating ports?

Question 56

How many interfaces can be added to an EtherChannel?

Question 57

How do you configure EtherChannel on Cisco switches?

Answer 55

All interfaces within an EtherChannel must have the same following configuration:

- Speed and duplex
- Interface mode (access or trunk)
- VLAN match
- Range of VLANs
- Native VLAN

Answer 56

EtherChannel can support up to eight interfaces.

NOTE   Because of the nature of the EtherChannel algorithm, it is best practice to have powers of two of the interfaces participating in an EtherChannel (for example, 2, 4, 8).

Answer 57

To configure EtherChannel, you configure the EtherChannel settings using the **interface port-channel** global command and then add ports to the EtherChannel using the **channel-group** *identifier* mode {active | on | auto} {passive | desirable} command. The following commands create an EtherChannel, setting it as a trunk link and adding interfaces g1/1 and g1/2 in the EtherChannel:

```
Switch(config)# interface port-channel 1
Switch(config-if)# switchport mode trunk
Switch(config-if)# interface range g 1/1-2
Switch(config-if-range)# channel-group 1 mode active
```

Question 58

What is HSRP?

Question 59

What is the HSRP Active router?

Question 60

What is the HSRP Standby router?

Answer 58

Hot Standby Routing Protocol (HSRP) is a Cisco-proprietary protocol that provides gateway redundancy by combining two or more routers in a group and creating a virtual IP and MAC address that is shared between the routers in the HSRP group. In other words, HSRP provides a mechanism to allow a single IP and MAC address to be shared by two or more routers, providing gateway redundancy for end devices.

In HSRP, one router is the active router performing the forwarding and one router can be the standby router, and if there are any other routers, they will be listening.

NOTE   The virtual MAC address is used to prevent ARP cache problems in the event that the primary router fails.

Answer 59

The HSRP Active router is the router that is forwarding packets for the virtual router in the HSRP group. It responds to the default gateway's ARP requests with the virtual router's MAC address. It sends hello messages to the other routers in the standby group every three seconds.

The Active router is the router with the highest priority value. The default is 100. If more than one router has the same priority, the router with the highest IP address on the HSRP-enabled interface becomes the Active router.

NOTE   Unlike STP, where lower values are always preferred, HSRP prefers higher values.

Answer 60

The HSRP Standby router is the primary backup router in the HSRP group. The Standby router listens for hello messages from the Active router. If the Standby router does not hear hello messages within a configurable period of time, called the holdtime, the Standby router becomes the Active router.

NOTE   In the event of a failure of the Active router, the Standby router becomes the Active router and assumes forwarding packets and responding to ARP requests to the virtual MAC address. When the old Active router comes back online, it does not automatically become the Active router.

Question 61

What is the default HSRP holdtime?

Question 62

What is HSRP preemption?

Question 63

What is HSRP interface tracking?

Answer 61

The default HSRP holdtime is 10 seconds.

If the Standby router does not receive hello messages from the Active router in the time outlined in the holdtime, the Standby router will assume the active role.

Answer 62

The HSRP preemption feature enables the router with the highest priority and preemption enabled to become the Active router. The active HSRP router is determined by the priority value that you configured, and then by the IP address. In each case, a higher value is preferred.

Preemption is configured using the **standby** *group_number* **preempt** interface command.

Answer 63

HSRP interface tracking enables the priority of a standby group router to be automatically adjusted, based on the availability of router interfaces.

When tracked interfaces become unavailable, the HSRP tracking feature ensures that the Active router with the unavailable interface will decrement its priority. If the Standby router's priority is greater than the current priority of the active device and if the Standby router has preemption configured, the active router will relinquish control of the Active role.

Question 64

How do you verify the HSRP state?

Question 65

What is HSRP load balancing?

Answer 64

The **show standby** EXEC command shows the HSRP state included in the HSRP role of the router, the virtual IP and MAC address of the HSRP group, and hello and holdtimers:

```
R2# show standby
Ethernet0 - Group 1
Local state is Active, priority 100
Hellotime 3 sec, holdtime 10 sec
Next hello sent in 2.592
Virtual IP address is 192.168.1.1 configured
Active router is local
Standby router is 192.168.1.2 expires in 8.020
Virtual mac address is 0000.0c07.ac05
2 state changes, last state change 00:02:08
```

Answer 65

Also called multigroup HSRP (MHSRP), this feature allows routers to be configured with multigroups for different VLANs to allow router load balancing. For example, using MHSRP, one router can be configured as the Active router for VLAN 10 and the Standby router for VLAN 20. The second router can be configured as the Active router for VLAN 20 and the Standby router for VLAN 10.

Question 66

What is the primary difference between HSRP and VRRP?

Question 67

What is GLBP?

Answer 66

Virtual Router Redundancy Protocol (VRRP) is the industry-standard protocol, whereas HSRP is Cisco proprietary. Both protocols provide the same functionality and operate in very similar ways.

Answer 67

Gateway Load Balancing Protocol (GLBP) is a Cisco-proprietary protocol that provides gateway redundancy like HSRP and VRRP but also provides automatic packet load sharing between a group of redundant routers. GLBP does this by providing a single virtual IP address and multiple virtual MAC addresses. There is one virtual MAC address for each additional router acting as a forwarder. A master router tracks the load on each router in the GLBP group and replies to ARP requests for the gateway IP using the MAC address of the least utilized router.

Section 3
Troubleshooting Basic Connectivity

As today's networks and systems have converged and become more mobile, complexity and interdependency have also increased. In addition to the complexity, more and more people rely on underlying systems and networks to function without any issues. As such, identifying issues and troubleshooting are important skills for any network administrator to possess.

To be successful in troubleshooting, you have to be prepared. First, you must be familiar with the network, protocols, and devices you are troubleshooting. Second, you must have a logical framework of troubleshooting methodology to follow. It would not be wise to unplug a network cable from a computer if a user is having an issue with his web browser crashing; this is why a logical methodology is so important.

In today's networks, issues arise within all the layers of the OSI model. Layer 1 issues typically deal with cabling problems, interface failures, NIC failures, and interface configuration issues. Layer 2 issues are duplex issues, STP, MAC address table inconsistencies, and interface configuration mismatches. Layer 3 issues deal with improper routers, dynamic protocols, and path selection. Layer 4 and 7 issues deal with applications not operating properly.

This section will cover some basic troubleshooting steps and tools, and provide common scenarios found while troubleshooting switched and routed IPv4 and IPv6 networks.

Question 1

List the six steps that can be taken to troubleshoot end-to-end connectivity.

Question 2

What command can be used to test IP connectivity between hosts?

Answer 1

The six steps that can be taken to verify and troubleshoot end-to-end connectivity are as follows:

Step 1.   Determine whether end-to-end connectivity is operational. If this fails, go to Step 2.

Step 2.   Determine whether there is a physical connectivity issue. If there is no physical issue, go to Step 3.

Step 3.   Determine whether the current path is the desired or proper path. If it is not, go to Step 4.

Step 4.   Determine whether the default gateway is correct. If it is, go to Step 5. If it is not, apply the correct gateway.

Step 5.   Determine whether DNS is working correctly. If it is, go to Step 6. If it is not, fix DNS.

Step 6.   Determine whether any ACLs are blocking traffic. If they are, reconfigure the ACLs.

Answer 2

The **ping** command can test IP connectivity between hosts.

NOTE   Other commands to test connectivity are tracert, traceroute, and application layer programs like Telnet and so on.

Question 3

What utilities can show you the path that packets take between two hosts?

Question 4

What IOS command can be used to test transport layer connectivity?

Answer 3

Tracert and traceroute can be used to observe the path that packets take between two hosts. It is useful to ensure that the packets are taking the proper path.

Tracert is used from a Windows host to observe the path that packets take, and traceroute is used from a Cisco device to trace the path that packets are taking. The command syntax for traceroute is **traceroute** *ip-address of host*.

Answer 4

The **telnet** IOS command can be used to test transport layer connectivity and also application layer connectivity.

Question 5

What command can you use on a Cisco device to view interface information, statistics, and errors?

Answer 5

To view interface information, such as interface type, speed, duplex settings, or statistics and errors, use the **show interface** *interface-id* privileged EXEC command. The following command shows the information for interface g0/1. You should be familiar with the highlighted areas.

```
core# show interface g0/1
GigabitEthernet0/1 is up, line protocol is up (connected)
  Hardware is Gigabit Ethernet Port, address is 000d.65ac.5040
(bia 000d.65ac.5040)
  MTU 1500 bytes, BW 1000000 Kbit, DLY 10 usec,
      reliability 255/255, txload 1/255, rxload 1/255
  Encapsulation ARPA, loopback not set
  Keepalive set (10 sec)
  Full-duplex, 1000Mb/s, link type is auto, media type is
      1000BaseSX
  [output omitted]
      Received 20320 broadcasts (12683 multicast)
      0 runts, 0 giants, 0 throttles
      0 input errors, 0 CRC, 0 frame, 0 overrun, 0 ignored
      0 input packets with dribble condition detected
      1680749 packets output, 880704302 bytes, 0 underruns
      0 output errors, 0 collisions, 0 interface resets
      0 babbles, 0 late collision, 0 deferred
      0 lost carrier, 0 no carrier
      0 output buffer failures, 0 output buffers swapped out
```

Question 6

When issuing the show interface **command, what does the Input queue drops counter signify?**

Question 7

When issuing the show interface **command, what does the Output queue drops counter signify?**

Question 8

When issuing the show interface **command, what does the Input errors counter signify?**

Answer 6

The Input queue drops counter signifies that, at some point, more traffic was sent to the router than it could process. If this number is consistently high, it means that the CPU cannot process the packets in time.

Answer 7

The Output queue drops counter indicates that packets were dropped because of congestion on the interface. Consistently seeing output drops means that there is too much congestion on the network, and mechanisms such as QoS should be implemented and/or the network bandwidth should be increased.

Answer 8

Input errors indicate that errors are experienced when receiving the frame. These errors can be CRC errors and could indicate cabling problems, interface hardware problems, or duplex mismatches.

Question 9

When issuing the show interface **command, what does the Output errors counter signify?**

Question 10

Traffic between two switches is slow. You issue the show interface command on the uplink between the two switches and you see the following:

```
!output omitted!
0 input packets with dribble condition detected
      180749 packets output, 8004302 bytes, 0 underruns
      0 output errors, 45345 collisions, 0 interface resets
      0 babbles, 45345 late collision, 0 deferred
      0 lost carrier, 0 no carrier
      0 output buffer failures, 0 output buffers swapped out
```

What is the problem?

Answer 9

Output errors indicate errors such as collisions that occur during the transmission of a frame.

Answer 10

The switch port is receiving a lot of late collisions. The problem can be a duplex mismatch or a faulty port, or the distance between the two switches might exceed the cable specifications.

NOTE   Duplex mismatches occur when the connecting ends are set to different duplex modes, or when one end's duplex is configured and the other is set to autonegotiation.

Question 11

What is the cause of multiple collisions on a port?

Question 12

While troubleshooting a switched network, you see the following on a switch interface that is having connectivity problems:

```
!output omitted!
  5 minute input rate 10000 bits/sec, 8 packets/sec
  5 minute output rate 10000 bits/sec, 7 packets/sec
     1476671 packets input, 363178961 bytes, 0 no buffer
     Received 20320 broadcasts (12683 multicast)
     2345 runts, 0 giants, 0 throttles
     0 input errors, 0 CRC, 0 frame, 0 overrun, 0 ignored
```

What could be the cause of the problem?

Answer 11

Multiple collisions are the number of times the transmitting port had more than one collision before successfully transmitting a frame. If you experience multiple collisions on a port, the problem usually lies with a duplex mismatch or an oversaturated medium.

Answer 12

The switch is receiving a lot of runts. Runts are frames that are smaller than 64 bytes with a bad frame check sequence (FCS). Bad cabling or inconsistent duplex settings usually cause runts, as do other physical layer issues.

Question 13

You have one computer that is connected to a switch that is having very slow and intermittent connections with the network. You log on to the switch and issue the show interface command on the port that the user is connected to. You see the following:

```
!output omitted!
  5 minute input rate 10000 bits/sec, 8 packets/sec
  5 minute output rate 10000 bits/sec, 7 packets/sec
     1476671 packets input, 363178961 bytes, 0 no buffer
     Received 20320 broadcasts (12683 multicast)
     0 runts, 325 giants, 0 throttles
     0 input errors, 0 CRC, 0 frame, 0 overrun, 0 ignored
```

What is most likely the cause of the problem?

Question 14

When users in VLAN 10 are having difficulty connecting to a server in VLAN 20, the connection is very slow. The users are having no problems communicating with each other, only with the server in VLAN 20. As the network administrator, you issue the show interface command on the switch that the server is connected to and you see the following:

```
!Output omitted!
Encapsulation ARPA, loopback not set
  Keepalive set (10 sec)
  Full-duplex, 1000Mb/s, link type is auto, media type is
10/100/1000-TX
```

The server has a Gigabit network card that is set to half-duplex. What is the problem?

Answer 13

The computer likely has a faulty NIC. The switch is receiving a lot of giants. Giants are frames greater than the Ethernet maximum transmission unit (MTU) of 1518 bytes. The cause of giants is usually a faulty NIC on the computer.

Answer 14

The problem lies with a duplex mismatch between the server and the switch. The **show interface** command shows that the port's duplex is set to full, but when you look at the server's NIC, its duplex setting is half-duplex. A duplex mismatch would cause a slow connection to the server.

Question 15

A hub is connected to a switch. Fifteen users are connected to the hub. All users are trying to connect to a server off of the switch, but are experiencing latency. What type of problem is this, and what are some of the causes for this problem?

Question 16

What are the five ways that a routing table can be populated?

Question 17

When issuing the show ip route **command on a Cisco router, what do the following codes mean?**

- L
- C
- S
- R
- O
- D

Answer 15

Because the users are connected to a hub, they are in the same collision domain and are experiencing collision domain connectivity problems.

Causes for the latency problem can include the following:

- The segment is overloaded or oversubscribed.
- Bad cabling on the segment.
- NICs on the segment do not have compatible settings.
- Faulty NICs.

Answer 16

The five ways that a routing table can be populated are as follows:

- **Directly connected networks:** Come from interfaces directly connected to a network segment.
- **Local host routes:** Come from the local IP address on the router interface. A host route for IPv4 has a /32 mask; for IPv6, it is a /128 mask.
- **Static routes:** Manually entered routes.
- **Dynamic routes:** Routes learned from a configured routing protocol.
- **Default routes:** Manually entered or dynamically established by a routing protocol, this is the path a packet will take when there is no specific route to a network in its routing table.

Answer 17

The first parts of the output from the **show ip route** command are the codes. The codes explain the letter representing associated source entries in the routing table. The code definitions are as follows:

- **L:** Local host route
- **C:** Directly connected networks
- **S:** Static routes
- **R:** RIP
- **O:** OSPF
- **D:** EIGRP

Question 18

A router receives a packet and does a route lookup. The router does not have the destination network in its routing table and also does not have a default gateway configured. What will the router do with the packet?

Question 19

A router receives several packets from a host and does a route lookup. The router has two equal-cost entries with the same prefix in its routing tables out two different interfaces. Where will the router send the packets?

Question 20

A router receives a packet and does a route lookup. The router has two equal-cost entries with different prefixes in its routing table out two different interfaces. Where will the router send the packet?

Answer 18

The router will discard or drop the packet.

If a router does not have a matching entry for a network in its routing table and a default route is not configured, the router will not know where to send the packet; thus, it will drop the packet.

Answer 19

The router will distribute the packets for the destination between the two different interfaces.

If a router has more than one entry for a destination in its routing table with the same prefix out multiple interfaces, the router will load-balance the packets received for the destination out of all the defined interfaces.

Answer 20

The router will send the packet to the interface that is associated with the route that has the longest prefix match.

The prefix is the network portion of the IP address designated by the subnet mask. If a router has multiple entries in its routing table with different prefixes, the most specific route will be chosen as the preferred route. The most specific route is the route with the longest prefix (subnet mask).

Question 21

What are the two ways that the mapping of computer names to an IP address can be accomplished?

Question 22

What Cisco IOS command can you use to see whether an IP access list is applied to an interface?

Answer 21

Mapping of computer names can be accomplished statically or dynamically.

Static entries are done in a text file called the HOSTS file by an administrator. This is done by manually entering the computer's name and IP address in the HOSTS file and storing it on all computers.

Dynamic entries are done using the DNS protocol and are entered in DNS servers.

NOTE   The HOSTS file is stored in the C:\windows\system32\etc\hosts directory on Windows computers. The **ip host** IOS command is similar to the HOSTS file and allows you to statically map computer names to IP addresses.

Answer 22

To determine whether an IP access list is applied to an interface, enter the following command:

```
show ip interface interface-type interface-number
```

For example:

```
RouterA# show ip interface s0
Serial0 is up, line protocol is up
  Internet address is 192.168.1.2/24
  Broadcast address is 255.255.255.255
  Address determined by non-volatile memory
  MTU is 1500 bytes
  Helper address is not set
  Directed broadcast forwarding is enabled
  Multicast reserved groups joined: 224.0.0.9
  Outgoing access list is not set
  Inbound  access list is 110
  Proxy ARP is enabled
  Security level is default
  Split horizon is enabled
  --Text Omitted--
```

Question 23

What Cisco IOS commands display the contents of all ACLs configured on the device?

Question 24

As a network administrator, you want to block all Telnet traffic originating from the network 192.168.1.0/24 that is connected to your router's Gigabit interface 0/0 and permit all other IP traffic. You create the following access list and apply it to Gigabit interface 0/0:

```
access-list 101 deny tcp 192.168.1.0 0.0.0.255 any eq 23
```

After you apply the access list, hosts connected to the router's Gigabit Ethernet interface cannot communicate with remote networks. Why?

Question 25

What utilities can be used to test end-to-end IPv6 connectivity?

Answer 23

The **show ip access-lists** and **show access-lists** commands display the contents of all ACLs configured on the device.

Answer 24

Hosts attached to network 192.168.1.0/24 cannot communicate with remote networks because the access list is denying all IP traffic. At the end of each access list is a deny all statement. Thus, access list 101 is not only denying Telnet traffic but is also denying all IP traffic as well. To resolve the problem, the access list needs to be configured as follows:

```
access-list 101 deny tcp 192.168.1.0 0.0.0.255 any eq 23
access-list 101 permit ip any any
```

Answer 25

Ping, tracert, and traceroute can be used to test end-to-end IPv6 connectivity.

Like IPv4, ping, tracert, and traceroute can test end-to-end connectivity for any IPv6 host.

NOTE   Troubleshooting connectivity in IPv6 is similar to IPv4; the primary difference is the address differences. Tools such as ping and traceroute operate the same way in the two versions.

Question 26

When issuing the show ipv6 neighbors **command, you see a host in the INCMP state. What does this mean?**

Question 27

When issuing the show ipv6 neighbors **command, you see a host in the STALE state. What does this mean?**

Answer 26

The INCMP, or incomplete, state means that address resolution is being performed on the host. A neighbor solicitation message has been sent to the host, but the corresponding neighbor advertisement message has not yet been received.

Answer 27

The STALE state means that the more than reachable time milliseconds have elapsed since the last positive confirmation was received. In the STALE state, the device takes no action until a packet is sent.

Section 4
Implementing an EIGRP-Based Solution

Enhanced Interior Gateway Routing Protocol (EIGRP) was introduced in Cisco IOS Release 9.21 as an enhancement to the limitations of IGRP. IGRP was developed by Cisco in the mid-1980s as a solution to Routing Information Protocol's (RIP's) limitation. RIP's limitation was based on its metric of hop count. In RIP, a hop larger than 15 was unreachable. As a result, RIP networks could contain no more than 15 hops. IGRP was developed to support larger networks than RIP. IGRP can support networks up to 255 hops in diameter. Additionally, IGRP could support multiple routed protocols. IGRP was created to support not only IP but also Internetwork Packet Exchange (IPX) and AppleTalk; RIP supports only IP.

Because of the limitation of IGRP, Cisco developed EIGRP. EIGRP is a classless protocol, meaning that it sends the subnet mask of its interfaces in routing updates. Although EIGRP is an enhancement of IGRP, it is not a distance vector routing protocol. EIGRP has some of the characteristics of a distance vector routing protocol and of a link-state protocol. As such, Cisco considers EIGRP an advanced distance vector routing protocol.

Like Open Shortest Path First (OSPF), EIGRP maintains awareness of the network through neighbor and topology tables, multicasts routing updates, and is fast to converge. However, EIGRP does not use the SPF algorithm to determine routes; instead, EIGRP uses the Diffusing Update Algorithm (DUAL).

EIGRP is a Cisco-proprietary protocol and supports IP, IPX, and AppleTalk. EIGRP also uses the same metric as IGRP.

This section provides flash cards that cover EIGRP concepts, configuring EIGRP, configuring EIGRP IPv6, and troubleshooting EIGRP.

Question 1

List some of the primary purposes of routing protocols.

Question 2

Define the administrative distance in routing.

Question 3

List the AD for each of the following:
- Directly connected interface
- Static route
- External BGP
- EIGRP
- OSPF
- IS-IS
- RIPv2
- External EIGRP
- Internal BGP
- Unknown

Answer 1

Some of the primary purposes of routing protocols are to

- Discover remote networks
- Maintain up-to-date routing information
- Choose the best path to destination networks when they are learned from the same protocol or routing process
- Find a new best path if the current path is no longer available

Answer 2

Administrative distance (AD) is an integer from 0 to 255 that rates the trustworthiness of the source of the IP routing information. It is only important when a router learns about a destination route from more than one source. The path with the lowest AD is the one given priority.

NOTE If a routing protocol has multiple paths within the same routing protocol to the same destination, the metric is used as the tiebreaker. The route with the lowest metric entered in the routing table is the preferred route.

Answer 3

The default ADs are as follows:
- Directly connected interface: 0
- Static route: 1
- External BGP: 20
- EIGRP: 90
- OSPF: 110
- IS-IS: 115
- RIPv2: 120
- External EIGRP: 170
- Internal BGP: 200
- Unknown: 255

Question 4

What is an autonomous system (AS)?

Question 5

What is a metric used by routing protocols?

Question 6

List some of the most common routing protocol metrics used by routing algorithms?

Answer 4

An AS is a collection of networks under common administrative control that share a common routing strategy.

Answer 5

Routing protocols use a metric as a factor that determines the desirability of a route that has been sent within routing protocol data. Each routing protocol uses a unique metric. For example, RIPv2 uses hop count as its metric. When building the routing table, the routing protocol metric is evaluated after the AD. A router uses the metric to determine the best or optimal path to which network traffic should be forwarded if the router learned multiple routes to the same destination.

Answer 6

The most common routing protocol metrics used by routing algorithms are as follows:

- **Bandwidth:** The data capacity of a link
- **Delay:** The length of time required to move a packet from source to destination
- **Hop count:** The number of routers a packet must take to reach its destination
- **Cost:** A value assigned by the network administrator, usually based on the bandwidth of the link

NOTE   Reliability and load are other metrics that can be used by routing algorithms, but they are not common.

Question 7

How do distance vector routing protocols function?

Question 8

How do distance vector routing protocols keep track of changes to the internetwork?

Question 9

What are link-state protocols? List two common link-state protocols.

Answer 7

Distance vector routing protocols pass complete routing tables to neighboring routers. Neighboring routers then combine the received routing table with their own routing tables. Each router receives a routing table from its directly connected neighbor. RIPv2 is the most common distance vector protocol used in today's internetworks. Distance vector routing protocols are often known as Bellman-Ford protocols because they use the Bellman-Ford algorithm.

Answer 8

Distance vector routing protocols keep track of changes to the internetwork by periodically broadcasting updates out all active interfaces, except the interface(s) where the router learned the update.

These broadcasts contain the entire routing table. This method is often called "routing by rumor."

Answer 9

Link-state protocols create a complete picture of the internetwork by determining the status of each interface (link) in the internetwork. When the interface goes down, link-state protocols send LSAs out all other interfaces, informing other routers of the downed link. Thus LSAs are only sent when there is a link change. Link-state protocols find the best paths to destinations by applying Dijkstra's algorithm against the link-state database.

As learned in ICND1, LSAs are link-state advertisements, sent by routers running a link-state protocol that include information regarding the router, link, and timers.

OSPF and IS-IS are two common link-state protocols.

Question 10

In routing, what is load balancing?

Question 11

What is per-destination and per-packet load balancing?

Question 12

What are the four components of EIGRP?

Answer 10

In routing, if a router has multiple paths with the same administrative distance and cost to a destination, packets are equally sent across the paths.

Load balancing is a function of Cisco IOS router software and is supported for static routes, RIPv2, Enhanced IGRP (EIGRP), OSPF, and the Intermediate System–to–Intermediate System (IS-IS) Protocol.

NOTE   This load balancing is what Cisco calls equal-cost load balancing, because multiple equal-cost paths to a destination exist. EIGRP also supports unequal-cost load balancing, which is when multiple unequal-cost paths to a destination exist.

Answer 11

Per-destination load balancing means that the router distributes packets based on the destination address.

Per-packet load balancing means that the router sends one packet for one destination over the first path, and the second packet for the same destination over the second path.

Answer 12

The four components of EIGRP are as follows:

- **Protocol-dependent modules:** Implement modules for IP, IPv6, IPX, and AppleTalk.
- **Reliable Transport Protocol (RTP):** Used to provide guaranteed delivery of EIGRP packets.
- **Neighbor discovery/recovery:** Used to discover and track neighbors through Hello packets.
- **Diffusing Update Algorithm (DUAL):** Used to perform distributed shortest-path routing while maintaining freedom from loops at every instant.

Question 13

By default, what does EIGRP use for calculating its metric?

Question 14

What are three general steps that EIGRP uses to add routes to the router's routing table?

Question 15

How does EIGRP discover neighbors?

Answer 13

EIGRP uses bandwidth and delay for calculating its metric.

By default, bandwidth and delay are used by EIGRP to calculate its metric. EIGRP can also be configured to use reliability, load, and maximum transmission unit (MTU). The metric of EIGRP is the metric of IGRP multiplied by 256 for improved granularity.

Answer 14

The three general steps that EIGRP uses to add routes to the router's routing table are as follows:

Step 1.   Discover other EIGRP routers attached to the EIGRP-enabled interface and form a neighbor relationship with the discovered routers. Routers that it forms a relationship with are kept in the router's EIGRP neighbor table.

Step 2.   Exchange update information with all discovered neighbors. This information is stored in the EIGRP topology table.

Step 3.   Run DUAL on all topology information and identify the lowest-metric routes in the routing table.

Answer 15

EIGRP neighbors are discovered through Hello messages. On most networks, Hello messages are multicast every five seconds to address 224.0.0.10. On Nonbroadcast Multi-Access (NMBA) links with speeds of T1 (1.544 Mbps) or slower, Hellos are unicast every 60 seconds.

Question 16

How does EIGRP send routing updates?

Question 17

What is the EIGRP neighbor table?

Answer 16

When routing information changes, EIGRP sends update messages to all neighbors, informing them of the change. If EIGRP has to send to multiple neighbors on the same interface, the update messages are multicast to IP address 224.0.0.10. If sending updates to one router, the messages are unicast to the neighbor.

NOTE   All update messages are sent using Reliable Transport Protocol (RTP) to ensure that delivery is guaranteed and that packets will be delivered in order.

Answer 17

The EIGRP neighbor table lists all adjacent routers. Each EIGRP router maintains a neighbor table.

The **show ip eigrp neighbors** command is used to observe the IP EIGRP neighbor table:

```
RouterA# show ip eigrp neighbors
```

```
IP-EIGRP Neighbors for process 10
```

Address	Interface	Holdtime (secs)	Uptime (h:m:s)	Q Count	Seq Num	SRTT (ms)	RTO (ms)
172.16.81.28	G0/0	13	0:00:41	0	11	4	20
172.16.80.28	G0/1	14	0:02:01	0	10	12	24
172.16.80.31	G1/0	12	0:02:02	0	4	5	20

Question 18

What is the EIGRP topology table?

Question 19

In EIGRP, what is the feasible successor?

Question 20

In EIGRP, what is the administrative distance (AD)?

Answer 18

The EIGRP topology table contains all learned routes to a destination. In other words, the topology table holds all feasible routes in its table. Every destination for one or more feasible existing successors will be recorded in the topology table along with the following items:

- The destination's feasible distance (FD)
- All feasible successors
- Each feasible successor's advertised distance to the destination
- The locally calculated distance to the destination through each feasible successor
- The interface connected to the network on which each feasible successor is found

The EIGRP topology table is viewed by issuing the **show ip eigrp topology** command.

Answer 19

The feasible successor is the backup route. These routes are selected at the same time the successors are identified, but they are typically kept in the topology table, not the routing table. They are used for fast convergence. If the successor fails, the router can immediately route through the feasible successor. Multiple feasible successors can exist for a destination.

If a neighbor router–advertised distance to a destination meets the feasible condition (FC), the neighbor becomes a feasible successor for that destination. The FC is a condition that is met if a neighbor's advertised distance to a destination is lower than the router's feasible distance to that same destination.

Answer 20

The AD is the cost between the next-hop router and the destination.

The AD is displayed in the EIGRP topology table using the **show ip eigrp topology** command.

Question 21

In EIGRP, what is the feasible distance (FD)?

Question 22

What Cisco IOS commands enable EIGRP on a Cisco router and advertise 192.168.3.0 and 192.168.4.0 as its directly connected networks?

Question 23

What command would you use to see EIGRP adjacencies?

Answer 21

The FD is the metric from the local router, through the next-hop router, and to the destination.

Answer 22

The **router eigrp** *process-id* command, followed by the **network** command, enables EIGRP on the router. The following commands enable EIGRP using 100 as the process ID and then advertise networks 192.168.3.0 and 192.168.4.0:

```
RouterA(config)# router eigrp 100
RouterA(config-router)# network 192.168.3.0
RouterA(config-router)# network 192.168.4.0
```

NOTE   All routers configured for EIGRP must be configured with the same process ID to share information. The process ID is a number from 1 to 65,535.

Answer 23

The **show ip eigrp neighbors** command displays EIGRP adjacencies and directly connected neighbors, as follows:

```
RouterA# show ip eigrp neighbors
```

```
IP-EIGRP Neighbors for process 100
Address          Interface    Holdtime Uptime   Q      Seq  SRTT  RTO
                              (secs)   (h:m:s)  Count  Num  (ms)  (ms)
192.168.10.2     Ethernet1    13       0:02:00  0      11   4     20
192.168.11.2     Ethernet0    14       0:02:01  0      10   12    24
```

Question 24

What IOS command allows you to view only the EIGRP routes in the routing table?

Question 25

How do you view the EIGRP neighbor table?

Question 26

How do you view the EIGRP topology table?

Answer 24

The **show ip route eigrp** command allows you to view only the EIGRP-learned routes in the routing table.

Answer 25

The **show ip eigrp neighbors** command shows the EIGRP neighbor table.

Answer 26

The **show ip eigrp topology** command shows the EIGRP topology table, including successors and feasible successors, as follows:

```
RouterB# show ip eigrp topology

IP-EIGRP Topology Table for process 100

Codes: P - Passive, A - Active, U - Update, Q - Query, R - Reply,
       r - Reply status

P 192.168.4.0 255.255.255.0, 1 successors, FD is 2172416
        via 192.168.3.2 (2172416/28160), Serial0
        via 192.168.2.2 (2684416/1794560), Serial1
```

Question 27

What Cisco IOS command would you use to view the EIGRP neighbor states?

Question 28

What are the two types of load balancing supported by EIGRP?

Question 29

Router A is running EIGRP and has four paths to network 192.168.100.0. All four paths have the same cost.

Which path(s) will Router A choose to route to network 192.168.100.0?

Answer 27

You would use the **show ip eigrp neighbors** command to check the EIGRP neighbor states. This command displays the contents of the Hello packet used in EIGRP as well as the neighbors discovered by EIGRP.

Answer 28

The two types of load balancing supported by EIGRP are equal-cost load balancing and unequal-cost load balancing.

Equal-cost load balancing is when the routes in the routing table have the same metric. By default, EIGRP supports load balancing on up to four equal-cost routes.

Unequal-cost load balancing is done over unequal-cost routes (for example, routes with different metrics to the same network). This is not enabled by default and load balancing can be performed through paths that are 128 times worse than the route with the lowest FD.

NOTE By default, Cisco IOS can load-balance across four equal-cost paths, but can support up to 32 equal-cost paths. The **maximum-paths** router configuration command allows you to change the default.

Answer 29

Router A will choose all four paths. By default, EIGRP can load-balance up to four equal-cost routes. This is called equal-cost load balancing. Because EIGRP has four equal-cost paths to network 192.168.100.0, all paths are included in Router A's routing table.

NOTE Remember, the default routing metrics that EIGRP uses are bandwidth of the interface and delay.

Question 30

Router A is connected to Router B through a point-to-point T1 link. Router B is connected to network 192.168.100.0 on its Fast Ethernet interface. EIGRP is running on both routers. You install a second point-to-point link between the two routers for redundancy. The new link has a bandwidth of 256 kbps. Because the new link has a higher cost than the T1 link, the new link is not installed in the routing table and is idle. EIGRP only uses the T1 link to route to network 192.168.100.0. You want to load-balance between the two links. How do you enable EIGRP to load-balance between the two links?

Question 31

While troubleshooting a router that is not receiving EIGRP updates, you issue the show ip protocols command and see the interfaces as passive. What does this mean?

Answer 30

By default, EIGRP can only load-balance equal-cost paths and not load-balance between unequal-cost paths. EIGRP needs to be configured to load-balance between unequal-cost paths. The goal is to configure EIGRP to spread the traffic load inversely proportionally to the metrics on the two links. EIGRP uses the **variance** command to perform unequal-cost load balancing. The **variance** command defines a multiplier by which a metric can vary from the lowest-cost route. A variance of 1 means that the metrics of multiple routes must be equal.

In this question, the metric of the T1 link is 1,657,856. The composite metric to network 192.168.100.0 (the total of the cost of the T1 link and the Fast Ethernet interface) is 2,172,416. The composite metric of the 256-kbps link is 10,514,432. To find the variance between the two paths to perform unequal-cost load balancing, divide the metric of the 256-kbps link by the T1 link: 10,514,432 / 2,172,416 = 4.8. Thus, to configure unequal-cost load balancing, the variance on Router A needs to be set to 5, as follows:

```
RouterA(config)# router eigrp 100
RouterA(config-router)# variance 5
```

NOTE The variance must be specified in whole numbers.

Answer 31

This means that the router is not sending EIGRP Hellos and that no adjacencies will be formed. Thus, no other EIGRP traffic will be sent.

The **passive-interface** command prevents an interface from sending EIGRP Hellos on a data link, blocking unnecessary Hellos and preventing neighbor adjacencies from forming. By issuing the **passive-interface** command on a router interface, the configured interface stops sending Hellos; however, incoming routing information is not stopped.

Question 32

How does EIGRP for IPv6 differ from EIGRP for IPv4?

Question 33

What Cisco IOS commands enable EIGRP routing for IPv6?

Answer 32

Enhanced IGRP (EIGRP) for IPv6 is the same EIGRP protocol as used with IPv4. It uses the same metric but includes a protocol-dependent module for IPv4 and IPv6. Also, EIGRP for IPv6 send updates to the reserved link-local multicast address FF02::A.

Answer 33

To enable a Cisco router with EIGRP routing for IPv6, take the following steps:

Step 1. Enable IPv6 routing.

Step 2. Create an EIGRP routing process in IPv6.

Step 3. Enable the EIGRP routing process.

Step 4. Enable EIGRP for IPv6 on specified interfaces.

The following example enables EIGRP for IPv6 in AS 10 and then enables interfaces G0/0 and G0/1 to participate in the EIGRP IPv6 process:

```
RouterA(config)# ipv6 unicast-routing
RouterA(config)# ipv6 router eigrp 10
RouterA(config-router)# no shutdown
RouterA(config-router)# interface g0/0
RouterA(config-if)# ipv6 eigrp 10
RouterA(config-router)# interface g0/1
RouterA(config-if)# ipv6 eigrp 10
```

NOTE If the router does not have an IPv4 address previously configured, the **router-id** *ip-address* EIGRP router mode command is needed to assign a fixed router ID.

Question 34

What Cisco IOS command allows you to display the EIGRP IPv6 topology table?

Question 35

What Cisco IOS command allows you to view the neighbors discovered by EIGRP IPv6?

Answer 34

The **show ipv6 eigrp topology** command allows you to display the EIGRP IPv6 topology table.

Answer 35

The **show ipv6 eigrp neighbors** command allows you to view the neighbors discovered by EIGRP IPv6.

Section 5
Implementing a Scalable Multiarea OSPF-Based Network

ICND1 introduced OSPF in a single area. OSPF is a link-state protocol that is highly scalable with fast convergence. One of the reasons that OSPF is so scalable is its ability to segment routing borders in OSPF using areas.

Area segmentation provides many benefits including route summarization between areas, link-state advertisements being confined to an area, and reduced overhead. Although multiarea OSPF has many benefits, one has to be careful when designing a multiarea OSPF solution. Multiarea OSPF adds additional complexity to the network, and a network administrator needs to ensure that the network topology is designed correctly, that IP addresses are allocated to take advantage of hierarchical routing and summarization, and that the correct placement of area border routers is done.

This section will cover the concepts of multiarea OSPF and describe how to configure multiarea OSPFv2 and OSPFv3.

Question 1

What is the routing metric that OSPF is based on?

Question 2

What does the Hello packet do in an OSPF network?

Answer 1

The routing metric that OSPF is based on is bandwidth. OSPF's metric is a cost value based on bandwidth. The default formula used to calculate OSPF cost is as follows:

Cost = 100,000,000 / Bandwidth in bps

The default OSPF costs are as follows:

- **10 Mbps:** 10
- **100 Mbps:** 1
- **1 Gbps:** 1
- **10 Gbps:** 1

NOTE Because the default OSPF costs for interfaces faster than 100 Mbps are the same, it is recommended to manually define the costs to ensure that higher-speed interfaces are preferred over lower-cost interfaces.

Answer 2

In OSPF, the Hello packet ensures that communication between OSPF-speaking routers is bidirectional.

The Hello packet is the means by which neighbors are discovered, and it acts as a keepalive between neighbors. It also establishes and maintains neighbor relationships and elects the designated router (DR) and the backup designated router (BDR) to represent the segment on broadcast and nonbroadcast multiaccess (NBMA) networks.

Question 3

What information does each Hello packet contain?

Question 4

What is the IP multicast address of OSPF Hello packets?

Answer 3

The Hello protocol packet contains the following information:

- Router ID of the originating router
- Area ID of the originating router interface
- IP address and mask of the originating router interface
- Authentication type and authentication password, if required, of the originating router interface
- HelloInterval
- DeadInterval
- Interface router priority
- Designated router (DR) and backup designated router (BDR)
- Neighbor field
- Router IDs of the originating router's neighbors

Answer 4

OSPF Hello packets are periodically sent out each interface using the IP multicast address 224.0.0.5 (AllSPFRouters). The HelloInterval each router uses to send out the Hello packet is based on the network link type. The default HelloInterval of point-to-point networks is 10 seconds; on point-to-multipoint broadcast networks and NBMA networks, the default is 30 seconds.

Question 5

For OSPF routers to become neighbors, what parameters must match in their Hello packets?

Question 6

Define the OSPF router ID, and describe how an OSPF router derives its router ID.

Answer 5

For OSPF routers to become neighbors, the parameters that must match in their Hello packets are as follows:

- HelloInterval
- DeadInterval
- OSPF area ID
- Authentication password (if enabled)
- Stub area flag

If any of these parameters differ, the routers cannot become OSPF neighbors. Additionally, for routers to establish an adjacency on an interface, the primary IP address on the router's interfaces must also be on the same subnet with the same mask, and the interface MTU must match.

Answer 6

The router ID is a 32-bit number that uniquely identifies the router in OSPF. It is required for OSPF to initialize.

A router can derive its router ID from several sources: manual configuration through the **router-id** command, by the numerically highest IP address set on the loopback interface, or by the highest numerical IP address on any active interface.

The loopback interface is a logical interface that never goes down. If no loopback address is defined, an OSPF-enabled router selects the numerically highest IP address on any active interface as its router ID.

Question 7

An OSPF-enabled router has the following IP addresses configured on its interfaces:

- Fast Ethernet 0/0: 192.168.9.5
- Serial 0/0: 172.16.3.1
- Fast Ethernet 0/1: 192.168.24.1

What is the router ID of the OSPF-enabled router?

Question 8

In OSPF, what is the designated router and backup designated router?

Question 9

On a multiaccess network, how is the DR elected?

Answer 7

192.168.24.1 is the router ID because it is the numerically highest IP address on all interfaces on the router. If the router had a loopback address configured, it would choose the loopback address as the router ID (even if the loopback IP address was numerically lower than other IP addresses configured on the router). The router ID can also be manually configured using the **router-id** route configuration command.

Answer 8

In multiaccess networks, a designated router (DR) must be elected on the subnet before database description packets can be exchanged between routers. All database description packets are forwarded to the DR, which in turn forwards them to other OSPF routers. The DR has the following duties:

- Represents the multiaccess network and attached routers for the OSPF area
- Manages the flooding process on the multiaccess network

The backup designated router (BDR) is the backup to the DR. In the event a DR fails, the BDR takes over as the DR.

Ethernet is an example of a multiaccess network.

Answer 9

On a multiaccess network, the DR is elected by the following criteria:

- The router with the highest OSPF interface priority becomes the DR.
- If two or more routers have the same OSPF interface priority, the router with the highest router ID becomes the DR.

If a new router is configured for OSPF that has a higher interface priority number than the current DR, the new higher interface priority router does not become the DR. The new router has to wait until the DR and BDR fail.

NOTE   The router with the second-highest router ID usually becomes the BDR.

Question 10

What is the OSPF neighbor table?

Question 11

What are link-state advertisements?

Question 12

What are the four types of OSPF update packets involved in building a link-state database?

Answer 10

The OSPF neighbor table is a list of the neighbors that OSPF has formed an adjacency with.

Answer 11

Link-state advertisements (LSA) are what OSPF-enabled routers send out all OSPF-enabled interfaces to describe the state of the routers' links. LSAs are also packets that OSPF uses to advertise changes in the condition of a specific link to other OSPF routers.

Answer 12

The four types of update packets used when building and synchronizing the link-state database (LSDB) are

- **DBD packet:** Describes the network routes of each neighbor.
- **LSR packet:** After DBD packets are exchanged, any missing information is sent using LSR packets.
- **LSU packet:** All missing information is sent to the neighbors by sending LSU packets that contain different LSAs.
- **LSAck packet:** Every packet is acknowledged with an LSAck packet to ensure reliable exchange of information.

Question 13

What is the OSPF area ID?

Question 14

In OSPF, what are the following router types?

- Backbone routers
- Internal routers
- Area border routers
- Autonomous system boundary routers

Answer 13

OSPF supports a two-layer hierarchical network structure. The area ID defines this hierarchical structure. In OSPF, there are two types of areas:

- Backbone (Area 0)
- Normal areas

The backbone area interconnects with other OSPF area types. OSPF requires that all areas connect directly to the backbone. Normal areas are used to connect users and resources. Typically, normal areas are set up according to functional or geographical groupings. By default, a normal area does not allow traffic from another area to use its links to reach other areas. All traffic from other areas must cross Area 0.

NOTE Normal areas can be special area types such as Stub, Totally Stub, Not-So-Stubby, and NSSA Totally Stub areas.

Answer 14

The OSPF router types are as follows:

- **Backbone routers:** All routers that have an interface in Area 0.
- **Internal routers:** Routers that have all interfaces in single area.
- **Area border routers (ABR):** Routers that connect Area 0 to nonbackbone areas.
- **Autonomous system boundary routers (ASBR):** Connect any OSPF area to a different routing administration. This is where external routes can be introduced into OSPF.

Question 15

What are the four characteristics of ABRs?

Question 16

How many LSAs exist in OSPF?

Answer 15

Area border routers (ABR) have the following characteristics:

- They separate LSA flooding zones.
- They are the primary point for area route summarization.
- They regularly function as the source for the default routes.
- They maintain the LSDB for each area with which it is connected.

Answer 16

Eleven distinct link-state packet formats are used in OSPF; each is used for a different purpose.

The ICND2 exam will only test you on five LSA types: Type 1–Type 5 LSAs:

- **Type 1:** Router LSAs. Describe the states of the router's links to the area and are flooded within a single area.
- **Type 2:** Network LSAs and are generated by the DR. They describe the set of routers attached to a particular network. They are flooded within a single area.
- **Type 3:** Network Summary LSAs. Sent by the ABR to advertise prefixes to other areas. They are flooded throughout the AS.
- **Type 4:** ASBR Summary LSAs. Inform the rest of the OSPF domain on how to get to the ASBR.
- **Type 5:** External link advertisements sent by the ASBR. Are flooded everywhere, except to special areas.

Question 17

If you have eight routers on an Ethernet network and you establish adjacencies on the DR and BDR, how many adjacencies will you have?

Question 18

An OSPF router has the OSPF interface priority set to 0. What does this mean?

Answer 17

You will have 14 adjacencies.

The formula for calculating the number of connections needed to establish adjacencies with the DR and BDR is $2(n-1)$, where n is the number of routers in the network. So, if you have eight routers in a network, $2(8-1) = 14$ adjacencies.

Answer 18

An OSPF interface priority setting of 0 means that the router can never become a DR.

Question 19

What are the four network types that OSPF defines?

Question 20

What are the eight OSPF neighbor states?

Answer 19

The four network types defined by OSPF are as follows:

- Broadcast networks
- NBMA networks
- Point-to-point networks
- Point-to-multipoint networks

OSPF routers on broadcast networks elect a designated router (DR) and a backup designated router (BDR); all routers form adjacencies with the DR and BDR. All OSPF packets are multicast to the DR and BDR.

NBMA networks are Frame Relay and ATM and have no broadcast capability. NBMA networks elect a DR and BDR, and all OSPF packets are unicast.

Point-to-point networks, such as a serial connection using HDLC or PPP, connect a single pair of routers and normally become adjacent without special configuration. This is because the OSPF network type will default to point-to-point.

Point-to-multipoint networks are configured NBMA networks. Routers on these networks do not elect a DR or BDR, and all OSPF packets are multicast.

Answer 20

The eight OSPF neighbor states are as follows:

- Down
- Attempt
- Init
- 2-Way
- Exstart
- Exchange
- Loading
- Full

Question 21

Define the OSPF Down state.

Question 22

What is the OSPF Attempt state?

Question 23

What is the OSPF Init state?

Answer 21

The OSPF Down state is the first OSPF neighbor state. It means that no Hellos have been received from the OSPF neighbor.

NOTE   During the fully adjacent state, if a router does not receive Hello packets from a neighbor within the RouterDeadInterval time (four missed Hellos), the neighbor state changes from Full to Down.

Answer 22

The OSPF Attempt state only applies to manually configured neighbors on NBMA networks. In this state, the router sends unicast Hello packets to a neighbor at the HelloInterval instead of at the PollInterval.

Answer 23

The Init state indicates that a router has received a Hello packet from its neighbor, but the receiving router's ID was not included in the Hello packet. As a result, two-way communication has not yet been established.

Question 24

Define the OSPF 2-Way state.

Question 25

What is the OSPF Exstart state?

Question 26

What is the OSPF Exchange state?

Answer 24

The OSFP 2-Way state indicates that bidirectional communication has been established between two routes. Bidirectional communication means that each router sees its router ID in its neighbor's Hello packets.

NOTE   On broadcast media and NBMA networks, a router becomes Full only with the DR and the BDR. The router stays in the 2-Way state with all other neighbors.

Answer 25

In the OSPF Exstart state, the router and the segment's DR and BDR establish a master-slave relationship and choose the initial sequence of numbers to form an adjacency. An adjacency should continue past this state. If it does not, there is a problem with the database description packet exchange.

Answer 26

In the OSPF Exchange state, a router sends database description packets describing its entire link-state database to neighbors that are in the Exchange or greater state.

Question 27

What is the OSPF Loading state?

Question 28

Define the OSPF Full state.

Question 29

Why would you want to configure multiarea OSPF?

Answer 27

In the Loading state, the exchange of link-state information occurs. Routers send link-state request packets to neighbors requesting more-recent LSAs that have been discovered but not received.

Answer 28

The OSPF Full state means that all routers are fully adjacent with each other.

Answer 29

Single-area OSPF puts all routers in a single area. The result is that LSAs are processed on every router and larger networks can have large routing tables.

Multiarea OSPF segments the network into different areas. As such, LSAs are confined to their area and there can be smaller routing tables with route summarization. This segmentation also confines any network instability to an area and can save router resources.

Question 30

How do you configure basic multiarea OSPF on a Cisco router?

Question 31

How can you display the OSPF neighbor information on a per-interface basis?

Answer 30

Multiarea OSPF configuration is similar to single-area OSPF configuration. The only difference is that you configure at least one router interface in one area while another or other interfaces are configured to a different area or areas. The following configuration example configures OSPF using process ID 1 and places the interface connected to network 172.16.0.0 255.255.0.0 in area 0 and the interface connected to network 192.168.1.0 255.255.255.0 in area 1:

```
RouterA(config)# router ospf 1
RouterA(config-router)# network 172.16.0.0 0.0.255.255 area 0
RouterA(config-router)# network 192.168.1.0 0.0.0.255 area 1
```

NOTE   Although the actual configuration of multiarea OSPF is not difficult, careful planning needs to be done to ensure that the IP addressing, network topology, ABRs, and ASBRs are all properly designed. The previous configuration configures the router as an ABR because it has two interfaces in two areas.

Answer 31

The **show ip ospf neighbor** and **show ip ospf interface** *interface-type interface-number* commands display OSPF neighbor information on a per-interface basis.

```
RouterB# show ip ospf neighbor

Neighbor ID    Pri    State      Dead Time    Address     Interface
172.16.0.1     1      FULL/  -   00:00:31     10.1.1.1    Serial0

RouterB# show ip ospf interface serial 0
Serial00 is up, line protocol is up
  Internet Address 10.1.1.1, Area 0
  Process ID 1, Router ID 1.1.1.1, Network Type POINT_TO_POINT,
    Cost: 64
  Transmit Delay is 1 sec, State POINT_TO_POINT
  Timer intervals configured, Hello 10, Dead 40, Wait 40,
    Retransmit 5
    <output excluded>
  Neighbor Count is 1, Adjacent neighbor count is 1
    Adjacent with neighbor 172.16.0.1
  Suppress hello for 0 neighbor(s)
```

Question 32

What Cisco IOS command will display all the routes the router learned by OSPF?

Question 33

What Cisco IOS command lists the OSPF area that the router interfaces belong in and the router's adjacent neighbors?

Answer 32

The **show ip route ospf** command shows all routes the router learned through OSPF and are in the routing table.

Answer 33

The **show ip ospf interface** command lists the area in which the router interface resides and the neighbors of the interface. Additionally, it lists the interface state, process ID, router ID, network type, cost, priority, DR and BDR, timer intervals, and authentication if it is configured. Here is an example of the **show ip ospf interface** command:

```
RouterB# show ip ospf interface ethernet 0
Ethernet0 is up, line protocol is up
  Internet Address 10.1.1.1/24, Area 0
  Process ID 1, Router ID 172.16.0.2, Network Type BROADCAST, Cost: 10
  Transmit Delay is 1 sec, State BDR, Priority 1
  Designated Router (ID) 172.16.0.1, Interface address 10.1.1.2
  Backup Designated router (ID) 172.16.0.2, Interface address 10.1.1.1
  Timer intervals configured, Hello 10, Dead 40, Wait 40, Retransmit 5
    Hello due in 00:00:06
  Index 1/1, flood queue length 0
  Next 0x0(0)/0x0(0)
  Last flood scan length is 2, maximum is 2
  Last flood scan time is 0 msec, maximum is 4 msec
  Neighbor Count is 1, Adjacent neighbor count is 1
    Adjacent with neighbor 172.16.0.1  (Designated Router)
  Suppress hello for 0 neighbor(s)
```

Question 34

What command can you use to view the OSPF neighbor state?

Question 35

You are trying to configure OSPF on a new router. When enabling OSPF, you receive an error that says "ospf unknown protocol". Why are you receiving this error message?

Question 36

When configuring a new router for OSPF, you receive the "failed to allocate unique router-id and cannot start" error message. Additionally, OSPF does not initialize. Why are you getting this error message?

Answer 34

The **show ip ospf neighbor** command shows the OSPF neighbor state.

Answer 35

Usually, the "ospf unknown protocol" error message means that the router's IOS license does not support OSPF. Purchasing the proper IOS license would remedy the issue.

Answer 36

For the OSPF process to initialize, the router must have one interface with a valid IP address in the up/line protocol up state. If an interface is not enabled and no IP address has been assigned, and no router ID is manually defined, you will receive the "failed to allocate unique router-id and cannot start" error message.

Question 37

As a network administrator, you are running OSPF in your network and you have two paths to the same destination; however, the costs of the paths are not the same. As a result, OSPF routes all traffic across the route with the lowest cost. You want to use the second path. How do you configure OSPF to load-balance between the two paths?

Question 38

What is the difference between OSPFv2 and OSPFv3?

Question 39

How is the OSPFv3 router ID determined?

Answer 37

Because OSPF's metric is based on cost, to load-balance between two paths with different costs, you must manually configure each interface with the same cost. The **ip ospf cost** *interface-cost* interface command sets the OSPF cost of an interface. In the example stated in the question, you would enter the following commands to make both interfaces have the same cost:

```
RouterA(config)# interface serial 0/0
RouterA(config-if)# ip ospf cost 10
RouterA(config-if)# interface serial 0/1
RouterA(config-if)# ip ospf cost 10
```

Answer 38

Open Shortest Path First version 3 (OSPFv3) is based on the current version of OSPF for IPv4, which is version 2. Like OSPFv2, OSPFv3 sends Hellos to neighbors, exchanges link-state advertisements (LSA), and exchanges database descriptor (DBD) packets. However, OSPFv3 runs directly over IPv6 and advertises using multicast groups FF02::5 and FF02::06, but uses its link-local address as the source address of its advertisements. OSPFv3 has some LSA types that are not included in OSPFv2.

FF02::5 is the address listened to by "all OSPF routers," and FF02::06 is the address listened to by the OSPF DRs and BDR. Another difference is that OSPFv3 does not include authentication because authentication in IPv6 is handled through IPsec. Finally, it is important to note that OSPFv3 and OSPFv2 run independently on a router.

Answer 39

The router ID in OSPFv3 is no longer based on the highest IPv4 address on the router. The OSPFv3 router ID is still a 32-bit address that looks like an IPv4 address. The router ID is set using the **router-id** *router_id* command.

Question 40

What do OSPFv3 adjacencies use to communicate?

Question 41

What does OSPFv3 use for the transport of LSAs?

Question 42

Is OSPFv3 enabled per prefix or per link?

Answer 40

OSPFv3 adjacencies use link-local addresses to communicate. Router next-hop attributes are neighboring router link-local addresses. Because link-local addresses have the same prefix, OSPF needs to store the information about the outgoing interface.

Answer 41

OSPFv3 uses IPv6 for the transport of LSAs. The IPv6 protocol number 89 is used.

Answer 42

OSPFv3 is enabled per link (interface) and identifies which networks are attached to the interface.

Question 43

How do you configure OSPFv3 on a Cisco router?

Question 44

What Cisco IOS command displays all OSPFv3 interfaces?

Question 45

What Cisco IOS command displays the OSPFv3 router ID, process ID, timers, areas configured, and reference bandwidth?

Answer 43

Configuring OSFPv3 consists of enabling OSPF for IPv6, configuring the router ID, and enabling OSPFv3 on an interface. The following commands enable OSPFv3 on a router with the router ID of 2.2.2.2 and place Gigabit interface 0/0 in area 0:

```
RouterA(config)# ipv6 router ospf 1
RouterA(config-rtr)# router-id 2.2.2.2
RouterA(config-rtr)# interface g 0/0
RouterA(config-if)# ipv6 ospf 1 area 0
```

Answer 44

The **show ipv6 ospf interface** command displays all interfaces enabled with OSPFv3.

Answer 45

The **show ipv6 ospf** command displays general OSPFv3 information such as router ID, process ID, timers, areas configured, and reference bandwidth.

Section 6
Wide-Area Networks and Point-to-Point Communication Links

Wide-area networks (WAN) connect local-area networks (LAN) that are separated over a geographic distance. WANs usually connect networks through a third-party carrier. These third-party companies are usually telephone or cable companies. The third-party carrier charges the company that connects the networks a monthly fee for the WAN connections.

Currently, several WAN implementations exist. These include point-to-point leased lines, packet-switched lines, and circuit-switched lines. Also, carriers are offering newer implementations such as Ethernet over Fiber.

This section provides an overview of the different types of WAN connections, WAN terminology, and encapsulation. You are introduced to two common types of WAN encapsulation used on serial point-to-point connections: HDLC and Point-to-Point Protocol (PPP).

HDLC is the default encapsulation type on serial interfaces for Cisco routers. It is proprietary to Cisco.

PPP is a Layer 2 encapsulation method that was created as an open standard. Because it is an open standard and not proprietary, such as HDLC, it can be used to connected Cisco and non-Cisco devices. As you read this and the following sections, keep this in mind. The ICND2 exam will thoroughly test your knowledge of WAN connections and their technologies.

Question 1

On what layers of the OSI model do WAN technologies operate?

Question 2

What are the four available WAN connection types?

Question 3

What is customer premises equipment (CPE)?

Answer 1

WAN technologies operate at the physical and data link layers of the OSI model.

A WAN interconnects LANs that are separated by a large geographical distance not supported by typical LAN media.

The physical layer defines the electrical, mechanical, and operation connections of WANs, in addition to the interface between the data terminal equipment (DTE) and data communications equipment (DCE).

The data link layer defines the WAN Layer 2 encapsulation, such as Frame Relay, ATM, Ethernet emulation, HDLC, and PPP.

Answer 2

The four available WAN connection types are as follows:

- Dedicated connections (leased lines)
- Circuit-switching connections
- Packet-switching connections
- Cell-switching connections

Answer 3

CPE is equipment that is typically located on the customer's (or subscriber's) premises. It is equipment owned by the customer or equipment leased by the service provider to the customer. CPE varies from country to country.

Question 4

In WAN terminology, what is the demarcation point (demarc)?

Question 5

In WAN technologies, what is the local loop?

Question 6

In WAN technologies, what is the central office (CO)?

Answer 4

The demarc is a point where the CPE ends and the local loop begins. It is the point between the wiring that comes in from the local service provider and the wiring installed to connect the customer's CPE to the service provider. It is the last responsibility of the service provider and is usually a network interface device (NID) located in the customer's telephone wiring closet. Think of the demarc as the boundary between the customer's wiring and the service provider's wiring.

Answer 5

The local loop is the physical cable that extends from the demarc to the service provider's network.

Answer 6

The CO is the WAN service provider's office where the local loop terminates and in which circuit switching occurs.

Question 7

What is the CSU/DSU?

Question 8

What is the difference between baseband and broadband?

Question 9

What is serial transmission?

Answer 7

The CSU/DSU is required for digital carrier lines such as T1s or T3s. The CSU provides termination for the digital signal and ensures connection integrity through error correction and line monitoring. The DSU converts the T-carrier line frames into frames that the LAN can interpret and vice versa.

Answer 8

Baseband is a network technology in which only one carrier frequency is used (such as Ethernet). Broadband is a network technology in which several independent channels are multiplexed into one cable (for example, a T1 line or broadband [TV] cable).

Answer 9

Serial transmission is a method of data transmission in which bits of data are transmitted sequentially over a single channel. WANs use serial transmission.

Question 10

What is the V.35 physical layer serial protocol?

Question 11

Define the EIA/TIA-232 physical layer serial protocol.

Question 12

In WAN communications, what is clocking?

Answer 10

V.35 is an ITU-T standard for synchronous communications between a network access device (NAD) and a packet network. V.35 supports speeds up to 2.048 Mbps using a 34-pin rectangular connector.

Answer 11

EIA/TIA-232 is a protocol that allows signal speeds of up to 64 kbps on a 25-pin D-connector over short distances.

Answer 12

Clocking is the method used to synchronize data transmission among devices on a WAN. The CSU/DSU (DCE device) controls the clocking of the transmitted data.

NOTE   If you are connecting two serial interfaces back to back in a lab, one interface must provide clocking.

Question 13

How many channels (time slots) are in a full point-to-point T1 line?

Question 14

WANs use a technology called multiplexing. What is multiplexing?

Question 15

On what layer of the OSI model does WAN multiplexing occur?

Answer 13

A T1 line has 24 channel, or time, slots. Each channel is 64 kbps.

This information is useful because not all companies buy a full T1 line. Internet service providers (ISP) might offer fractional T1 lines that are less expensive than a full T1; this can be an option for branch offices that do not require a full T1. However, these are very rare in today's high-speed data networks. When configuring a router for a fractional T1, you need to configure the proper time slots on the CSU/DSU. If the CSU/DSU is internal to the router (a WAN interface card [WIC]), you configure the time slots in the serial interface of the router. If the CSU/DSU is external, you need to configure the external device. The default configuration on a Cisco interface is a full T1 (all 24 channels).

Answer 14

Multiplexing is a technology that enables multiple logical signals to be transmitted simultaneously across a single physical channel and then be combined into a single data channel at the source. This enables the signals to appear as one, combining the speeds of all channels.

Answer 15

WAN multiplexing occurs on the physical layer. Because multiplexing combines signals across a single physical channel, it occurs at the physical layer of the OSI model.

Question 16

How many DS0s are bundled to create a T1 line?

Question 17

How many T1 lines make up a T3 line?

Question 18

Describe packet-switched WAN connections.

Answer 16

Twenty-four DS0s are bundled to create a T1 line. One DS0 is 64 kbps.

NOTE   This is a perfect example of multiplexing. Twenty-four DS0 signals are combined to make one WAN line with a transfer rate of 1.544 Mbps.

Answer 17

Twenty-eight T1 lines make up a T3 line.

A T3 line is 45 Mbps and is made up of 28 T1 lines.

Answer 18

Packet-switched WAN connections use virtual circuits (VC) to provide end-to-end connectivity. Packet-switched WAN connections are similar to leased lines, except that the line is shared by other customers. A packet knows how to reach its destination by the programming of switches. Frame Relay is an example of a packet-switched connection. MPLS functions similarly to a packet-switched connection but also incorporates some advanced features.

Question 19

Define circuit-switched WAN connections?

Question 20

What type of WAN link is a leased line?

Question 21

What are synchronous links?

Answer 19

Circuit-switched WAN connections are connections dedicated for only the duration of the call or the time required to transmit data. The telephone system is an example of a circuit-switched network.

Answer 20

A leased line is a point-to-point link that provides a single, preestablished WAN communication path from the customer to the remote network.

Answer 21

Synchronous links have identical frequencies and contain individual characters encapsulated in control bits, called start/stop bits, which designate the beginning and end of each character. Synchronous links try to use the same speed as the other end of a serial link. Synchronous transmission occurs on V.35 and other interfaces, where one set of wires carries data and a separate set of wires carries clocking for that data.

Question 22

What are asynchronous links?

Question 23

Describe HDLC.

Question 24

What is the default encapsulation on a Cisco serial interface?

Answer 22

Asynchronous links send digital signals without timing. Asynchronous links agree on the same speed, but no check or adjustment of the rates occurs if they are slightly different. Only 1 byte per transfer is sent. Modems are asynchronous.

Answer 23

High-Level Data Link Control (HDLC) was derived from Synchronous Data Link Control (SDLC). It is the default encapsulation type on point-to-point dedicated links and circuit-switched connections between Cisco routers. It is an ISO-standard, bit-oriented, data-link protocol that encapsulates data on synchronous links. HDLC is a connection-oriented protocol that has little overhead. HDLC lacks a protocol field and therefore cannot encapsulate multiple network layer protocols across the same link. Because of this, each vendor has its own method of identifying the network layer protocol. Cisco offers a proprietary version of HDLC that uses a type field that acts as a protocol field, making it possible for multiple network layer protocols to share the same link.

Answer 24

HDLC is the default encapsulation on a Cisco serial interface.

Question 25

By default, Cisco uses HDLC as its default encapsulation method across synchronous serial lines (point-to-point links). If a serial line uses a different encapsulation protocol, how do you change it back to HDLC?

Question 26

What is the Point-to-Point Protocol (PPP)?

Question 27

List three characteristics of PPP.

Answer 25

To change a serial line back to HDLC, use the following interface command on the serial interface you want to change:

```
Router(config-if)# encapsulation hdlc
```

If the serial interface was previously configured for Frame Relay, you could also use the **no encapsulation frame-relay** interface command to set the encapsulation back to HDLC.

Answer 26

PPP is an industry-standard protocol that provides router-to-router or router-to-host connections over synchronous and asynchronous links. It can be used to connect WAN links to other vendors' equipment. It works with several network layer protocols, such as IP and Internetwork Packet Exchange (IPX). PPP provides authentication (which is optional) through Password Authentication Protocol (PAP), Challenge Handshake Authentication Protocol (CHAP), or Microsoft CHAP (MS-CHAP).

Answer 27

Three characteristics of PPP are as follows:

- It can be used over dial (analog) or switched lines.
- It provides error correction.
- It encapsulates several routed protocols.

Question 28

What two WAN encapsulations on a serial link are considered to be the most useful?

Question 29

How do you view the encapsulation type on a serial interface?

Answer 28

HDLC and PPP are considered to be the most useful because they are the most common and easiest to configure on a Cisco router.

NOTE   This might seem like a tricky question because it is hard to decide what are considered to be the most useful WAN encapsulations, but you might see questions like this on the CCNA exam, and you would have to choose the best answer even though multiple correct ones might exist.

Answer 29

The **show interface serial** *interface-number* command, as follows, allows you to view the encapsulation type on a serial interface:

```
RouterB# show interface serial 0
Serial0 is up, line protocol is up
  Hardware is HD64570
  Internet address is 192.168.1.1/24
  MTU 1500 bytes, BW 1544 Kbit, DLY 20000 usec, rely 255/255,
    load 1/255
      Encapsulation HDLC, loopback not set, keepalive set (10 sec)
  Last input 00:00:00, output 00:00:03, output hang never
  Last clearing of "show interface" counters never
  Input queue: 0/75/0 (size/max/drops); Total output drops: 0
  Queueing strategy: weighted fair
  Output queue: 0/1000/64/0 (size/max total/threshold/drops)
    Conversations  0/1/256 (active/max active/max total)
    Reserved Conversations 0/0 (allocated/max allocated)
  5 minute input rate 0 bits/sec, 0 packets/sec
  5 minute output rate 0 bits/sec, 0 packets/sec
```

Question 30

What provides clocking for a serial line?

Question 31

What command should be entered when connecting two routers without external DCE devices through a serial link?

Question 32

What command changes the clock rate of a Cisco interface acting as a DCE to 128 kbps?

Answer 30

The data communications equipment (DCE) provides clocking for a serial line. Examples of DCE devices are a data service unit/channel service unit (DSU/CSU) or another serial interface on a Cisco router configured for clocking.

Answer 31

The **clock rate** command should be entered. When connecting two routers without an external DCE device, the **clock rate** interface command changes one of the router's serial interfaces from a data terminal equipment (DTE) device to a DCE device.

Answer 32

The **clock rate 128000** command changes the clock rate to 128 kbps.

NOTE   Remember that the clock rate is in bits per second, not kilobits per second, and that you must insert a space between **clock** and **rate**.

Question 33

What is the default bandwidth of a serial interface on a Cisco router?

Question 34

How would you change the bandwidth of a serial interface on a Cisco router to 256 kbps?

Answer 33

The default bandwidth is 1544 kbps, or T1. This can be viewed with the **show interface serial** *interface-number* command, as follows:

```
RouterA# show int s0
Serial0 is up, line protocol is up
  Hardware is HD64570
  Internet address is 192.168.1.2/24
  MTU 1500 bytes, BW 1544 Kbit, DLY 20000 usec, rely 255/255,
    load 1/255
  Encapsulation PPP, loopback not set, keepalive set (10sec)
(Text omitted)
```

Answer 34

You would change the bandwidth by issuing the **bandwidth 256** interface command.

The command to change the bandwidth of a serial interface is the **bandwidth** *bandwidth-in-kbps* interface command. The correct command to change the bandwidth to 256 kbps is as follows:

```
RouterA(config-if)# bandwidth 256
```

Question 35

PPP is a data link layer protocol that provides network layer services. What are the two sublayers of PPP?

Question 36

What features does LCP offer to PPP encapsulation?

Answer 35

The two sublayers of PPP are as follows:

- **Network Control Protocol (NCP):** The component that encapsulates and configures multiple network layer protocols. Some examples of these protocols are IP Control Protocol (IPCP) and Internetwork Packet Exchange Control Protocol (IPXCP).

- **Link Control Protocol (LCP):** Used to establish, configure, maintain, and terminate PPP connections.

NOTE   The PPP protocol stack is specified at the physical and data link layers. For the exam, remember that PPP uses LCP to set up and configure the link and to negotiate the authentication, compression, and multilink before a connection is established. PPP uses NCP to allow communication of multiple network layer protocols across a PPP link.

Answer 36

LCP is used to establish, configure, and maintain PPP connections. It also offers authentication, callback, compression, error detection, and multilink to PPP encapsulation.

Question 37

How does PPP carry packets from several different protocol suites?

Question 38

What two methods of authentication can be used with PPP links?

Question 39

What two protocols are available for compression on PPP links?

Answer 37

PPP uses NCP to carry packets from several protocol suites.

Answer 38

The two methods of authentication that can be used with PPP links are as follows:

- Password Authentication Protocol (PAP)
- Challenge Handshake Authentication Protocol (CHAP)

PAP is the less-secure of the two methods; passwords are sent in clear text and are exchanged only upon initial link establishment. CHAP is used upon initial link establishment and periodically to make sure that the router is still communicating with the same host. CHAP passwords are exchanged as message digest algorithm 5 (MD5) encrypted values.

NOTE   In reality, there are more than two PPP authentication types. However, for the CCNA exam, only PAP and CHAP are covered.

Answer 39

The two protocols are Stacker and Predictor. As a rule, Predictor uses more memory than Stacker, and Stacker is more CPU intensive than Predictor.

NOTE   Cisco routers also support LZS and MPPC PPP compression. However, these are not covered in the CCNA exam.

Question 40

What Cisco IOS command enables PPP on a Cisco router serial interface?

Question 41

If PPP is enabled on an interface, how do you view the LCP and NCP states of the interface?

Question 42

A Cisco router and a router from another manufacturer are directly connected through a dedicated serial link. What command can be used on a Cisco router to form a WAN connection between the two routers?

Answer 40

The **encapsulation ppp** interface command, as follows, enables PPP on a Cisco router serial interface:

```
RouterB(config-if)# encapsulation ppp
```

Answer 41

Issue the **show interface serial** *interface-number* command, as follows, to view LCP and NCP states:

```
Router# show interface s0/3/0
Serial0/3/0 is up, line protocol is up (connected)
  Hardware is HD64570
  Internet address is 192.168.1.2/24
  MTU 1500 bytes, BW 128 Kbit, DLY 20000 usec,
     reliability 255/255, txload 1/255, rxload 1/255
  Encapsulation PPP, loopback not set, keepalive set (10 sec)
  LCP Open
  Open: IPCP, CDPCP0
  (text omitted)
```

Answer 42

The **encapsulation ppp** interface command can be used to form a WAN connection between the two routers. Because the Cisco router is connecting to another manufacturer's router over a dedicated serial link, PPP needs to be configured as the Layer 2 WAN protocol. If both routers were Cisco routers, HDLC or PPP encapsulation could be used.

Question 43

What three phases are used to establish a PPP session?

Question 44

How do you enable PPP authentication using CHAP on a Cisco router?

Answer 43

The three phases used to establish a PPP session are as follows:

Step 1.   **Link establishment phase:** Each PPP device sends LCP packets to configure and test the link (Layer 1).

Step 2.   **Authentication phase (optional):** If authentication is configured, either PAP or CHAP is used to authenticate the link. This must take place before the network layer protocol phase can begin (Layer 2).

Step 3.   **Network layer protocol phase:** PPP sends NCP packets to choose and configures one or more network layer protocols to be encapsulated and sent over the PPP data link (Layer 3).

NOTE   The **debug ppp authentication** command is a great troubleshooting command that allows you to view the results of PPP authentication. It shows you whether the username and password were found and verified.

Answer 44

Follow these steps to enable PPP authentication using CHAP on a Cisco router:

Step 1.   Make sure that each router has a host name assigned to it using the **hostname** command.

Step 2.   On each router, define the username of the remote router and the password that both routers will use with the **username** *remote-router-name* **password** *password* command.

Step 3.   Configure PPP authentication with the **ppp authentication** {chap | **chap pap** } interface command. (If both CHAP and PAP are enabled, the first method you specify in the command is used. If the peer suggests the second method or refuses the first method, the second method is used.)

```
RouterB(config)# hostname RouterB
RouterB(config)# username RouterA password cisco
RouterB(config)# int s0/0
RouterB(config-if)# ppp authentication chap
```

NOTE   CHAP uses a three-way handshake process to perform one-way authentication on a PPP serial interface.

Section 7
Establishing a WAN Connection
Using Frame Relay

Frame Relay was a popular technology used to connect WAN links in the 1990s and early 2000s because of its speed, reliability, and cost. Frame Relay is a packet-switched technology. Packet-switched networks enable end devices to dynamically share the WAN medium and bandwidth. Currently, Frame Relay has been largely replaced by newer technologies such as MPLS and Ethernet emulation. However, because of its early popularity, you can still find Frame Relay networks today.

In a Frame Relay network, data travels through the service provider's network along with other customers' data. The service provider programs switches to switch data in the right direction so that it does not get crossed with another customer's data. Because the data is shared in the switch with other customers' data, users are not going to always get 100 percent of the WAN link. To counteract this, most service providers guarantee a set speed of data transfer along the Frame Relay cloud; at times, this rate can be exceeded.

Frame Relay operates at the two lower layers of the OSI model and is a specification on how to encapsulate your data across a WAN link. It is considered a non-broadcast multiaccess (NBMA) technology because multiple routers can access the frame cloud but they do not have broadcast ability. This section quizzes you on the different terminology of Frame Relay and describes how to enable Frame Relay encapsulation on a Cisco router.

Question 1

What does Frame Relay rely on for error correction?

Question 2

What is the difference between switched virtual circuits (SVC) and permanent virtual circuits (PVC)?

Question 3

What is a data-link connection identifier (DLCI)?

Answer 1

Frame Relay relies on upper-layer protocols.

Frame Relay does not rely on any certain protocol for error correction. Instead, it relies on upper-layer protocols to provide error correction. For example, Frame Relay relies on TCP to provide error checking in an IP network.

NOTE Frame Relay does not provide error correction, but does provide error checking known as the cyclic redundancy check (CRC). The CRC compares two calculated values to determine whether errors occurred during the transmission from source to destination. Frame Relay reduces network overhead by implementing error checking rather than error correction.

Answer 2

SVCs are dynamically established. PVCs are permanent. SVCs are virtual circuits that are dynamically established when data needs to be transferred and are terminated when data transmission is complete. SVCs consist of four states: call setup, data transfer, idle, and call termination. PVCs are permanently established virtual circuits that operate in one of two states: idle or data transfer. When the PVC is idle, the connection between the data terminal equipment (DTE) devices is still active.

Answer 3

A DLCI is a number that identifies the logical circuit between the router and the Frame Relay switch. It is the Frame Relay Layer 2 address.

The Frame Relay switch maps DLCIs between each pair of routers to identify a PVC. For IP devices at the end of each virtual circuit to communicate, their IP addresses need to be mapped to DLCIs. Mapping DLCIs is done automatically using Inverse ARP or statically. DLCIs have local significance. Think of DLCIs as the MAC address of the Frame Relay network.

NOTE DLCIs are usually assigned by the Frame Relay provider.

Question 4

What does the Frame Relay switch use to distinguish between each PVC connection?

Question 5

What is the committed information rate (CIR)?

Question 6

How does Frame Relay use Inverse ARP?

Answer 4

The Frame Relay switch uses DLCIs to distinguish between each PVC connection.

Answer 5

The CIR is the rate that the service provider commits to transferring data. The service provider sends any data in excess of this rate if its network has capacity at that time. The CIR is expressed in bits per second.

Answer 6

Frame Relay uses Inverse ARP as a way to dynamically map a network layer address to a DLCI.

Frame Relay uses Inverse ARP to determine the remote node's IP address by sending the Inverse ARP to the local DLCI. With Inverse ARP, the router can discover the network address of a device associated with a virtual circuit (VC).

Question 7

What is the Local Management Interface (LMI)?

Question 8

In Frame Relay, what is the forward explicit congestion notification (FECN)?

Question 9

What is the backward explicit congestion notification (BECN)?

Answer 7

The LMI is a signaling standard between a customer premises equipment (CPE) device (a router) and the Frame Relay switch that is responsible for managing and maintaining status between the devices. It is autosensed with Cisco IOS Release 11.2 and later.

Answer 8

The FECN is the bit in the Frame Relay header that signals to anyone receiving the frame that congestion is occurring in the same direction in which the frame was traveling.

Answer 9

The BECN is the bit in the Frame Relay header that signals to devices receiving the frame that congestion is occurring in the direction opposite to which the frame was traveling.

If devices detect that the BECN bit in the Frame Relay header is set to 1, they slow the rate at which data is sent in that direction.

Question 10

In the Frame Relay header, what is the discard eligibility (DE) bit?

Question 11

The Frame Relay circuit between two routers is experiencing congestion. Which types of notifications are used to alleviate the congestion?

Question 12

What is the default LMI type for Cisco routers that are configured for Frame Relay?

Answer 10

The DE bit is turned on for frames that are in excess of the CIR. The DE bit tells a switch which frames to discard if they must be discarded.

For example, if your CIR is 256 kbps and you are using 512 KB of bandwidth, any frame above the first 256 KB will have the DE bit turned on. If the Frame Relay switch becomes congested, it will discard any frame above the first 256 KB with the DE turned on.

Answer 11

FECNs, BECNs, and DE notifications alleviate the congestion.

Answer 12

The default LMI for Cisco routers configured for Frame Relay is Cisco. By default, Cisco routers autosense the LMI type the Frame Relay switch is using. If it cannot autosense the LMI type, the router uses Cisco as its LMI type. The three types of LMIs supported by Cisco routers are as follows:

- Cisco
- ANSI
- Q933a

Question 13

When a router receives LMI information, it updates its VC status to one of three states. What are these three states?

Question 14

What is the default network connectivity type for a Frame Relay WAN?

Answer 13

The three states of a VC are as follows:

- **Active state:** The connection is active, and routers can exchange data.

- **Inactive state:** The local connection to the Frame Relay switch is working, but the remote router's connection to the Frame Relay switch is not working.

- **Deleted state:** Indicates that no LMIs are being received from the Frame Relay switch or that no service exists between the router and the local Frame Relay switch.

Answer 14

The default network connectivity type for a Frame Relay WAN is nonbroadcast multiaccess (NBMA). Nonbroadcast means that the network does not support broadcasts. Multiaccess means that the communication medium is shared by multiple devices, such as a LAN. An NBMA environment is treated like other broadcast media environments, such as Ethernet, where all the routers are on the same subnet.

Question 15

What three problems do Frame Relay NBMA networks cause when using multipoint interfaces?

Question 16

How do you enable Frame Relay on a Cisco router?

Answer 15

Frame Relay's NBMA network can cause reachability issues when a single multipoint interface is used to connect to multiple sites. Three issues caused by this are as follows:

- **Split horizon:** In EIGRP and RIP, split horizon reduces routing loops by preventing a routing update that is received on an interface from being forwarded out the same interface.

- **Neighbor discovery and DR/BDR elections:** By default, OSPF over NBMA works in nonbroadcast mode and neighbors are not automatically discovered. Also, one has to make sure that the hub router becomes the DR because NBMA networks behave like Ethernet, and a DR and BDR are needed to exchange routing information.

- **Broadcast replication:** Routers connected to many PVCs over a single interface must replicate broadcasts such as routing updates to remote routers. These broadcasts can consume bandwidth.

Answer 16

To enable Frame Relay on a Cisco router, you must first enable the serial interface for Frame Relay encapsulation with the **encapsulation frame-relay** interface command, as follows:

```
RouterB(config)# int s 0
RouterB(config-if)# ip address 192.168.1.1 255.255.255.0
RouterB(config-if)# encapsulation frame-relay
```

NOTE When enabling Frame Relay, you might need to configure some optional parameters, such as the DLCI, LMI type, and **bandwidth** to define your VC, its speed, and its LMI type. In its simplest form, Frame Relay configuration is merely the process of specifying the interface's encapsulation.

Question 17

What is the command used to configure DLCI 16 on interface s0?

Question 18

What Cisco IOS command displays the LMI traffic statistics and LMI type?

Question 19

The default encapsulation for a serial interface configured for Frame Relay is cisco. If you are connecting to a non-Cisco router, how do you change the encapsulation type?

Answer 17

The command used to configure DLCI 16 on interface s0 is **frame-relay interface-dlci 16.**

Answer 18

The **show frame-relay lmi** command, as follows, displays the LMI traffic statistics and LMI type:

```
RouterA# show frame-relay lmi
LMI Statistics for interface Serial0 (Frame Relay DTE) LMI  TYPE
= CISCO
   Invalid Unnumbered info 0          Invalid Prot Disc 0
   Invalid dummy Call Ref 0           Invalid Msg Type 0
   Invalid Status Message 0           Invalid Lock Shift 0
   Invalid Information ID 0           Invalid Report IE Len 0
   Invalid Report Request 0           Invalid Keep IE Len 0
   Num Status Enq. Rcvd 1748          Num Status msgs Sent 1748
   Num Update Status Sent 0           Num St Enq. Timeouts 0
```

Answer 19

If you are connecting to a non-Cisco router in a Frame Relay network, you need to specify ietf as the encapsulation type, as follows:

```
Router(config)# interface s0/3/0
RouterB(config-if)# encapsulation frame-relay ietf
```

Question 20

If Inverse ARP is disabled on your router, how do you reenable it?

Question 21

If a remote router does not support Inverse ARP, what must you configure on the router?

Answer 20

Inverse ARP is enabled by default on a Cisco router. If it is disabled, reenable it by using the following command:

```
RouterB(config-if)# frame-relay inverse-arp [protocol] [dlci]
```

Supported protocols indicated by the *protocol* option include **ip**, **ipx**, **decnet**, and **appletalk**.

Answer 21

If a remote router does not support Inverse ARP, you must configure a static mapping between the local DLCI and the remote protocol address.

Question 22

If a remote router does not support Inverse ARP, you must define the address-to-DLCI table statically. How do you create these static maps?

Question 23

How do you enable Frame Relay on a subinterface?

Answer 22

To define static maps on a Cisco router, use this command:

```
RouterA(config-if)# frame-relay map protocol remote-protocol-
address local-dlci
  [broadcast] [ietf | cisco] [payload-compress packet-by-packet]
```

The *protocol* option defines the supported protocol: AppleTalk, DECnet, DLSW, IP, IPX, LLC2, and RSRB.

The *protocol-address* option is the remote router's network layer address.

The *dlci* option defines the local router's local DLCI.

The **broadcast** statement specifies whether you want to forward broadcasts over the VC, permitting dynamic routing protocols over the VC.

The **ietf | cisco** statement is the encapsulation type.

For example, the following command tells the router to get to IP address 192.168.1.2 using DLCI 110:

```
RouterB(config-if)# frame-relay map ip 192.168.1.2 110 broadcast
cisco
```

Answer 23

To enable Frame Relay on a subinterface, you remove the IP address from the primary interface with the **no ip address** interface command, enable Frame Relay encapsulation on the serial interface, and then configure each subinterface with the IP address. For example, if you wanted to configure interface serial 0 with a subinterface, you would issue the following commands:

```
West-SD(config-if)# no ip address
West-SD(config-if)# encap frame-relay
West-SD(config-if)# int s0.1 point-to-point
West-SD(config-if)# ip address 192.168.1.5 255.255.255.0
West-SD(config-if)# frame-relay interface-dlci 110
West-SD(config-if)# int s0.2 point-to-point
West-SD(config-if)# ip address 192.168.2.5 255.255.255.0
West-SD(config-if)# frame-relay interface-dlci 120
```

NOTE   The **int s0.1 point-to-point** command tells the router to create subinterface s0.1 and to configured the link as a point-to-point link, not an NBMA link. To configure the subinterface as an NBMA link, use the **multipoint** command instead. If you do not configure the subinterface as multipoint, all interfaces connected to the Frame Relay WAN need to be on a different IP subnet.

Question 24

What command displays the status of a Frame Relay virtual circuit as well as traffic statistics?

Question 25

How do you display the current Frame Relay map entries and information about these connections on a Cisco router?

Question 26

How do you clear dynamic Frame Relay map entries that were created by Inverse ARP?

Answer 24

The **show frame-relay pvc** command shows the status of the Frame Relay circuit and traffic statistics. It also lists all the configured PVCs and DLCI numbers and the status of each PVC.

Answer 25

To view the current map entries and information about the connections, use the **show frame-relay map** command, as follows:

```
RouterA# show frame-relay map
Serial0 (up): ip 192.168.1.2 dlci 100(0x64,0x1840), dynamic,
              Broadcast, status defined, active
```

Answer 26

Use the **clear frame-relay-inarp** privileged EXEC command to clear dynamic Frame Relay maps created by Inverse ARP.

Question 27

As a network administrator, you configured Frame Relay on your Cisco routers; however, the Frame Relay link is down. You issue the show interface serial 0/0 command on your Cisco routers and you see the following:

```
RouterA# show int s0/0
Serial0/0 is down, line protocol is down
   Hardware is HD64570
   Internet address is 192.168.1.2/24
```

What are possible reasons that the Frame Relay link is down?

Question 28

You configure Frame Relay between two Cisco routers; however, you cannot ping the remote network. You issue the show interface serial 0 command and you see the following:

```
RouterA# show int s0
Serial0 is up, line protocol is down
   Hardware is HD64570
   Internet address is 192.168.1.2/24
```

What are possible reasons that you cannot ping the remote network?

Answer 27

Because the **show interface** command shows that the interface is down and the line protocol is down, the error is at the physical layer. This means that the problem is with the cable, the channel service unit/data service unit (CSU/DSU), or the serial line. To troubleshoot the problem, perform the following steps:

Step 1. Check the cable to make sure that it is a DTE serial cable and that the cables are securely attached.

Step 2. If the cable is the correct type, try a different serial port.

Step 3. If the cable does not work on the second port, try replacing the cable. If replacing the cable does not work, the problem might lie with the CSU/DSU.

Answer 28

Because the line is up but the line protocol is down, the router is getting a carrier signal from the CSU/DSU and the problem is with the data link layer. Causes for the line protocol being down include the following:

- The Frame Relay provider did not activate its port.
- An LMI mismatch has occurred.
- An encapsulation mismatch has occurred.
- The DLCI is inactive or has been deleted.
- The DLCI is assigned to the wrong subinterface.
- There are missing keepalives.

Question 29

How do you display the encapsulation type, DLCI, and LMI type, and determine whether the device is a DTE or DCE on a serial interface?

Answer 29

To display the interface's encapsulation type, DLCI number, and LMI type, and determine whether the device is a DTE or DCE, use the **show interface** *interface-type interface-number* command, as follows:

```
RouterA# show int s0
Serial0 is up, line protocol is up
  Hardware is HD64570
  Internet address is 192.168.1.2/24
  MTU 1500 bytes, BW 1544 Kbit, DLY 20000 usec, rely 255/255,
    load 1/255
  Encapsulation FRAME-RELAY, loopback not set, keepalive set (10 sec)
  LMI enq sent   3, LMI stat recvd 0, LMI upd recvd 0, DTE LMI up
  LMI enq recvd 5, LMI stat sent   0, LMI upd sent   0
  LMI DLCI 1023  LMI type is CISCO  frame relay DTE
  Broadcast queue 0/64, broadcasts sent/dropped 0/0, interface
    broadcasts 0
  Last input 00:00:05, output 00:00:07, output hang never
  Last clearing of "show interface" counters never
  Input queue: 0/75/0 (size/max/drops); Total output drops: 0
  Queueing strategy: weighted fair
<Output omitted>
```

Section 8
Introducing VPN Solutions

Virtual Private Networks (VPN) provide an Internet-based wide-area network (WAN) infrastructure for connecting branch offices, home offices, and telecommuters to the network. In other words, VPNs allow office locations and remote users to interconnect with each other securely through the Internet. After they are connected through the secure VPN connection, the interconnected networks become part of the network as if they were connected through a leased line such as a classic WAN link. This is done by tunneling and encrypting all traffic between the defined locations.

VPNs are growing in popularity because most locations already have an Internet connection, and instead of purchasing a separate dedicated leased line to interconnect offices, the interconnection can be done through the existing Internet connection.

Two categories of VPN connections exist:

- **Site-to-site:** Site-to-site connections are dedicated VPN connections that are usually always on, connecting entire networks. They act like a dedicated WAN link to interconnect locations much like a classic WAN link. Site-to-site connections are usually created in a firewall or a dedicated VPN concentrator.

- **Remote access:** Remote connections allow remote users to connect to the VPN through client software or Secure Shell (SSL). These connections are initiated by the remote user when the user wants to access the network.

To secure the connection between sites, an industry-standard protocol is typically used. One such protocol, IPsec, creates a connection between two endpoints and encrypts and decrypts traffic between the endpoints.

This section covers the basic topics of VPN solutions that you will find on the INCD2 exam.

Question 1

What is a Virtual Private Network (VPN)?

Question 2

What are the two types of VPNs?

Answer 1

A VPN is an encrypted connection between private networks over a public network such as the Internet. VPNs encrypt the traffic between connections to ensure that the traffic stays private. VPNs use virtual connections routed through the Internet to form a private network of the company to the remote site or employee host.

Answer 2

The two types of VPNs are as follows:

- Site-to-site
- Remote access

Site-to-site VPNs are an extension of a classic WAN network. They connect entire networks to each other. All traffic is sent and received through a VPN "gateway." The VPN gateway is responsible for encapsulating any encrypted outbound traffic for all traffic from a particular site to the destination site. The destination VPN gateway decrypts the traffic and forwards it to the private network.

Remote access VPNs are used for telecommuters, mobile users, and extranet traffic. They connect individual hosts securely to the company's private network. Remote VPNs can use any Internet-based medium to connect to the VPN, and each host connects through VPN client software. This VPN client software is responsible for encrypting and decrypting the traffic.

Question 3

What types of devices can be VPN gateways?

Question 4

What is an SSL VPN?

Question 5

What are the two Cisco SSL VPN solutions?

Answer 3

The following types of devices can be VPN gateways:

- Routers
- Firewalls
- Specialty VPN devices

Answer 4

An SSL VPN provides remote-access connectivity from almost any Internet-enabled location using a web browser and its native Secure Socket Layer (SSL) encryption.

Answer 5

The two Cisco SSL VPN solutions are

- Cisco AnyConnect SSL VPN
- Clientless Cisco SSL VPN

Cisco AnyConnect SSL VPN uses the Cisco AnyConnect client and SSL encryption for the VPN solution. The Clientless Cisco SSL VPN solution does not require client software to be installed and provides VPN access using almost any Internet-enabled web browser and SSL.

Question 6

What is IPsec?

Question 7

What four security services does IPsec provide?

Question 8

What are the two main IPsec framework protocols?

Answer 6

IPsec is an industry-standard protocol suite that acts at the network layer, protecting and authenticating IP packets between IPsec peers (devices). IPsec secures a path between a pair of gateways, a pair of hosts, or a gateway and a host.

IPsec is not bound to any specific encryption or authentication algorithm, keying technology, or security algorithms, thus allowing IPsec to support newer and better algorithms.

Answer 7

IPsec provides the following four security services:

- **Confidentiality (encryption):** Packets are encrypted before being transmitting across a network.

- **Data integrity:** The receiver can verify that the transmitted data was not altered or changed. This is done through checksums.

- **Authentication:** Ensures that the connection is made with the desired communication partner.

- **Antireplay protection:** Verifies that each packet is unique and not duplicated. This is done by comparing the sequence number of the received packets with a sliding window of the destination host or gateway.

Answer 8

The two main IPsec framework protocols are as follows:

- **Authentication Header (AH):** AH provides authentication, data integrity, and optional replay-detection services for IPsec using the authentication and data integrity algorithms. AH acts as a digital signature to ensure that data in the IP packet has not been tampered with. AH does not provide data encryption and decryption services. It can be used by itself or with ESP.

- **Encapsulation Security Protocol (ESP):** ESP provides encryption with optional authentication and replay-detection services. ESP encrypts the IP packet and the ESP header, thus concealing the data payload and the identities of the source and destination.

Question 9

List three types of encryption algorithms supported by IPsec.

Question 10

What two authentication methods are used by IPsec to authenticate peers?

Question 11

For IPsec encryption to work in a VPN, what must both the sender and receiver be configured with?

Answer 9

Three types of encryption algorithms supported by IPsec are as follows:

- **Data Encryption Standard (DES):** Uses a 56-bit key that ensures high-performance encryption. Uses a symmetric key cryptosystem.

- **Triple DES (3DES):** A variant of DES that breaks data into 64-bit blocks. 3DES then processes each block three times, each time with an independent 56-bit key, thus providing significant improvement in encryption strength over DES. Uses a symmetric key cryptosystem.

- **Advanced Encryption Standard (AES):** Provides stronger encryption than DES and is more efficient than 3DES. Key lengths can be 128-, 192-, and 256-bit keys.

Answer 10

The following two authentication methods are used by IPsec to authenticate peers:

- **Pre-Shared Keys:** Pre-Shared Keys are secret key values entered into each peer manually that authenticate the peer.

- **Rivest, Shamir, and Adelman (RSA) digital signatures:** RSA signatures use the exchange of digital certificates to authenticate the peers.

Answer 11

For IPsec encryption to work in a VPN, the sender and receiver must be configured with the same transform set.

A transform set is the rules used to encrypt the traffic through the VPN. These rules are based on algorithms and a key. If each end had a different transform set, the receiving device would not know how to decrypt the traffic of the sending device.

Question 12

What is the Diffie-Hellman Key Exchange?

Question 13

How does IPsec ensure data integrity?

Question 14

What are two common HMAC algorithms used by IPsec?

Answer 12

The Diffie-Hellman (DH) Key Exchange is a public key exchange that exchanges shared secret keys used for encryption and decryption over an insecure channel. DH is used within IKE to establish session keys.

Answer 13

To ensure data integrity, IPsec uses a data integrity algorithm that adds a hash to the message. The hash guarantees the integrity of the original message. A hash function or algorithm condenses a variable-length input message into a fixed-length hash of the message output, which can then be used as the message's "fingerprint."

Data integrity through IPsec protocols uses Hash-based Message Authentication Code (HMAC). To derive HMAC, IPsec uses hash algorithms MD5 and SHA to calculate a hash.

Answer 14

Two common HMAC algorithms used by IPsec are as follows:

- **Message digest algorithm 5 (MD5):** Uses a 128-bit shared secret key. The message and 128-bit shared secret key are combined and run through the MD5 hash algorithm, producing a 128-bit hash. This hash is added to the original message and forwarded to the remote host.

- **Secure Hash Algorithm 1 (SHA-1):** Uses a 160-bit secret key. The message and 160-bit shared secret key are combined and run through the SHA-1 hash algorithm, producing a 128-bit hash. This hash is added to the original message and forwarded to the remote host.

Question 15

What are GRE tunnels?

Question 16

What are the four characteristics of GRE?

Question 17

What IP protocol defines GRE packets?

Answer 15

Generic Routing Encapsulation (GRE) tunnels transport multiprotocol and IP multicast traffic between two or more remote sites that have only IP connectivity. GRE tunnels do this by encapsulating any OSI Layer 3 protocol. GRE tunnels allow routing information to be passed between connected networks.

GRE tunnels are not encrypted.

Answer 16

GRE has the following four characteristics:

- Uses a protocol type field in the GRE header to support the encapsulation of any OSI Layer 3 protocol
- Stateless with no flow-control mechanisms
- No encryption to protect encapsulated packets
- Creates 24 bytes of additional overhead for tunneled packets

Answer 17

IP protocol 47 defines GRE packets.

Question 18

What are the six steps to implement a GRE tunnel?

Answer 18

The six steps to implement a GRE tunnel are

Step 1.   Identify the IP addresses of all connecting sites that will be used to communication between sites.

Step 2.   Create a tunnel interface.

Step 3.   Specify GRE tunnel mode as the tunnel interface mode (optional).

Step 4.   Specify the tunnel source IP address.

Step 5.   Specify the tunnel destination IP address.

Step 6.   Configure an IP address for the tunnel interface.

The following example configures a GRE tunnel between Router A and Router B.

Router A configuration:

```
RouterA(config)# interface Tunnel0
RouterA(config-if)# ip address 192.168.255.1 255.255.255.0
RouterA(config-if)# tunnel mode gre ip
RouterA(config-if)# tunnel source 192.168.1.1
RouterA(config-if)# tunnel destination 192.168.1.2
```

Router B configuration:

```
RouterB(config)# interface Tunnel0
RouterB(config-if)# ip address 192.168.255.2 255.255.255.0
RouterB(config-if)# tunnel mode gre ip
RouterB(config-if)# tunnel source 192.168.1.2
RouterB(config-if)# tunnel destination 192.168.1.1
```

Section 9
Network Device Management

After a network is installed and running, the next and longest phase of any system life cycle is the management and operation phase. During the management and operation phase, the primary function is to ensure that the network and devices are functioning as originally configured; that any change in the network or system is properly tested, implemented, and documented; and that disaster recovery procedures are in place.

This section covers topics to help you manage a Cisco network. These topics include configuring SNMP, logging with a Syslog server, understanding NetFlow, and maintaining router configurations.

Question 1

What is SNMP?

Question 2

How many versions of SNMP exists?

Question 3

How do you configure SNMP on a Cisco router?

Answer 1

Simple Network Management Protocol (SNMP) is a standards-based application layer protocol that provides a means to monitor and control network devices. SNMP consists of an SNMP manager, an SNMP agent, and a Management Information Base (MIB).

The SNMP manager queries the SNMP agent, makes changes to the MIB variables, and provides a central place to analyze data gathered by agents.

The SNMP agent runs on a network device and gathers statistics and information on the device. The SNMP manager queries the agent for this information.

The MIB is the database of information maintained by the agent that the manager can query or set.

Answer 2

Currently, there are three versions of SNMP, as follows:

- **SNMPv1:** Uses plain text with community strings to authenticate communication between managers and agents.

- **SNMPv2c:** Uses plain text with community strings to authenticate communication like version 1, but also introduces bulk retrieval mechanisms.

- **SNMPv3:** Introduces security with strong authentication, confidentiality, and integrity as well as the v2 bulk retrieval mechanisms.

Answer 3

Follow these steps to configure SNMP on a router:

Step 1.   Configure the community string with read-write privileges.

Step 2.   Set the system contact and location.

The following example configures SNMP for read-write access with the community string of Ciscopress, the location of San Diego, and the contact information:

```
RouterA(config)# snmp-server community Ciscopress RW
RouterA(config)# snmp-server location San Diego
RouterA(config)# snmp-server contact John Smith
```

NOTE   This method is a minimum basic configuration for SNMP on a Cisco router. Best practice is to configure read-write access with authentication.

Question 4

What is Syslog?

Question 5

By default, Cisco network devices send what type of messages to the logging process?

Question 6

What are the various destinations that syslog messages can be forwarded to on Cisco devices?

Answer 4

Syslog is a protocol that allows network devices to send event notification messages across IP networks to event message collectors.

An event message collector can be a server or network management station that supports Syslog.

Answer 5

By default, Cisco devices send the output from system messages and **debug** privileged EXEC commands to a logging process.

Answer 6

Cisco devices can be configured to generate syslog messages and forward them to the following destinations:

- Logging buffer
- Console line
- Terminal lines
- Syslog server

Question 7

What are the eight severity syslog levels?

Question 8

How do you configure syslog on a Cisco router or switch?

Question 9

What is NetFlow?

Answer 7

The eight severity syslog levels used on Cisco devices are

- **Severity 0:** Emergency. System is unusable.
- **Severity 1:** Alert. Immediate action is needed.
- **Severity 2:** Critical. Critical condition with the device.
- **Severity 3:** Error. An error condition has occurred.
- **Severity 4:** Warning. A warning condition has occurred.
- **Severity 5:** Notification. Normal but significant condition.
- **Severity 6:** Information. Informational message.
- **Severity 7:** Debugging.

Answer 8

The **logging** *ip-address* and **logging trap** *severity* commands are used to configure a Cisco router or switch to send information to a syslog server. The *ip-address* is the IP address of the syslog server, and the *severity* tells the device what messages to send to the syslog server based on the severity level. By default, syslog servers receive informational messages. The **logging trap** command, if used, will change the default logging level.

Answer 9

NetFlow is a Cisco application that provides statistics on packets flowing through routing devices on a network.

NetFlow can provide network traffic accounting, provide usage-based network reports, and be used for network planning, security, and denial of service monitoring.

Question 10

What are the two components of NetFlow?

Question 11

What are the seven key fields that define a unique flow in NetFlow?

Answer 10

The two components needed for NetFlow are a network device configured for NetFlow and a NetFlow collector.

A NetFlow collector receives NetFlow information from network devices and then filters, aggregates, and stores the data. The collector also performs traffic analysis.

Answer 11

The seven key fields that define a unique flow in NetFlow are

- Source IP address
- Destination IP address
- Source port number
- Destination port number
- Layer 3 protocol type
- Type of service (ToS)
- Input logical interface

NOTE ToS is a field in the IP header. It is used to mark IP packets with different priorities in order to receive different treatment in terms of throughput, reliability, and latency.

Question 12

How many released versions of NetFlow exist?

Question 13

What are the steps used to configure NetFlow on a Cisco router?

Question 14

What Cisco IOS command displays the version of NetFlow configured on a router?

Answer 12

Five versions of NetFlow exist.

NetFlow exports data in UDP in one of five formats or versions: 1, 5, 7, 8, and 9.

Version 9 is the most versatile export data format, but it is not backward compatible with version 8 or 5.

Answer 13

The steps used to configure NetFlow are as follows:

Step 1.   Configure NetFlow data capture from ingress and egress packets using the **ip flow ingress** and **ip flow egress** interface commands.

Step 2.   Configure NetFlow data to be exported to the NetFlow collector using the **ip flow-export destination** *ip-address* global command.

Step 3.   Configure the NetFlow export version using the **ip flow-export version** *version* global command.

Answer 14

The **show ip flow export** command displays the version of NetFlow configured on the router, the host of the NetFlow connector, the UDP port number used, and the accounting data export.

Question 15

On a Cisco router, what is RAM used to store?

Question 16

What is the function of ROM on a Cisco router?

Question 17

What is flash memory used for on a Cisco router?

Answer 15

RAM is used on a Cisco router to store the following:

- IOS
- Router running configuration file
- IP routing table
- ARP cache
- Packet buffer

Answer 16

On a Cisco router, ROM is a form of permanent storage and contains the microcode for basic router functions. The major areas of this microcode in ROM are

- **Bootstrap code:** Brings up the router during initialization. Reads the configuration register to determine how to boot and then loads the Cisco IOS.
- **POST:** Tests the basic functionality of the router hardware.
- **ROMMON:** A low-level OS that is used for manufacturing, testing, troubleshooting, and password recovery.

Answer 17

Flash memory stores the Cisco IOS Software image and, if room exists, multiple configuration files or multiple IOS files. Flash memory is not erased when the router or switch is reloaded.

Question 18

What is the function of NVRAM on a Cisco router?

Question 19

What is the main purpose of the configuration register on a Cisco router?

Question 20

How do you enter ROM Monitor (ROMMON)?

Answer 18

Nonvolatile random-access memory (NVRAM) holds the saved router configuration (it also holds the switch configuration). Cisco IOS uses NVRAM to store the startup configuration file. All configuration changes are made in the running configuration file in RAM and stored to NVRAM when saved. This configuration is maintained when the device is turned off or reloaded.

Answer 19

The configuration register is used to control how the router boots. It is a 16-bit software register value that is stored in NVRAM.

Answer 20

To enter ROMMON, while connected to the console port, reboot the router or switch and press the **Break** key during router bootup.

Question 21

When a Cisco router powers up, what steps does the router take in the boot sequence?

Question 22

How do you change the configuration register on a Cisco router?

Answer 21

The seven steps a router takes in the power-on boot sequence are as follows:

Step 1.   Perform a power-on self-test (POST).

Step 2.   Load and run the bootstrap code from ROM.

Step 3.   Find the Cisco IOS Software in flash. If the IOS is not found in flash, it can be located elsewhere, such as a TFTP server. If a complete IOS version is not found, a scaled-down version of the IOS is copied from ROM to RAM.

Step 4.   Load the Cisco IOS Software into RAM.

Step 5.   Find the configuration file in NVRAM. If no configuration file exists, the router or switch will enter the setup utility or attempt an AutoInstall to look for a configuration file from a TFTP server.

Step 6.   Load the configuration file from NVRAM to RAM.

Step 7.   Run the configured Cisco IOS Software.

Answer 22

To change the configuration register on a Cisco router, use the **config-register** command from global configuration mode.

Question 23

What Cisco IOS command would you use to view the current configuration register value?

Question 24

Before installing a new, upgraded version of the Cisco IOS, what should be checked on the router? What IOS command gathers this information?

Answer 23

The **show version** command, as follows, displays the router's current configuration register:

```
cisco2960-1# sh version
Cisco IOS Software, C2960 Software (C2960-LANBASEK9-M), Version
15.1SE3, RELEASE SOFTWARE (fc1)
Technical Support: http://www.cisco.com/techsupport
Copyright (c) 1986-2010 by Cisco Systems, Inc.
Compiled Thu 02-Dec-10 08:16 by prod_rel_team
Image text-base: 0x00003000, data-base: 0x01800000
<Output omitted>
Configuration register is 0x2102
```

NOTE   For the exam, you must know that the **show version** command displays the system hardware, software version, names and location of the IOS images, boot images, and configuration register.

Answer 24

Before upgrading the IOS on a router, the amount of available flash and RAM should be checked. You need to verify that the router can support the new image.

The **show version** privileged command displays the amount of flash and RAM available on a router.

Question 25

What IOS command configures the router to boot from an alternate IOS located in flash?

Question 26

How do you make a Cisco router a TFTP server?

Answer 25

The **boot system flash** *ios-file-name* global configuration command instructs the router to boot from a different IOS located in flash memory.

Answer 26

To configure a Cisco router as a TFTP server, use the **tftp-server** global configuration command.

NOTE   You might want to configure a Cisco router as a TFTP server to allow other devices to access IOS files or configuration files.

Question 27

What Cisco IOS command merges the running configuration in RAM from a saved configuration file on a TFTP server?

Question 28

How do you upload and save your current router configuration to a TFTP server?

Answer 27

The **copy tftp running-config** privileged EXEC command merges the running configuration in RAM from the saved configuration file on a TFTP server. Sample command output is as follows:

```
RouterB# copy tftp running-config
Address or name of remote host []? 192.168.0.2
Source filename []? routerb-confg
Destination filename [running-config]?
Accessing tftp://192.168.0.2/routerb-confg...
Loading routerb-confg from 192.168.0.2 (via Ethernet0): !
[OK - 780/1024 bytes]
780 bytes copied in 4.12 secs (195 bytes/sec)
RouterB#
01:40:46: %SYS-5-CONFIG: Configured from tftp:  //192.168.0.2/
routerb-confg
```

NOTE   When a configuration file is copied into RAM from any source, the configuration merges with any existing configuration in RAM rather than overwriting it. New configuration parameters are added, and changes to existing parameters overwrite the old parameters.

Answer 28

The **copy running-config tftp** command uploads and saves the current configuration to a TFTP server.

Question 29

During router startup, you see the following error message:

`Boot cannot open "flash"`

What will the router try to do next?

Question 30

As a network administrator, you are locked out of a Cisco router and must go through password recovery. What must you set the configuration register to in ROMMON mode to allow you to change the router password?

Answer 29

The router will attempt to locate the IOS image from a TFTP server. If the router cannot find the IOS image from a TFTP server, the router will load a limited IOS from ROM.

The Cisco IOS boot process is as follows:

1. Router performs a power-on self-test (POST).
2. Router loads and runs bootstrap code from ROM.
3. Router finds the IOS and loads it. The router looks for the IOS in the following order: flash, TFTP, ROM.
4. Router looks for and finds the configuration file and loads it into running configuration. If the router does not find a configuration file, it runs setup mode.

Answer 30

The configuration register in ROMMON must be set to 0x2142. The hexadecimal number of 4 will instruct the router to ignore the startup configuration at the next reload.

Section 1
VLANs and Trunk Links

VLANs and Trunks

The virtual LAN (VLAN) organizes physically separate users into the same broadcast domain. The use of VLANs improves performance, security, and flexibility. The use of VLANs can also decrease the cost of arranging users, because no extra cabling is required.

VLAN Characteristics

VLANs allow logically defined user groups rather than user groups defined by their physical locations. For example, you can arrange user groups such as accounting, engineering, and finance, rather than everyone on the first floor, everyone on the second floor, and so on. Some defining VLAN characteristics are as follows:

- VLANs define broadcast domains that can span multiple physical LAN segments.
- VLANs improve segmentation, flexibility, and security.
- VLAN segmentation is not bound by the physical location of users.
- Each switch port can be assigned to a data VLAN and voice VLAN, or a trunk.
- Ports assigned to the same VLAN share broadcasts and are in the same broadcast domain.
- A VLAN can exist on one or several switches.

Figure 1-1 shows a VLAN design. Note that VLANs are defined by user functions rather than locations.

Figure 1-1   *VLAN Design*

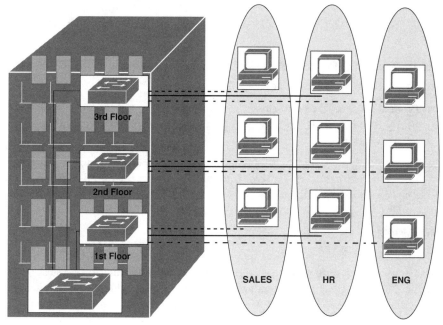

VLAN Operation

Figure 1-2 shows that each VLAN on a switch behaves as if it were a separate physical bridge. The switch forwards packets (including unicasts, multicasts, and broadcasts) only to ports assigned to the same VLAN from which they originated. This drastically cuts down on network traffic.

Figure 1-2   *VLAN Operation*

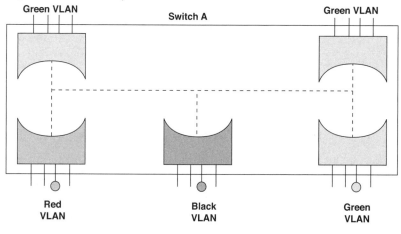

VLANs require a trunk or a physical connection for each VLAN to span multiple switches. Each trunk can carry traffic for multiple VLANs.

VLAN Port Membership Modes

A port must be assigned (configured) to a VLAN or configured as a trunk by assigning a membership mode that specifies the kind of traffic the port carries:

- **Static access:** The port belongs to only one VLAN and is manually assigned.

- **Trunk (IEEE 802.1Q):** The port is a member of all VLANs.

- **Dynamic access:** The port belongs to one VLAN and is dynamically assigned by a VLAN Membership Policy Server (VMPS). Dynamic access ports cannot connect to another switch.

- **Voice VLAN:** The port is an access port attached to a Cisco IP Phone that is configured to use one VLAN for voice traffic and another VLAN for data traffic from a device connected to the IP Phone.

Trunking

The IEEE 802.1Q is a standard that defines a system of VLAN tagging for Ethernet frames and the procedures to be used by bridges and switches in handling such frames. 802.1Q tagging provides a standard method of identifying frames that belong to a particular VLAN by using an internal tag that modifies the existing Ethernet frame with the VLAN identification.

Cisco supports 802.1Q trunking over Fast Ethernet and above links. 802.1Q defines how to carry traffic from multiple VLANs over a single point-to-point link.

Configuring VLANs and Trunks

The steps to configure VLANs on Cisco Catalyst series switches are as follows:

STEP 1.   Create the VLAN.

STEP 2.   Name the VLAN.

STEP 3.   Add the desired ports to the VLAN.

STEP 4.   Verify VLANs.

The steps to configured trunk links on Cisco Catalyst series switches are as follows:

STEP 1.   Properly configure the interface to the proper modes (for example, Trunk, DTP, Auto, DTP desirable).

STEP 2.   Define allowed VLANs on trunk links.

STEP 3.   Ensure that VLANs have been properly configured on the switch so that they can be trunk links.

Adding, Modifying, and Deleting a VLAN

The **vlan** *vlan-id* global command adds a VLAN to a Catalyst switch, as demonstrated here:

```
Switch(config)# vlan 10
Switch(config-vlan)# name Accounting
```

To modify a VLAN name, enter the VLAN you want to modify and change its name to the desired name, as follows:

```
Switch(config)# vlan 10
Switch(config-vlan)# name Sales
```

The **no vlan** *vlan-id* global command removes a VLAN from a Catalyst switch, as demonstrated here:

```
Switch(config)# no vlan 10
```

Configuring a Trunk Link

Cisco switches can use a proprietary protocol, DTP (Dynamic Trunking Protocol), to negotiate a trunk link. The **switchport trunk** command sets a switch ports to trunk mode.

```
switchport mode [dynamic {auto | desirable} | trunk]
```

- **mode dynamic auto** allows the interface to convert to a trunk link if the connecting neighbor interface is set to **trunk** or **desirable**.

- **mode dynamic desirable** allows the interface to actively attempt to convert the link to a trunk link. The link becomes a trunk if the neighbor interface is set to **trunk, desirable,** or **auto. trunk** sets the interface to trunking on.

```
Cat2960(config)# interface g0/1
Cat2960(config-if)# switchport mode trunk
Cat2960(config-if)# interface g0/2
Cat2960(config-if)# switchport mode dynamic desirable
```

Defining Allowed VLANs

By default, all VLANs (1–4094) are allowed to propagate on all trunk links. To limit a trunk to allow only specified VLANs, use the following command:

```
switchport trunk allowed vlan {add | all | except | remove}
    vlan-list
```

The following command allows only VLANs 10–50 on a trunk link:

```
Cat2960(config-if)# switchport trunk allowed vlan 10-50
```

Assigning Ports to a VLAN

Assigning a single port:

```
Cat2960(config)# interface fastethernet 0/1
Cat2960(config-if-range)# switchport mode access
Cat2960(config-if-range)# switchport access vlan 10
```

Assigning a range of ports:

```
Cat2960(config)# interface range fastethernet 0/1 - 12
Cat2960(config-if-range)# switchport mode access
Cat2960(config-if-range)# switchport access vlan 10
```

VLAN Troubleshooting

Use the following high-level steps to troubleshoot VLAN issues:

STEP 1.   Use the **show vlan** command to check whether a port is configured for the proper VLAN. If not, use the **switchport access vlan** command to correct the VLAN membership.

STEP 2.   Use the **show mac address-table** command to check which MAC addresses were learned on the port of the switch and to which VLAN that port is assigned.

STEP 3.   If the port shows inactive, that means the VLAN was deleted from the switch. Use the **show vlan** or **show interfaces switchport** command to verify whether the VLAN is configured on the switch.

Use the following steps to troubleshoot trunking issues:

STEP 1.   Use the **show interfaces trunk** command to check whether a trunk has been established between the switches. Cisco switches use DTP by default to negotiate a trunk link. If negotiation is not working, statically configure the trunk links.

STEP 2.   Make sure that the local and peer native VLANs match by using the **show interfaces trunk** command. If the native VLANs do not match, VLAN leaking occurs.

Section 2
Building Redundant Switched Topologies

Issues in Redundant Topologies

A redundant topology has multiple connections to switches or other devices. Redundancy ensures that a single point of failure does not cause the entire switched network to fail. In the absence of the Spanning Tree Protocol (STP), Layer 2 redundancy can cause problems in a network, including broadcast storms, multiple copies of frames, multiple loops, and MAC address table instability. Figure 2-1 shows a redundant topology.

Figure 2-1   *Redundant Switched Topology*

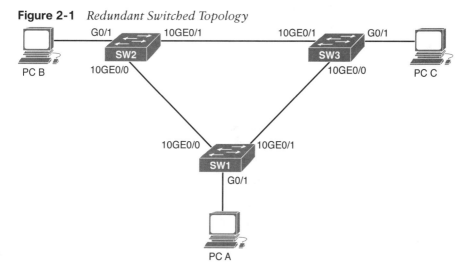

Broadcast Storms

Switches flood broadcasts out all interfaces in the same VLAN, except the interface in which the frame arrived. The flooding of broadcast frames can cause a broadcast storm (indefinite flooding of frames) unless a mechanism is in place to prevent it.

An example of a broadcast storm is shown in Figure 2-2. The dashed lines show how the switches forward the frame when STP does not exist and can be described as follows:

1. PC A sends a broadcast frame, which is received by switch SW1 on interface G0/1.

2. Switch SW1 checks the destination and floods the frame out interfaces 10GE0/0 and 10GE0/1.

3. Switches SW2 and SW3 receive the frame on interface 10GE0/0, and both switches flood the frame out their interface 10GE0/1.

4. Switch SW3 will receive the broadcast sent from SW2 on interface 10GE0/1 and flood it out interfaces G0/1 and 10GE0/0. SW2 does the same thing. Switch SW1 will receive the broadcast it originally sent from SW3 and SW2 and floods the broadcasts out all interfaces except the interface in which the frame arrived. In this case, SW1 will again forward the broadcast it received from SW2 out interface 10GE0/1 and the broadcast it received from SW3 out interface 10GE0/0. The frame travels continuously in both directions.

Figure 2-2 *Broadcast Storm*

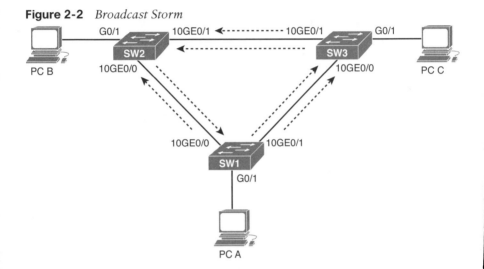

Multiple Frame Transmission

Some protocols cannot correctly handle duplicate transmissions. Protocols that use sequence numbering see that the sequence has recycled. Other protocols process the duplicate frame with unpredictable results. As depicted in Figure 2-3, multiple frame transmissions occur, as follows:

1. PC A sends a frame to PC C. The frame is received by SW1 on interface G0/1.

2. Switch SW1 checks the destination address. If the switch does not find an entry in the MAC address table for PC C, it floods the frame on all ports except the originating port. In this case, switch SW1 will flood the frame out interfaces 10GE0/0 and 10GE0/1.

3. Switch SW2 receives the frame on interface 10GE0/0 and checks the destination address. If the switch does not find an entry in the MAC address table for PC C, SW2 floods the frame on all ports except the originating port. This means that SW2 will flood the frame out interface 10GE0/1.

4. Switch SW3 receives the frame sent from SW1 on interface 10GE0/0 and checks the destination address. Switch SW3 sees that PC C is directly connected on interface G0/1 and sends the frame to interface G0/1. Switch SW3 also receives

the frame sent from SW2 on interface 10GE0/1 and sees that it is intended for PC C and forwards the frame to interface G0/1.

Note that PC C has now received the same frame twice.

Figure 2-3   *Multiple Frame Transmission*

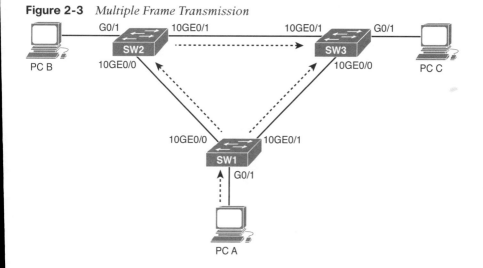

MAC Database Instability

Database instability occurs when a switch receives the same frame on different ports. MAC address instability means that the switches' MAC address tables will keep changing the information listed for the source MAC address of the looping frame. For example, in Figure 2-4:

1. PC A sends a frame to PC C. Switch SW1 receives the frame from PC A on interface G0/1. SW1 adds an entry in its MAC address table that the MAC address for PC A is associated with interface G0/1.

2. If SW1 does not have an entry for PC C in its MAC address table, it floods the frame out interfaces 10GE0/0 and 10GE0/1.

3. Switches SW2 and SW3 receive the frame from SW1.

4. With the switch-learning process, SW2 and SW3 will learn about the source address of PC A on interfaces 10GE0/0 and 10GE0/0. When the looping frame goes to SW2 and SW3, the switches will update their MAC address tables with the associated port and MAC address of PC A. For example, with switch SW3, it will continually update its MAC address table to reflect that PC A is associated with port 10GE0/0 and then 10GE0/1.

This process repeats indefinitely.

Figure 2-4   *MAC Database Instability*

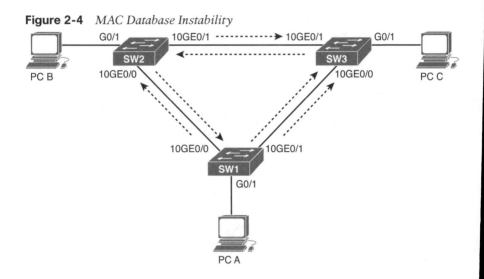

Spanning Tree Protocol

Spanning Tree Protocol (STP) prevents looping traffic in a redundant switched network by blocking traffic on the redundant links. If the main link goes down, Spanning Tree activates the standby path.

STP was developed by Digital Equipment Corp. (DEC) and was revised in the IEEE 802.1d specification. The two algorithms are incompatible. Catalyst 2960s switches use the IEEE 802.1w PVST+ by default.

Spanning Tree Operation

STP assigns roles to switches and ports so that only one path is available through the switch network at any given time. This is accomplished by assigning a single root bridge, root ports for nonroot bridges, and a single designated port for each network segment. The root bridge is automatically chosen but should be manually chosen. On the root bridge, all ports are designated ports. Assignment is made by cost. Table 2-1 shows the costs for switch interfaces.

Table 2-1   *Spanning Tree Costs*

Link Speed	Cost
10 Gbps	2
1 Gbps	4
100 Mbps	19
10 Mbps	100

On the root bridge, all ports are set to the forwarding state. For the nonroot bridge, only the root port is set to the forwarding state. The port with the lowest-cost path to the root bridge is chosen as the root port.

One designated port is assigned on each segment. The bridge with the lowest-cost path to the root bridge is the designated port. Figure 2-5 shows a root bridge, nonroot bridge, and port status. One port on each segment will be blocking to prevent loops.

Figure 2-5   *Root Bridge, Nonroot Bridge, and Port Status*

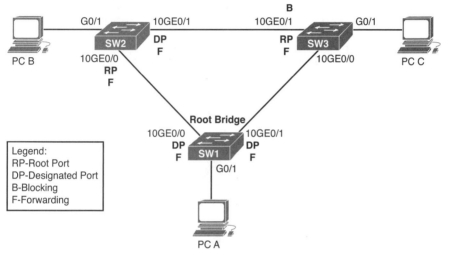

Spanning Tree must select the following:

■ One root bridge.

■ One root port per nonroot bridge.

■ One designated port per network segment.

■ The decision on which switch is elected the root bridge is based on the lowest BID.

■ The decision for which ports become the root port on nonroot bridges is based on the lowest root path cost. If two ports have an equal path cost to the root, the switch looks at the BID values in the received BPDUs to make a decision. If the BID values are the same because both ports are connected to the same upstream switch, the switch looks at the Port ID field in the BPDUs and selects its root port based on the lowest value in that field.

■ The designated port for each segment is the port with the lowest root path cost. Ties are broken by upstream BID and port ID.

Selecting the Root Bridge

Switches running STP exchange information at regular intervals using a frame called the bridge protocol data unit (BPDU). Each bridge has a unique bridge ID. The bridge ID contains the bridge MAC address and a priority number. The midrange value of 32768 is the default priority. The bridge with the lowest bridge ID is selected as the root bridge. When switches have the same priority, the one with the lowest MAC address is the root bridge. Figure 2-6 shows switch SW1 as the root bridge.

Figure 2-6   *Root Bridge Selection*

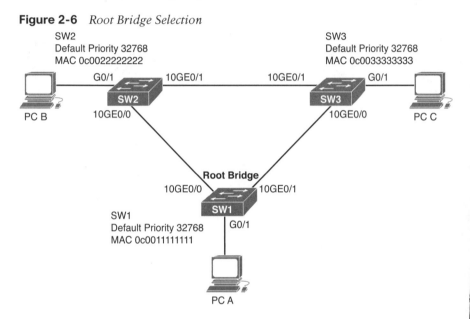

Spanning Tree Election Criteria

Spanning Tree builds paths from the root bridge along the fastest links. It selects paths according to the following criteria:

1. Lowest path cost to the root bridge

2. Lowest sender bridge ID

3. Lowest sender port ID

Port States

When a link goes down, Spanning Tree converges and a switch chooses transition interfaces from one state to another. This transition from blocking to forwarding is not done immediately because an immediate change to forwarding could temporarily cause frames to loop. To prevent these temporary loops, STP transitions an interface through two intermediate interfaces states: listening and learning. Each switch port in a network running STP is in one of the following states listed in Table 2-2.

Table 2-2   *Spanning Tree Port States*

Port State	Timer	Actions
Blocking	Max Age (20 sec)	Receives BPDUs, discards frames, does not learn MAC addresses
Listening	Forward Delay (15 sec)	Receives BPDUs to determine its role in STP, does not learn MAC addresses
Learning	Forward Delay (15 sec)	Receives and transmits BPDUs, learns MAC addresses
Forwarding	—	Forwards frames, learns MAC addresses, receives and transmits BPDUs

The Max Age timer determines how long any switch should wait, after hearing Hellos, before trying to change the STP topology. The forward delay is the time it takes for a port to go to a higher state. It usually takes 50 seconds for a port to go from the blocking state to the forwarding state, but the timers can be adjusted.

Spanning Tree is considered converged when all ports are either in the forwarding or blocking state.

Spanning Tree Recalculation

When a link fails, the network topology changes. Connectivity is reestablished by placing key blocked ports in the forwarding state.

In Figure 2-7, if interface 10GE0/1 on SW1 fails, switch SW3 does not receive the BPDUs. If the BPDU is not received before the MAXAGE timer expires, Spanning Tree begins to reconverge. In the figure, switch SW3's MAXAGE timer expires and it transitions interface 10GE0/1 from blocking to listening. If interface 10GE0/1 on SW1 is repaired and comes back online, STP will reconverge again.

Figure 2-7   *Spanning Tree Recalculation*

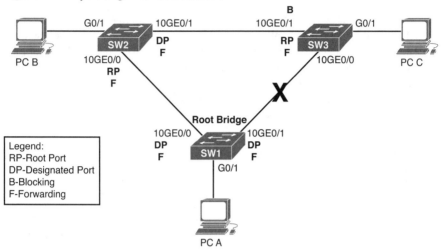

Time to Convergence

A network is said to have converged when all ports in a switched network are in either a blocking or forwarding state after a topology change.

Types of Spanning Tree

STP is a network protocol that ensures a loop-free topology. There are several varieties of spanning-tree protocols, as discussed in the sections that follow.

Per-VLAN STP+ (PVST+)

PVST+ creates a different spanning-tree instance for each VLAN on a switch. Each VLAN has its own root bridge, root ports, designated ports, and nondesignated ports.

PVST+ is enabled by default on Cisco switches running 802.1D. In PVST+, the spanning-tree topology can be configured so that each VLAN has a different root bridge. PVST+ is Cisco proprietary.

PVST+ provides a separate instance of Spanning Tree for each VLAN. STP requires that each switch have a unique bridge ID (BID). The original 802.1D standard BID consisted of the bridge priority and MAC address. Because PVST+ provides a separate instance of Spanning Tree for each VLAN, the BID field is required to carry VLAN ID (VID) information. This is accomplished by using a portion of the Priority field as the extended system ID to carry the VID. Therefore, in PVST+, the BID consists of the following:

- **Bridge priority:** A 4-bit field. The default is 32,768.

- **Extended system ID:** A 12-bit field carrying the VID.

- **MAC address:** A 6-byte field containing the MAC address of the switch.

Rapid Spanning Tree Protocol (RSTP)

IEEE 802.1w, or RSTP, is an enhancement of STP that provides faster STP convergence. RSTP addresses many convergence issues but still only provides a single instance of STP. RSTP improves convergence by either eliminating or significantly reducing the waiting periods that 802.1d STP needs to avoid loops during convergence. RSTP does this by only having to wait for three Hellos in the MAXAGE timer (6 seconds) and eliminates the forward delay time in both the listening and learning states. RSTP convergence times are typically less than 10 seconds and in some cases as low as 1 to 2 seconds.

RSTP Port States

Table 2-3 lists the RSTP port states.

Table 2-3   *Port State Comparison*

Operational Status	STP Port State	RSTP Port State	Port Included in Active Topology?
Enabled	Blocking	Discarding	No
Enabled	Listening	Discarding	Yes
Enabled	Learning	Learning	Yes
Enabled	Forwarding	Forwarding	Yes
Enabled	Disabled	Discarding	No

In RSTP, all ports are either in the forwarding or discarding state. Discarding means that the port does not forward frames, process received frames, or learn MAC addresses, but it listens for BPDUs.

RSTP Port Roles

RSTP has new port roles. The root port and designated port roles are the same as they are in 802.1D. However, the blocking port in 802.1D is split into the backup and alternate port roles. Also, in RSTP, the Spanning Tree algorithm determines the role of a port based on BPDUs. The port roles in RSTP are as follows:

- **Root port:** The port that received the best BPDU on a switch.

- **Designated port:** The port that sends the best BPDU on the segment.

- **Backup port:** Defined as not being the designated or root port. It is a port that receives more useful BPDUs from the same switch it is on and is in a blocking state.

- **Alternate port:** A port that receives more useful BPDUs from another switch and is in a blocking state.

In RSTP, if the root port fails, the alternate port will become the new root port and the backup port will become the new designated port.

Figure 2-8 shows the new port roles in RSTP.

Figure 2-8   *RSTP Port Roles*

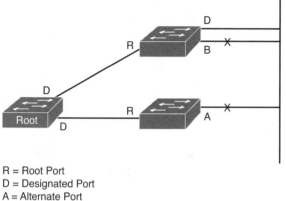

R = Root Port
D = Designated Port
A = Alternate Port
B = Backup Port

New BPDU Format

RSTP uses a new BPDU format. Additionally, RSTP uses BPDUs as a keepalive mechanism. RSTP sends a BPDU every hello-time (2 seconds by default). If a port does not receive three consecutive BPDUs (6 seconds), the switch considers it has lost connectivity to its direct neighbor and begins to transition to the forwarding state.

Edge Port

An RSTP edge port is a port that is directly connected to end stations. Because directly connected end stations cannot create bridging loops in a switched network, the edge port directly transitions to the forwarding state.

Edge ports are configured using the **spanning-tree portfast** interface command.

Point-to-Point Link

A point-to-point link is a link in RSTP that directly connects two switches (an uplink) in full-duplex.

Link Type

In RSTP, a link can only rapidly transition to a forwarding state on edge port and on point-to-point links. The link type is automatically derived from the duplex mode of a port. Full-duplex is assumed to be point-to-point, and a half-duplex link is considered a shared point.

Per-VLAN Rapid Spanning Tree Plus (PVRST+)

Like the original 802.1D standard, the 802.1w standard uses Common Spanning Tree (CST), which uses one spanning-tree instance for the entire switched network. PVRST+ defines a spanning-tree protocol that has one instance of RSTP per VLAN.

Configuring the Root and Backup Root Switch

In STP, the root switch is the switch with the lowest bridge ID (BID). The BID consists of the bridge priority and the switch MAC address. Because all Cisco switches have the same bridge priority (32768), the switch with the lowest MAC address will be the root bridge. In many cases, this is not desired. For example, an older (and potentially slower) switch will have a lower MAC address than a newer switch, and the older switch will be the root bridge.

To specify a switch to be the root switch, use the following global command:

```
spanning-tree vlan vlan-number root primary
```

For example, the following command configures the switch to be the root switch for only VLAN 1:

```
Cat2960(config)# spanning-tree vlan 1 root primary
```

The **spanning-tree root primary** command increases the switch priority (lowering the numerical value) so that the switch becomes the root bridge and forces Spanning Tree to perform a recalculation.

To configure the backup root switch, use the **spanning-tree vlan** *vlan-number* **root secondary** global command, as follows:

```
Cat2960(config)# spanning-tree vlan 1 root secondary
```

PortFast and BPDU Guard

Spanning Tree PortFast is a Cisco feature that causes an access port on a switch to transition immediately from the blocking state to the forwarding state, thus bypassing the listening and learning states.

When a switch port that is configured with PortFast is configured as an access port, that port transitions from the blocking to the forwarding state immediately. PortFast is useful if a workstation is configured to acquire an IP address through Dynamic Host Configuration Protocol (DHCP). The workstation can fail to get an IP address because the switch port to which the workstation is connected might not have transitioned to the forwarding state by the time DHCP times out.

In valid PortFast configurations, BPDUs should never be received on the port. If they were, that would mean the port was connected to another switch, potentially causing a spanning-tree loop. BPDU Guard will put a port in an error-disabled state if a BPDU is received.

PortFast should only be used on access ports. If you enable PortFast on a port connecting to another switch, you risk creating a STP loop. An exception to this is when a trunk connects to a nonswitch device.

Configuring PortFast

PortFast is configured using the following interface command:

```
SwitchA(config-if)# spanning-tree portfast
```

PortFast can be configured globally on all nontrunking links using the following global command:

```
SwitchA(config)# spanning-tree portfast default
```

After enabling PortFast globally, it can be disabled using the **no spanning-tree portfast** interface command on a per-interface basis.

Configuring BPDU Guard

BPDU Guard can be configured using the following interface command:

```
SwitchA(config-if)# spanning-tree bpduguard enable
```

BPDU Guard can be enabled globally using the following global command:

```
SwitchA(config)# spanning-tree portfast bpduguard default
```

The **show running-config interface** *interface-id* and **show spanning-tree interface** *interface-id* **portfast** commands show whether an interface is configured with PortFast and BPDU Guard.

Verifying Spanning Tree

The following steps can help analyze and verify the proper operation of Spanning Tree:

STEP 1.   Discover the physical Layer 2 topology using the **show cdp neighbors** command.

STEP 2.   Locate the root bridge using the **show spanning-tree vlan** *vlan-id* command.

STEP 3.   Use the **show spanning-tree vlan** *vlan-id* command on all switches to find which ports are in the blocking or forwarding states.

Improving Redundant Switched Topologies with EtherChannel

EtherChannel is a feature that allows combining of up to eight physical links into one logical connection. This logical connection load-shares traffic between the physical links and is seen by Spanning Tree as one link. With EtherChannel, instead of a redundant link not being used, all physical links are forwarding traffic.

EtherChannel provides an easy way to increase network bandwidth. Fast Ethernet, Gigabit Ethernet, and 10 Gigabit Ethernet links can be configured for EtherChannel. If one of the physical links in the EtherChannel group fails, the other links still forward traffic.

EtherChannel Advantages

EtherChannel provides the following benefits:

- Logical aggregation of up to eight links between switches or EtherChannel-capable devices

- High bandwidth by load-balancing across aggregated links

- Viewed as one logical port by Spanning Tree

- Provides redundancy in the event that one port fails

EtherChannel Protocols

Two protocols exist to negotiate the creation and maintenance of EtherChannel links. These protocols are

- **Port Aggregation Group Protocol (PAgP):** A Cisco-proprietary protocol that helps the automatic creation of EtherChannel links. PAgP works by sending packets between EtherChannel-capable ports to negotiate the forming of the EtherChannel. PAgP also manages the EtherChannel by checking for configuration consistency and manages link additions and failures between two switches.

- **Link Aggregation Control Protocol (LACP):** LACP is an IEEE 802.3ad standard that functions similarly to the Cisco PAgP in enabling automatic creation of EtherChannel links.

PAgP Modes

There are three PAgP modes, as follows:

- **On:** Forces the interface to be an EtherChannel without PAgP.

- **Desirable:** Places an interface in an active negotiation state, asking whether the other side can or will participate in the EtherChannel. Will form an EtherChannel if the other end of the link is configured as Desirable or Auto.

- **Auto:** Places an interface in a passive negotiation state waiting for the other end of the link to form the EtherChannel. Will form an EtherChannel only if the other end of the link is configured as Desirable.

Table 2-4 shows the channel establishment phases using PAgP.

Table 2-4 *PAgP Channel Establishment*

Channel Establishment	On	Desirable	Auto
On	Yes	No	No
Desirable	No	Yes	Yes
Auto	No	Yes	No

LACP Modes

Like PAgP, there are three LACP modes, as follows:

- **On:** Forces the interface to participate in an EtherChannel without LACP.

- **Active:** Places a port in an active negotiation state. Will form an EtherChannel if the other end of the link is configured as either Active or Passive.

- **Passive:** Places a port in a passive negotiation state. Will form an EtherChannel if the other end of the link is configured as Active.

Table 2-5 shows the channel establishment phases using LACP.

Table 2-5 *LACP Channel Establishment*

Channel Establishment	On	Desirable	Auto
On	Yes	No	No
Active	No	Yes	Yes
Passive	No	Yes	No

Configuring EtherChannel

When configuring interfaces for EtherChannel, all interfaces on the local and remote switch must have the same configuration, as follows:

- Speed and duplex settings.

- Interface mode of either access or trunk.

- All interfaces in the EtherChannel must be assigned to the same VLAN or be trunk links.

- For trunk ports, the range of VLANs allowed on the trunk must match.

- Native VLAN.

EtherChannel can support up to eight interfaces. Because of the nature of the EtherChannel algorithm, it is best practice that the number of interfaces participating in an EtherChannel group be in the powers of 2 (2, 4, 8).

To configure EtherChannel, you must first configure the EtherChannel settings using the **interface port-channel** global command and then add ports to the EtherChannel using the **channel-group** *identifier* mode {active | on | auto} {passive | desirable} interface command. The following command creates an EtherChannel, setting it as a trunk link and adding interfaces g1/1 and g1/2 in the EtherChannel:

```
Switch(config)# interface port-channel 1
Switch(config-if)# switchport mode trunk
Switch(config-if)# interface range g 1/1-2
Switch(config-if-range)# channel-group 1 mode active
```

Verifying EtherChannel

The following commands are used to determine whether EtherChannel is functioning properly:

- **show interface Port-channel** [*channel-number*]: Displays the general status of the EtherChannel interface. It will let you know whether the EtherChannel is up and functioning properly.

- **show etherchannel summary:** Displays all the EtherChannels configured on a switch. Useful for when more than one EtherChannel is configured.

- **show etherchannel port-channel:** Displays information about specific EtherChannel interfaces. It will display the number of physical interfaces in a port channel, indicate whether PAgP or LACP is being used, and show whether the channel is up.

Layer 3 Redundancy

Client devices such as servers, computers, laptops, and tablets can only be configured with one gateway, even if multiple routers exist. If multiple gateways do exist, by default there is no dynamic method by which devices can determine the address of the new default gateway.

Layer 3 redundancy provides default gateway backup by running a protocol allowing two or more routers to act as a single virtual router. The virtual router is configured as the default gateway for devices. When ARP frames are sent to the default gateway, the virtual router will reply with the virtual MAC address. This is done to prevent any ARP caching issues if the primary physical router in the virtual group fails.

Figure 2-9 shows how two routers configured for Layer 3 redundancy operates.

Figure 2-9 *Gateway Redundancy*

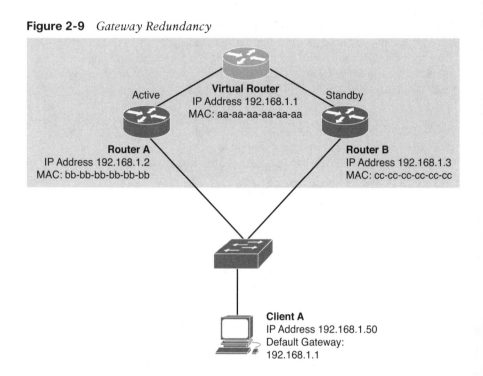

Client A is configured with the virtual IP for its default gateway. Router A is the active router in the group and responds to client A's ARP requests with the group's virtual IP address and MAC address. Router A also handles the forwarding of all traffic destined to the virtual IP address. When client A sends an ARP request to its default gateway, Router A will respond with the source IP address of 192.168.1.1 and source MAC address of aa-aa-aa-aa-aa-aa.

In Figure 2-10, the active router fails.

Figure 2-10   *Failure of Active Router*

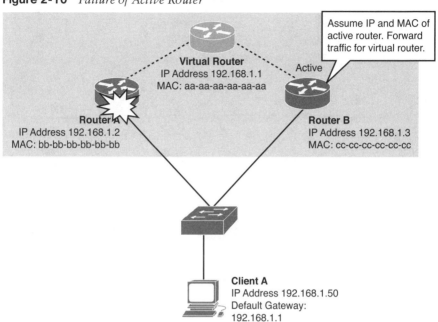

In the event that the active router fails or there is a link failure, the following occurs:

1. The standby router (Router B) stops seeing hello messages from the active router (Router A).

2. The standby router (Router B) assumes the role of the forwarding router.

3. The standby router (Router B) assumes both the IP and MAC addresses of the virtual router.

Because the standby router (Router B) assumes the IP and MAC addresses of the virtual router, client A sees no disruption in service. The standby router now becomes the active router.

In the event that Router A comes back online, by default, it will not assume the role of the active router if using HSRP; Router A will become the active router again only if Router B fails or has a link failure, as shown in Figure 2-11.

Figure 2-11 *Old Active Comes Back Online*

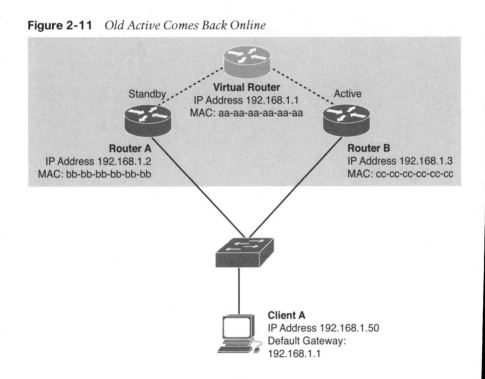

HSRP

Hot Standby Router Protocol (HSRP) is a Cisco-proprietary protocol that provides gateway redundancy by combining two or more routers by creating a virtual IP and MAC address that is shared between the routers in the HSRP group.

In HSRP, one router is the active router performing the forwarding and one router is the standby router. Any other routers are in the listening state. The set of routers participating in HSRP that jointly emulate the virtual router is called the standby group.

HSRP Active Router

The HSRP active router is the router that is forwarding packets for the virtual router in the HSRP group. It responds to the default gateway's ARP requests with the virtual router's MAC address. It sends hello messages to the multicast address 224.0.0.1 every 3 seconds.

The active router is the router with the highest priority value. The default is 100. If more than one router has the same priority, the router with the highest IP address on the HSRP-enabled interface becomes the active router.

HSRP Standby Router

The HSRP standby router is the primary backup router in the HSRP group. The standby router listens for hello messages from the active router. If the standby router does not hear hello messages within a configurable period of time, called the hold-time, the standby router becomes the active router.

In the event of a failure of the active router, the standby router becomes the active router and assumes forwarding packets and responding to ARP requests to the virtual MAC address. When the old active router comes back online, it does not automatically become the active router.

HSRP Interface Tracking

HSRP interface tracking enables the priority of a standby group router to be automatically adjusted, based on the availability of router uplink interfaces.

When tracked interfaces become unavailable (leave the Up/Up state), the HSRP tracking feature ensures that the active router with the unavailable interface will automatically decrement the priority on that interface. If the standby router is configured with preemption, it will see the lower priority from the active router and take over the role of the active router.

In Figure 2-12, Router A is the active router and Router B the standby. Both router interfaces connecting to the core network have interface tracking enabled. Because Router A is the active router, all traffic from Client A to the core network is processed through Router A. If the uplink interface to the core network on Router A becomes unavailable, Client A will no longer be able to access the core network. Because Router A did not fail it, Router B will not automatically assume the role of the active router. With interface tracking configured, as soon as Router A's uplink interface to the core becomes unavailable, HSRP will decrement the priority of Router A, and Router B becomes the active router if it is configured with preemption.

Figure 2-12   *HSRP Interface Tracking*

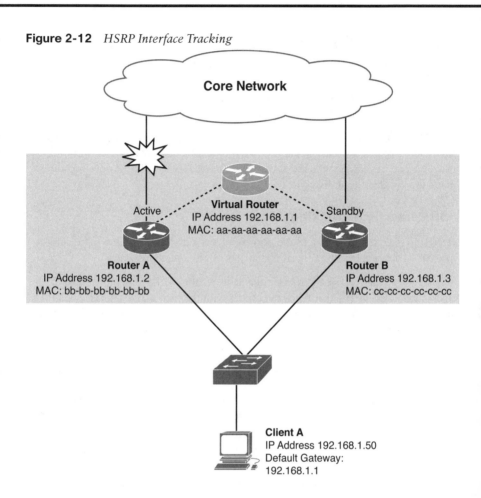

HSRP Load Balancing

In HSRP, there is only one active router per subnet at a time. The active router forwards all traffic for the virtual gateway while the standby router forwards no traffic.
HSRP load sharing is achieved by configuring the active router for one subnet or
VLAN and the other router as the active router for different subnets or VLANs. This
is done by configuring a router to be active for one HSRP group, and be in standby
or in the listening state for another HSRP group. For example, Router A would be
configured to be the active router for VLANs 1–5, and Router B would be configured to be the active router for VLANs 6–10.

VRRP

Virtual Router Redundancy Protocol (VRRP) is similar to HSRP but is an industry standard created by IEFT. In VRRP, preemption is enabled by default. Also, you can use the same IP address on a configured interface as the virtual IP address, whereas HSRP requires a different IP address for the virtual IP. VRRP routers communicate through multicast address 224.0.0.18.

Gateway Load Balancing Protocol

Gateway Load Balancing Protocol (GLBP) is a Cisco-proprietary protocol that provides gateway redundancy like HSRP and VRRP but also provides automatic packet load sharing between a group of redundant routers. GLBP does this by providing a single virtual IP address and multiple virtual MAC addresses.

Section 3
Troubleshooting Basic Connectivity

Network issues can occur at any layer of the OSI model. Typical network issues occur at Layers 1–3. Physical issues can include cabling or interface failures, network interface card (NIC) failures, and port configuration issues.

Data-link issues can include links not properly trunking, MAC address table inconsistencies, or spanning-tree issues.

IP issues can include incorrectly configured hosts—whether this is an IP address, default gateway, or subnet mask—and routing issues.

General Troubleshooting Suggestions

The following are three suggestions to general network connectivity troubleshooting:

- Become familiar with normal network operation.
- Have an accurate physical and logical map of the network.
- Do not assume that a component is working without checking it first.

General Troubleshooting Steps

The following six steps can be taken to verify and troubleshoot end-to-end connectivity:

STEP 1.   Determine whether end-to-end connectivity is operational. If this fails, go to Step 2.

STEP 2.   Determine whether there is a physical connectivity issue. If there is no physical issue, go to Step 3.

STEP 3.   Determine whether the current path is the desired or proper path. If it is not, go to Step 4.

STEP 4.   Determine whether the default gateway is correct. If it is, go to Step 5. If it is not, apply the correct gateway.

STEP 5.   Determine whether DNS is working correctly. If it is, go to Step 6. If it is not, fix DNS.

STEP 6.   Determine whether any ACLs are blocking traffic. If they are, reconfigure the ACLs.

Verification of End-to-End Connectivity

End-to-end connectivity can be verified using the **ping** and **traceroute** commands. Connectivity of upper-layer protocols can be done by using **telnet**.

Ping is a utility that uses ICMP to test whether another host is reachable. Ping sends an ICMP echo request message to a host, expecting an ICMP echo reply to be returned. If ping fails, you typically do not have IP connectivity with a host.

Traceroute is also a utility that uses ICMP. Traceroute maps the path that IP datagrams follow when communicating between two hosts. Use the **traceroute** Cisco IOS command or the **tracert** Windows command to observe the path between two hosts.

Although Telnet is an application, you can use Telnet to test transport layer connectivity. For example, say that you are troubleshooting access to a web server. Users cannot access pages on the web server; however, pings to the web server are successful. By telnetting to port 80, you can determine whether the transport layer is functioning properly and whether the server is accepting requests on port 80.

Troubleshooting Physical Connectivity Problems

Common causes for physical connectivity problems include hardware issues, configuration issues, and connectivity issues.

Hardware Issues

When troubleshooting hardware issues, perform the following:

- Check the interface status of the interfaces involved. Make sure that the interfaces are enabled.

- Check the cable. Make sure that the cable is good and that the proper cable type is used.

- Check for loose connections.

- Make sure that the cable is plugged into the correct port.

Cable Type

When using copper cabling, make sure that you are using the correct cable type for the connection you are making.

Straight-through RJ-45 cables connect nonsimilar devices to each other: data terminal equipment (DTE) devices (end stations, routers, or servers) to a data communications equipment (DCE) device (switch or hub).

Crossover cables typically connect similar devices (DTE to DTE or DCE to DCE), such as when connecting one switch to another. Figure 3-1 shows the pinouts for a crossover cable.

Figure 3-1   *Crossover Cable and Pinouts*

Cable 10 BASE T/
100BASE T Crossover

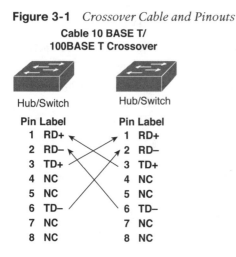

Hub/Switch	Hub/Switch
Pin Label	**Pin Label**
1 RD+	1 RD+
2 RD–	2 RD–
3 TD+	3 TD+
4 NC	4 NC
5 NC	5 NC
6 TD–	6 TD–
7 NC	7 NC
8 NC	8 NC

Verify Interface Information

To view interface information, such as interface type, speed, duplex settings, or statistics and errors, use the **show interface** *interface-id* privileged EXEC command. The following command shows the information for interface g0/1. The highlighted areas are areas you should be familiar with.

```
SwitchA# show interface g0/1
GigabitEthernet0/1 is up, line protocol is up (connected)
  Hardware is Gigabit Ethernet Port, address is 000d.65ac.5040
    (bia 000d.65ac.5040)
  MTU 1500 bytes, BW 1000000 Kbit, DLY 10 usec,
     reliability 255/255, txload 1/255, rxload 1/255
  Encapsulation ARPA, loopback not set
  Keepalive set (10 sec)
  Full-duplex, 1000Mb/s, link type is auto, media type is 1000BaseSX
  input flow-control is on, output flow-control is off
  ARP type: ARPA, ARP Timeout 04:00:00
  Last input 00:00:09, output never, output hang never
  Last clearing of "show interface" counters never
  Input queue: 0/2000/0/0 (size/max/drops/flushes); Total output
     drops: 0
  Queueing strategy: fifo
  Output queue: 0/40 (size/max)
  5 minute input rate 10000 bits/sec, 8 packets/sec
  5 minute output rate 10000 bits/sec, 7 packets/sec
     1476671 packets input, 363178961 bytes, 0 no buffer
```

```
Received 20320 broadcasts (12683 multicast)
0 runts, 0 giants, 0 throttles
0 input errors, 0 CRC, 0 frame, 0 overrun, 0 ignored
0 input packets with dribble condition detected
1680749 packets output, 880704302 bytes, 0 underruns
0 output errors, 0 collisions, 0 interface resets
0 babbles, 0 late collision, 0 deferred
0 lost carrier, 0 no carrier
0 output buffer failures, 0 output buffers swapped out
```

Input queue drops signify at some point in time that more traffic was delivered to the router than it could process. This is not necessarily a problem and can be normal during traffic peaks. However, it can be an indication that the CPU cannot process packets in time.

The output queue drops signify that packets were dropped because of interface congestion. Output queue drops are normal if the aggregate input traffic is higher than the output traffic; for example, going from a 1-Gbps interface to a 100-Mbps interface. However, consistently seeing output drops can be a good indicator that queuing technologies like QoS need to be implemented.

Input errors indicate that errors were experienced when receiving a frame. Examples include CRC errors and can mean that there are cabling problems or interface duplex mismatches.

Output errors indicate errors that occurred during the transmission of a frame. An example includes collisions.

Interface Errors

The following are reasons for common interface errors:

- "errDisable" message: EtherChannel misconfiguration, duplex mismatch, BPDU Guard has been enabled on the interface, Unidirectional Link Detection (UDLD), native VLAN mismatch, or port security violations.

- Excessive collisions: Duplex mismatch, faulty port, oversaturated medium, or distance between the two devices exceeds the cable specifications.

- Excessive runts: Runts are frames smaller than 64 bytes with a bad frame check sequence (FCS). Bad cabling or inconsistent duplex settings cause runts.

- Excessive giants: Giants are frames greater than the Ethernet maximum transmission unit (MTU) of 1518 bytes. The cause is usually a faulty NIC or a misconfiguration.

Interface Speed and Duplex

Common network performance problems in Ethernet-based networks are due to duplex or speed mismatches between two devices. When configuring duplex settings, the following guidelines are recommended:

- Point-to-point Ethernet links should always be configured in full-duplex mode.

- Half-duplex is not common in today's networks and is mostly encountered if hubs are used.

- Autonegotiation of speed and duplex is recommended on interfaces connected to noncritical endpoints.

- Manually set the speed and duplex on links between networking devices and ports connected to critical endpoints.

Troubleshooting Path Issues

In troubleshooting Layer 3 path issues, one has to have a good understanding of the path that packets take to reach their final destination. This can be accomplished by inspecting the routing tables of routers along the path using the **show ip route** command.

The routing table can be populated by the following ways:

- **Directly connected networks:** Come from interfaces directly connected to a network segment. The most certain method of populating the routing table with an AD of 0. Are only removed from the routing table if the interface fails or is administratively shut down.

- **Local host routes:** Come from the local IP address on the router interface. The subnet mask represents the host route.

- **Static routes:** Manually entered routes. The default AD is 1.

- **Dynamic routes:** Routes learned from a configured routing protocol and neighbor relationships to other routers are established. These routes change based on any network topology changes.

- **Default routes:** Manually entered or dynamically learned by a routing protocol, these are the paths a packet will take when there is no specific route to a network in its routing table.

The **show ip route** command displays the routing table as shown here. The highlighted codes detail how the router (the source) learned the routing entries.

```
Router# show ip route

Codes: I - IGRP derived, R - RIP derived, O - OSPF derived,
       C - connected, S - static, E - EGP derived, B - BGP derived,
       * - candidate default route, IA - OSPF inter area route,
       i - IS-IS derived, ia - IS-IS, U - per-user static route,
       o - on-demand routing, M - mobile, P - periodic downloaded
           static route,
       D - EIGRP, EX - EIGRP external, E1 - OSPF external type 1
           route,
       E2 - OSPF external type 2 route, N1 - OSPF NSSA external type
           1 route,
```

```
       N2 - OSPF NSSA external type 2 route


Gateway of last resort is 10.119.254.240 to network 10.140.0.0


O E2 10.110.0.0 [160/5] via 10.119.254.6, 0:01:00, Ethernet2
E    10.67.10.0 [200/128] via 10.119.254.244, 0:02:22, Ethernet2
O E2 10.68.132.0 [160/5] via 10.119.254.6, 0:00:59, Ethernet2
O E2 10.130.0.0 [160/5] via 10.119.254.6, 0:00:59, Ethernet2
E    10.128.0.0 [200/128] via 10.119.254.244, 0:02:22, Ethernet2
E    10.129.0.0 [200/129] via 10.119.254.240, 0:02:22, Ethernet2
E    10.65.129.0 [200/128] via 10.119.254.244, 0:02:22, Ethernet2
E    10.10.0.0 [200/128] via 10.119.254.244, 0:02:22, Ethernet2
E    10.75.139.0 [200/129] via 10.119.254.240, 0:02:23, Ethernet2
E    10.140.0.0 [200/129] via 10.119.254.240, 0:02:23, Ethernet2
```

If the destination address in a packet does not match an entry in the routing table, the default route is used. If there is no default route configured, the packet is dropped.

If the destination address in a packet matches a single entry in the routing table, the packet is forwarded through the interface defined in the route.

If the destination address in the packet matches more than one entry in the routing table and the routing entries have the same network mask, the packets for the destination are load balanced among the routes in the routing table.

If the destination address in the packet matches more than one entry in the routing table and the routing entries have different network masks, the packet is forwarded out the interface of the routing entry that has the longest prefix match.

Troubleshooting Default Gateway Issues

If a destination address in a packet has no match in the router's routing table, the packet will be sent to the default gateway only if a default gateway is configured. If a default gateway is not configured, the router will drop the packet, and communication between two endpoints on different networks will not work. The **show ip route** command on a Cisco device will display if a default gateway is configured. In the following example, the default gateway (gateway of last resort) is configured as network 170.170.3.4 and will send all packets that do not have a specific entry in the routing table out Fast Ethernet interface 0/0:

```
Router# show ip route
Codes: C - connected, S - static, I - IGRP, R - RIP, M - mobile, B
  - BGP    D - EIGRP, EX - EIGRP external, O - OSPF, IA - OSPF inter
  area    N1 - OSPF NSSA external type 1, N2 - OSPF NSSA external
  type 2    E1 - OSPF external type 1, E2 - OSPF external type 2, E -
  EGP    i - IS-IS, L1 - IS-IS level-1, L2 - IS-IS level-2, * - candi-
  date default    U - per-user static route, o - ODR
```

```
Gateway of last resort is 170.170.3.4 to network 0.0.0.0

170.170.0.0/24 is subnetted, 2 subnets
  C 170.170.2.0 is directly connected, Serial0/0
  C 170.170.3.0 is directly connected, FastEthernet0/0
  S* 0.0.0.0/0 [1/0] via 170.170.3.4
```

The **route print** Windows command will display if a Windows computer is configured with a default gateway.

Troubleshooting Name Resolution Issues

Mapping of computer names to IP addresses can be done the following ways:

- **Statically:** Done in a text file called the HOSTS file by an administrator. This is done by manually entering the computer's name and IP address in the HOSTS file and storing it on all computers.

- **Dynamically:** Done using the DNS protocol and is entered in DNS servers.

A quick way to verify whether name resolution is working properly is by pinging or telnetting to a device by its host name instead of IP address.

The host file serves as a function for translating host names to IP addresses. In Windows operating systems, the host file is located at C:\Windows\System32\drivers\etc\hosts. It can be edited using a text editor.

To make a static name resolution entry on a Cisco router or switch, use the **ip host** *name ip_address* command.

Troubleshooting ACL Issues

Access control lists (ACL) are used for access control on VTY lines, packet filtering on interfaces, and identifying which IP address can be translated by NAT. If a router's interface(s) is configured with ACLs, the ACLs might be prohibiting traffic from passing inbound or outbound on the interface.

The **show ip access-lists** command displays the contents of all ACLs configured on a router.

The **show ip interface** *interface-type interface-number* command shows whether an ACL is configured on an interface and what direction the ACL is applied:

```
RouterA# show ip interface s0
Serial0 is up, line protocol is up
  Internet address is 192.168.1.2/24
  Broadcast address is 255.255.255.255
  Address determined by non-volatile memory
  MTU is 1500 bytes
```

```
Helper address is not set
Directed broadcast forwarding is enabled
Multicast reserved groups joined: 224.0.0.9
Outgoing access list is not set
Inbound  access list is 110
Proxy ARP is enabled
Security level is default
Split horizon is enabled
```

Only one access list per interface, per protocol is allowed.

Troubleshooting IPv6 Connectivity

Troubleshooting IPv6 is similar to IPv4. However, one needs to remember the different types of addresses in IPv6. The different IPv6 addresses are

- **Unicast:** An address that identifies a single device. It has a one-to-one mapping. Unicast addresses include global, link local, loopback (::1), and unspecified (::).

- **Anycast:** An address that represents a group of devices that support similar service. Anycast addresses have a one-to-nearest mapping.

- **Multicast:** Identifies a set of devices called a multicast group. It has a one-to-many mapping and also replaces IPv4 broadcast addresses. Use the reserved address space FF00::0/8.

The IETF reserved the following IPv6 addresses:

- **Subnet-router anycast address:** The lowest address within each subnet prefix.

- **Anycast address:** The highest 128 interface identifier values within each subnet mask.

NOTE   Ping, traceroute, and **telnet** are tools that can be used to troubleshoot IPv6 connectivity. Instead of using an IPv4 address, an IPv6 address would be specified.

The **show ipv6 neighbors** command displays the neighbor discovery table on a Cisco router. This table includes the IPv6 address of the neighbor, age in minutes since the address was confirmed to be reachable, and state.

```
Router# show ipv6 neighbors
```

```
IPv6 Address                     Age Link-layer Addr State Interface
2000:0:0:4::2                      0 0003.a0d6.141e  REACH Ethernet2
FE80::203:A0FF:FED6:141E           0 0003.a0d6.141e  REACH Ethernet2
3001:1::45a                        - 0002.7d1a.9472  REACH Ethernet2
```

Table 3-1 outlines the meaning of each state.

Table 3-1   show ipv6 neighbors *Table State*

State	Description
ICNMP (Incomplete)	Address resolution is being performed on the host. A neighbor solicitation message has been sent to the host, but the corresponding neighbor advertisement message has not yet been received.
REACH (Reachable)	Positive confirmation from the neighbor was received within the last ReachableTime milliseconds. No special action is needed because packets are being sent.
STALE	More than ReachableTime milliseconds have elapsed since the last positive confirmation was received. In the STALE state, the device takes no action until a packet is sent.
DELAY	More than ReachableTime milliseconds have elapsed since the last positive confirmation was received. A DELAY_FIRST_PROBE_TIME packet is sent.
PROBE	A response to the DELAY_FIRST_PROBE_TIME packet did not occur, and a reachability confirmation is activity being sought by the resending neighbor.

The **show ipv6 route** command displays the IPv6 routing table.

The **show ipv6 access-lists** command displays whether there are any IPv6 ACLs configured on a router.

The **show ipv6 interface** command displays whether an ACL is attached to an interface.

Section 4
Implementing an EIGRP-Based Solution

Routing Overview

Routing is the process of getting packets and messages from one location to another.

In Figure 4-1, for hosts in network 10.120.2.0 to communicate with hosts in network 172.16.1.0, a router needs the following key information:

- **Destination address:** The destination (typically an IP address) of the information being sent. This includes the subnet address.

- **Sources of information:** Where the information came from (typically an IP address of the router sending the route). Can also be a routing protocol or directly connected route.

- **Possible routes:** Likely routes to get from source to destination.

- **Best route:** The best path selected by the router to reach the intended destination.

- **Status of routes:** Known paths to destinations.

Figure 4-1   *Information Needed by a Router to Communicate with Other Networks*

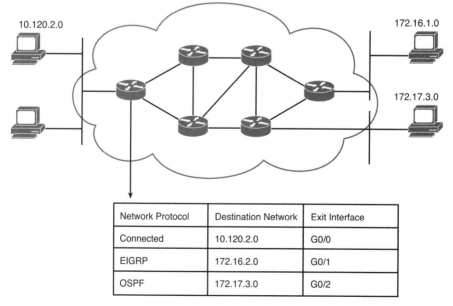

Network Protocol	Destination Network	Exit Interface
Connected	10.120.2.0	G0/0
EIGRP	172.16.2.0	G0/1
OSPF	172.17.3.0	G0/2

A router is constantly learning about routes in the network and storing this information in its routing table. The router uses its table to make forwarding decisions. The router learns about routes in one of two ways:

- Manually (routing information entered by the network administrator)
- Dynamically (a routing protocol running in the network)

Dynamic Routing Overview

Routing protocols learn paths to destination networks and maintain routing tables. Dynamic routing uses routing protocols to allow routers to communicate with each other. This communication allows routers to learn possible paths to destination networks. A routing protocol defines communication rules and interprets network layer address information. Routing protocols describe the following:

- Routing advertisement methods
- Information contained in updates
- When updates are sent
- Paths to destination networks

Autonomous Systems

An autonomous system refers to a group of networks under a common administrative domain. Interior gateway protocols (IGP), such as Routing Information Protocol v2 (RIPv2), Enhanced IGRP (EIGRP), and Open Shortest Path First (OSPF), exchange routing information within an autonomous system. Exterior gateway protocols (EGP) advertise routes between autonomous systems. The Border Gateway Protocol (BGP) is an example of an EGP. Figure 4-2 shows autonomous systems and where IGPs and EGPs are used.

Figure 4-2   *Autonomous Systems*

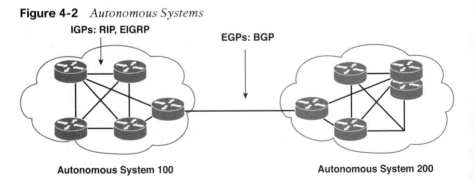

IGPs: RIP, EIGRP

EGPs: BGP

Autonomous System 100

Autonomous System 200

Administrative Distance

Several routing protocols can be used at the same time in the same network. When more than a single source of routing information exists, the router uses an administrative distance (AD) value to rate the trustworthiness of each routing information source. The administrative distance is an integer from 0 to 255. In general, a route with a lower AD is considered more trustworthy and is more likely to be used. Figure 4-3 shows that Router A has two paths to network E, one learned from RIPv2 and another from EIGRP. Because EIGRP has a lower AD than RIPv2, Router A will pick the path advertised by EIGRP.

Figure 4-3   *AD Determines Path*

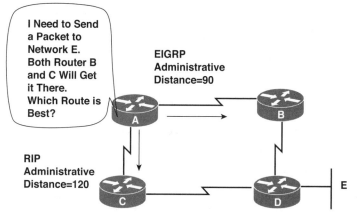

Table 4-1 shows the default administrative distance values.

Table 4-1   *Default Administrative Distance Values*

Route Source	Default Distance
Connected interface	0
Static route	1
EIGRP	90
IGRP	100
OSPF	110
RIP	120
External EIGRP	170
Unknown	255

Routing Protocol Classes

The following three basic routing protocol classes exist:

- **Distance vector:** Uses the direction (vector) and distance (such as hops) to other routers as metrics. RIPv2 is a distance vector protocol.

- **Link-state:** Also called shortest path first, this protocol re-creates the topology of the entire network. Open Shortest Path First (OSPF) and Intermediate System–to–Intermediate System (IS-IS) are link-state protocols.

- **Advanced distance vector:** Combines the link-state and distance vector algorithms. EIGRP is a balanced hybrid protocol.

Classful and Classless Routing

Routing protocols also fall into two types of routing categories: classful or classes routing.

- **Classful routing:** Subnet masks are not advertised in the routing advertisements. When used, all subnetworks of the same major network (Class A, B, or C) must use the same subnet mask, which is not necessarily a default major class subnet mask. Perform automatic route summarization across network boundaries.

- **Classless routing:** Subnet masks are advertised in routing advertisements. Found in the routing protocols RIPv2, EIGRP, OSPF, and IS-IS.

Summarizing Routes

In large networks, it is impractical for a router to maintain tables with hundreds of thousands of routes. Route summarization (also called route aggregation or super-netting) reduces the number of routes that a router must maintain by representing a series of network numbers in a single summary address.

Route summarization reduces the size of routing tables while maintaining routes to all the destinations in the network. This helps improve routing performance, and memory can be saved.

Route summarization also improves convergence time. The router that summarized the route no longer has to announce any changes to the status of individual subnets. Instead, the router that summarized the route advertises the entire summary route as either up or down, and the routers that learn the summary route do not have to reconverge every time one of the individual subnets goes up or down.

Route summarization is performed in two ways: manually or automatically. Manual summarization provides the best control for managing routes.

Classless routing protocols, such as RIPv2, IS-IS, EIGRP, and OSPF, support route summarization using subnets and VLSMs. RIPv2 and EIGRP automatically perform route summarization to the classful network boundary when routing updates cross between two major networks. OSPF must be configured to manually perform summarization.

Summarizing Routes in Discontiguous Networks

RIPv2 and EIGRP (in IOS releases earlier than 15.0) automatically perform route summarization to the classful network boundary when routing updates cross a different classful network. This works fine if the network is contiguous; however, this automatic summarization causes problems if the network is discontiguous. Figure 4-4 shows that Routers A and C are connected to networks 10.1.1.0/24 and 10.1.2.0/24. Because the network is discontiguous, Routers A and C automatically summarize that they are connected to network 10.0.0.0/8. As a result, Router B thinks it has two routes to network 10.0.0.0/8.

Figure 4-4   *Autosummarization in a Discontiguous Network*

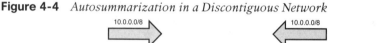

Implementing EIGRP

Enhanced IGRP (EIGRP) is a Cisco-proprietary routing protocol. EIGRP is a classless routing protocol, meaning that it sends the subnet mask of its interfaces in routing updates, which use a complex metric based on bandwidth and delay.

EIRGP is an advanced distance vector protocol with some link-state features.

EIGRP Features

EIGRP is an advanced distance vector routing protocol that includes the following features:

- **Protocol-dependent modules:** EIGRP supports IP, IPv6, Internetwork Packet Exchange (IPX), and AppleTalk.

- **Reliable Transport Protocol:** RTP controls sending, tracking, and acknowledging updates and EIGRP messages.

- **Neighbor discovery/recovery:** EIGRP discovers neighboring devices using periodic Hello messages.

- **Diffusing Update Algorithm (DUAL):** EIGRP uses DUAL to calculate and maintain loop-free paths and provide fast convergence.

- **Partial updates:** EIGRP sends partial triggered updates instead of periodic updates.

EIGRP Terminology

As an advanced distance vector protocol, EIGRP uses some features that help improve convergence time. Important EIGRP terminology is as follows:

- **Neighbor table:** Lists all adjacent routers. Includes the neighbor's address and the interface through which it can be reached. EIGRP routers keep a neighbor table for each routed Layer 3 protocol (IP, IPv6).

- **Topology table:** Contains all learned routes to a destination. The topology table holds all successor and feasible successor routes in its table.

- **Routing table:** Holds the best routes (the successor routes) to each destination.

EIGRP Path Calculation

DUAL uses distance information (metric) to select the best, loop-free path to a destination. It does this by selecting a successor with the best feasible distance. A backup route, called the feasible successor, is selected if the advertised distance is less than the feasible distance. The following is a list of the terminology DUAL uses to select a route:

- **Successor:** The primary route used to reach a destination. The successor route is kept in the routing table.

- **Feasible successor:** The backup route. Must have an advertised distance (AD) less than the feasible distance (FD) of the current successor route.

- **Advertised distance (AD):** The lowest-cost route between the next-hop router and the destination.

- **Feasible distance (FD):** The metric with the best route to reach a subnet. It is the sum of the advertised distance (AD) plus the cost between the local router and the next-hop router.

EIGRP Metric

The EIGRP metric can be based on several different things; however, by default, the EIGRP metric is based on

- **Bandwidth:** The smallest bandwidth of all outgoing interfaces between the source and destination in kilobits.

- **Delay:** The sum of all interface delays along the path in tens of microseconds.

The calculation EIGRP uses to determine the total metric is

{256 * [(K1 * Bandwidth) + (K2 * Bandwidth)]} / {(256 − Load) + (K3 * Delay) * [K5 / (Reliability + K4)]}

where if K5 = 0, the [K5 / (Reliability + K4)] part is not used (that is, equals to 1). Using the default K values, the metric calculation is simplified to:

256 * (Bandwidth + Delay)

Configuring and Verifying EIGRP

The **router eigrp** *as_number* command enables EIGRP on the router. This is followed by the **network** command to enable EIGRP on the specified interfaces. The following commands enable EIGRP using AS 100 and then enable EIGRP on all router interfaces with IP addresses in the networks 192.168.3.0 and 192.168.4.0:

```
RouterA(config)# router eigrp 100
RouterA(config-router)# network 192.168.3.0
RouterA(config-router)# network 192.168.4.0
```

- **show ip eigrp neighbors:** Displays the EIGRP neighbor table. This displays the neighbors the EIGRP discovered and when neighbors become active and inactive.

- **show ip route eigrp:** Displays all EIGRP routes in the routing table.

- **show ip eigrp topology:** Displays the EIGRP topology table, including successors and feasible successors.

- **debug eigrp neighbors:** Used to display the active process of neighbors discovered by EIGRP.

Load Balancing with EIGRP

Load balancing is a router's ability to balance traffic over all its network's ports that are the same metric to the destination address.

EIGRP uses a complex metric based on bandwidth, delay, load, reliability, and MTU to select the best path to a destination. By default, EIGRP only uses bandwidth and delay to calculate its metric.

By default, EIGRP can automatically load-balance up to four equal-cost routes (16 routes being the maximum); this is called equal-cost load balancing.

Unequal-cost load balancing is when a router can load-balance traffic to a destination through links of different metrics. In Figure 4-5, Router A has two unequal paths to network 10.1.2.x.

Figure 4-5   *EIGRP Unequal-Cost Load Balancing*

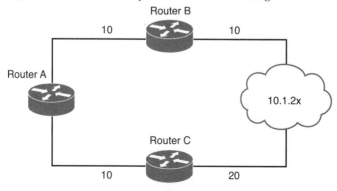

Because the path through Router B has a lower metric than the path through Router C, Router A will route all traffic to network 10.1.2.x through Router B.

To configure Router A to perform unequal-cost load balancing, you need to use the **variance** *multiplier* command on Router A. The multiplier is a variance value between 1 and 128, with the default set to 1.

To determine the variance, divide the metric between Router C by the metric of Router B. In this case, it would be 30/20, which equals 1.5. So the variance to perform unequal-cost load balancing to network 10.1.2.x is the next whole number—2. The following configuration sets the variance on Router A to 2:

```
RouterA(config)# router eigrp 100
RouterA(config-router)# variance 2
```

Troubleshooting EIGRP

After EIGRP is configured, connectivity should be tested. If connectivity fails, basic items to look at are

- Are the router interfaces enabled?
- Are the IP addresses and subnet masks correct?
- Do both routers have the same EGIRP AS number configured?
- Are the IP addresses and subnet masks for the interfaces in the EIGRP advertising range in the **network** statement?
- Are any interfaces configured as passive?

EIGRP Neighbor Troubleshooting

When EIGRP is not forming neighbor relationships with other EIGRP routers, there might be several reasons for this. Some include

- The interface between the devices is down.
- Neighbor routers are not attached to the same primary network.
- The routers have mismatching EIGRP autonomous systems.
- Proper interfaces are not enabled for the EIGRP process.
- An interface is configured as passive.
- Inbound ACLs are configured on the neighboring interface that is blocking traffic.
- Misconfigured authentication.
- A manual change of the K values that EIGRP uses to calculate its metric.

EIGRP will not form neighbor adjacencies over secondary networks; thus, the neighboring routers should be on the same primary network. Also, the primary address assigned to an interface must be part of the network used by the **network** configuration command under EIGRP. Using the **passive-interface** command prevents EIGRP Hellos from being sent on a data link, blocking unnecessary Hellos and preventing neighbor adjacencies from forming.

Commands to troubleshoot EIGRP neighbor issues are as follows:

- **show ip route eigrp:** Displays whether there are EIGRP routes in the routing table.

- **show ip eigrp interfaces:** Lists the interfaces on which the routing protocol is enabled (based on the **network** commands), except on passive interfaces.

- **show ip protocols:** Lists the contents of the **network** configuration commands for each routing process and lists enabled but passive interfaces. Will also show whether K-values are changed.

- **show ip interface brief:** Verifies that the protocol and status of the link between the neighboring routers is up.

- **debug eigrp neighbors:** Used to display the active process of neighbors discovered by EIGRP.

- **debug eigrp packets:** Used to determine whether there is an authentication problem.

EIGRP Route Troubleshooting

If EIGRP neighbor relationships are up, and connectivity to a remote network fails, there might be a routing problem. Some issues that can cause a connectivity problem for EIGRP are as follows:

- Proper networks are not being advertised on remote routers.

- An access list is blocking advertisements of remote networks.

- Automatic summary is causing confusion in discontiguous networks.

EIGRP can be configured to automatically summarize routes at classful boundaries. If there are discontiguous networks in your environment, automatic summarization will cause routing confusion. Auto-summarization is disabled by default in IOS version 15.0 and higher. Earlier IOS versions have it enabled by default.

Commands to help you troubleshoot EIGRP route issues are as follows:

- **show ip protocols:** Lists the contents of the **network** configuration commands for each routing process and lists enabled but passive interfaces. This will help determine what networks are being advertised on routers. Also, displays whether any access lists are applied to the EIGRP network advertisements.

- **show ip route:** Verifies routes for remote networks.

- **no auto-summary:** Disables automatic summarization in the router EIGRP configuration mode.

Implementing EIGRP for IPv6

EIGRP has multiprotocol support. As such, IPv6 support was added as a separate module, and it is configured and managed separately from IPv4 EIGRP. That said, EIGRP for IPv6 is similar to EIGRP for IPv4.

The basic components of EIGRP for IPv6 remain the same as in IPv4; these include

- Neighbor discovery using hello packets

- Incremental updates

- Fast convergence with DUAL

- Composite metric

- Load balancing

In EIGRP for IPv6, hello packets and updates are sent to the well-known link-local multicast address FF02::A.

Configuring and Verifying EIGRP for IPv6

The steps to configure EIGRP routing for IPv6 are as follows:

STEP 1.   Enable IPv6 routing.

STEP 2.   Create an EIGRP routing process in IPv6.

STEP 3.   Enable the EIGRP routing process.

STEP 4.   Enable EIGRP for IPv6 on specified interfaces.

The following example enables EIGRP for IPv6 in AS 10 and then enables interfaces G0/0 and G0/1 to participate in the EIGRP IPv6 process:

```
RouterA(config)# ipv6 unicast-routing
RouterA(config)# ipv6 router eigrp 10
RouterA(config-rtr)# no shutdown
RouterA(config-rtr)# interface g0/0
RouterA(config-if)# ipv6 eigrp 10
RouterA(config-rtr)# interface g0/1
RouterA(config-if)# ipv6 eigrp 10
```

The **show ipv6 eigrp topology** command displays the EIGRP IPv6 topology table.

The **show ipv6 eigrp neighbors** command displays the neighbors discovered through EIGRP IPv6.

The **show ipv6 route eigrp** command displays the EIGRP routes in the IPv6 routing table.

Section 5
Implementing a Scalable Multiarea OSPF-Based Network

OSPF was introduced in ICND1. To provide a brief recap, OSPF is an open-standard, link-state routing protocol.

When a router is configured for OSPF, routers create adjacencies with neighboring routers and exchange information to create a link-state database (LSDB) outlining the topology of the network.

Link-State Routing

The link-state-based routing algorithm (also known as shortest path first [SPF]) maintains a database of topology information. Unlike the distance vector algorithm, link-state routing maintains full knowledge of distant routers and how they interconnect. Network information is shared in the form of link-state advertisements (LSA). See Figure 5-1.

Figure 5-1 *Link-State Routing*

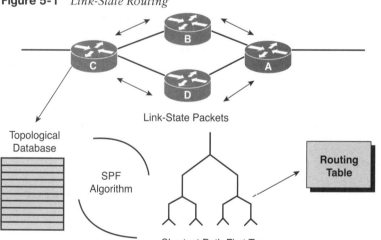

With link-state routing protocols, each router has a full map of the network topology. As such, a router can independently make a decision based on its map of the network.

Each link-state router must keep a record of the following:

- Immediate neighbor routers

- All other routers in the network

- The best paths to each destination

Link-state routing provides better scaling than distance vector routing for the following reasons:

- Link-state sends only topology changes (called triggered updates). Distance vector sends complete routing tables.

- Link-state advertisements are sent less often than distance vector updates.

- Link-state uses a hierarchy by dividing large routing domains into smaller routing domains called areas. Areas limit the scope of route changes.

- Link-state supports classless addressing and summarization. An exception to this is RIPv2.

- Link-state routing converges fast and is robust against routing loops, but it requires a great deal of memory and strict network designs.

OSPF Overview

OSPF is a routing protocol that is often used in networks because of scalability, fast convergence, and multivendor environment support. It is important to understand OSPF terminology and operation.

OSPF Metric

OSPF uses path cost as a metric. A lower cost indicates a better path. On Cisco devices, the cost of an interface is based on the bandwidth of an interface. Thus, a high bandwidth of an interface equals a lower cost.

The formula to calculate the OSFP cost is

Cost = Reference bandwidth / Interface bandwidth (bps)

The default reference bandwidth is 10^8 (100,000,000), or the equivalent of the bandwidth of a Fast Ethernet interface.

OSPF assigns a cost of 10 to a 10-Mbps Ethernet interface; a 100-Mbps interface has a cost of 1. A 10-Gbps and a 1-Gbps interface have the same default cost of 1. In the event that higher-bandwidth interfaces are used, it is recommended to manually change the cost of an interface.

Establishing OSPF Neighbor Adjacencies

OSPF-enabled routers establish adjacencies with OSPF routers on a common data link to share link-state information. OSPF depends on the status of the link between two routers; this is done using the Hello protocol.

The Hello protocol establishes and maintains neighbor relationships and ensures that there is two-way communication between neighbors. Two-way communication is verified when a router recognizes itself in the hello packet received from a neighbor router.

Hello packets are periodically sent to multicast address 224.0.0.5. Routers must agree on the following information inside the hello packet before a neighbor relationship can be established:

- Subnet mask and subnet number

- Hello and dead intervals

- Neighbors

- Area ID

- Authentication data

- Value of the stub area flag

When two-way communication has been established, adjacencies can be formed. However, not all neighbors will become adjacent. Whether an adjacency is formed or not depends on the type of network to which the two neighbors are attached. OSPF network types are covered in the "OSPF Network Types" section, later in this guide.

Building a Link-State Database

There are four types of packets used when building and synchronizing the link-state database (LSDB):

- **DBD packets:** Used to describe the network routes of each neighbor. DBD packets contain the LSA entry header that appears in the link-state database (LSDB). Each LSA entry header includes information about the link-state type, the address of the advertising router, the cost of the link, and the sequence number.

- **LSR packets:** After DBD packets are exchanged, routers request missing information using link-state request (LSR) packets.

- **LSU packets:** Update packets sent to adjacent neighbors that contain all missing information.

- **LSAck packets:** Every packet is acknowledged to ensure reliable transport and exchange of information.

When two routers discover each other and form adjacencies, they perform the following to exchange information:

1. The routers exchange one or more DBD packets to understand the network each router is connected to.

2. The routers acknowledge the receipt of each DBD packet using LSAck packets.

3. The routers compare the information they received from the information they already have. If the DBD has a more up-to-date link-state entry, the router sends an LSR to the other router requesting the updated link-state entry.

4. The other router responds with the complete information in an LSU packet, and the receiving router adds the new link-state entries in its LSDB.

5. When the router receives the LSU, it sends an LSAck.

OSPF Area Structure

Large and complex networks can take a long time for routes to converge. To help reduce the frequency that the Dijkstra algorithm runs, OSPF can be implemented with more than one area. By implementing areas, the number of routers in an area and the number of LSAs that flood within the area are smaller than a single network, thus helping with the Dijkstra calculation time. Routers in an area maintain detailed information about the links and routers in their area and only general or summary information about routers and links in other areas. Also, LSAs are only flooding within their own area.

OSPF supports a two-tier hierarchy structure. As shown in Figure 5-2, this two-tier structure consists of

- Backbone area (always Area 0)
- Normal areas (any area that is not Area 0)

Figure 5-2 *OSPF Area Structure*

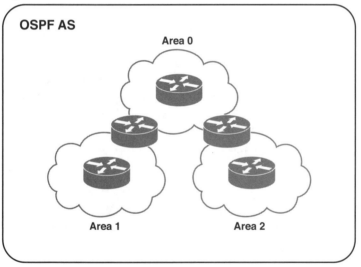

The backbone or transit area function is to interconnect other OSPF area types. OSPF requires that all areas connect to Area 0. In Figure 5-2, direct links between Area 1 and Area 2 routers are not allowed. If Area 1 routers want to communicate with Area 2 routers, Area 0 is used as the transit area. Typically, end users are not found in Area 0.

Normal areas function is to connect users and resources. By default, a normal area does not allow traffic from another area to use its links to reach other areas. All traffic from other areas must cross Area 0.

OSPF Router Types

Routers that connect to Area 0 are backbone routers. In Figure 5-3, Routers R1, R2, and R3 are backbone routers.

Routers that have all interfaces in a normal area are known as internal routers. In Figure 5-3, Routers R1, R4, and R5 are internal routers.

Routers that connect Area 0 to normal areas are call area border routers (ABR). In Figure 5-3, Routers R2 and R3 are ABRs.

Figure 5-3   *OSPF Router Types*

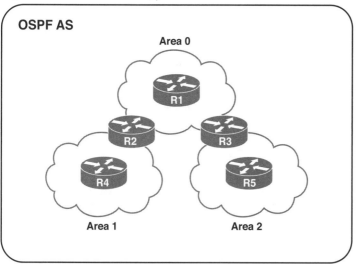

ABRs have an important role in OSPF. They perform the following functions:

■ Separate LSA flooding zones.

■ Are the primary point for area address summarization.

■ Regularly are the source for default routes.

■ Maintain the LSDBs for each area they are connected to.

Routers that connect any OSPF area to a different routing administration (for example, BGP) are called ASBRs. The ASBR is the point where external routers can be introduced in the OSPF AS.

LSA Types

LSAs are used to exchange link-state information after routers form full adjacencies. LSAs report the state of routers' links and have the following characteristics:

■ LSAs are reliable.

■ LSAs are flooded throughout the OSPF area.

- LSAs have a sequence number and a timer. The sequence number and timer ensure that each router has the most current LSA.

- LSAs are refreshed every 30 minutes.

There are 11 different and distinct LSAs used in OSPF. Cisco does not support all 11 LSA types, and the ICND2 exam will test you on the following LSA types:

- **Type 1:** Router LSAs. Describe the state of the router's links to the area and are flooded only within that area.

- **Type 2:** Network LSAs. Created by the designated router (DR) and are flooded in the area that contains the network.

- **Type 3:** Network summary LSAs. Used by the ABR to advertise prefixes to other areas. Are not flooded throughout the AS. Summarization is not on by default.

- **Type 4:** ASBR summary LSAs. Tell the OSPF domain (AS) how to get to the ASBR.

- **Type 5:** Autonomous system LSAs. External link advertisements created by the ASBRs. They are flooded in all areas expect special areas.

Figure 5-4 displays the different LSA types.

Figure 5-4   *LSA Types*

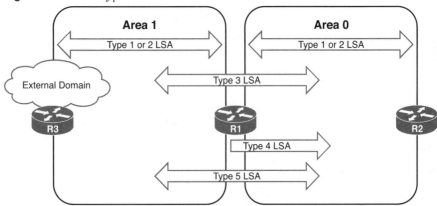

Multiarea OSPF Implementation

Single-area OSPF puts all routers into a single OSPF area. Every router processes all LSAs, and for larger networks, there will be large routing tables.

Multiarea OSPF is a more scalable solution than single-area designs. In multiarea designs, LSAs are limited to their area, routing tables are smaller, and summarization can be used.

Planning for Multiarea OSPF

Multiarea OSPF designs need to be planned properly. Things to plan for and consider are

- **IP addressing design:** A proper IP addressing scheme will determine how well OSPF might scale. Detailed IP addressing plans and subnetting information should be created.

- **Network topology:** Primary and backup links need to be identified and planned.

- **ABRs and ASBRs:** The different OSPF areas should be outlined as well as the routers that will be acting as ABRs and ASBRs.

- **Implementation plan:** Outlining how OSPF will be implemented throughout the organization.

OSPF Network Types

OSPF defines the following four network types:

- Broadcast networks
- Nonbroadcast multiaccess (NBMA) networks
- Point-to-point networks
- Point-to-multipoint networks

Ethernet is an examples of a broadcast network but is better defined as a broadcast multiaccess network. OSPF routers on broadcast multiaccess networks elect a designated router (DR) and backup designated router (BDR). All routers on the broadcast multiaccess segment form adjacencies with the DR and BDR. On broadcast multiaccess networks, all LSA packets are multicast to the DR and BDR address of 224.0.0.6; Hellos are still multicast to the all-OSPF routers address of 224.0.0.5. The router with the highest OSPF interface priority is elected the DR, and the router with the second-highest OSPF interface priority is the BDR. The OSPF interface priority defaults to 1 but should be administratively configured to manually define the DR and BDR. If the default priority value of 1 is left on all router interfaces, the DR/BDR election relies on the router ID (RID): The highest RID on the segment becomes the DR, and the second highest becomes the BDR.

NBMA networks include Frame Relay and ATM; they are capable of connecting more than two routers but have no broadcast capability. NBMA networks elect a DR and BDR, and all OSPF packets are unicast.

Point-to-point networks, such as a serial connections using HDLS or PPP, connect a single pair of routers and normally become adjacent without special configuration. This is because the OSPF network type will default to point-to-point. No DR/BDR elections take place.

Point-to-multipoint networks are configured as NBMA networks, in which networks are treated as a collection of point-to-point links. Routers on these networks do not elect a DR or BDR, and because all links are seen as point-to-point, all OSPF packets are multicast.

Multiarea OSPF Configuration and Verification

Multiarea OSPF configuration is similar to single-area OSPF configuration. The only difference is that you configure a router with different areas. The following configuration example configures OSPF using process ID 1 and places the interfaces connected to network 172.16.0.0 255.255.0.0 in area 0 and interfaces connected to network 192.168.1.0 255.255.255.0 in area 1:

```
RouterA(config)# router ospf 1
RouterA(config-router)# network 172.16.0.0 0.0.255.255 area 0
RouterA(config-router)# network 192.168.1.0 0.0.0.255 area 1
```

OSPF can also be configured directly on an interface using the **ip ospf** *process-id* **area** *area_id* interface command. Configuring OSPF on an interface simplifies the configuration by only enabling OSPF on defined interfaces. The following example configures OSFP on interface G0/0 in area 0 and interface G0/1 in area 1:

```
RouterA(config)# interface g 0/0
RouterA(config-if)# ip address 172.16.0.1 255.255.255.0
RouterA(config-if)# no shut
RouterA(config-if)# ip ospf 1 area 0
RouterA(config-if)# interface g 0/1
RouterA(config-if)# ip address 192.168.1.1 255.255.255.0
RouterA(config-if)# no shut
RouterA(config-if)# ip ospf 1 area 1
RouterA(config-if)# exit
RouterA(config)# router ospf 1
```

The **show ip ospf neighbor** command displays the OSPF neighbors, neighbor router ID, neighbor priority, OSPF state, dead timer, neighbor interface IP address, and the interface that the neighbor is accessible through.

The **show ip ospf interface** command displays OSPF-related information on OSPF-enabled interfaces. This command displays the OSPF process ID that the interface is assigned to, area that the interfaces are in, Hello and Dead timers, and cost of the interface.

The **show ip protocols** command displays the OSPF status. It displays which routing protocols are configured on a router, the contents of the **network** command for each routing process, enabled interfaces, and routing protocol specifics such as Router ID.

Troubleshooting OSPF

Troubleshooting OSPF can be complex. However, troubleshooting OSPF is no different than troubleshooting any other routing protocol. The cause can be one of the following:

- Missing routing information

- Inaccurate route information

Viewing the routing table is the primary source of troubleshooting information. When troubleshooting OSPF, consider the following:

- Verify that all interfaces have the correct address and mask.

- Verify that the **network area** statements have the correct inverse mask to match the correct interfaces.

- Verify that the **network area** statements put all interfaces in the correct areas.

- Verify that the router has established adjacency with a neighboring router. This is done with the **show ip ospf neighbors** command. If adjacency is not established, the routers cannot exchange routes.

- If adjacency between routers is not established, verify that all interfaces are operational and enabled for OSPF and configured for the same OSPF area. Also, make sure that the interfaces are not configured as passive.

Troubleshooting Neighbor States

When OSPF is enabled on a router, the router starts to discover other OSPF-enabled devices by exchanging Hello messages. During the process and throughout the OSPF process, neighbors go through various neighbor states. When troubleshooting OSPF, it is important to know the different OSPF neighbor states. Table 5-1 lists these states.

Table 5-1 *OSPF Neighbor States*

State	Definition
Down	The first OSPF neighbor state. Means that no Hello messages have been received from OSPF neighbors.
Attempt	Applies only to manually configured neighbors in an NBMA environment. The router sends unicast Hello packets every poll interval to the neighbor from which Hellos have not been received within the dead interval.
Init	Specifies that the router has received a Hello packet from its neighbor, but the receiving router's ID was not included in the Hello packet.
2-Way	Bidirectional communication has been established between two routers. This means that each router has seen the other's Hello packet. This occurs when the router receiving the Hello packets sees its own Router ID within the received Hello packet's neighbor field. On broadcast and NBMA networks, a router only becomes Full with the DR and BDR. The router stays in the 2-Way state with all other neighbors.

State	Definition
Exstart	The router and the segment's DR and BDR establish a master-slave relationship and choose the initial sequence of number to form an adjacency. An adjacency should continue past this state. If it does not, there is a problem with the database description packet exchange.
Exchange	OSPF routes exchange database descriptor (DBD) packets describing their entire link-state database to neighbors that are in the Exchange or greater state too.
Loading	The state where the actual exchange of link-state information occurs. Routers send link-state request packets to neighbors requesting more-recent LSAs that have been discovered but not received.
Full	All routers are fully adjacent with each other.

A prerequisite for neighbor relationships to form between routers is Layer 3 connectivity. Also remember that for OSPF-enabled routers to become neighbors, they must meet the following criteria:

- Both routers must be in the same subnet and same area.
- The Hello and hold/dead timers must match.
- Both routers must have unique Router IDs.
- If configured for authentication, both routers must have matching authentication.

When troubleshooting neighbor states and adjacencies, consider the following:

- Verify that Hellos are being sent from both neighbors.
- Verify that the timers are the same between neighbors.
- Verify that the interfaces are configured on the same subnet.
- Verify that the neighboring interfaces are the same network type.
- If authentication is being used, make sure that authentication is properly configured between the routers.
- Make sure that no ACLs are blocking OSPF.

Troubleshooting OSPF Routing Table

If OSPF routers are adjacent and routes are missing from the routing table, it might be because of multiple routing protocols enabled on the router. When you have more than one routing protocol configured in a network, you might receive routing information about a network through an undesired routing protocol. The **show ip route** command will display the routing table of a router, and the **show ip protocols** command will display all routing protocols configured on the router and specific information regarding each routing protocol to help assist with the troubleshooting process.

Troubleshooting Commands

The following commands can be used to help you troubleshoot OSPF, OSPF neighbor states, and routing table issues:

- **show ip protocols:** Lists the configured routing protocols, their administrative distances, the interfaces configured for each routing protocol, and the contents of the **network** configuration commands for each routing process, and lists enabled but passive interfaces. This will help determine what networks are being advertised on routers.

- **show ip ospf interface:** Lists the area in which the interface belongs and neighbors adjacent on the interface. Displays the hold and dead timers.

- **show ip ospf neighbor:** Lists neighbors and current neighbor status.

- **show ip route ospf:** Lists all OSPF routes that the router learned.

- **debug ip ospf packet:** Shows log messages that describe the contents of all OSPF packets.

- **debug ip ospf hello:** Shows messages describing Hello packets and Hello failures.

- **debug ip ospf adj:** Shows the authentication process if OSPF authentication is configured.

- The **debug ip ospf adj** command is an important command for troubleshooting OSPF adjacencies. OSPF routers exchange Hello packets to create neighbor adjacencies. For an OSPF adjacency to occur, the following five items in an OSPF Hello packet must match:

  - Area ID

  - Hello/dead intervals

  - Authentication password

  - Stub area flag

  - Subnet and network

To determine whether any of these Hello packet options do not match, use the **debug ip ospf adj** command. The following output shows a successful adjacency on the serial 0 interface:

```
RouterA# debug ip ospf adj
00:50:57: %LINK-3-UPDOWN: Interface Serial0, changed state to down
00:50:57: OSPF: Interface Serial0 going Down
00:50:57: OSPF: 172.16.10.36 address 192.16.64.1 on Serial0 is dead,
    state DOWN
00:50:57: OSPF: 70.70.70.70 address 192.16.64.2 on Serial0 is dead,
    state DOWN
00:50:57: %OSPF-5-ADJCHG: Process 10, Nbr 70.70.70.70 on Serial0 from
    FULL to DOWN, Neighbor Down: Interface down or detached
```

```
00:50:58: OSPF: Build router LSA for area 0, router ID 172.16.10.36,
seq 0x80000009
00:50:58: %LINEPROTO-5-UPDOWN: Line protocol on Interface Serial0,
changed state to down
00:51:03: %LINK-3-UPDOWN: Interface Serial0, changed state to up
00:51:03: OSPF: Interface Serial0 going Up
00:51:04: OSPF: Build router LSA for area 0, router ID 172.16.10.36,
seq 0x8000000A
00:51:04: %LINEPROTO-5-UPDOWN: Line protocol on Interface Serial0,
changed state to up
00:51:13: OSPF: 2 Way Communication to 70.70.70.70 on Serial0,
state 2WAY
00:51:13: OSPF: Send DBD to 70.70.70.70 on Serial0 seq 0x2486 opt
0x42
  flag 0x7 len 32
00:51:13: OSPF: Rcv DBD from 70.70.70.70 on Serial0 seq 0x19A4 opt
0x42
  flag 0x7 len 32 mtu 1500 state EXSTART
00:51:13: OSPF: First DBD and we are not SLAVE
00:51:13: OSPF: Rcv DBD from 70.70.70.70 on Serial0 seq 0x2486 opt
0x42
  flag 0x2 len 72 mtu 1500 state EXSTART
00:51:13: OSPF: NBR Negotiation Done. We are the MASTER
00:51:13: OSPF: Send DBD to 70.70.70.70 on Serial0 seq 0x2487 opt
0x42
  flag 0x3 len 72
00:51:13: OSPF: Database request to 70.70.70.70
00:51:13: OSPF: sent LS REQ packet to 192.16.64.2, length 12
00:51:13: OSPF: Rcv DBD from 70.70.70.70 on Serial0 seq 0x2487 opt
0x42
  flag 0x0 len 32 mtu 1500 state EXCHANGE
00:51:13: OSPF: Send DBD to 70.70.70.70 on Serial0 seq 0x2488 opt
0x42
  flag 0x1 len 32
00:51:13: OSPF: Rcv DBD from 70.70.70.70 on Serial0 seq 0x2488 opt
0x42
  flag 0x0 len 32 mtu 1500 state EXCHANGE
00:51:13: OSPF: Exchange Done with 70.70.70.70 on Serial0
00:51:13: OSPF: Synchronized with 70.70.70.70 on Serial0, state FULL
00:51:13: %OSPF-5-ADJCHG: Process 10, Nbr 70.70.70.70 on Serial0 from
LOADING
  to FULL, Loading Done
00:51:14: OSPF: Build router LSA for area 0, router ID 172.16.10.36,
seq 0x8000000B
```

OSPFv3

OSPFv3 is a complete rewrite of OSPFv2 to support IPv6; however, for the most part, OSPFv3 is similar to OSPFv2. The packet types and neighbor discovery mechanisms are the same between the two as are the LSA flooding.

Key OSPFv3 differences are as follows:

- The router ID is no longer based on an IPv4 address of the router. It needs to be manually assigned using the **router-id** *router_id* command and is a 32-bit number that looks like an IPv4 address. If not manually set, the router ID will be the same as the highest configured loopback address on the router. If there is no configured loopback address, the highest IP address on the router's physical interface will be used.

- Router adjacencies use link-local addresses to communicate.

- Uses IPv6 for transport of LSAs using protocol number 89.

- Is enabled per link and identifies which networks are attached to the link for determining prefix reachability propagation and the OSPF area.

- Uses IPv6 multicasting by using FF02::5 for all OSPF routers and FF02::6 for the OSPF DR and the OSPF BDR.

OSPFv2 and OSPFv3 run independently on a router.

OSPFv3 Configuration and Verification

Configuring OSFPv3 consists of enabling OSPF for IPv6, configuring the router ID, and enabling OSPFv3 on an interface. The following commands enable OSPFv3 on a router with a router ID of 2.2.2.2 and place Gigabit interface 0/0 in area 0:

```
RouterA(config)# ipv6 router ospf 1
RouterA(config-rtr)# router-id 2.2.2.2
RouterA(config-rtr)# interface g 0/0
RouterA(config-if)# ipv6 ospf 1 area 0
```

The **show ipv6 ospf interfaces** command displays OSPFv3-enabled interfaces, the OSPFv3 area, process ID, router ID, and adjacent OSPF neighbors.

The **show ipv6 ospf** command displays general OSPFv3 information such as process ID, router ID, timers, areas configured, and reference bandwidth.

Section 6
Wide-Area Networks and Point-to-Point Communication Links

WANs connect networks, users, and services across a broad geographic area. Companies use the WAN to connect company sites for information exchange (see Figure 6-1).

Figure 6-1   *WAN Connections*

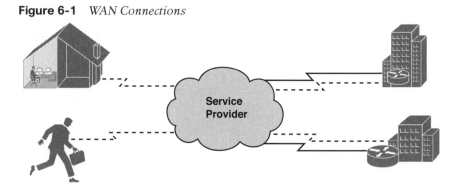

Understanding Serial WAN Interfaces

WAN serial interfaces, defined as follows, are either synchronous or asynchronous:

- **Synchronous links** have identical frequencies and contain individual characters encapsulated in control bits, called start/stop bits, which designate the beginning and end of each character. Synchronous links try to use the same speed as the other end of a serial link. Synchronous transmission occurs on V.35 and other interfaces, where one set of wires carries data and a separate set of wires carries clocking for that data.

- **Asynchronous links** send digital signals without timing. Asynchronous links agree on the same speed, but no check or adjustment of the rates occurs if they are slightly different. Only 1 byte per transfer is sent. Modems are asynchronous.

Serial interfaces are specified as DTE (data terminal equipment) or data communications equipment (DCE). DCE converts user data into the service provider's preferred format; in other words, DCEs provide clocking for the serial link. An example of a DCE is a channel service unit/data service unit (CSU/DSU) or a serial interface configured for clocking. The port configured as DTE requires external clocking from the CSU/DSU or other DCE device.

Digital lines, such as T1 or T3 carrier lines, require a CSU/DSU. The CSU provides termination for the digital signal and ensures connection integrity through error correction and line monitoring. The DSU converts the T-carrier line frames into frames that the LAN can interpret and vice versa.

WAN Review

Figure 6-2 shows the typical WAN topology with explanations as follows:

Figure 6-2 *Typical WAN Topology*

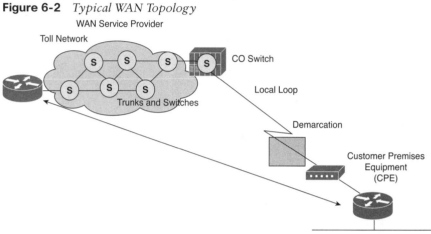

Point-to-Point or Circuit-Switched Connection

- **Customer premises equipment (CPE):** Located on the subscriber's premises and includes both equipment owned by the subscriber and devices leased by the service provider.

- **Demarcation (or demarc):** Marks the point where CPE ends and the local loop begins. Usually it is located in the telecommunications closet.

- **Local loop (or last mile):** The cabling from the demarc into the WAN service provider's central office.

- **Central office (CO):** A switching facility that provides a point of presence for WAN service. The central office is the entry point to the WAN cloud, the exit point from the WAN for called devices, and a switching point for calls.

- **Toll network:** A collection of trunks inside the WAN cloud.

WAN Connection Types

WAN services are generally leased from service providers on a subscription basis. The following three main types of WAN connections (services) exist:

- **Leased-line:** A leased line (or point-to-point dedicated connection) provides a preestablished connection through the service provider's network (WAN) to a remote network. Leased lines provide a reserved connection for the client but are costly. Leased-line connections typically are synchronous serial connections.

Figure 6-3   *Leased-Line*

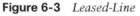

Synchronous Serial

- **Circuit-switched:** Circuit switching provides a dedicated circuit path between sender and receiver for the duration of the call. Circuit switching is used for basic telephone service or ISDN.

Figure 6-4   *Circuit-Switched WAN*

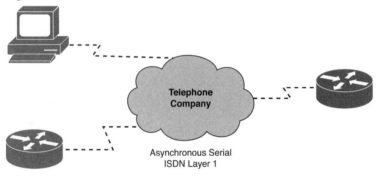

Telephone Company

Asynchronous Serial
ISDN Layer 1

- **Packet-switched:** With packet switching, devices transport packets using virtual circuits (VC) that provide end-to-end connectivity. Programmed switching devices provide physical connections. Packet headers identify the destination. Packet switching offers leased line–type services over shared lines, but at a much lower cost. Frame Relay, ATM, X.25, and Metro Ethernet are types of packet-switched connections.

Figure 6-5   *Packet-Switched WAN*

Service Provider

Synchronous Serial

Layer 2 Encapsulation Protocols

The following are examples of Layer 2 encapsulation protocols:

- **High-Level Data Link Control (HDLC):** The default encapsulation type on point-to-point dedicated links and circuit-switched connections.

- **Point-to-Point Protocol (PPP):** Provides connections between devices over several types of physical interfaces, such as asynchronous serial, High-Speed Serial Interface (HSSI), ISDN, and synchronous. PPP works with many network layer protocols, including IP and IPX. PPP uses Password Authentication Protocol (PAP) and Challenge Handshake Authentication Protocol (CHAP) for basic security.

- **Frame Relay:** Industry-standard switched data link layer protocol. Frame Relay (based on X.25) can handle multiple virtual circuits.

- **Asynchronous Transfer Mode (ATM):** International standard for cell relay using fixed-length (53-byte) cells for multiple service types. Fixed-length cells allow hardware processing, which greatly reduces transit delays. ATM takes advantage of high-speed transmission media such as E3, T3, and Synchronous Optical Network (SONET).

- **Ethernet:** Typically found in LANs, the deployment in fiber to business areas has caused Ethernet to be a popular point-to-point and multipoint WAN solution.

- **Broadband:** Data transmission where multiple pieces of data are sent simultaneously to increase the rate of transmission. In networking, broadband refers to transmissions methods where two or more signals are a medium, such as

  - **DSL:** PPPoE and PPPoA. Provides digital data transmission over the telephone network.

  - **Cable Ethernet:** Provides digital data transmission over the cable television infrastructure with the use a of a cable modem.

Figure 6-6 shows the typical WAN connections that each Layer 2 encapsulation protocol supports.

Figure 6-6 *WAN Connection Support by Layer 2 Encapsulation Protocols*

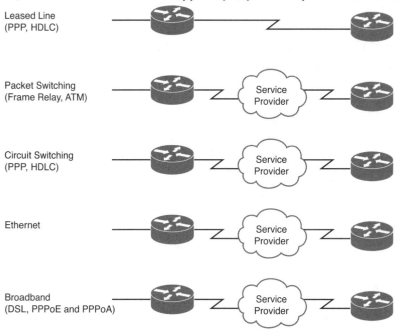

Configuring Serial Encapsulation

A point-to-point serial link provides a single, established WAN communications path from the customer's premises through a carrier network to a remote destination. Point-to-point links are typically more expensive than shared lines but have benefits that can outweigh their cost.

A router serial port is required for each leased-line connection, and the underlying network is based on T-carrier or E-carrier technologies. The leased line connects to the network through a CSU/DSU. The purpose of the CSU/DSU is to provide clocking. Table 6-1 shows typical WAN speeds for the UC and Europe. Note that these speeds are routed values.

Table 6-1 *U.S. and European WAN Speeds*

Country	Type	Speeds
U.S.	T1	1.544 Mbps
	T2	6 Mbps (4 T1 lines)
	T3	45 Mbps (28 T1 lines)
	T4	275 Mbps (168 T1 lines)
Europe	E1	2 Mbps
	E2	8 Mbps (128 E0 lines)
	E3	34 Mbps (16 E1 lines)
	E4	140 Mbps (64 E1 lines)

Configuring and Verifying a Serial Interface

Configuring a serial interface consists of entering the serial interface, configuring the bandwidth, configuring the clock rate (if a DCE device), enabling the interface, and configuring the encapsulation type. The following example configures a RouterA interface S0/0, sets the bandwidth to 128K, and sets the clock rate to 128,000:

```
RouterA(config)# interface s 0/0
RouterA(config-if)# bandwidth 128
RouterA(config-if)# clock rate 128000
RouterA(config-if)# no shutdown
```

The **bandwidth** *bandwidth* command sets the bandwidth metric used by a dynamic routing protocol in kilobits per second. It does not change the physical bandwidth of the interface.

The **clock rate** *clock_rate* command sets the interface clock rate in bits per second. This command is only used when not connecting to a CSU/DSU and is typically found when connecting to routers directly in a lab with the router acting as a DCE device. A special DTE/DCE cable is required for these types of connections, and clocking only needs to be configured on the DCE end of the cable.

The **show controllers** command can be used to determine the type of cable that is connect to a serial interface.

HDLC

HDLC is a data-link protocol used on synchronous serial data links. HDLC cannot support multiple protocols on a single link, because it lacks a mechanism to indicate which protocol it is carrying.

The Cisco version of HDLC uses a proprietary field that acts as a protocol field. This field makes it possible for a single serial link to accommodate multiple network layer protocols. Cisco HDLC is a point-to-point protocol that can be used on leased lines between two Cisco devices. PPP should be used when communicating with non-Cisco devices. Figure 6-7 shows the frame format of HDLC.

Figure 6-7   *HDCL Frame Format*

Cisco HDLC

Flag	Address	Control	Proprietary	Data	FCS	Flag

Because HDLC is the default encapsulation type on Cisco router serial links, you don't need to configure HDLC. However, if the encapsulation type has been changed to another protocol, the following command changes the serial interface encapsulation back to HDLC:

```
Router(config-if)# encapsulation hdlc
```

Point-to-Point Protocol

As shown in Figure 6-8, PPP uses a Network Control Protocol (NCP) component to encapsulate multiple protocols and the Link Control Protocol (LCP) to set up and negotiate control options on the data link.

Figure 6-8 *PPP*

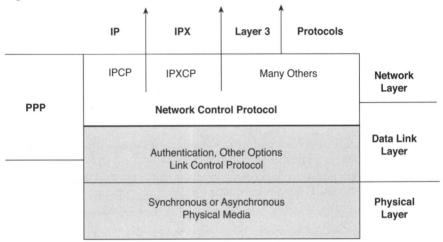

PPP Configuration Options

Cisco routers using PPP encapsulation include the LCP options shown in Table 6-2.

Table 6-2 *PPP Configuration Options*

Feature	How It Operates	LCP Feature
Authentication	Requires a password; performs challenge handshake	PAP, CHAP
Compression	Compresses data at the source; reproduces data at the destination	Stacker or Predictor
Error detection	Disables an interface that exceeds an error percentage threshold	Link Quality Monitoring
Multilink	Load balancing across multiple links	Multilink Protocol (MP)
Loop link detection	Detects whether a link is looped and disables it	Magic number

Establishing a PPP Session

The three phases of PPP session establishment are link establishment, authentication, and the network protocol phase, as follows:

STEP 1. **Link establishment:** Each PPP device sends LCP packets to configure and test the link (Layer 2).

STEP 2. **Authentication phase (optional):** If authentication is configured, either PAP or CHAP is used to authenticate the link. This must take place before the network layer protocol phase can begin (Layer 2).

STEP 3. **Network layer protocol phase:** PPP sends NCP packets to choose and configure one or more network layer protocols to be encapsulated and sent over the PPP data link (Layer 3).

Enabling PPP

To enable PPP encapsulation on a serial interface, enter the **encapsulation ppp** interface command, as follows:

```
RouterB(config-if)# encapsulation ppp
```

PPP Authentication Protocols

The two methods of authentication on PPP links are as follows:

■ **Password Authentication Protocol (PAP):** The less-secure of the two methods. Passwords are sent in clear text and are exchanged only upon initial link establishment.

■ **Challenge Handshake Authentication Protocol (CHAP):** Used upon initial link establishment and periodically to make sure that the router is still communicating with the same host. CHAP passwords are exchanged as MD5 hash values. CHAP uses a three-way handshake process to exchange a shared secret on a PPP serial interface.

Configuring PPP Authentication

The three steps to enable PPP authentication on a Cisco router are as follows:

STEP 1. Make sure that each router has a host name assigned to it using the **hostname** command.

STEP 2. On each router, define the username of the remote router and password that both routers will use with the **username** *remote-router-name* **password** *password* command.

STEP 3. Configure PPP authentication with the **ppp authentication** {**chap** | **chap pap** | **pap chap** | **pap**} interface command. (If both PAP and CHAP are enabled, the first method you specify in the command is used. If the peer suggests the second method or refuses the first method, the second method is used.)

The following commands configure CHAP and PAP for authentication with the pass-word of cisco. The remote router's host name is RouterA:

```
Router(config)# hostname RouterB
RouterB(config)# username RouterA password cisco
RouterB(config)# int s0
RouterB(config-if)# ppp authentication chap
```

Verifying the Serial Encapsulation Configuration

The **show interface** *interface-number* command, as follows, shows the encapsulation type configured on the router's serial interface and the LCP and NCP states of an interface if PPP authentication is enabled:

```
RouterA# show int s0
Serial0 is up, line protocol is up
  Hardware is HD64570
  Internet address is 192.168.1.2/24
  MTU 1500 bytes, BW 1544 Kbit, DLY 20000 usec, rely 255/255,
  load 1/255
  Encapsulation PPP, loopback not set, keepalive set (10sec)
  LCP Open
  Open: IPCP, CDPCP
  Last input 00:00:02, output 00:00:02, output hang never
  Last clearing of "show interface" counters never
  Input queue: 0/75/0 (size/max/drops); Total output drops: 0
  (text omitted)
```

Troubleshooting Serial Connections

Issues with serial lines typically arise from misconfigured encapsulation, authentica-tion issues, or carrier issues. To troubleshoot serial connections, the following should be checked:

- Check whether the correct cable is connected to the device (DTE/DCE).

- Verify that the encapsulation configuration is the same on both sides of the connections.

- If using PPP and authentication is configured, verify that CHAP or PAP authen-tication is configured correctly. If the host name on one side does not match the username on the other side, authentication will fail.

- If encapsulation and authentication are successful, the link should be operational. If ping still does not work, make sure that the IP addresses are properly configured.

Section 7
Establishing a WAN Connection Using Frame Relay

Frame Relay is a connection-oriented Layer 2 protocol that allows several data connections (virtual circuits) to be multiplexed onto a single physical link. Frame Relay relies on upper-layer protocols for error correction. Frame Relay specifies the interconnection process between a router and a service provider's local access switching equipment. It does not define how the data is transmitted within the Frame Relay service provider cloud.

A connection identifier maps packets to outbound ports on the service provider's switch. When the switch receives a frame, a lookup table maps the frame to the correct outbound port. The entire path to the destination is determined before the frame is sent.

Frame Relay Stack

As Figure 7-1 shows, the bulk of Frame Relay functions exist at the lower two layers of the OSI reference model. Frame Relay is supported on the same physical serial connections that support point-to-point connections. Cisco routers support the EIA/TIA-232, EIA/TIA-449, V.35, X.21, and EIA/TIA-530 serial connections. Upper-layer information (such as IP data) is encapsulated by Frame Relay and is transmitted over the link.

Figure 7-1 *Frame Relay Functions at Layer 1 and 2 of the OSI Model*

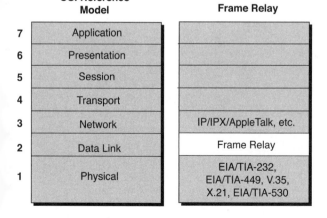

OSI Reference Model		Frame Relay
7	Application	
6	Presentation	
5	Session	
4	Transport	
3	Network	IP/IPX/AppleTalk, etc.
2	Data Link	Frame Relay
1	Physical	EIA/TIA-232, EIA/TIA-449, V.35, X.21, EIA/TIA-530

Frame Relay Terminology

The following terms are used frequently when referring to Frame Relay:

- **VC (virtual circuit):** A logical circuit between two network devices. A VC can be a permanent virtual circuit (PVC) or a switched virtual circuit (SVC). PVCs save bandwidth (no circuit establishment or teardown) but can be expensive. SVCs are established on demand and are torn down when transmission is complete. VC status can be active, inactive, or deleted. Today, most Frame Relay circuits are PVCs.

- **DLCI (data-link connection identifier):** Identifies the logical connection between directly connected sets of devices. Identifies the VC. The DLCI is locally significant.

- **CIR (committed information rate):** The minimum guaranteed data transfer rate agreed to by the service provider and customer.

- **Inverse ARP (Inverse Address Resolution Protocol):** Routers use Inverse ARP to discover the network address of a device associated with a VC.

- **LMI (Local Management Interface):** A signaling standard that manages the connection between the router and the Frame Relay switch. LMIs track and manage keepalive mechanisms, multicast messages, and status. LMI is configurable, but routers can autosense LMI types by sending a status request to the Frame Relay switch. The router configures itself to match the LMI type response. The three types of LMIs supported by Cisco Frame Relay switches are Cisco (developed by Cisco, StrataCom, Northern Telecom, and DEC), ANSI Annex D (ANSI standard T1.617), and q933a (ITU-T Q.933 Annex A).

- **FECN (forward explicit congestion notification):** A message sent to a destination device when a Frame Relay switch senses congestion in the network.

- **BECN (backward explicit congestion notification):** A message sent to a source router when a Frame Relay switch recognizes congestion in the network. A BECN message requests a reduced data transmission rate.

Frame Relay Topologies

Frame Relay networks can be designed using star, full-mesh, and partial-mesh topologies. Figure 7-2 shows the three topologies in Frame Relay.

Figure 7-2 *Frame Relay Topologies*

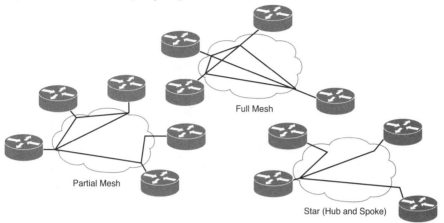

Full Mesh

Partial Mesh

Star (Hub and Spoke)

A star topology, also known as a hub-and-spoke configuration, is the common network topology. Remote sites are connected to a central site, which usually provides services. Star topologies require the fewest PVCs, making them relatively inexpensive. The hub router provides a multipoint connection using a single interface to interconnect multiple PVCs.

In a full-mesh topology, all routers have virtual circuits to all other destinations. Although it is expensive, this method provides redundancy, because all sites are connected to all other sites. Full-mesh networks become very expensive as the number of nodes increases. The number of links required in a full-mesh topology that has *n* nodes is [*n* * (*n* − 1)] / 2.

In a partial-mesh topology, not all sites have direct access to all other sites. Connections usually depend on the traffic patterns within the network.

By default, a Frame Relay network provides nonbroadcast multiaccess (NBMA) connectivity between remote sites. An NBMA environment is treated like other broadcast media environments, such as Ethernet, where all the routers are on the same subnet.

However, to reduce costs, NBMA clouds are usually built in a hub-and-spoke topology. With this topology, the physical network does not provide the multiaccess capabilities that Ethernet does, so each router might not have a separate PVC to reach the other remote routers on the same subnet. When running Frame Relay with multiple PVCs over a single interface, you can encounter split horizon when running RIPv2 or EIGRP.

Frame Relay Reachability Issues

In any Frame Relay topology, when a single interface must be used to interconnect multiple sites, you can have reachability issues because of the NBMA nature of Frame Relay.

Frame Relay NBMA connectivity causes problems with routing protocols. The following problems are caused:

- **Split horizon:** Split horizon is one way to eliminate routing loops and speed convergence in RIPv2 and EIGRP. The idea behind split horizon is that a routing update that is received on an interface is prevented from being forwarded out the same interface. If the router has no valid alternative path to the network, it is considered inaccessible. Split horizon also eliminates unnecessary routing updates, thus speeding convergence. In a hub-and-spoke Frame Relay network, split horizon will prevent the hub router from sending updates to spoke routers if it received a routing update from another spoke router on the same interface.

- **Neighbor discovery and DR and BDR elections:** OSPF over NBMA Frame Relay works in nonbroadcast mode by default. This results in neighbors not automatically being discovered. Neighbors will need to be manually configured and the hub router configured as the DR.

- **Broadcast replication:** Routers that support multipoint connections over a single interface that terminate several PVCs must be able to replicate broadcast packets on each PVC to remote routers. These replicated broadcasts consume bandwidth.

In Figure 7-3, Router A receives a routing update from Router B. Because Router A received the update on its serial interface, and because of the split horizon rule, Router A cannot send the updated route information to Routers C and D, causing Routers C and D to not learn about networks attached to Router B.

Figure 7-3   *Frame Relay Reachability Issues*

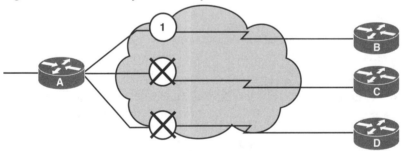

These reachability issues can be solved by disabling split horizon, implementing a fully meshed network, or configuring subinterfaces on the router.

Disabling split horizon increase the chances of routing loops in a network, and implementing a fully meshed network is costly. The best option is to configure subinterfaces. These logically assigned interfaces let the router forward broadcast updates in a Frame Relay network.

As Figure 7-4 shows, subinterfaces are logical subdivisions of a physical interface into three subinterfaces (labeled 1, 2, and 3). Routing updates received on one subinterface can be sent out another subinterface without violating split horizon rules. By configuring virtual circuits as point-to-point connections, the subinterface acts similarly to a leased line. It is also possible (and sometimes recommended) to turn off split horizon to solve this problem.

Figure 7-4 *Subinterface Example*

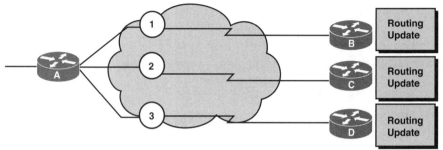

Frame Relay Signaling

The Local Management Interface (LMI) is a set of enhancements to the basic Frame Relay specification that defines signaling between a router and a Frame Relay switch. LMI is responsible for managing the Frame Relay connection and maintaining the status between the devices.

The LMI signaling process is as follows:

1. The router connects to a Frame Relay switch through a channel service unit/data service unit (CSU/DSU).

2. The router sends a VC status inquiry to the Frame Relay switch.

3. The switch responds with a status message that includes DLCI information for the usable PVCs.

4. The router advertises itself by sending an Inverse ARP to each active DLCI.

5. The routers create map entries with the local DLCI and network layer address of the remote routers. Static maps must be configured if Inverse ARP is not supported.

6. Inverse ARP messages are sent every 60 seconds.

7. LMI information is exchanged every 10 seconds.

Cisco routers support three LMI types:

- Cisco
- ANSI
- Q.933A

The LMI type can be configured manually. By default, Cisco routers will try to auto-sense the LMI type.

Frame Relay Address Mappings

DLCIs are numbers that identify the logical connection between the router and the Frame Relay switch. The DLCI is the Frame Relay Layer 2 address, and it is locally significant. DLCIs are usually assigned by the Frame Relay service provider. A Frame Relay router learns about a remote router's DLCI by either Inverse ARP (which is automatically enabled on Cisco routers) or by static mappings.

Static mappings are configured in the following situations:

- A Frame Relay peer does not support Inverse ARP.

- You want to control broadcast traffic across a PVC.

- You want to have different Frame Relay encapsulations across PVCs.

Configuring Frame Relay

The three commands used to configure basic Frame Relay on a router select the Frame Relay encapsulation type, establish the LMI connection, and enable Inverse ARP. The commands used are as follows:

```
encapsulation frame-relay [cisco | ietf]
frame-relay lmi-type {ansi | cisco | q933i}
frame-relay inverse-arp [protocol] [dlci]
```

Configuring Basic Frame Relay

To configure basic Frame Relay, enter the following:

```
RouterA> enable
RouterA# config term
RouterA(config)# int ser 1
RouterA(config-if)# ip address 10.16.0.1  255.255.255.0
RouterA(config-if)# encapsulation frame-relay frame-relay
RouterA(config-if)# frame-relay lmi-type   cisco
RouterA(config-if)# bandwidth 64
RouterA(config-if)# frame-relay inverse-arp ip 16
RouterA(config-if)# exit
RouterA(config)# exit
RouterA#
```

Configuring a Static Frame Relay Map

A router's address-to-DLCI table can be defined statically when Inverse ARP is not supported. These static maps can also be used to control broadcasts. To statically configure the map table, use the following command:

```
frame-relay map protocol protocol-address dlci [broadcast]
[ietf | cisco | payload-compress]
```

where:

- *protocol* specifies bridging or logical link control.

- **broadcast** is an optional parameter that controls broadcasts and multicasts over the VC.

- **payload-compress** enables payload compression.

The **frame-relay interface-dlci** *dlci* command also statically maps a local DLCI to a configured Layer 3 protocol on a subinterface. The difference is that map statements are used in multipoint Frame Relay configurations and the **frame-relay interface-dlci** *dlci* command is used in point-to-point subinterface configurations.

Configuring Subinterfaces

To enable Frame Relay on a subinterface, you must remove the IP address from the primary interface with the **no ip address** interface command, enable Frame Relay encapsulation on the serial interface, and then configure each subinterface with the IP address.

Subinterfaces can be configured as either point-to-point or multipoint.

With point-to-point configuration, one PVC connection is established with another physical interface or subinterface on a remote router using a single subinterface. In other words, each point-to-point subinterface is a different subnet.

With multipoint configuration, multiple PVC connections are established with multiple physical interfaces or subinterfaces on remote routers on a single subinterface. All interfaces involved use the same subnet, and each interface has its own local DLCI.

To select a subinterface, use the following command:

```
interface interface.subinterface-number {multipoint | point-to-
point}
```

To configure a subinterface, use the following command:

```
frame-relay interface-dlci dlci-number
```

The range of subinterface numbers is 1 to 4,294,967,295. The number that precedes the period (.) must match the physical interface number to which this subinterface belongs.

The *dlci-number* option binds the local DLCI to the Layer 3 protocol configured on the subinterface, as evidenced by the **show frame-relay map** command. This is the only way to link an LMI-derived PVC to a subinterface (LMI does not know about subinterfaces).

Configuring Point-to-Point Subinterfaces

To configure point-to-point subinterfaces, enter the following sample commands:

```
West-SD(config-if)# no ip address 192.168.1.5 255.255.255.0
West-SD(config-if)# encap frame-relay
West-SD(config-if)# int s0.1 point-to-point
West-SD(config-if)# ip address 192.168.1.5 255.255.255.0
West-SD(config-if)# frame-relay interface-dlci 110
West-SD(config-if)# int s0.2 point-to-point
West-SD(config-if)# ip address 192.168.2.5 255.255.255.0
West-SD(config-if)# frame-relay interface-dlci 120
```

Configuring Multipoint Subinterfaces

To configure multipoint subinterfaces, enter the following sample commands:

```
West-SD(config-if)# no ip address 192.168.1.5 255.255.255.0
West-SD(config-if)# encap frame-relay
West-SD(config-if)# int s0.1 multipoint
West-SD(config-if)# ip address 192.168.1.5 255.255.255.0
West-SD(config-if)# frame-relay map ip 192.168.1.1 110 broadcast
```

Verifying Frame Relay

You can use the following commands to verify and display Frame Relay information:

- **show interface:** Displays Layer 1 and Layer 2 status, LMI type, and the LMI DLCIs used for the local management interface.

- **show frame-relay lmi:** Displays LMI traffic statistics (LMI type, status messages sent, and invalid LMI messages).

- **show frame-relay pvc:** Displays the status of all configured connections, traffic statistics, and BECN and FECN packets received by the router.

- **show frame-relay map:** Displays the current map entries for static and dynamic routes. The **frame-relay-inarp** command clears all dynamic entries.

Troubleshooting Frame Relay

The **show interface** command provides a wealth of information for troubleshooting Frame Relay. What follows are different examples of output from the **show interface** command and possible reasons for the Frame Relay link failures:

```
RouterA# show int s0
Serial0 is down, line protocol is down
  Hardware is HD64570
  Internet address is 192.168.1.2/24
```

If the **show interface** command shows that the interface is down and the line proto-col is down, and the error is at the physical layer. This means that the problem is with the cable, the CSU/DSU, or the serial line. To troubleshoot the problem, perform the following:

- Check the cable to make sure that it is a DTE serial cable and that the cables are securely attached.

- If the cable is correct, try a different serial port.

- If the cable does not work on the second port, try replacing the cable. If replacing the cable does not work, the problem lies with your carrier.

```
RouterA# show int s0
Serial0 is up, line protocol is down
  Hardware is HD64570
  Internet address is 192.168.1.2/24
```

In the preceding example, the line is up but the line protocol is down. This means that the router is getting carrier signal from the CSU/DSU, and the problem is with the data link layer. Causes for the line protocol being down include the following:

- Frame Relay provider not activating its port

- LMI mismatch

- Encapsulation mismatch

- DLCI is inactive or has been deleted

Section 8
Introducing VPN Solutions

Virtual Private Networks (VPN) provide an Internet-based WAN infrastructure of connecting branch offices, home offices, and telecommuters to the network. In other words, VPNs allow office locations and remote users to interconnect with each other securely through the Internet. After they are connected through the secure VPN connection, the interconnected networks become part of the network as if they were connected through a leased line such as a classic WAN link.

Benefits of VPNs

VPNs provide the following benefits:

- **Cost savings:** VPNs enable organizations to use the Internet to interconnect offices.

- **Security:** VPNs use advanced encryption and authentication protocols to protect data from unauthorized access.

- **Scalability:** Because VPNs use the Internet, adding new users or organizations is easily done without changing the organization's network infrastructure.

Types of VPNs

The following two types of VPN networks exist:

- Site-to-site
- Remote-access

Site-to-site VPNs are an extension of a classic WAN network. They connect entire networks to each other. All traffic is sent and received through a VPN "gateway." The VPN gateway is responsible for encapsulating and encrypting outbound traffic for all traffic from a particular site to the destination site. The destination VPN gateway decrypts the traffic and forwards it to the private network. A VPN gateway can be a router or a firewall such as an ASA (Adaptive Security Appliance). Figure 8-1 shows an example of a site-to-site VPN.

Figure 8-1   *Site-to-Site VPN*

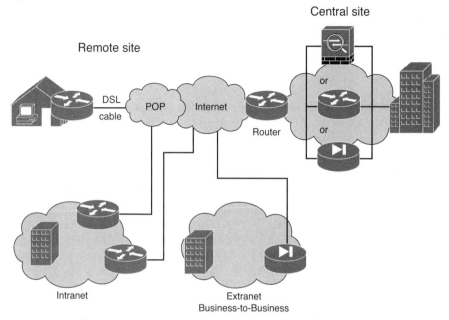

Remote-access VPNs are used for telecommuters, mobile users, and extranet traffic. They connect individual hosts' security to the company private network. Remote VPNs can use any Internet-based medium to connect to the VPN, and each host connects through VPN client software. Figure 8-2 shows an example of remote-access VPNs.

Figure 8-2   *Remote-Access VPN*

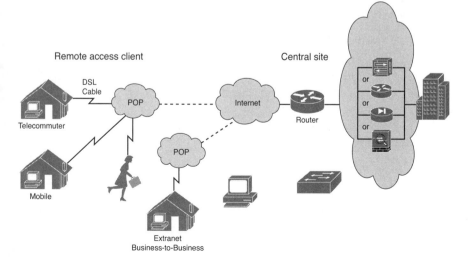

Cisco SSL VPN Solutions

SSL VPNs provide remote-access connectivity from almost any Internet location using a web browser and the browser's native Secure Socket Layer (SSL) encryption. Cisco also supports SSL VPNs using the Cisco AnyConnect VPN Client.

Cisco supports two SSL VPN solutions:

- Cisco AnyConnect
- Clientless

The Cisco AnyConnect SSL VPN uses the Cisco AnyConnect Client and SSL as the encryption protocol.

The Cisco Clientless SSL VPN solution provides VPN access using almost any Internet web browser and SSL for encryption without the need for an installed client.

Introducing IPsec

IPsec is an industry-standard suite of protocols that acts at the network layer, protecting and authenticating IP packets between IPsec peers (devices). IPsec secures a path between a pair of gateways, a pair of hosts, or a gateway and a host.

IPsec is not bound to any specific encryption or authentication algorithm, keying technology, or security algorithms, thus allowing IPsec to support newer algorithms.

IPsec provides the following four functions:

- **Confidentiality (encryption):** Packets are encrypted before being transmitting across a network.

- **Data integrity:** The receiver can verify that the transmitted data was not altered or changed. This is done through checksums.

- **Authentication:** Ensures that the connection is made with the desired communication partner.

- **Anti-replay protection:** Verifies that each packet is unique and not duplicated. This is done by comparing the sequence number of the received packets with a sliding window to the destination host or gateway.

Confidentiality

IPsec provides confidentiality by encrypting the data before transmitting it across the network, making the data unreadable if intercepted.

As shown in Figure 8-3, for encryption to work, both the sender and receiver must know the rules to transform the original message into its coded form. These rules are based on an algorithm.

Figure 8-3   *Encryption Confidentiality*

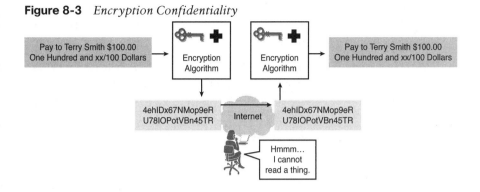

Encryption Algorithms

Encryption rules are based on an algorithm and key. The degree of security depends on the length of the key of the encryption algorithm; the shorter the key, the easier it is to break. IPsec supports the following encryption algorithms:

■ **Data Encryption Standard (DES):** Uses a 56-bit key that ensures high-performance encryption. Uses a symmetric key cryptosystem.

■ **Triple DES (3DES):** A variant of DES that breaks data into 64-bit blocks. 3DES then processes each block three times, each time with an independent 56-bit key, thus providing signification encryption strength over DES. Uses a symmetric key cryptosystem.

■ **Advanced Encryption Standard (AES):** Provides stronger encryption than DES and is more efficient than 3DES. Key lengths can be 128-, 192-, and 256-bit keys.

Diffie-Hellman Key Exchange

Encryption algorithms that use a symmetric shared secret key to perform encryption and decryption need to have a secure way to send the key values to each other. The Diffie-Hellman (DH) Key Exchange is a public key exchange that exchanges shared secret keys used for encryption and decryption over an insecure channel. DH is used with IKE to establish session keys.

Data Integrity

To ensure data integrity, IPsec uses a data integrity algorithm that adds a hash to the message. The hash guarantees the integrity of the original message. A hash function or algorithm condenses a variable-length input message into a fixed-length hash of the message output. The message hash can then be used as the message's "fingerprint."

Data integrity through IPsec protocols uses the Hash-based Message Authentication Code (HMAC). To service HMAC, IPsec uses hash algorithms MD5 and SHA to calculate a hash. MD5 and SHA work as follows:

- **HMAC - Message Digest Algorithm 5 (MD5):** Uses a 128-bit shared secret key. The message and 128-bit shared secret key are combined and run through the MD5 hash algorithm, producing a 128-bit hash. This hash is added to the original message and forwarded to the remote host.

- **HMAC - Secure Hash Algorithm-1 (SHA-1):** Uses a 160-bit secret key. The message and 160-bit shared secret key are combined and run through the SHA-1 hash algorithm, producing a 160-bit hash. This hash is added to the original message and forwarded to the remote host.

Authentication

In a VPN, before a communication path is considered secure, the end devices must be authenticated. The two peer authentication methods are as follows:

- **Pre-Shared Keys (PSK):** Pre-Shared Keys are a secret key value entered into each peer manually that authenticates the peer.

- **Digital signatures:** Also called Rivest, Shamir, and Adelman (RSA) signatures, they use the exchange of digital certifications to authenticate the peers.

IPsec Protocol Framework

IPsec is a framework of open standards that spells out the rules for secure communications. To do this, IPsec relies on existing algorithms to implement encryption, authentication, and key exchange. As shown in Figure 8-4, the two main IPsec framework protocols are as follows:

- **Authentication Header (AH):** AH provides authentication, data integrity, and optional replay-detection services for IPsec using the authentication and data integrity algorithms. AH acts as a digital signature to ensure that data in the IP packet has not been tampered with. AH does not provide data encryption and decryption services. Can be used by itself or with ESP.

- **Encapsulation Security Protocol (ESP):** ESP provides encryption with optional authentication and replay-detection services. ESP encrypts the IP packet and the ESP header, thus concealing the data payload and the identities of the source and destination.

Figure 8-4   *IPsec Framework Protocols*

Authentication Header

AH provides the following:
• Authentication
• Integrity

Encapsulating Security Payload

ESP provides the following:
• Encryption
• Authentication
• Integrity

Figure 8-5 show the algorithms that IPsec uses.

Figure 8-5   *IPsec Framework and Authentication Protocols*

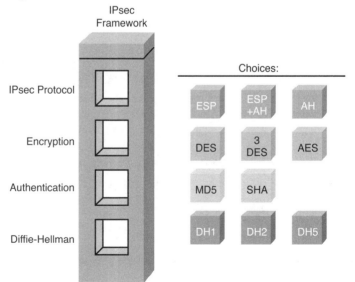

Configuring GRE Tunnels

Generic Routing Encapsulation (GRE) tunnels transport multiprotocol and IP multicast traffic between two or more sites that have IP connectivity. GRE encapsulates any Layer 3 protocol, allowing non-IP traffic and routing information to be passed between tunneled networks. Figure 8-6 shows how GRE tunneling networks.

Figure 8-6 *GRE Tunnel Overview*

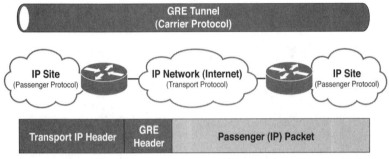

IP protocol 47 defines GRE packets, and GRE has the following characteristics:

- Uses a protocol type field in the GRE header to support encapsulation of any Layer 3 protocol

- Is stateless without flow-control mechanisms

- Does not encrypt its payload

- Adds at least 24 bytes of additional overhead for tunneled packets

GRE Tunnel Configuration and Verification

The following steps create a GRE tunnel:

STEP 1.   Identify the IP addresses of all connecting sites that will be used to communicate between sites.

STEP 2.   Create a tunnel interface.

STEP 3.   Specify GRE tunnel mode as the tunnel interface mode (optional).

STEP 4.   Specify the tunnel source IP address.

STEP 5.   Specify the tunnel destination IP address.

STEP 6.   Configure an IP address for the tunnel interface.

The following example configures a GRE tunnel between Router R1 and Router R2.

Router R1 configuration:

```
R1(config)# interface Tunnel0
R1(config-if)# ip address 192.168.255.1 255.255.255.0
R1(config-if)# tunnel mode gre ip
R1(config-if)# tunnel source 192.168.1.1
R1(config-if)# tunnel destination 192.168.1.2
```

Router R2 configuration:

```
R2(config)# interface Tunnel0
R2(config-if)# ip address 192.168.255.2 255.255.255.0
R2(config-if)# tunnel mode gre ip
R2(config-if)# tunnel source 192.168.1.2
R2config-if)# tunnel destination 192.168.1.1
```

The **show ip interface brief** command will display if a GRE tunnel is up or down.

The **show ip interface tunnel** *tunnel_number* command is used to verify the state of the GRE tunnel. This includes whether the tunnel is up or down, the IP address of the tunnel, the tunnel source and destination IP addresses, and the tunnel transport and protocol.

Section 9
Network Device Management

SNMP Overview

Simple Network Management Protocol (SNMP) is a standards-based application layer protocol that provides a way to monitor and control network devices. SNMP consists of an SNMP manager, an SNMP agent, and a Management Information Base (MIB).

The SNMP manager queries the SNMP agent, makes changes to the MIB variables, and provides a central place to analyze data gathered by agents.

The SNMP agent runs on a network device and gathers statistics and information on the device. The SNMP manager queries the agent for this information.

The MIB is the database of information maintained by the agent that the manager can query or set.

SNMP Versions

SNMP is implemented in three versions: 1, 2c, and 3. Each version provides an enhancement to the prior version.

The three versions of SNMP and their features are outlined in Table 9-1.

Table 9-1   *SNMP Versions*

Version	Security	Bulk Retrieval Mechanism
1	Plain text authentication with community strings	No
2c	Plain text authentication with community strings	Yes
3	Authentication, confidentiality, and integrity	Yes

SNMP Configuration

Basic SNMP configuration consists of the following steps:

STEP 1.   Configure the SNMP community string with read-write access.

STEP 2.   Configure the SNMP contact.

STEP 3.   Configure the SNMP location.

To configure the SNMP community string, use the **snmp-server community** global command:

```
snmp-server community string [view view-name] [ro | rw] [ipv6
  nacl] [access-list-number | extended-access-list-number |
  access-list-name]
```

To configure the SNMP contact, use the **snmp-server contact** global command:

```
snmp-server contact text
```

To configure the SNMP location, use the **snmp-server location** global command:

```
snmp-server location text
```

The following example configures SNMP for read-write access with the community string of Ciscopress, the location of San Diego, and John Smith as the contact:

```
RouterA(config)# snmp-server community Ciscopress RW
RouterA(config)# snmp-server location San Diego
RouterA(config)# snmp-server contact John Smith
```

This is a very basic and minimum configuration for SNMP on a Cisco router. It is recommended to configure read-write access with authentication.

Syslog Overview

Syslog is a standards-based protocol used for data logging. Syslog allows a device to send event notification messages across IP networks to event collectors called Syslog servers.

Syslog utilizes three layers:

- **Syslog content:** The management information in the syslog message.

- **Syslog application:** Handles generation, interpretation, routing, and storage of syslog messages.

- **Syslog transport:** Places and removes messages on the wire.

By default, a Cisco device sends the output from system messages and debug commands to the logging process. The logging process controls where system messages go. One can configure a Cisco device to forward syslog messages to the following destinations:

- Logging buffer
- Console buffer
- Terminal lines
- Syslog server

Table 9-2 lists the eight Syslog severity levels.

Table 9-2   *Syslog Severity Levels*

Severity Level	Meaning
0	Emergency. The system is unusable.
1	Alert. Immediate action needed.
2	Critical. There is a critical condition.
3	Error. An error condition occurred.
4	Warning. A warning condition occurred.
5	Notification. Normal but signification condition.
6	Informational.
7	Debugging.

Syslog Configuration

Syslog configuration on a Cisco device consists of configuring a Syslog server for the destination of syslog messages and the logging severity level.

The **logging** {*ip-address* | *hostname*} global command configures system messages going to a Syslog server, and the **logging trap** *level* global command limits the syslog messages sent to the Syslog server based on severity. Messages at or numerically lower than the specified level are logged. For example, if severity 5 (notification) was set, all notification and lower messages (levels 0–5) will be logged.

The following example configures RouterA to send system messages to Syslog server 192.168.1.150 with a severity level of 4:

```
RouterA(config)# logging 192.168.1.150
RouterA(config)# logging trap warning
```

NetFlow

NetFlow is an embedded Cisco IOS application that provides visibility into network statistics. NetFlow does this by characterizing and monitoring IP traffic flows. NetFlow examines each packet that is forwarded within a router or switch for a set of unique IP attributes. These unique IP attributes are

■ Source IP address

■ Destination IP address

■ Source port number

- Destination port number
- Layer 3 protocol type
- Type of service (ToS)
- Input logical interface

All packets with the same unique IP attributes are grouped into a flow, and then packets and bytes are tallied. This allows network administrators to have granular visibility into network traffic, allowing them to

- Analyze the impact of network applications
- Account and charge for network utilization
- Troubleshoot
- Provide security and anomaly detection

The two components of NetFlow are

- NetFlow collector
- NetFlow end devices

The NetFlow collector is a central server running NetFlow collector software that NetFlow end devices send flows to.

NetFlow Configuration and Verification

The steps to configure NetFlow are as follows:

STEP 1.   Configure NetFlow data capture from ingress and egress packets using the **ip flow ingress** and **ip flow egress** interface commands.

STEP 2.   Configure NetFlow data to be exported to the NetFlow collector using the **ip flow-export destination** *ip-address udp-port* global command.

STEP 3.   Configure the NetFlow export version using the **ip flow-export version** *version* global command.

The following example configures NetFlow RouterA Gigabit interface G0/0 for both inbound and outbound packets, sending the flows to the NetFlow collector on IP address 192.168.1.250 using UDP port number 9991, and sets the NetFlow version to 9:

```
RouterA(config)# interface g 0/0
RouterA(config-if)# ip flow ingress
RouterA(config-if)# ip flow egress
RouterA(config-if)# exit
RouterA(config)# ip flow-export destination 192.168.1.250 9991
RouterA(config)# ip flow-export version 9
```

NetFlow exports data using UDP packets in one of five formats: 1, 5, 7, 8, and 9. Version 9 is the most recent and recommend version to use.

The **show ip interface** command verifies whether NetFlow is enabled on an interface.

The **show ip flow export** command verifies the status and NetFlow accounting statistics.

The **show ip cache flow** command displays a summary of NetFlow statistics.

Managing Cisco Devices

When a router or switch boots, it performs a series of steps to ensure proper startup. When managing a network, it is important to know this boot sequence and the components that make up your routers and switches.

Router Components

The major router components are as follows:

■ **RAM:** Random-access memory contains key software (IOS), running configuration, IP routing table, ARP cache, and packet buffer.

■ **ROM:** Read-only memory contains startup microcode.

■ **NVRAM:** Nonvolatile RAM stores the configuration.

■ **Configuration register:** Controls the bootup method.

■ **Interfaces:** The interface is the physical connection to the external devices. Physical connections can include Ethernet, serial, USB, and console and AUX ports.

■ **Flash memory:** Flash contains the Cisco IOS Software image. Some routers run the IOS image directly from flash and do not need to transfer it to RAM.

ROM Functions

ROM contains the startup microcode and consists of the following three areas:

■ **Bootstrap code:** Brings the router up during initialization. Reads the configuration register to determine how to boot.

■ **POST:** Tests the basic function of the router hardware and determines the hardware present.

■ **ROMMON:** A low-level operating system normally used for manufacturing, testing, troubleshooting, and password recovery.

Router Power-On Boot Sequence

When a router is booted up, it goes through the following sequence:

1. The router checks its hardware with a power-on self-test (POST).

2. The router loads a bootstrap code.

3. The Cisco IOS Software is located and loaded using the information in the boot-strap code.

4. The configuration is located and loaded.

The bootstrap code locates and loads the Cisco IOS image. It does this by first look-ing at the configuration register. The default value for the configuration register is 0x2102. Changing the configuration register changes the location of the IOS load.

If the configuration register's fourth character is from 0x2 to 0xF, the bootstrap parses the startup config file in NVRAM from the **boot system** command that spec-ifies the name and location of the Cisco IOS Software image to load.

After the IOS is loaded, the router must be configured. Configurations in NVRAM are executed. If one does not exist in NVRAM, the router initiates an auto-install or setup utility. The auto-install routine attempts to download a configuration file from a TFTP server.

The Configuration Register

The config register includes information that specifies where to locate the Cisco IOS Software image.

Before changing the configuration register, use the **show version** command to deter-mine the current image. The last line contains the register value. Changing this value changes the location of the IOS load (and many other things). A **reload** command must be used for the new configuration to be set. The register value is checked only during the boot process.

Table 9-3 shows the configuration register values and meanings.

Table 9-3 *Configuration Register Values*

Configuration Register Boot Field Value	Meaning
0x0	Use ROM monitor mode (manually boot using the **boot** command).
0x1	Automatically boot the first image in flash memory as a system image.
0x2 to 0xF	Examine NVRAM for boot system commands (0x2 is the default if the router has flash).

The **show version** command verifies changes in the configuration register setting.

The **show flash** command displays contents in flash memory, including the image filenames and sizes.

The **show running-config** command shows the current running configuration in RAM.

The **show startup-config** command shows the configuration file saved in NVRAM. This is the configuration that will be used if the router is reloaded and the running config is not saved.

Managing IOS Images

The boot field value in the config register specifies the name and location of the Cisco IOS Software to load. The **boot system** {*file-url* | *filename*} global command allows one to configure the source for the Cisco IOS Software image to load. The uniform resource locator (URL) (*file-url*) convention allows you to specify files on network devices.

URL prefixes for Cisco network devices are as follows:

- **bootflash:** Boot flash memory
- **flash:** Available on all platforms
- **flh:** Flash load helper log files
- **ftp:** File Transfer Protocol (FTP) network server
- **nvram:** NVRAM
- **rcp:** Remote Copy Protocol (RCP) network server
- **usbflash0:** First USB flash memory slot
- **usbflash1:** Second USB flash memory card
- **system:** Contains the system memory and the running configuration
- **tftp:** Trivial File Transfer Protocol (TFTP) network server

Backing Up and Upgrading IOS Images

The following commands allow you to back up your IOS to a TFTP server or upgrade your IOS from a TFTP server:

```
wg_ro_a# show flash
wg_ro_a# copy flash tftp
wg_ro_a# copy tftp flash
```

The **show flash** command is used to determine the amount of flash a router has available and verify the size of the IOS image you are going to back up.

When using the **copy flash tftp** command, you must enter the IP address of the remote host and the name of the source and destination system image file.

The router prompts you for the IP address of the remote host and the name of the source and destination system image file.

The **copy tftp flash** command is used to upgrade or install a different version of IOS to your router.

Cisco IOS **copy** Command

As shown in Figure 9-1, the **copy** commands are used to move the configuration from one component or device to another. The syntax is as follows:

```
copy source-url destination-url
```

For example:

```
copy running-config startup-config
```

Figure 9-1   *IOS* copy *Command*

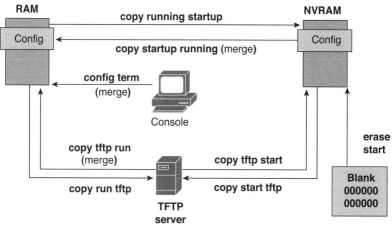

When a configuration is copied into RAM, it merges with the existing configuration in RAM. It does not overwrite the existing configuration. In Cisco IOS Release 12.3T and later, the **configure replace** command allows you to overwrite the running configuration.

The **show running-config** and **show startup-config** commands are useful troubleshooting aids. These commands allow you to view the current configuration in RAM or the startup configuration commands in NVRAM.

Password Recovery

Password recovery allows one to access privileged EXEC mode if the password is forgotten. Password recovery procedures differ for different router and switch platforms. However, the general steps to password recovery are

STEP 1.   Turn of or shut down the router/switch.

STEP 2.   Turn on the router/switch. Upon power on, press the **Break** key to interrupt the boot process to access ROMMON.

STEP 3.   In ROMMON mode, set the config register to 0x2142.

STEP 4.   Reset the router/switch. When the router/switch boots, the new config register setting tells the device to ignore the saved configuration.

STEP 5.   Enter privileged EXEC mode.

STEP 6.   Copy the startup config to the running config to load the saved router/switch configuration.

STEP 7.   Enable all interfaces using the **no shutdown** command.

STEP 8.   Enter global configuration and change the enable password.

STEP 9.   Change the config register back to its original value of 0x2102.

STEP 10. Copy the running config to the startup config.

Cisco IOS Licensing

Prior to IOS version 15.x, one would purchase and install the appropriate IOS version based on the feature sets needed. There were eight different IOS files for specified features. Starting with IOS 15.x, there is one universal IOS image that contains all IOS packages and features. Desired features need to be activated with a license file. The available license types are

- **IP Base:** Entry-level IOS features. Features include OSPF, EGIRP, and multicast support.

- **Data:** Provides features found in service provider images, including MPLS, L2VPN, IP SLAs, and multiprotocol support.

- **Unified Communications:** Offers features needed for Cisco UC, including VoIP and IP telephony.

- **Security:** Provides security features such as the IOS firewall, IPS, IPsec, and VPNs.

The **show license feature** command displays the installed license and features supported on a router.

The **show license** command displays information about all the Cisco IOS Software licenses installed on the router.

The **license install** *stored-location-url* privileged EXEC command is used to install a permanent license file.

New with IOS 15.0 is the ability to try other advanced features. For example, one can evaluate the Unified Communications features for a specific trial period of 60 days without having to purchase a permanent license file during the trial period. The **license boot module** *module-name* **technology-package** *package-name* command allows the installation of a 60-day license.

The **license save** *file-sys://lic-location* command saves all licenses on a device to the location specified in the *//lic-location* syntax.

The **license clear** *feature-name* command removes a license from a router.

ciscopress.com: Your Cisco Certification and Networking Learning Resource

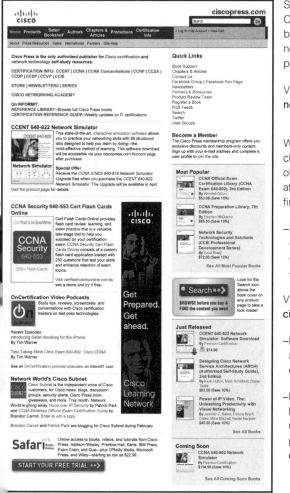

Subscribe to the monthly Cisco Press newsletter to be the first to learn about new releases and special promotions.

Visit **ciscopress.com/ newsletters.**

While you are visiting, check out the offerings available at your finger tips.

Podcasts

–Free Podcasts from experts:
· OnNetworking
· OnCertification
· OnSecurity

View them at **ciscopress.com/podcasts.**

–Read the latest author **articles** and **sample chapters** at **ciscopress.com/articles.**

–Bookmark the Certification Reference Guide available through our partner site at **informit.com/ certguide.**

nnect with Cisco Press authors and editors via Facebook and itter, visit **informit.com/socialconnect.**

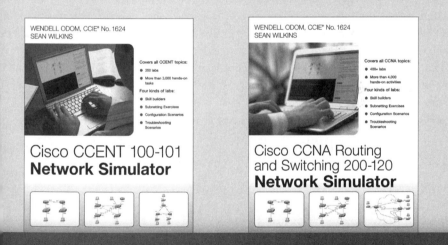